THE ARCHAEOLOGY OF ENGLISH BATTLEFIELDS

CONFLICT IN THE PRE-INDUSTRIAL LANDSCAPE

THE ARCHAEOLOGY OF ENGLISH BATTLEFIELDS

CONFLICT IN THE PRE-INDUSTRIAL LANDSCAPE

by Glenn Foard and Richard Morris

ENGLISH HERITAGE

CBA Council for British Archaeology www.britarch.ac.uk

CBA Research Report 168
Council for British Archaeology
2012

Published in 2012 by the Council for British Archaeology
St Mary's House, 66 Bootham, York YO30 7BZ

British Library cataloguing in Publication Data
A catalogue record for this book is available from the British Library
ISBN 978-1-902771-88-5

Typeset by Carnegie Publishing Ltd
Printed and bound by Information Press, Oxford

The publisher acknowledges with gratitude a generous grant from English Heritage towards the cost of publication

Front cover: Flodden monument on Piper's Hill

Back cover: (from top left, clockwise) Survey work underway at Bosworth; the battle of Sedgemoor, 1685, from a contemporary plan by Dummer (© Pepys Library, Magdalene College, Cambridge); ridge and furrow on Edgehill battlefield; bullets and powder box caps from Naseby battlefield; (centre) silver gilt boar badge found on Bosworth battlefield

Contents

List of figures and tables

Acknowledgements

This book has been largely researched and written by Glenn Foard, based upon work undertaken for the report *Conflict in the Pre-Industrial Landscape of England*. That report and the present book have also benefited from extensive help in design, management and editing by Richard Morris. He has also contributed additional material, particularly on the early medieval period and on memorialisation. Rob Janaway and Andy Wilson of the University of Bradford have provided text on taphonomy. John Baker, Stuart Brookes, David Parsons and Andrew Reynolds assisted approaches to the location of early medieval battlefields, with which their research project 'Beyond the Burghal Hidage' is partly concerned. Aleksandra Maclain of the University of York carried out the local bibliographic searches and analysis for the more intensive survey of Cumbria and the West Riding of Yorkshire.

The methodology for the assessment of fields of conflict used here was based upon that previously developed in collaboration with Tracey Partida for the assessment of Scottish sites. Tracey also undertook most of the digital mapping, refining these in GIS to create the published plans. Other information has been provided by David Hall (on open-field systems), Ian Wood (on Heavenfield), and Rodney Burton (on soils). Charles Haecker arranged visits to, and fieldwork on, battlefield sites in the USA, and both he and Douglas Scott advised on the investigation and management of battlefields in the USA. Damian Shiels advised on Irish battlefields. Information on specific sites was given by Susanne Wilbers-Rost (Kalkriese), Simon Richardson and Tim Sutherland (Towton), Ian Sanderson (Adwalton Moor), Lillian Ladel (Wareham), Tony Pollard (his and Barry Sagar's work at Sedgemoor), and Les Rees (his detecting at Boarstall). Alex Hildred provided information on, and access to, material from the *Mary Rose*. Various individuals advised on buildings with impact damage, with Paul Stamper providing more substantial assistance with the research on Civil War sieges sites in Shropshire. All of England's HER officers, bar one, provided information on battlefields and siege sites in their records, as did many Finds Liaison Officers. Andy Holland prepared the Pourbaix drawings. Anne Curry drew attention to Holmer's thesis on Yorkist armies. Additional help was given by many other people, including Steven Moorhouse, Jane Morris, Axel Müller, and members of staff of the Institute for Medieval Studies, University of Leeds.

During preparation of the original report, comments and guidance were provided by an advisory panel consisting of John Childs (Chair), Paul Stamper, Rob Janaway, Karen Watts, and Michael Rayner. In addition, a seminar was held at Leeds in 2008, where the results of the study were discussed. Various comments made there have been taken into account in the final drafting. The text for the present book, having been changed substantially from that of the original report, was reviewed again by Paul Stamper.

Principal funding was provided by English Heritage, with additional support from the University of Leeds and in-kind contributions from the Battlefields Trust. Finally we must acknowledge the support of the University of Huddersfield in enabling us to bring the work to publication. Several of the research objectives defined in the book are also now being carried forward at Huddersfield.

Unless otherwise specified, all references to Naseby are from Foard 1995 and to Towton from Fiorato *et al* 2000 (2nd edn 2007). For Edgehill they are from Foard 2008c, with acknowledgements to the late Clive Kibblewhite and the rest of the team that worked with me on that HLF-funded project for the Battlefields Trust. For Bosworth they are from Foard and Curry in prep, with acknowledgements to Richard Mackinder and the team who worked with me on that HLF-funded project for Leicestershire County Council and the Battlefields Trust. Geological information indicating alluvial and related areas is based on British Geological Survey 1:10,000 scale mapping. Unless otherwise specified, contours on all maps are from out of copyright Ordnance Survey mapping; likewise, unless otherwise specified, all photographs are by Glenn Foard.

Abbreviations

Adomnán	*Life of Columba* / Adomnán of Iona, ed Richard Sharpe. London: Penguin, 1995
Annales Cambriae	*British History and the Welsh Annals*, ed and trans J Morris. London: Phillimore, 1980
ASC	*Anglo-Saxon Chronicle*
Audley	*Arte of Warre*, ed W St P Bunbury, *Journal of Army Historical Research*, **6**, 1927
Historia Brittonum	*British History and the Welsh Annals*, ed and trans J Morris. London: Phillimore, 1980
HE	Bede, *Ecclesiastical History of the English People*, ed B Colgrave and R A B Mynors. Oxford: Clarendon Press, 1969
Gerald	Gerald of Wales, *The Description of Wales*, ed L Thorpe. London: Penguin, 1978
Itinerary	*The Itinerary of John Leland in or about the years 1535–1543*, ed L Toulmin Smith, 5 vols. London: G Bell, 1906–10
Nennius	*British History and the Welsh Annals*, ed and trans J Morris, London: Phillimore, 1980
Plummer	C Plummer, *Venerabilis Baedae Opera Historica*, 2 vols. Oxford, 1896
Raine	J Raine ed, *Priory of Hexham* 2 vols. Durham: Surtees Society, 1864–5
Vegetius	N P Milner, ed and trans, *Epitome of Military Science*. Liverpool: Liverpool University Press, 1996

Summary

The study of battlefields is one of the most recent areas of archaeological investigation. Originating in the USA in work at the Little Bighorn in 1984, the first archaeological investigations in England were undertaken in the mid 1990s, at Naseby (Northamptonshire) and then at Towton (North Yorkshire). Over the last ten years several more large-scale projects have been carried out. In the process, important advances have been made in refining and applying systematic methods.

The present book is based upon a resource assessment of English battlefields of the pre-industrial era, prepared for English Heritage in 2006–08. This has been revised and updated to include results of subsequent research up to the end of 2010. While the focus of the book is on the nature and recognition of archaeological evidence, some consideration is also given to interpretative and commemorative aspects of the subject.

A key objective has been to describe the evolving methodology for the investigation of battlefields. Such study involves the integration of techniques of military history, archaeological survey (particularly with metal detectors), and landscape history. It divides into four main stages, the first of which is analysis of primary written sources for the action. Next comes reconstruction of the historic terrain in which the battle was fought, using written, physical and (where available) graphical evidence. A third step is to place the events of the battle in that landscape context using the topographical clues in the accounts. After this, the resulting hypotheses are tested by investigation of battle archaeology in the field.

The main thrust of the book is accordingly towards the unstratified metal artefact scatters which form the core component of battle archaeology – material left by the fighting itself. It is also in this area that the most important advances are to be made, and where effective conservation management is most urgently required.

Mass graves are discussed. However, since this is a specialist area in which England has seen only one modern excavation, and since publication of that work has already demonstrated the rich potential of its field, no attempt is made here to repeat that discussion. Instead, the focus is upon the challenge of actually locating mass graves, for if their potential is to be realised then they must be found, and in practice they are extremely elusive. Until this problem is solved they are a resource which cannot be exploited or conserved.

The analysis of battlefields presented here is underpinned by a newly revised database of fields of conflict in England, which provides the basis for period surveys from prehistory to the early modern age. In each phase the current state of knowledge is discussed and the research potential explored.

While some attention is given to other types of place where fighting occurred, the main emphasis is upon battles – from earliest times to 1685. This is because it is on battlefields that the majority of information currently exists and where the main research potentials have been revealed. While general observations are made on other fields of conflict, only for the early modern period has a consideration of sieges been attempted.

A key conclusion is that battlefields older than 1066 are at present almost improssible to locate, and, accordingly, little is currently possible in the way of their investigation. This may change, but for present purposes the last millennium is the centre of attention, for it is here that historically rewarding analysis of individual battlefields is now possible. Moreover, as one moves closer to the present both written and physical evidence and research potential increase. The most extensive discussion is of the period from 1450 to 1685, for it is here that substantial archaeological evidence appears to exist for the battles themselves.

Within this period, two important themes are explored. One is the military character of the Anglo-Scottish border, which is identified as a special zone worthy of more detailed and integrated study than it has thus far received, exploring conflict and garrisons on both sides of the border.

The other, and by far the most important, focus is

upon gunpowder weapons and the physical evidence they have deposited. The projectiles, mainly of lead, are the single most important type of evidence on battlefields from the late 15th to 17th centuries. They offer potential for research into the technology of warfare as well as the actions on the individual battlefields on which they were used. In exploring this theme attention is given to the result of scientific and experimental research, particularly of live firing.

The book brings together strands of hitherto disparate evidence to form the corpus of battlefield archaeology in England. At present there are only a few major case studies available – Towton, Bosworth and Edgehill – none of which has yet been fully published. These are complemented here by a series of smaller studies, some of which have been undertaken specifically for the present work. However, a good deal – arguably, too much – of the evidence we have had to use derives from non-archaeological collecting. The limitations of such acquisition are discussed.

The study reveals gaps in understanding and identifies important research opportunities, both for the investigation of individual battlefields and of the history of warfare itself. The book is, however, written against a background of extreme urgency, because the evidence left by past actions is under great and imminent threat, and such management mechanisms as are available are neither adequate nor being as effectively used as they could be.

The single most important message from this study is that unless action to limit the decay and destruction is taken soon, in future decades there will be little left to study.

Résumé

L'étude des champs de bataille et autres zones de conflit constitue un des développements les plus récents en recherche archéologique. Elle a ses racines aux Etats Unis où les premières enquêtes archéologiques furent conduites à Little Bighorn en 1984 ; en Angleterre elles remontent au milieu des années 1990 sur les sites de Naseby (Northamptonshire) et de Towton (North Yorkshire). Plusieurs projets d'envergure se sont ajoutés à ces projets au cours des dix dernières années. Des progrès importants ont été réalisés dans la mise au point de méthodologies systématiques dans le domaine de la recherche sur les champs de bataille anglais.

Le volume présenté ici se base sur un diagnostic des ressources concernant les champs de bataille de l'ère préindustrielle en Angleterre, préparé pour le gouvernement anglais (English Heritage) en 2006–2008 et mis à jour afin d'inclure les résultats de recherches entreprises jusqu'à fin 2010. L'accent est placé sur la nature et l'identification des données archéologiques mais on trouvera aussi un bref aperçu sur les aspects interprétatifs et commémoratifs du sujet.

L'objectif principal est de présenter l'évolution des méthodes appliquées à l'étude des champs de bataille. Ceci comprend l'intégration des techniques appartenant à l'histoire militaire, les relevés archéologiques (y compris l'usage des détecteurs de métaux) et l'histoire du paysage. Quatre étapes sont proposées, la première étant l'analyse des sources historiques qui décrivent les combats. La reconstruction du terrain de bataille, par l'étude des sources historiques, physiques et graphiques (si disponibles) suit. La troisième étape consiste à réintégrer les événements dans le contexte du paysage affecté en utilisant les indices donnés par les sources. Enfin les hypothèses ainsi échafaudées sont soumises à des interventions archéologiques sur le terrain.

L'accent est porté sur l'étude des objets en métal non-stratifiés qui jonchent les champs de bataille, c'est-à-dire les témoignages concrets de scènes de combat. C'est dans ce domaine que de grands progrès sont à faire et où des mesures de protection sont à développer urgemment.

Quant aux charniers, il s'agit d'un sujet spécialisé qui n'a fait l'objet que d'une campagne de fouilles récentes en Angleterre ; comme les résultats de cette campagne ont déjà été publiés et ont démontré le potentiel de ce genre d'étude, nous ne reprenons pas la discussion dans ce volume. Par contre nous relevons le défi de localiser ces charniers : en effet, si nous voulons réaliser leur potentiel, il nous faut d'abord les trouver, ce qui se révèle fort difficile en pratique. Cette ressource demeure donc encore inexploitée et non conservée.

L'analyse des champs de batailles présentée ici se base sur les données relatives aux zones de conflit en Angleterre regroupées dans une banque de données récemment révisée ; cette dernière permet une mise au point chronologique, de la préhistoire aux temps modernes. On trouvera ainsi pour chaque phase un examen de l'état de nos connaissances, ainsi qu'une évaluation du potentiel pour de futures études.

Quoique nous touchons à d'autres types de zones de conflit, l'intérêt principal se porte sur les champs de bataille — des temps les plus anciens jusqu'en 1685. C'est en effet dans ce domaine que réside la vaste majorité de nos données et qu'existe le plus grand potentiel pour de futures recherches. Tout en donnant quelques indications générales sur les autres zones de conflit, nous n'avons considéré les formes de siège que pour les débuts de l'époque moderne.

Nous concluons qu'il est pratiquement impossible d'examiner les champs de bataille datant d'avant 1066. Ceci peut changer mais pour l'instant ce n'est que le dernier millénaire qui offre la possibilité de conduire des recherches significatives sur des champs de bataille spécifiques. De plus, plus nous avançons vers l'époque moderne, plus nos sources, tant écrites que matérielles, augmentent. La période la plus amplement considérée s'étend de 1450 à 1685, car c'est seulement pour cette époque que nous disposons d'une documentation suffisamment importante pour pouvoir appréhender les champs de batailles eux-mêmes.

Nous examinons deux thèmes pertinents pour cette époque. Le premier concerne le caractère militaire de la frontière entre l'Ecosse et l'Angleterre. En effet il s'agit d'une zone qui mérite un examen plus approfondi que n'a été effectué jusqu'à présent, prenant en compte en particulier les combats et les garnisons établies des deux côtés de la frontière.

Notre second thème, le plus important, considère l'usage des armes à feu et les vestiges que ces armes ont laissé. Les projectiles, surtout en plomb, sont les plus importants documents retrouvés sur les champs de bataille du 15ème au 17ème siècle. Ils permettent de cerner les techniques de combat ainsi que les actions menées sur des champs de bataille spécifiques. L'exploration de ce thème est rehaussée par les résultats d'analyses scientifiques et de recherches expérimentales, en particulier sur le tir d'armes à feu.

Notre volume rassemble des données jusqu'à présent éparses et constitue ainsi un inventaire de l'archéologie des champs de bataille en Angleterre. Il n'existe actuellement que quelques études de cas — Towton, Bosworth et Edgehill — et aucune n'a été publiée intégralement. Celles-ci sont complétées ici par d'autres contributions plus brèves, dont certaines spécialement écrites pour ce volume. Cependant une très grande — peut-être trop grande — partie des données utilisées par nos auteurs dérive de collections récupérées hors contexte archéologique, ce qui forme un sujet de discussion dans le volume.

Notre étude révèle qu'il existe des lacunes dans nos connaissances et met en relief d'importantes possibilités pour de nouvelles recherches, tant pour l'examen de champs de bataille spécifiques que pour l'histoire de la guerre en général. Notre volume sort dans un climat d'extrême urgence, car les preuves concrètes, surtout les indices de combats, se trouvent sévèrement menacées. Les auteurs démontrent que la gestion en place actuellement est en partie inadéquate et que même le système actuel pourrait être utilisé de manière plus efficace.

La leçon la plus importante à tirer de notre étude est qu'il ne restera plus grand-chose à étudier dans les décennies à venir si un programme efficace pour limiter la destruction et la détérioration des champs de bataille n'est pas mis sur pied rapidement.

Zusammenfassung

Die Untersuchung von Schlachtfeldern und anderen Konfliktfeldern ist eine der jüngsten Disziplinen der archäologischen Forschung. Ihr Ursprung liegt in den Vereinigten Staaten, wo Little Bighorn in 1984 untersucht wurde; danach kamen die ersten Erkundigungen in England, die in der Mitte der 90er Jahren in Naseby (Northamptonshire) und dann in Towton (North Yorkshire) stattfanden. Einige größere Projekte sind auch während der letzten zehn Jahren durchgeführt worden. Somit wurden bedeutende Fortschritte in der Anwendung von systematischen Ausgrabungsmethoden auf englischen Schlachtfeldern gemacht.

Eine Auswertung von englischen Schlachtfeldern aus der vorindustriellen Epoche, die für das englische Amt English Heritage zwischen 2006 und 2008 unternommen wurde, unterstützt das vorliegende Werk. Diese Auswertung wurde revidiert und ergänzt, sodass die Forschungsergebnisse bis Ende 2010 eingeschlossen werden konnten. Obschon der Band vornehmlich die Charakterisierung der Eigenschaften des archäologischen Befundes betrifft, werden die Interpretation und die Erinnerungsaspekte des Themas auch kurz betrachtet.

Eine wichtige Zielstellung war die Entwicklung von Methoden, die für die Untersuchung von Schlachtfeldern angebracht sind, zu beschreiben. Solche Untersuchungen umfassen verschiedene Fächer, wie die archäologische Geländeaufnahme (vor allem mit Metallsuchgeräten), die Militärgeschichte oder die Landschaftsgeschichte. Man kann solch ein Verfahren in vier Abschnitte einteilen. Eine erste Stufe entspricht der Auswertung der schriftlichen Quellen, die die Schlacht betreffen. Danach kommt eine Modellierung des Geländes, die die Belege aus dem Boden, die schriftlichen, und (wenn vorhanden) die bildlichen Quellen in Betracht ziehen. In einer dritten Stufe wird der Ablauf der Schlacht, auf Grund von topographischen Hinweisen, mit der Landschaft in Zusammenhang gebracht. Schließlich werden die so aufgebauten Hypothesen durch archäologische Bodenforschungen geprüft.

Dementsprechend wird der Schwerpunkt auf die Auswertung von unstratifizierten Metallstreufunden – die Kernkomponente der Schlachtfelderarchäologie, die eigentlichen Spuren einer Schlacht – gelegt. Weitere Fortschritte müssen in diesem Bereich noch gemacht werden. Es ist auch in diesem Bereich, dass eine effektive Bodenschutzstrategie dringend nötig ist.

Massengräber werden auch besprochen. Da es sich aber um ein spezialisiertes Feld handelt, und weil in England nur eine moderne Ausgrabung, die die reichen Möglichkeiten solcher Untersuchungen bewiesen hat, stattgefunden hat, wird das Thema in dieser Hinsicht nur kürzlich betrachtet. Anstatt dessen behandeln wir hier die Probleme, die mit der Auffindung von Massengräber verknüpft sind, da man sie zuerst finden muss, um ihr Potenzial auszubeuten, und da es in der Tat sehr schwierig ist solche Gräber, zu entdecken. Bis eine Lösung gefunden wird, bleiben sie eine Quelle, die nicht ausgebeutet oder erhalten werden kann.

Die Auswertung der Schlachtfelder, die in diesem Band auftreten, stützt sich auf eine neu revidierte Datenbank für England; diese dient als Basis für die Auswertung von ur- und frühgeschichtlichen bis modernen Zeitstufen. Der Wissensstand und die Möglichkeiten für weitere Auswertungen werden für jede Periode abgewertet.

Obschon auch andere Typen von Konfliktfeldern betrachtet werden, liegt der Schwerpunkt auf den Schlachten – von vorgeschichtlichen Zeiten bis 1685. Der Grund ist, dass die Mehrzahl der Angaben zurzeit in diesem Feld liegen und es ist auch in diesem Bereich, dass die wichtigsten Forschungsmöglichkeiten am deutlichsten sind. Obschon allgemeine Beobachtungen über andere Konfliktfelder vorhanden sind, ist es nur in der frühmodernen Zeitstufe, dass es möglich ist, einige Überlegungen über Belagerungen anzubieten.

Eine wichtige Schlussfolgerung ist, dass es zurzeit kaum möglich ist, Schlachtfelder, die älter als 1066 sind, zu untersuchen. Diese Situation kann sich ändern, aber der Mittelpunkt des Interesses ist hier das letzte Jahrtausend, eine Epoche, für welche es jetzt möglich ist, sinnvolle Auswertungen von bestimmten

Schlachtfeldern zu erarbeiten. Außerdem gibt es mehr materielle Spuren und Forschungsmöglichkeiten, als man näher an die Gegenwart rückt. Am ausführlichsten wird die Zeitspanne zwischen 1450 und 1685 besprochen, weil es die einzige Zeitstufe ist, in welcher es umfangreiche archäologische Daten über eigentliche Schlachten gibt.

In dieser Zeitstufe untersuchen wir zwei wichtige Themen. Erstens die militärischen Eigenschaften der Grenze zwischen England und Schottland, eine eigenartige Zone, wo es sich lohnt, genauere und besser integrierte als bisher unternommene Untersuchungen von Schlachten und Besatzungen beidseitig der Grenze, durchzuführen.

Das zweite, und wichtigste, Thema betrifft Schusswaffen und die Spuren, die diese Waffen hinterlassen haben. Das Geschoss, vor allem aus Blei, ist das bedeutendste Material, das von Schlachtfeldern des 15. bis 17. Jahrhunderts geborgen worden ist. Es bietet neue Möglichkeiten, die Kriegstechnologie sowie der Ablauf der Kämpfe auf bestimmten Schlachtfeldern, auszuwerten. In diesem Thema werden die Resultate von experimentellen und wissenschaftlichen Untersuchungen, vor allem von scharfer Munition, betrachtet.

Verschiedene, bisher getrennte Informationstypen werden in diesem Buch zusammengebracht, um ein Gesamtbild der englischen Schlachtfelderarchäologie aufzubauen. Zurzeit gibt es nur wenige bedeutende Auswertungen – Towton, Bosworth und Edgehill – und keine ist völlig veröffentlicht. Eine Reihe von geringeren Studien werden hier vorgestellt; einige davon wurden für dies Werk speziell unternommen. Wir müssen aber betonen, dass eine große (vielleicht zu große) Menge der Daten die vorhanden sind, von nicht-archäologischen Sammlungen stammen. Die Schwächen von solchen Sammlungen werden im Band bewertet.

Unsere Arbeit zeigt, wo es Lücken in unserer Kenntnis gibt, und weist auf Forschungsmöglichkeiten für bestimmte Schlachtfelder auch wie für die Kriegsgeschichte hin. Das Werk wurde in einem Zeitpunkt der höchsten Dringlichkeit unternommen, da die konkreten Beweise, vor allem die Spuren der eigentlichen Schlachten, bedroht sind. Die Autoren zeigen, dass die gegenwärtige Bewirtschaftung der Ressourcen nicht ganz geeignet ist, und dass der Bodenschutz nicht als effektiv ist, als es möglich wäre.

Am wichtigsten ist die Erkenntnis, dass, sofern etwas Gründliches um den Verfall und die Zerstörung anzuhalten nicht bald unternommen wird, verbleibt dann sehr wenig in den nächsten Jahrzehnten.

1

Introduction

Warfare has long been a subject of archaeological research. Weapons from prehistory onwards have received detailed study, while fortifications, among the earliest monuments to be studied by antiquaries, have been extensively investigated and are relatively well understood. In contrast, the archaeology of combat, be that open battle or assaults upon fortified positions, has been largely ignored. As a result the nature, scale, and survival of such evidence are still poorly understood. In large part this is because the physical traces left by battles, sieges, and skirmishes are far more ephemeral than those of defensive works.

The present book sets out to begin to redress the balance. In doing so it reviews evidence from recent work, principally in England, to describe the character of surviving battlefield archaeology of the pre-industrial era. It examines the factors influencing the condition of surviving sites, seeks to define their research potential, and suggests ways in which that potential may be realised. Finally it examines the main threats faced by these sites and considers management action to secure their survival.

Battles and sieges are complementary aspects of warfare, but they have left different kinds of evidence and must be separately assessed. A siege site will normally have defensive remains that enable investigations to be focused, even if the archaeology left by the action extends far beyond those defences. In contrast, a battlefield is 'just a field', and it can be difficult even to establish exactly where the fighting took place. This is particularly true for earlier battles, the surviving evidence for which becomes more ephemeral as one moves back in time. Furthermore, whatever advances are made in battlefield archaeology, in most cases we will remain dependent upon written records to identify the existence of a battle and to establish the general location of the site.

The principal focus of the book is thus on battlefields. In the following chapter we seek to define the character and importance of battlefields as archaeological sites, and to show how investigation of the physical remains they contain (Fig 1.1) can cast light upon both individual events and the wider history of warfare. In England their importance as historic sites has been recognised, since 1995, by the inclusion of nationally important examples on the Register of Historic Battlefields (hereafter the Register) (English Heritage 1995). These sites have been the setting for turning points in our history; they were places where the reputations of great leaders were made or lost; and where the evolving tactics and technology of war were put to the test. Above all, they are places where people risked their lives fighting for a cause, and the resting places of thousands who died while doing so.

If a battlefield is to have more than commemorative value, however, we need to place its events securely within the landscape. In Europe this has been achieved by building upon pioneering work in battlefield archaeology in the USA. Beginning in 1984 with the systematic use of metal detectors on the site of the 1867 battle of the Little Bighorn, research in the United States has pushed back through the earlier battlefields of the Indian wars, the American Civil War, and the Revolutionary War (Connor and Scott 1998; Scott and McFeaters 2011). Archaeologists have begun to refine these methods to explore the much longer chronology of large-scale warfare in Europe, where the history of landscape evolution is also far more complex. Battlefield study accordingly demands interdisciplinary work in which the approaches of military history are integrated with those of historical geography and landscape archaeology, all underpinned by systematic use of the metal detector. This methodology continues to be refined, especially to tackle the increasingly difficult problems that are encountered as one moves back into the medieval period and beyond.

Where the general location of a battlefield has been established, the next step is to use written and archaeological evidence to reconstruct a map of the landscape as it was at the time of the action. Of particular concern is the battlefield terrain, taken here to mean elements of the contemporary landscape which are likely to have had tactical significance. Events of the battle recorded in primary written sources are then placed within the

Fig 1.1 A small sample of bullets and powder box caps from more than 1000 artefacts from Naseby battlefield, collected in the late 1980s and early 1990s by two metal detectorists whose principal interest was the history of the battle (Foard 1995)

reconstructed terrain, using the topographic clues in those accounts. For the earliest periods such topographical detail often amounts to little more than the name of the action. Inevitably, this places severe limitations on what can be achieved, and unless the topographical detail is exceptionally specific such reconstructions of action within the terrain will remain hypothetical. The final step, therefore, is to test such hypotheses by sampling the battle archaeology. This is done through systematic metal-detecting survey, since the principal physical evidence is normally a scatter of metal artefacts in the plough soil. The nature of this evidence will vary, depending on the scale, location, character, and, most importantly, the period of the action.

A survey of the battle archaeology may show beyond reasonable doubt how the main elements of a battle fitted within its contemporary landscape. Where this is achieved it becomes possible to analyse the way in which terrain influenced the deployments and action and to do so with a confidence not previously available to military historians. This may reveal for example the success of a commander in exploiting the opportunities presented by the terrain, or in mitigating the threats posed by his opponents' use of that terrain.

Mass graves are the other major component of battle archaeology. Their locations and information to be derived from the numbers buried are of obvious significance. Moreover, palaeo-pathology can reveal physical attributes of the soldiers themselves and the use and effectiveness of different weapons. Unfortunately, with the exception of Towton, such remains have yet to make a substantial contribution to the understanding of English battlefields. This is principally because the graves are difficult to locate. They may lie anywhere across several square kilometres and, in the absence of reliable tradition, place-name evidence or chance finds, there is currently no dependable method which we can use to locate them. While geophysics may be effective in cases when a small target area has been identified, such survey is not currently practicable on a battlefield-wide scale.

Investigation of battlefields which have good documentary and physical evidence can do more than simply improve our understanding of the actions themselves. A comparison of the written and archaeological records, complemented by scientific analysis and experiment, may lead to advances in the methodology of battlefield archaeology that enable the effectiveness of particular survey techniques to be assessed, or revealing the archaeological signatures of different types of action. In exceptional conditions, for instance where colluviation enables the survival of ferrous artefacts, we may begin to understand the nature of the evidence that has been lost elsewhere. The wider patterning of artefacts may also assist in estimating the size and composition of the armies involved and suggest how they were deployed – issues that for medieval battles are poorly understood.

In the present study we were able to build upon the work that was undertaken to underpin the creation of the Register in 1995 (Fig 1.2), which then led the way in the conservation of fields of conflict in Europe (English Heritage 1995). Fifteen years on, we can review its achievement in the light of our current knowledge of the archaeology of such sites and suggest ways in which their management can be refined to ensure the long-term survival of all aspects of these nationally important places.

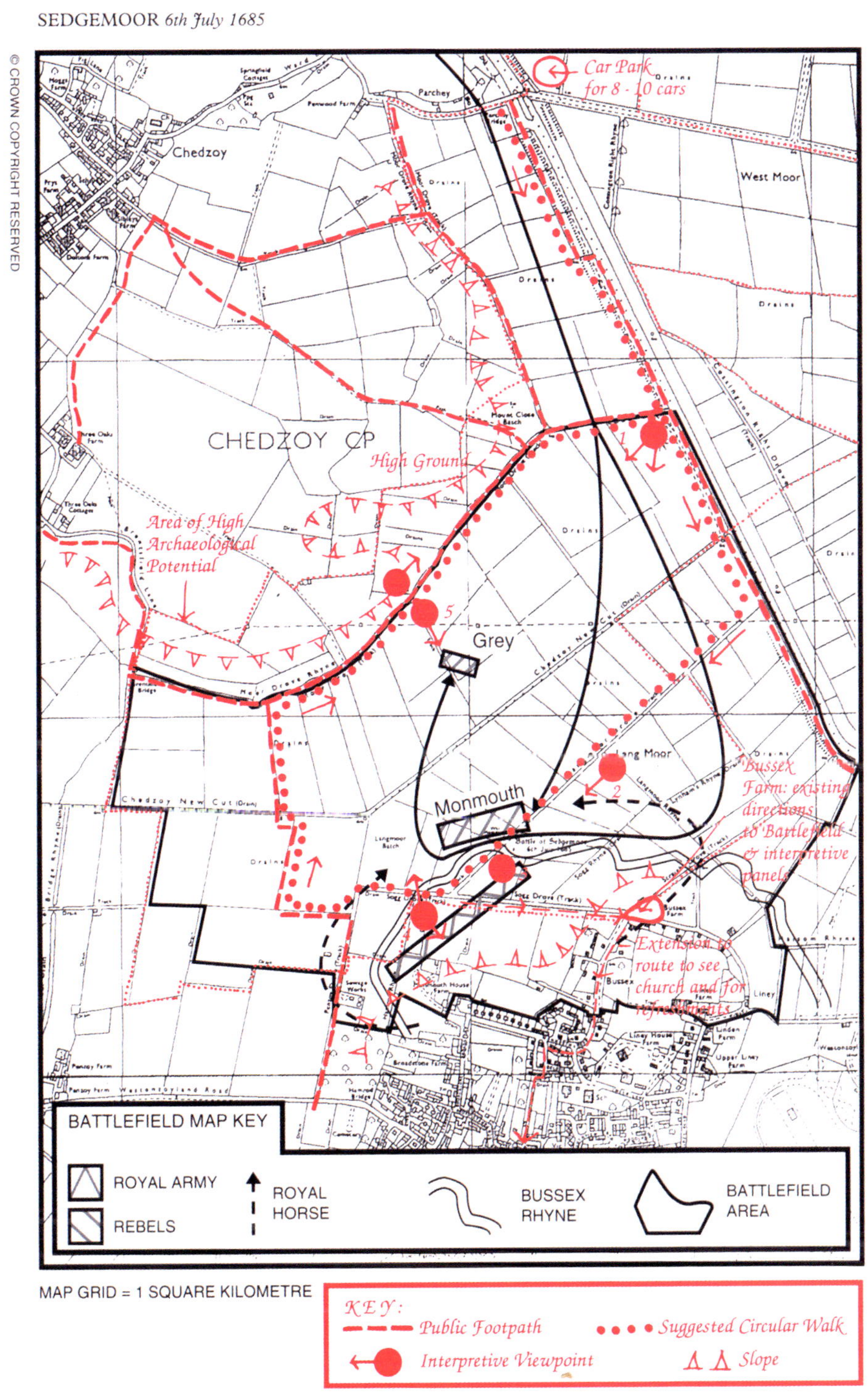

Fig 1.2 The plan from the Register entry published in 1995 for the battle of Sedgemoor (1685). In addition to the Register boundary it shows troop deployments, existing access and interpretation, and potential for enhancement (© English Heritage / Crown copyright 2012. Ordnance Survey Licence number 100024900)

Phases of warfare

Four main phases of warfare can be defined in England, according to the character of the evidence. For the pre-Roman period the absence of written records means that we have no knowledge of when or where battles took place. Without such information it may rarely be possible to identify a battlefield, though chance discovery of a mass grave or a scatter of projectiles might provide the basis for a search. This assumes, of course, that meaningful battle archaeology survives from this period and that an effective methodology can be designed to recover it. In contrast, evidence of sieges has occasionally been identified during investigations of pre-Roman defensive sites.

In the Roman (AD 43–410) and, especially, the early medieval (AD 410–1065) periods references to battles become progressively more common. Despite this, the quantity and character of the written record is rarely sufficient even to establish the general location of a battlefield. In England the existence of battle archaeology from this period has yet to be demonstrated, although two Roman-period battlefields in Germany, at Kalkriese and Harzhorn, have been identified from battle archaeology (Wilbers-Rost 2009; Geschwinde *et al* 2009). If distinctive siege archaeology of the period can be identified in England, as it has for several prehistoric sites, then this may provide a guide to the types of physical evidence to be expected on contemporary battlefields and suggest how these might be investigated.

During the later medieval period (AD 1066–1500) written evidence for battles becomes more detailed, and the locations of many battles and sieges, and some lesser actions, are thus known. Terrain reconstruction at a level of detail sufficient for the interpretation of a battlefield also becomes possible. This is especially true for the later centuries, from which detailed documentary sources are often available to complement evidence in the landscape itself. This can enable accurate mapping of the patterns of hedgerows, ridge and furrow, roads and other features as they may have been at the time of the battle, but apart from the elusive mass graves, we do not know whether significant battle archaeology from before 1450 survives on most battlefields or, if it does, what form it may take. In Europe there appears to be just one earlier site that has produced a surface scatter – Masterby in Sweden (1361), a small action which preceded the battle of Wisby (Knarrstrom 2009). In England the earliest substantial battle archaeology so far recovered dates from the later 15th century: Towton (1461) has yielded several thousand artefacts and it was at first believed that a similar signature might be present on most other medieval battlefields. However, recent work at Bosworth (1485) suggests this may not be the case: with the exception of lead round shot, the scatter of battle-related metal artefacts at Bosworth is far slighter than that seen at Towton. Without the focus provided by the artillery rounds the other evidence at Bosworth would have been very difficult to locate. Thus, the absence of battle archaeology, even after systematic metal detecting of a wide area, may not prove that the area in question was *not* part of the battlefield. If we cannot depend upon such negative evidence then the investigation of early battlefields becomes far more complicated.

As we enter the early modern period (from 1500 onwards) an increasingly wide range of documentary and physical evidence survives for both terrain and action. Artefact scatters in particular become more substantial in the 17th century, when the extensive use of handguns deposited lead bullets in their tens of thousands on major battlefields. An effective methodology has been demonstrated for the investigation of such archaeology on a battlefield-wide scale which can also ensure comparability between separate investigations of different sites or different areas of the same site. Such consistency is essential if the potential of the archaeological evidence is to be fully realised.

In addition to advancing understanding of individual battles, battlefield archaeology also has the potential to contribute to wider questions about the evolution of warfare. This can be demonstrated by comparison of the evidence from Towton (1461), Bosworth (1485), and Edgehill (1642). The very different battle archaeology from these sites reflects the transformation in the character of warfare resulting in large part from the introduction of gunpowder weapons. The ferrous arrowheads recovered from Towton show the warbow still dominant, with little in the way of firepower. In contrast, Bosworth appears to reveal the large-scale use of gunpowder artillery, but a continuing absence of gunpowder small arms. By the time of Edgehill one sees, in tandem with other important tactical changes, the highly effective large-scale use of handguns by both cavalry and infantry, carefully integrated with the use of hailshot by the artillery.

The early stages in the application of firepower to the battlefield, in the 14th and 15th centuries, are poorly evidenced in the written record. In the 16th and even the 17th century some of the detail of implementation and effectiveness remains unclear. Battlefield archaeology, however, can provide new evidence regarding when particular types of weapons came into use, in what numbers they did so, and how they were used tactically. The calibre of lead projectiles will indicate the bore of the guns and hence, with certain caveats, their type – such as musket, carbine, or pistol. This may show, in turn, where on the battlefield different types of troops – infantry, cavalry, dragoons, and artillery – were engaged and the intensity of fire they laid down. This is an important theme, for by the 19th century the application of firepower to the battlefield enabled Europeans to dominate the world.

Other changes in the nature of warfare were seen in earlier centuries. They include the transitions between actions fought wholly on foot in the early medieval period to those in which the use of heavy cavalry predominated after the Conquest, and then a return to the dominance of infantry in the 14th century (Prestwich 1996). This last change was associated with the rise to dominance of the warbow, making English armies feared across Europe thanks to victories like Crécy (1346) and Agincourt (1415). The arrowheads from Towton suggest that these transitions form another key theme which may be usefully investigated.

Battlefield archaeology thus has the potential to address overarching themes as well as to cast new light on individual events. To realise this potential carefully focused research is needed to establish the character of the evidence, where it survives, the range of questions which could be posed of it, and how it can best be investigated and conserved. Such action is urgent because, as we shall see, the evidence is under great threat from both uncontrolled metal detecting and the impact of modern agriculture.

Types of action

For the purposes of this study four broad classes of action are distinguished: battle, skirmish, siege, and raid. To an extent these categories are artificial, but they make a useful framework with which to organise

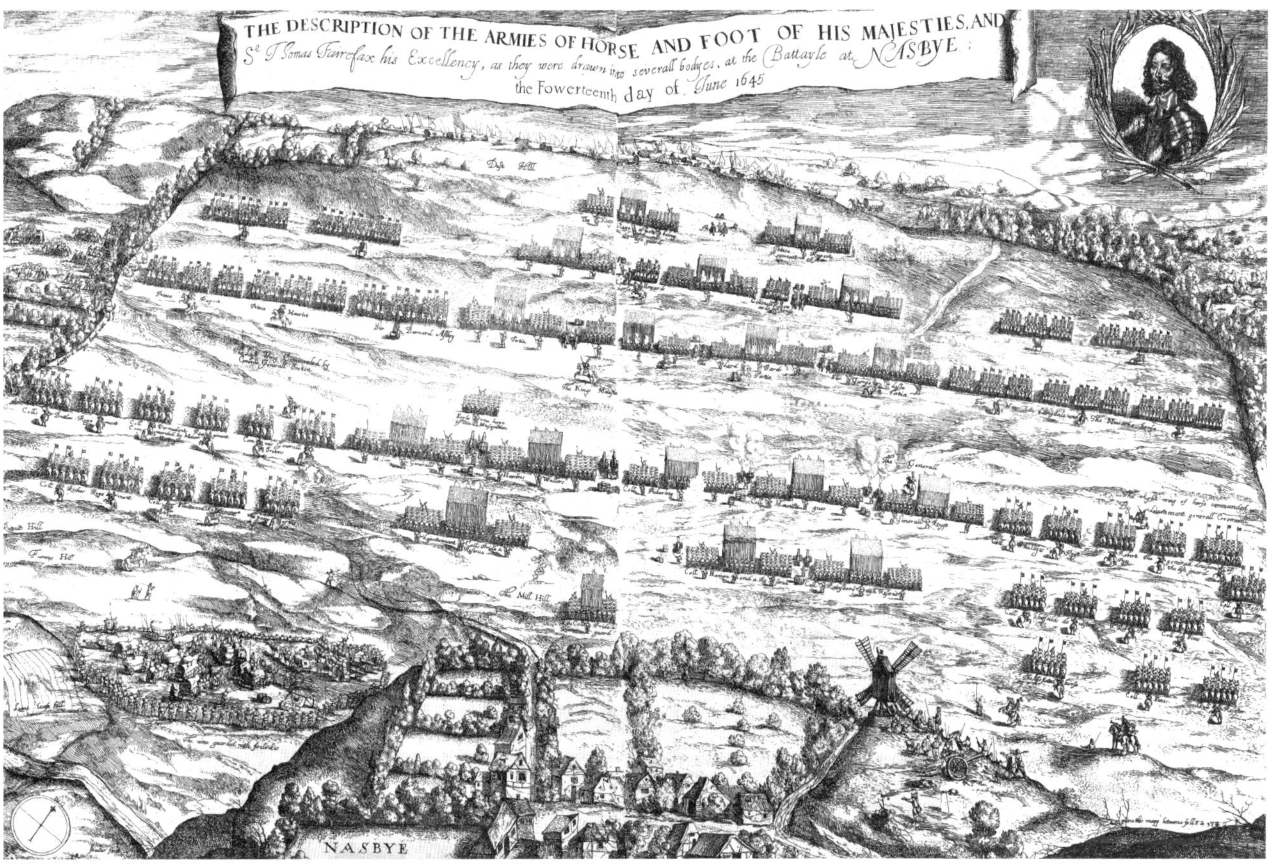

Fig 1.3 Troops deployed in battle array at Naseby (1645), depicted on an engraving prepared within a year or so of the event and published by Sprigge in 1647. Note the wide but shallow formations, organised with two or three supporting lines of troops, with infantry battalions interspersed with artillery in the centre, and with cavalry divisions placed on either wing. Such formations are typical of 17th-century battles (Reproduced by permission of the Naseby Battlefield Trust)

evidence. The principal focus is upon battles, and especially the chief actions, because they provide the greatest potential for combined documentary and archaeological study. A battle is taken to be an action involving wholly or largely military forces, present on each side in numbers totalling *c* 1000 or more, and normally deployed in formal battle array. There can, however, be exceptions – for example, where enclosed terrain required the use of disbanded tactics.

Defining the lower limit can be difficult, particularly with regard to the many actions of the Civil War in which fewer than 5000 troops were engaged; 1000 has been chosen because it was almost impossible, at least in open ground, to marshal larger numbers of troops without employing a formal battle array – and the use of a battle array represents a very distinct way of fighting (Fig 1.3). The slightly arbitrary nature of this limit of 2000 – for the combined forces of both sides – is demonstrated by the action at Middlewich (1643). It was fought in the town, probably with no more than 2000 troops, and so is listed here as a skirmish. However, for such a small action it is exceptional in having a surviving contemporary battle plan. This indicates that the troops were deployed in a formal battle array, not in loose order as might be expected in an urban skirmish (Liddiard and McGuicken 2007, 29).

Skirmishes, though sometimes subsidiary to battles, tended to form a separate part of a military campaign. A skirmish is taken here to be an engagement between forces not in battle array. Typically this occurred when small numbers of troops were involved, because the rigid order of a battle array was not so essential for the control of substantially fewer than 1000 men. As a result of the smaller numbers engaged, these sites tend to be less extensive than battlefields. Fighting by mainly disbanded forces did occasionally involve large numbers, but normally only when the action took place in an enclosed landscape of walled or hedged fields, in very heavily broken mountainous terrain, or in an urban area. In England by far the most substantial example is the complex action at Lostwithiel in 1644, in the largely enclosed landscape of Cornwall. Indeed, in 1995 this action was excluded from the Register because of its complexity. Such major events, some of which had important military and political outcomes, need to be dealt with alongside the more typical battles.

Border raids are taken to be relatively small-scale cross-border incursions, often by irregular or civilian forces, though they could comprise part of a larger military campaign by regular forces, sometimes termed a 'chevauchée' (Prestwich 1996, 10). The latter were sometimes major punitive actions that ended in a genuine battle, such as the Scottish incursion which led to the battle of Solway Moss (1542). All the examples identified here are from the Scottish Marches, where until the beginning of the 17th century security was poor and there was considerable reliance on direct action. We have not attempted to identify all border raids, but more intensive pilot work undertaken on Cumbria revealed such raids to be heavily under-represented in our data. Hence, many more sites than are currently present on our distribution maps are to be expected in the Scottish Marches, particularly in Northumberland. In the later Middle Ages similar actions may also be identifiable in the Welsh Marches, while a few seaborne incursions are noted along the south coast in the early modern period.

A small number of sites have been identified where large armies faced each other but engaged only in skirmishing, or in no significant action at all: Turnham Green (1642), where a major battle was narrowly avoided, is such a case. Various other sites are classed as 'unverified' in our data because of the limited or dubious nature of the evidence associated with them. Often this is local tradition, including finds of human remains, cairns and standing stones, with no contemporary written record. These sites are likely to be spurious, although continuing research may demonstrate that a few are genuine.

Sieges form the other major class of actions. These can normally be distinguished from battles and skirmishes because they were fought wholly or largely against fixed positions. While troops involved in battles might occasionally dig-in their artillery, construct temporary defensive works, or take cover behind existing non-defensive earthworks or buildings, the greater part of the action did not centre upon prepared defensive positions. Sieges, in contrast, were mounted to gain control of more permanent and substantial defensive sites which had been constructed to modify the strategic landscape and give long-term tactical advantage to the defenders.

2

THE EVIDENCE AND ITS INVESTIGATION

This volume is based upon the results of a largely desk-based project funded by English Heritage and undertaken at the University of Leeds (Foard 2008a). The project examined how the physical evidence for military action and the landscape in which it took place can be better integrated into the investigation and management of England's historic environment. The survey began by enhancing the Battlefield Trust's *UK Fields of Conflict* Database and the associated Bibliography (hereafter 'Database' and 'Bibliography').[1] We then assessed the battles, determined which could be located with reasonable confidence, and undertook a basic assessment of the sites' condition and potential. Finally, we carried out more detailed examination of a few representative sites. This involved an examination of secondary sources alongside limited work with primary documentary and physical evidence, supported by field visits. Where not specifically referenced in the present text, information on individual actions and features or other evidence related to them will be found in the Database and Bibliography. Both will be made accessible online via the Archaeology Data Service (ADS) at http://ads.ahds.ac.uk/ (doi:10.5284/1000399). The Database does not claim to be comprehensive; its principal focus has been on battles, and it aims to include all located battles (a list of which is given in Appendix 1) as well as iconic lesser actions. To allow direct comparison between English and Scottish battlefields, the methodology and classification used in the enhancement of the database for England followed that developed in our earlier enhancement of the Database for fields of conflict in Scotland (Foard and Partida 2005).

This work should be extended across Europe. England's battlefields belong within a wider tradition of European warfare, and there are variations in the character of warfare across Europe, such as the English dependence on the warbow as a battle-winning weapon in the 14th and 15th centuries. Ideally, therefore, it is within this wider context that English battlefields should be assessed, and the relative importance of some sites may well be viewed differently when they are placed in a European context. Until such a database is established that evaluation will not be practicable. However, to provide some feeling for the wider context, evidence from Ireland is included in some graphs and a few individual battlefields outside England are examined in the later phases of the study.

The end date of the study was set at 1799, thus including all English land battles, the last being Sedgemoor in 1685. So too are all skirmishes, as the last genuinely military land action was in 1778, during the American War of Independence, when American troops landed in Whitehaven. A number of topics were excluded from the study. Warfare in the industrial period is not considered because of its very different scale, character and archaeological signature. All naval actions are excluded for similar reasons. Memorialisation and public interpretation are not dealt with at length, except where memorials were raised within living memory of the event and might thus help locate the action; however, both these issues are briefly examined because they are of such popular interest. Siege sites are not addressed except insofar as their archaeology proves to be an essential complement to that of battlefields. (The limited work we were able to undertake on sieges showed that they require more intensive assessment than battlefields.) Skirmishes and raids have been added where data for them were revealed by our survey, but with the exception of a pilot study we did not make a national search for such sites.

To enhance the Database we first worked from secondary published sources. Further information was then gathered from Pastscape (the online database of the National Monuments Record (NMR)), from all but one of England's HERs, and from data made available online by the Archaeology Data Service (ADS).[2] An online search of the finds database of the Portable Antiquities Scheme (PAS) was also undertaken. The PAS search did not reveal artefacts which might indicate additional battlefields, and nor were any substantial assemblages noted that related to known battlefields.

Key facts about each site recorded on the Database

normally included name, date, location, and type of action, distinguishing between battles and skirmishes, border raids, sieges, and episodes of civil unrest. Where possible, component features of each battlefield were also identified. These include the locations of burials, memorials, specific battle finds, and modern surveys and excavations. All substantial published references, together with a small number of 'grey literature' reports relating to named battles, were listed in the Bibliography.

Evidence from the secondary works allowed us to classify 100 actions according to the number of combatants, although this proved impossible for 25 later medieval battles. Except for Lincoln II (1217), which is described in most secondary works as a battle, all actions with 2000 or fewer engaged were classified as skirmishes. This category includes two Registered battlefields, Chalgrove and Powick, which the Register reports show were merely skirmishes. The problem of classification is greatest when dealing with the mid-17th century because there were far more lesser actions, or at least there are many more reported in secondary works. As noted above, since there were already 88 actions from 1066 onwards that were classed as battles it was impractical to review skirmish sites in detail. If the full potential of archaeology in the study of early warfare is to be realised, this issue will need to be revisited and a representative sample of these lesser actions selected for investigation and conservation.

Next, the importance and potential of each battle was graded based on quality of sources, locational certainty, the number and survival of associated features, the scale of the event, and its probable military and political significance. For a rough-and-ready perspective on perceived cultural importance we assessed citations from a selection of 'all period' secondary sources, scoring each battle according to the number of such books in which it appeared.[3] This bibliographic score broadly reflects a combination of the perceived importance of the action together with the degree of certainty over its location and the quality of associated records and current understanding. Some early and unlocated battles earn a high rating simply because of their historical reputation or legendary status: Mount Badon (*c* AD 500) is an example. Some other battles, such as Sedgemoor (1685), have a high score because they are particularly well documented and understood, despite perhaps being of smaller scale or, arguably, of lesser military importance.

The initial scoring yielded a list in which the upper levels contained only a handful of surviving sites which had been omitted from the Register. Through this process it also became clear that no battlefield before 1066 is sufficiently well located to enable its detailed assessment. The second stage of enhancement was therefore restricted to 88 actions generally described as battles from the later Middle Ages onwards in which more than 2000 troops were engaged and which were considered potentially locatable. To improve on the crude assessment of perceived cultural importance described above, the Bibliography for these 88 actions was enhanced via a search by battle name in three online bibliographic databases: the National, Academic, and Specialist Library Catalogue (COPAC), the Royal Historical Society's Bibliography of British and Irish History (BBIH), and the British and Irish Archaeological Bibliography (BIAB).

For well-located sites, the modern Ordnance Survey Explorer mapping and online vertical aerial photography were examined for current land use, state of development, and the survival of ridge and furrow and other earthworks.[4] The Land Utilisation Survey of the 1930s and surface geology from the British Geological Survey (BGS) 1:10,000 scale mapping were also examined (Stamp 1931–35). Where exact location and extent were in doubt, this assessment was made around a conjectural centre-point grid reference for the site. Associations with Listed Buildings and Scheduled Ancient Monuments (SAMs) were not noted in the assessment because an initial review revealed few of significance. For many sites it was not practical consistently to assess other attributes, such as whether the troops were deployed in battle array, or to score documentary potential for both military history and terrain, since to do so would have called for time-consuming recourse to primary sources. The graded list for the battles, following the second level of assessment, is given in Appendix 2.

In this phase of work it was not possible systematically to search local historical and archaeological journals, volumes of record societies and related sources, which have proliferated since the 1840s. However, to gain a sense of what such a nationwide search might reveal, two sample areas were examined in such detail. The areas chosen were historical administrative units, because most local history literature is organised by historic county. One was Cumberland and Westmorland (essentially modern Cumbria), which was selected as a border region where numerous raids and other lesser actions were to be expected. The other was the historical West Riding of Yorkshire, which lay well away from a land border during the last millennium and hence was expected to be more representative of England's experience of warfare. The bibliographic search on these two areas began with antiquarian and local histories listed in Currie and Lewis's guide to English county histories (1994). In addition to yielding evidence, these works also helped to identify further potential sources of information on fields of conflict. For the sample areas online searches were repeated on COPAC and the BBIH using a variety of keywords likely to produce local history sources, including combinations of the county name with the following topics: history, civil war, battle, border, Scottish, rebellion, Jacobite, peel, castle, military, and siege. This method proved effective in finding article titles which do not appear in traditional library searches. Finally, a search was undertaken in the University of Cambridge Library. Here the main search of county histories and society journals was complemented by sources in the relevant local history sections of the library. Potential sources were then searched via their indexes (including for the names of specific actions, where possible), contents lists, or scanning rapidly through historical overviews in these works. Some sources, particularly antiquarian ones, were poorly indexed or not indexed at all; others were well indexed, but primarily by site or name rather than subject. A number of county histories were organised by parish or township, with in-depth historical discussions of each site. However, given the fixed time available and the number of parishes in each county, it was impossible to search each of the parish descriptions.

Such local searching was time consuming and erratic indexing makes it likely that some references to military actions were missed. References to actions were found in a wide variety of books and articles, so it is unwise to suppose that certain types of source, such as histories of major military conflicts or works on castles and fortified sites, should be prioritised. The large proportion of newly found actions with three or fewer references (34 out of 57 for Cumbria) demonstrates that most medieval and early modern military actions are not sufficiently well known to be noted in every local history source. Their citation, rather, appears highly dependent on the particular subject or focus of the author.

In Cumbria, as noted, 57 new battles, sieges and skirmishes were found, and additional references were identified for nine of the eighteen sites already on the Database. Five known events for which no additional references were found are either doubtful or are actions for which a number of possible locations have been proposed. Of the four added which might be battles, none is *certainly* of this scale and character: Dunmail Raise (AD 945); Burgh-by-Sands (1031); Naworth (1570) and Great Salkeld (1644). The most significant enhancement was in the category of sieges, where 41 are now recorded, in contrast with the 5 previously listed. Of these, 26 were sieges of Carlisle, the greatest of the border garrisons, which took place during the later Middle Ages, the Civil War, and the Jacobite rebellions. The remainder were primarily sieges of smaller castles or minor skirmishes. In all, there are now 30 skirmishes, as against six before. The vast majority of actions newly identified in this intensive enhancement for Cumbria were the 110 medieval border raids, none of which had previously been entered on the Database.

In the West Riding, 42 actions were added to the 47 already known. Nearly all them were sieges and minor skirmishes, with just eight recorded raids. Of the 42, over half took place in the Civil War. Only one additional battle was found: a spurious mention of a 5th-century encounter referencing a 'tumulus near the castle' which supposedly marks the burial place of the Saxon general Hengist, killed in battle by Aurelius Ambrosius. Additional references were also found for 38 of the previously known actions. As with Cumbria, rarely did previously unknown actions produce many references, and none yielded more than six.

This assessment demonstrates that intensive enhancement, although unlikely to identify additional battles, may be expected to yield additional sieges and skirmishes. It also highlights the different character and chronology of the actions in the two sample areas. The West Riding saw far more action in the Wars of the Roses and the Civil War whereas, not surprisingly for a border region, Scottish incursions characterised Cumbria's military history. When raids are excluded the West Riding appears to have suffered far more recorded military actions. This is not simply because the county is larger and less remote than Cumbria, but also because it is better-documented. Indeed, there are so many local history and antiquarian works available for Yorkshire that a comprehensive search would have been extremely lengthy. Most importantly, the study showed that our decision to concentrate our bibliographic search at the national level is unlikely to have resulted in a significant number of battles being missed, although it is clear that local sources must be included in any future assessment of sieges and lesser actions.

The final phase of our study involved intensive case studies of representative sites from among the 88 late medieval and early modern battles. In these investigations we drew upon research previously undertaken for the Battlefields Trust in 2002–05. At that time the files held by English Heritage's Heritage Protection team for each Registered battlefield, for 'Battle Sites', and for other sites assessed for the Register were consulted. Each of the Registered battlefields was also visited and its condition and potential considered in the light of the information presented in the relevant Register report. The online catalogues of the British Library, The National Archives, and Access to Archives (A2A) were consulted for historic maps of each site. Additionally, for selected battlefields a search was made of the indexes of the relevant County Record Offices. Where significant evidence was forthcoming we undertook digital mapping of relevant historic landscape detail. The RAF vertical aerial photographs of the 1940s and the oblique air photography in the National Monuments Record were searched for the Registered battlefields, enabling an assessment to be made of the extent of survival of earthwork evidence for the historic terrain. The primary focus of this work was upon ridge and furrow, but it also included abandoned drainage systems, roads, and enclosed field systems. To assist in the quantification of threats to the sites we consulted all local authority archaeologists on planning-related issues and all Finds Liaison Officers on metal-detecting rallies that had been held on battlefields.

Following the assessment of all this evidence these battle sites were selected as case studies: Sedgemoor, Naseby, Adwalton Moor, Marston Moor, Braddock Down, Edgehill, Bosworth, Towton, and Heavenfield. Hastings was also considered, but the large degree to which archaeological reports and other data for this site remain unpublished precluded more than a basic assessment of its topography. Sites of some other types of action, including the Civil War siege sites of Beeston Castle, Sandal Castle, Wareham, Morton Corbet, and Grafton Regis, were also selected for study. In addition, several prehistoric sites, particularly Crickley Hill and Danebury, were briefly reviewed from published sources.

In the analysis that follows we will draw upon each level of the data collected. We begin with the broad overview provided by the Database, which enables an understanding of the distribution of English battlefields through time and space. Later, we expand into the fine detail of individual exemplar sites: the threats to them and their research potential, the types of evidence they contain, and the ways in which they can be investigated. Before both, we briefly review the themes of interpretation and commemoration.

Interpretation and commemoration

Since 'evidential value' is the principal subject of the present study the interpretative and commemorative aspects of English battlefields were recorded only on an incidental basis (English Heritage 2008). As a result, the analysis that follows is not definitive. Despite this, the review demonstrates the degree to which fields of conflict have, for at least a thousand years, been a significant aspect of England's historic landscape.

There is today considerable public and educational interest in battlefields and other fields of conflict (Pollard 2003). Hastings (1066) and Bosworth (1485), both turning points in English national history, have substantial interpretative facilities which in 2009–10 received 131,480 and 48,500 paying visitors, respectively.[5] On a smaller scale, at Shrewsbury a visitor centre linked to a farm shop has been established by private enterprise (Jagger 2010). Potential for the development of visitor centres is being explored at several other sites. At Naseby the Naseby Battlefield Trust has applied for planning permission to construct a Visitor Centre adjacent to the battlefield, and at Towton discussions are underway to secure the use of part of an existing building close to the battlefield for a similar purpose (M Marix Evans and M Taylor pers comm). Although facilities on English battlefields are more modest than those found on major battlefields in the USA, they are – with a few exceptions, such as Kalkriese (Germany, AD 9) and Culloden (Scotland, 1746) – more substantial than those elsewhere in Europe.[6]

Effective interpretation, as distinct from a rehash of inherited tales, requires secure understanding of the battle and battlefield. Whether it is currently interpreted or not it also demands that surviving terrain features are effectively managed to maintain the overall interpretative potential of the site. Without understanding, conservation management may focus on the wrong area of landscape or overlook significant survivals from the time of the battle. Such knowledge is, therefore, the best defence against uninformed land use change. It was partly for these reasons that the

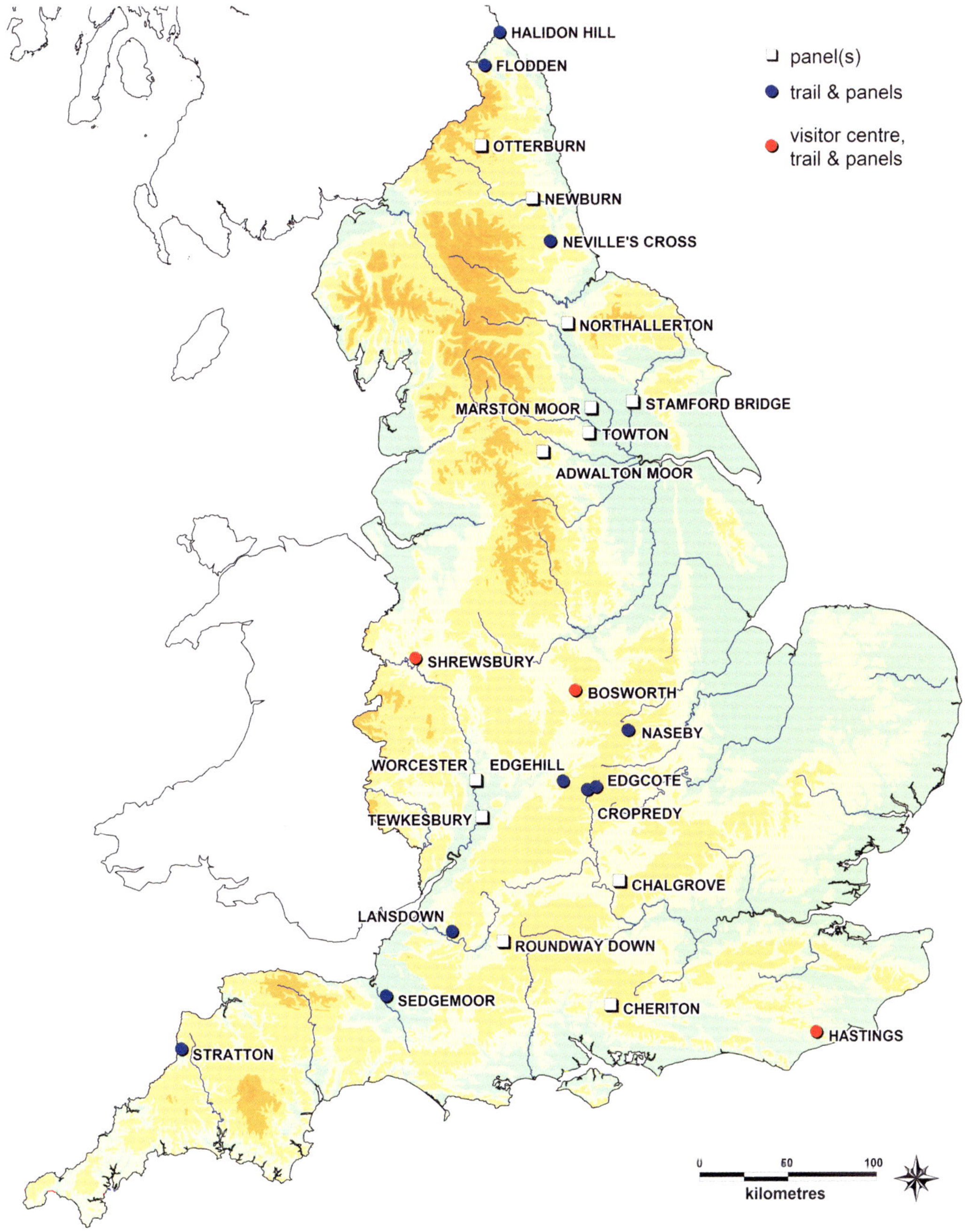

Fig 2.1 Map of the main interpretative resources on battlefields in England

Heritage Lottery Fund (HLF) required that the interpretation they were funding at Bosworth should be informed by a study to locate the true site of the battle.

Many battlefields are valued by their local communities; in many cases local societies, local authorities, or individual owners have established battlefield trails and interpretative panels (Fig 2.1). An example is Flodden (1513), which was estimated as having some 11,400 visitors in 2009 (C Hallam-Baker pers comm). The extent of interest here is also reflected in the number of published books and guides, and in the events developed to mark major anniversaries, such as that being planned for Flodden's 500th anniversary in 2013 (C Burgess pers comm).

At least twenty English battlefields have one or more on-site interpretation panels (Fig 2.2). Of these, twelve have battlefield trails, as at Lansdown (1643) and Shrewsbury (1403). The most elaborate is at Hastings, which also includes an audio tour. At Towton (1461) interpretative material was provided in 2010 in the grounds of the nearby Crooked Billet pub, in addition to a small panel beside the battlefield monument. Our study also found at least two interpretative schemes that had fallen into decay: at Stoke

Fig 2.2 An interpretation panel close to the supposed English deployment on the Halidon Hill (1333), Northumberland. The Scottish army is presumed to have deployed on the rising ground in the distance, where hundreds of shelters for the modern pig farm now stand. Innovative signage such as this does not always provide the visitor with the most useful information by which to understand the battlefield

(1487) the trail set up in the anniversary year of 1987 has long since disappeared, though the interpretation panels are now displayed in the church; and at Tewkesbury (1471) one decayed and illegible panel can be seen beside Bloody Meadow. While the need for continuing maintenance of interpretation schemes is obvious, such cases remind us that the need is not always observed. Maintenance is most likely to occur where there is active local interest, as at Worcester (1651), where vandalised panels were recently replaced.

Battlefield tourism has its origins in the 17th and 18th centuries, if not before. It can be seen, for example, in the brief visits of Celia Fiennes to Bosworth and of Robert Burns to Culloden, while Naseby shows well the evolution of battlefield tourism in the 19th century (Fiennes and Morris 1949; Foard 1995, 343–88).[7] Despite this early interest, apart from the minor signage erected in the late 19th century at Naseby, on-site interpretation is largely a development of the later 20th century. In earlier centuries commemorative structures were the norm: monuments, crosses, and, occasionally, chapels have been constructed on battlefields at least from the early Middle Ages, and monuments are still being erected today (Figs 2.3 and 2.4).

A total of 54 commemorative features, comprising 43 battlefield monuments and eleven memorial plaques, has been identified by the study. The most substantial are the chapels, which were constructed *de novo*, modified from existing chapels, or constructed as chantries within existing buildings. Then there are the various crosses; and finally there are the pre-existing features, such as prehistoric standing stones and isolated trees, which became linked with battles in local tradition. Most monuments were erected in the 19th and 20th centuries and their location will reflect the prevailing interpretations of the day. Those few earlier monuments which survive, such as those at Blore Heath (1459) and Lansdown (1643), may embody a genuine oral tradition that derived directly from the battle itself. For medieval and especially pre-Conquest battles, where there is so much uncertainty as to location, the existence of such monuments can be of considerable significance. The number of battle-related monuments that are scheduled or listed reflects the extent to which they have become elements of the historic environment in their own right. Indeed, it is ironic that these memorials are much better protected today than the sites of the events they were erected to commemorate!

Where battle-related crosses or chapels survive in their original location, or their earlier sites are known, they may be a strong indicator as to the general location of the action. The same may also be true of some springs, standing stones and other features that have a traditional or place-name link to a battle. But such a memorial need not be on the battlefield itself. A good example is King Richard's Well at Bosworth. First recorded in the late 18th century, it is now known to be *c* 3km north-east of the battlefield, its location perhaps indicating the site of Richard's camp on the eve of the battle. At Heavenfield, an action fought in the mid-AD 630s, the medieval chapel also lies several kilometres from the battlefield (see pp 48–9).

At least nine medieval chapels or religious houses stood upon battlefields or were associated with battles.

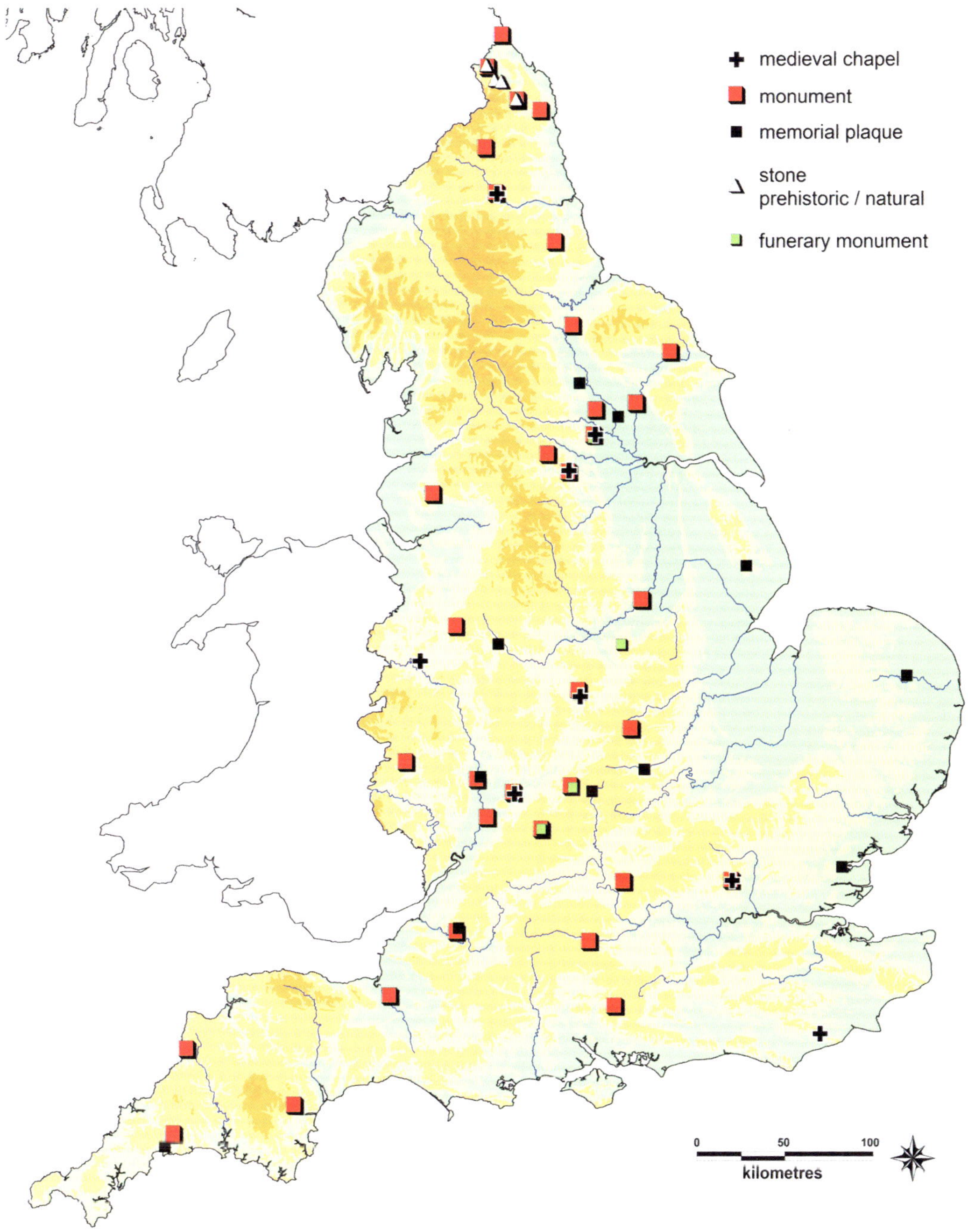

Fig 2.3 Commemorative features, including monuments, chapels and other monastic foundations (some of which no longer survive), on or associated with English fields of conflict[8]

The earliest known is associated with the action at *Assandun* in 1016, although the site of both the battle and the chapel is disputed (Rodwell 1993). The greatest is Battle Abbey, constructed by William I on the site of the battle of Hastings in memory of those killed. A collegiate church was built on the site of the 1403 battle at Shrewsbury; known as Battlefield church, it was given its own parish and, though heavily restored, it survives today in the care of the Churches Conservation Trust (Fig 2.5). Lesser chapels are documented at Towton, Barnet, Wakefield, and (probably) Evesham. That at Wakefield (1460) still stands, on the bridge to the north of the battlefield. The Towton chapel must have lain close to the mass grave excavated in the village in 1996, for the adjacent ground is called Chapel Hill; it is now thought likely that the building lay beneath the present hall (T Sutherland pers comm).

While the locations of some chapels are well known, the sites of others have been lost. At Barnet (1471) documentary research has recently identified the site of the chapel raised to the dead of that battle: it lies within an isolated moated enclosure near the former Kitts End, north of Monken Hadley (Warren 2009). This may prove to be the true site of the battle but,

Fig 2.4 Modern art, drawing upon 17th-century themes, enhances one of a series of small markers that add interest to the battlefield trail at Lansdown (1643)

Fig 2.5 Battlefield church, built to commemorate the dead of the battle of Shrewsbury (1403), viewed from the battlefield trail. This trail leads from a specially constructed car park and viewing platform on the southern edge of the battlefield. The new Visitor Centre lies to the north-east of the church in a converted farm complex

given the preceding catalogue, the location of the chapel cannot alone provide proof. At Evesham a well or spring said to lie close to where Simon de Montfort was killed in 1265 afterwards became a place of pilgrimage and a scene of miracles. Later a chapel was apparently constructed nearby, although geophysical survey undertaken in 2006 with the aim of identifying the site failed to produce definitive evidence of its location (Cox 1988, 21–8; Smalley 2008). There were wells on other battlefields which did not see the construction of chapels, the earliest being Oswald's Well, said to lie on or close to the site of the battle of Maserfield, where King Oswald of Northumbria was killed in AD 641.

The last battlefield chapel to be planned was that meant for Bosworth, but it was never built, and instead a chantry was established in the chapel at Dadlington – if, indeed, it was not intended all along to use this pre-existing chapel (Foss 1998, 38–9). That at Towton also appears to have been developed out of a pre-existing chapel of ease which, although lacking burial rights, had seen the burial of some of the bodies of those killed in the rout. There are a number of other chapels for which links have been claimed with battles or kings killed in battle, but which do not stand on a battlefield. One example is the 7th-century chapel which by tradition was constructed near Edwinstowe in memory of King Edwin, who was killed at the battle of Hatfield Chase in AD 632. A related group of sites are religious houses founded in expiation for acts of violence, such as the monastery established by King Oswiu at Gilling after AD 651 following the murder there, at Oswiu's instigation, of his rival Oswine (HE iii 14).

At least seven crosses stand or stood in supposedly significant relationship to English battlefields. That known as Neville's Cross, just to the south of Durham, already existed in 1346 and gave its name to the battle fought nearby in that year. In contrast, most battlefield-related crosses are believed to have been erected as memorials to the deaths of important individuals, as is the case with the Percy Cross on Hedgeley Moor (1464), which bears the heraldic badges of the Percy family and was presumably raised in memory of Sir Ralph Percy, a Lancastrian commander who died in the battle (Haigh 1995, 82). Others have a more tenuous traditional association: that on Stainmore, for instance, is linked to the violent death of Eric Bloodaxe in AD 950 or 954. The stump of a medieval cross survived there into the 20th century but is said to have since been lost in road works. Perhaps more secure is

Fig 2.6 The medieval cross said to mark the location where Lord Audley was killed at Blore Heath (1459). It is possibly the earliest surviving memorial on an English battlefield to an individual who died in action

Malcolm's Cross on the battlefield at Alnwick, which commemorates the Scottish king's death there in 1093. Nearby lay Malcolm's Well, where a leper hospital was later established; however, it is unclear whether the hospital was actually associated with the battlefield. The most substantial cross, said to have been erected in the 14th century as a memorial to the battle of Boroughbridge (1322), is a 5.5m column comprising four shafts banded together; unfortunately in 1852 this was moved a kilometre or so from Boroughbridge to the centre of nearby Aldborough. Probably the most useful cross, in terms of locating the action, is that at Blore Heath (1459), which is said to mark the place where Lord Audley fell during the battle (Fig 2.6). Its position in relation to the terrain seems to fit well with the original descriptions of action, although this interpretation will need to be archaeologically tested.

The history of battlefield crosses demonstrates that using them to locate a battle is not always simple. The cross on the battlefield of Otterburn (1388), for example, said to have marked the place where the

Scottish commander James, earl of Douglas died in action, originally lay beside the main road. In the 19th century the cross was moved by several hundred metres, probably because the main road had by then been realigned (National Army Museum 1995m). Although that cross had been constructed in 1777, Armstrong's map of Northumberland of 1769 shows that a 'Battle Cross' already existed at that time. Nonetheless, 381 years separate map and battle, so even the earlier cross may not represent a secure link in local tradition to the event itself. The cross on Towton battlefield appears even less secure, having been erected around 1900 using a medieval cross head, found nearby, which may originally have had no association with the battle (Sutherland 2000a, 155). At North Walsham a different problem arises, for there one finds the remains of three medieval crosses linked in local tradition with the battle of 1381, separated in all by more than 1km.

Of the early monuments three are reasonably securely linked to individuals: one, already mentioned, is the cross to Lord Audley; a second is the 17th-century monument on Wigan battlefield that marks the place where the royalist commander Sir Thomas Tyldesley died in 1651; the third is the 18th-century monument said to mark the place where Sir Bevil Grenville fell on Lansdown battlefield in 1643.

While some early constructions have a good chance of representing direct knowledge of the events themselves, later monuments usually lack such a link. They may have been placed more for convenience or visibility and so create confusion rather than accurately locate the action. Examples are the monuments to Colonel John Hampden at Chalgrove and to Lord Falkland at Newbury, both of which were placed beside main roads rather than where the individuals fell. The best example, however, is the obelisk at Naseby, erected in 1826 on a windmill mound in a prominent position more than a kilometre from the battlefield (Foard 1995, 358–9). Most of these general monuments belong to the 19th or 20th century, though the earliest may be that erected in 1709 at Mortimer's Cross (1461). This lies on the western edge of Kingsland, on the southern periphery of the battlefield as currently interpreted (Hodges 2001, 50; Haigh 1995, 42–3).

The study identified six genuine funerary monuments marking the graves of individuals who fell in a particular battle, erected within living memory of their deaths. Some lie in churches and churchyards close to the battlefield, others are more distant. The monument and effigy of Captain Kingsmill lie in Radway church, for Kingsmill fell in that parish during the battle of Edgehill. In contrast, the grave of Captain Gourdon, also a casualty of that battle, is in Warmington churchyard, some 6km from the centre of the action (Fig 2.7). This is presumably because, having been wounded in the battle, he was taken back to that village and died there of his wounds.[9] Others examples are in the church at Stow on the Wold (1646), in Saxton churchyard beside Towton (1461), in the church at Willoughby on the Wolds (1648), and in Middlezoy church near Sedgemoor (1685).

Fig 2.7 The gravestone of Captain Gourdon, in the churchyard at Warmington, Warwickshire, where he was buried in 1642, after the battle of Edgehill

As noted above, there are other features that have come to be treated as battle memorials, including prehistoric standing stones, natural erratics, and even some trees. In Northumberland several standing stones were already linked to battlefields on Armstrong's map of Northumberland of 1767. These include examples at Homildon Hill (1415), at nearby Yeavering or *Geteryne* (1415), and the so-called (King) James's 'chair' and 'stone' at Flodden (1513). The trees, which seem most often to be oaks, include the Battle Oak at Mortimer's Cross (1461) and Wardington Oak at Cropredy (1644). While most are now lost they have occasionally been replaced by memorial stones, such as the Burrand Bush Stone on Stoke Field (1487) (Barrett 1896, 149). Some may be spurious associations, as might be suggested for Charles's Oak in Sibbertoft, on Naseby battlefield, because the earliest reference to this name seems to be from the 1930s. Yet, even here, there is doubt, because the tree stood on an ancient enclosure boundary in an area that was dominated by open fields in 1645, and is close to a bullet scatter indicating an intense fire-fight during the battle (Foard 1995, 377).

Investigating fields of conflict

While the antiquaries who first studied battles sought to exploit all the available evidence, both documentary and physical, this holistic approach was abandoned as archaeology developed as a separate discipline during the 19th century (Foard 2008c, ch 1). As a result, for more than a century the study of offensive military action became almost the sole preserve of military historians. Working mainly from written records of the events and of the armies that fought, they brought important advances in understanding, although they rarely exploited the full range of archaeological and written sources for the historic terrain over which the battles were fought. This was left to local historians, who occasionally achieved important insights into individual battles, as did Twemlowe (1912) at Blore Heath (1459) and Foss (1990) at Bosworth (1495). Rarely, however, did that kind of work have a direct influence on the mainstream of battlefield study.

Almost never did military historians exploit the potential of battle archaeology. This was left to the amateur metal detectorist, once detecting had developed as a widespread hobby in the 1970s. Unfortunately, the collection of material by detectorists was not governed by the systematic methods of archaeological field survey. As a result, much of the potential information that could have been derived from the material they retrieved has been lost, while the pattern of the distribution that remains *in situ* has probably been distorted.

There is one notable exception in all this: the work of the historian Peter Newman at Marston Moor in the late 1970s (Newman 1978; 1979; 1981). He attempted to draw together all three strands of evidence, with some success, even though he lacked expertise in landscape history and archaeology. But Newman's work was never fully published – the first distribution plan did not appear until 2007, for example (Foard 2007a) – and as a result this important initiative did not influence the development of the subject in the way that it could have done. It was only in the mid-1990s that such evidence was effectively drawn into the study of battlefields, first at Naseby and then at Towton. This revealed the potential for archaeology to advance the understanding of fields of conflict in Europe, just as had already been recognised in the USA.

The fragmentation of antiquarian endeavour in the 19th century into separate fields of archaeological and historical study caused battlefield study to be abandoned by archaeologists. Without their involvement there was no effective way to place the events of a battle accurately within the terrain as it was at the time of the action. As a result, many battlefields still lack a secure location. The recent reintegration of archaeology with history in the study of battlefields is a good example of how major advances can be made by bridging the gap between disciplines – something that is now seen as an important objective (Smail 2009). As a result of such work over the last decade, European battlefield archaeology has now taken its place alongside that in the USA (Scott *et al* 1989; Meller 2009). The next challenge is to apply a fully scientific approach, supported by other specialist areas of expertise such as ballistics and computer modelling.

There are five main stages within the methodology for the investigation of battlefields. First, the general location of the battlefield must be identified. Next, the topographical evidence in primary accounts of the action should be isolated. A reconstruction of the historic terrain then follows, which subsequently enables the creation of a hypothesis through the placing of the documented events into the reconstructed terrain. Finally, the hypothesis can be tested by sampling the independent evidence provided by battle archaeology. Such investigation generates varied and complex data sets, so it is essential that they are integrated in a Geographical Information System (GIS).[10] Taking these now in turn:

Identifying the location

Secondary works often imply that battle sites are known. It is true that most early modern battlefields are securely located, but for later medieval battles there is often uncertainty. For early medieval battles this appears to be complete: with the possible exception of

Maldon (AD 991) (National Army Museum 1995j) no pre-Conquest battle site is currently located beyond reasonable doubt. Recent research into both the location of burials and the visual and physical networks of military communications and fortifications in Anglo-Saxon Wessex may offer ways to address the issue (Reynolds 2009, esp ch 2). For example, it may be that sites such as Ringmere in Essex and Woden's Barrow in Wiltshire, through the known location of burial features themselves, provide a good indication of the location of the battlefields. Examination of pre-Conquest actions against *burhs*, which are normally well located, could provide another avenue of approach. Elsewhere, however, battles in the early Middle Ages are not yet archaeologically approachable

The inability to locate battles arises mainly from lack of detail in the primary accounts – a difficulty that tends to increase the earlier the date of the battle. Uncertainty also tends to increase as the scale of fighting shrinks, with lesser actions normally being more poorly documented than major ones. Thus, while most battles of the early modern period are well documented, many of the skirmishes are not.

In looking for the general location of a battlefield, the first task is to review the secondary sources to establish current interpretations. Then, as Richmond did for Bosworth, one must return to the primary written accounts. These will show the degree to which current interpretations are supported by the primary evidence – particularly by the topographical detail and any alternative battle names. This information can, with care, be complemented by place-names, traditions, physical evidence reported by antiquaries, and more recent chance finds. These combined data will often enable a general area to be identified, although in some cases alternative sites may be revealed. It is to be hoped that Bannockburn (1314), in Scotland, for which at least nine possibilities have been given, is an exceptional example (Foard and Partida 2005).

Where problems remain, one can usefully look beyond the tactical terrain and consider the wider strategic landscape. This may include the major road network, river crossings and towns. In some periods and regions this landscape will have been modified by the establishment of garrisons or even by the construction of specific roads for military purposes, as seen over many centuries along the Anglo-Scottish border. Understanding the strategic landscape can often help in determining the direction of approach of the armies to the field, so complementing evidence in the primary accounts of the battle. To further narrow down the search one may, with care, resort to the principle of inherent historic military probability, considering what a soldier of the period is likely to have done in a given terrain and military context.[11]

Reconstructing the historic terrain

Once the battle's general location has been identified, the next step is to reconstruct in GIS the character of the landscape at the time of the battle, focusing especially upon the historic terrain. This comprises the militarily significant elements of the landscape contemporary with the action which are known or are likely to have affected where and how the battle was fought. In the past most battles have been analysed and presented in the context of a modern Ordnance Survey map, although certain authors have attempted to provide more. At Hastings, in 1869, E A Freeman employed the high-resolution relief shading recently made available by the Ordnance Survey, thanks to collaboration with Captain Edward James, whose father had been director-general of the Ordnance Survey. In 1907, by now a Major-General, James produced a new plan for F H Baring presenting deployments set on a high-resolution contour survey of the battlefield (Lawson 2002, fig 45 and plate 4). The role of physical geography in shaping the context within which a battlefield was selected, and its implications for the approach of the armies to the site, has also been considered for Hastings. Evidence of coastline changes over the last millennium reveals why Senlac Hill was chosen by Harold as the place to challenge the Norman army: it was a strong defensive location, controlling a narrow neck of land where the only major road led out from William's bridgehead at Hastings (Morillo 1996, maps 1 and 2).

Occasionally historic maps have also been used in an attempt to tackle major changes in the battlefield landscape. Hence in 1893, when Gardiner wrote on the first battle of Newbury (1643), he used Rocque's 1762 map of Berkshire as a base for his plan of the deployments. He chose this because it showed both Wash Common and Enborne Heath still unenclosed, and these open areas were where he believed certain troops had deployed and fought (Gardiner 1893, 1, 211) (Fig 2.8). For most battlefields the evidence is not so easily retrieved, but techniques exist that enable more to be achieved in many cases.

Such reconstruction has two objectives: first, to enable the topographical detail mentioned in primary accounts to be securely located, so allowing the events

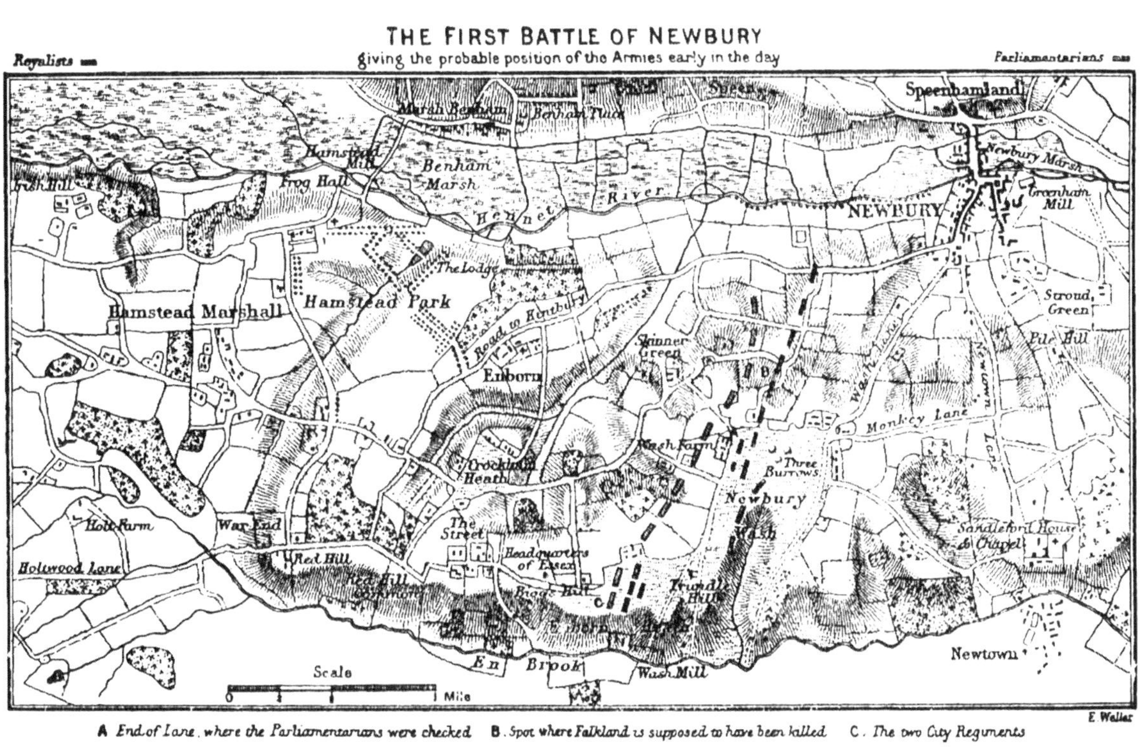

Fig 2.8 Rocque's 1762 map of Berkshire shows both Wash Common and Enborne Heath still unenclosed, as they had been in 1643. This map was used by Gardiner as a base on which to suggest the deployments in the 1643 battle of Newbury (Gardiner 1893)

to be accurately placed; and second, to provide an understanding of the wider terrain, which is the context within which the events of the battle should be analysed. That terrain was of great significance in warfare of all periods is shown by military manuals from *c* AD 400 (Vegetius) through to the 17th century (Cockle 1957). The impact of terrain on the way in which battles were fought was certainly understood throughout the medieval period. Thus, in the 12th century, Gerald of Wales discussed the suitability of heavy armour for use in the plain, but its disadvantage when used in restricted spaces, or in woody or boggy grounds. There, he said, the foot were at an advantage and light armour was preferable for mobility (Gerald, I, 8).

Terrain includes the underlying landform and the pattern of roads, watercourses, buildings, fields, woodland, and marsh. Some aspects, such as relief and geology, are normally stable within the historic period, so modern mapping can be used with little correction. While Ordnance Survey 'panorama' contours are normally adequate to understand the relief at a strategic level, they are not suitable for more detailed analysis because even slight changes of landform across a battlefield may have tactical significance. The fine detail needed is most easily met, at present, by the 5m digital terrain model (dtm) from NEXTMap Britain, though it must be validated by field examination and documentary research to isolate any modern changes. It can be used in GIS for viewshed analysis to determine, for example, which ground is likely to have been within and which outside the range of artillery set in particular locations.

Most other elements of the historic landscape have been altered by man, often undergoing striking changes since the time of the battle. Some of these, such as the former extent of marsh or meadow, may be suggested by drift and solid geology, mapping of which is available from the British Geological Survey at 1:50,000. Yet more detail can be provided by soils mapping, available from the Soils Survey. Unfortunately there are large tracts of England for which mapping at 1:25,000 scale or better is not available. At Bosworth an existing survey covered half of the battlefield, but the remainder required new specialist fieldwork and analysis. For man-made or man-altered aspects, therefore, one must draw upon documentary, archaeological, or palaeo-environmental data. Yet even with the advances achieved by the English landscape school over the last 50 years (Fleming 2007), the reconstruction of a day in the life of a landscape remains a difficult challenge. The potential for reconstruction will vary considerably by period, region, historic landscape character, and specific location, depending on the complexity of the landscape, the trajectories of change, and the quality of documentary and physical evidence. There may even be variation between different parts of the same battlefield. The earlier the battle, the more difficult reconstruction will tend to prove.

The broad regional variations in the character and evolution of England's historic landscape are reasonably well understood (Aalen 2006; Cunliffe 2006; Hooke 2006; Kain 2006; Short 2006; Stocker 2006; Williamson 2006; Winchester 2006). During the medieval period a large area of England was under open-field cultivation. In the 'central province', from Northumberland to Dorset, enclosure of these open landscapes tended to be late. Open-field systems were still running in many places into the 19th century, though enclosure did happen in other townships as early as the 15th century (Roberts and Wrathmell 2000; Hall forthcoming; Tate and Turner 1978). On either side of the central zone, in regions such as East Anglia or Cheshire, enclosure tended to happen well before the parliamentary enclosure acts of the 18th and 19th centuries. In the most peripheral areas, such as the far south-west, largely enclosed landscapes existed throughout the last millennium. Right across England there could also be large tracts of heath, fen, and woodland, with extensive pastures on downland and many upland areas dominated by moorland.

As an example of the varying potential for terrain reconstruction at different times and in different zones one may take the open-field landscapes of Central England. Here arable furlongs, comprising bundles of parallel strips, are believed to have reached their maximum extent in the early 14th century. Thus, where there is good survival of headlands and of ridge and furrow on the ground or on aerial photographs, and where furlong patterns are well documented on historic maps or in written sources, it is possible to suggest the maximum extent and layout of the open-field system at around 1300. Where furlongs can be shown never to have existed then informed analysis, taking into account drainage, relief, and geology, as well as documentary evidence, may allow the extent of meadow, heath, wood, or moor also to be defined (Foard *et al* 2009; Hall forthcoming; Hall 1982). Reconstruction proves more problematic the earlier or later one moves from *c* 1300. In later centuries the open-field systems tended to contract as a result of enclosure for pasture. Where the landscape remained largely in open field until the early modern period, then reconstruction may still be practicable. If it was still open at parliamentary enclosure or is depicted as such on an early map, then it is unlikely that it had ever been enclosed beforehand and reverted to open field. In areas characterised by ancient enclosures, however, it may not be possible, in the absence of written records, to determine what was open and what enclosed at the time of an early modern battle. Similar issues arise over the enclosure of moor, fen, and heath. Where documentary sources such as maps, terriers or charters survive they may shed light upon the chronology of enclosure. Thus, at Adwalton Moor (1643) the western part of the battlefield was mapped in great detail in 1599, but no relevant sources for the more important eastern part of the battlefield have yet been located (see Fig 8.15). When one looks back in time from *c* 1300, the picture becomes even more uncertain. Here the question is when land was incorporated into the open-field system from former pastures, heath, moor, or woodland. There is far less chance of relevant documents surviving for these earlier centuries. Thus, at Stamford Bridge (1066), while it may be possible to reconstruct much of the open-field system and to define areas which had not been converted to arable by the height of medieval expansion (see Fig 3.15), it is unlikely that it will ever be possible to define the extent of arable when the battle was fought. Different, if not more complex, problems will be posed when working in other regions and landscape types.

Finally, there are problems posed by individual places, whether as a result of the unique trajectory of their evolution or the vagaries in the survival of evidence. At Edgehill (1642), for example, a large area of open fields continued to function well into the 18th century in Kineton and Radway, whereas some adjacent townships had been enclosed long before 1642 (see Fig 7.21). Radway has a surviving 'draft' enclosure map which covers the open areas in that township where the battle was fought and shows that almost the whole township was still open in the mid-18th century. As is usual with these drafts, the map reveals fine detail for the pre-existing furlongs and roads, together with the few hedges and enclosures that did exist. In contrast, there is no map for either Great or Little Kineton townships, where far more of the action took place. Here one can only attempt a crude reconstruction of the extent of ancient enclosures and open-field land using the 18th-century enclosure awards. These awards and the enclosure maps which often accompany them provide little other detail on the character of the pre-existing landscape (Hollowell 2000).

It is rare that such variation in potential between or within battlefields can be predicted from a search of the indexes of record offices: the potential becomes clear only when the documents themselves are examined in detail. It is possible to make an initial assessment of the historic landscape using the English Heritage Landscape Characterisation mapping, but it must be used with great care. When applied in our case study of Braddock Down (1643) the characterisation data failed to provide detail sufficient to enable meaningful analysis (see Fig 7.3).[12]

Other aspects of terrain may always remain elusive, particularly if they varied according to the time of year and the particular crop rotation. For example, given the great height of cereals prior to the modern era, when they could be as tall as a man, the presence of a standing crop in summer might provide cover that was missing at other times. Establishing which land was under cereal and which fallow in a particular year will be impossible on most battlefields, for although such information can occasionally be found in the field orders in court rolls of the 17th century it is extremely unlikely that such documents will survive for the specific year of the battle.

Placing deployments and action within the historic terrain

Topographical detail in the primary accounts of the battle can now be used to suggest the location of the deployments and action. If there are more than one or two primary accounts then a concordance can be constructed, creating a coherent single structure, as has been demonstrated for Edgehill (Foard 2008c, 341 et seq). This enables all documentary evidence for each element of the battle to be correlated to provide a sequence of events, each with its linked topographical information.

Where the battle accounts are detailed and terrain reconstruction has identified relevant topographical features it may be possible to place the deployments and action with a high degree of accuracy, as at Naseby (1645) and Sedgemoor (1685) (see Figs 8.13 and 7.9). Where accounts are less specific, the terrain reconstruction less complete, or terrain had less influence on the events, then uncertainties are likely to remain. The earlier a battle, the more difficult this task is likely to prove, because battle accounts will be less detailed and the terrain more difficult to reconstruct. Even with such limitations, however, if there was highly constricted terrain then accurate placing of events may still be possible. This is the case at Towton, where the accounts show that fighting took place on land between the villages of Towton and Saxton (see Figs 5.5 and 5.6). Since there is a precipitous slope to the west and there was, apparently, wet moor to the east, there is only one area within which the battle could have been fought. Here, too, the principle of inherent historic military probability may safely be applied: the high ground is divided by a single shallow valley, and the only logical place to deploy would have been on either side of the valley, where troops could have stood well out of the range of opposing archers.

Achieving the level of accuracy seen for Naseby and Sedgemoor demands knowledge of the likely width of the frontage of each army when deployed in battle array. This in turn requires information on both the numbers of troops present and the tactical formations used. The latter may be reported in the accounts; if not then informed conjecture must be employed, based on an understanding of practice in the period or even the preferences of particular commanders as demonstrated in other battles (Roberts 2010). The tactical deployments of early modern battles, unless fought in an enclosed landscape, are sufficiently well understood that a reconstruction of the battle arrays, down to the level of battalion, can usually be suggested (Foard 2008c, ch 2). This will be far more difficult for medieval battles, however, as can be seen by comparing the alternative frontages that have been suggested at Hastings (see Fig 3.14). This is because we lack reliable information on troop numbers, which are often exaggerated in the primary sources, and our knowledge of battle formations in the period is likewise poor (Strickland and Hardy 2005). As a result, it may only be through archaeological investigation that the width of medieval frontages will ultimately be understood. Thus, at Towton, whatever tactical formation one might apply, the constricted terrain precluded the deployment of the vast numbers of troops claimed in some primary accounts (Boardman 2000, 90–2).

The greatest limitation normally lies with the topographical detail in the primary accounts. A comparison of the primary accounts for two major battles, Bosworth (1485) and Edgehill (1642), illustrates the point. The numbers of significant primary accounts for each battle are 5 and 24 respectively; first-hand accounts 1 and 21; and total topographical references in all accounts 13 and 143. There are, of course, exceptions: the battle of Hastings (1066) is far better documented than Bosworth, for example (Morillo 1996; Allen Brown 1984; Lawson 2002). Before 1066, however, the topographical evidence is so vague or non-existent, and subsequent landscape change so great, that reconstruction may lie beyond the reach of current methodology.

Surveying the battle archaeology

The hypothesis as to the placement of deployments and action must now be tested by surveying the battle archaeology. The physical evidence is principally in the form of a scatter of metal artefacts in the topsoil. In limited areas of a few battlefields a proportion of the finds may have been protected through secondary stratification – for example by colluviation. Primary stratified evidence is normally restricted to the burials of those killed in action, in mass graves on or close to the battlefield. Defensive features were not normally constructed on battlefields, although there were exceptions. Only in the case of sieges, where the action was against a fortified site, are substantial defensive and offensive structures normally found. On early modern sites there may also be impact scars on buildings. These are most common on siege sites, but are occasionally seen on battlefields, where they provide evidence for troops taking cover behind or within existing structures.

The spread of artefacts deposited during a battle can provide detailed information about the action, although the character, density, and spatial extent of scatters will vary dramatically according to the period and type of action. This has implications not only for what they can tell us, but also for the survey methods needed to recover the evidence. From the great arrowstorms loosed by English warbows in the 14th and 15th centuries to the relentless fire of machine guns in the 20th, the tactical use of projectile weapons is central to the archaeological understanding of warfare.

On battlefields of the 17th to the 19th century by far the most common artefact is the lead bullet. Tens of thousands of them were fired during major battles. They are accompanied by smaller numbers of fitments from military equipment or personal possessions, such as buttons, strap ends and buckles, which have often survived in good condition because many were of copper alloy (Fig 2.9). For this period the character of the scatter will vary significantly across a battlefield, reflecting the nature of the action in each sector. Thus, at Edgehill (1642) the cavalry action produced a scatter of smaller calibre bullets at relatively low density, whereas the infantry action yielded a far higher density of bullets, most of larger calibre and including some fired from artillery (see Figs 7.15–7.16 and 7.21–7.22). The archaeology of early modern battles is so distinctive and substantial that if a sufficiently large area has been surveyed the lack of an artefact scatter can normally be taken to indicate that the action occurred elsewhere.

In England before the mid-16th century, small arms were in very limited use on the battlefield and thus bullets will not be common. However, what may be present from the later 15th and earlier 16th centuries are lead round shot fired from artillery (see Figs 5.8–5.10). These scatters are much thinner than those of bullets because artillery have a lower rate of fire and are present in far smaller number than small arms. Hence, although Bosworth has so far produced the

Fig 2.9 A silver coin recovered from Edgehill battlefield, which may have been deposited during the fighting. Like other non-projectile artefacts, it could represent casual loss unrelated to the battle (Reproduced courtesy of D Beaumont)

Fig 2.10 Heavily decayed arrowheads of ferrous metal from Towton (1461) (Reproduced courtesy of T Sutherland)

largest assemblage of round shot from archaeological survey on any site of the period in Europe, the total recovered is just 34.

Until recently, it was believed on the evidence reported from Towton (1461) that the absence of bullets from medieval battlefields was compensated for by the presence of large numbers of artefacts from personal and military equipment lost in the action. These have been recovered from Towton in far greater numbers than are seen on Civil War battlefields (see Figs 5.5–5.6). Even arrowheads, manufactured from vulnerable ferrous metal, have been recovered from Towton in substantial numbers – the count by 2010 exceeded 300 (T Sutherland pers comm) (Fig 2.10). However, the results from Bosworth, supported by small-scale investigation at sites such as Flodden (1513), suggest that most sites yield only small numbers of such finds (Pollard and Oliver 2002, 118–83).[13] If so, then for most medieval battlefields, unless lead projectiles were used, it may prove very difficult to demonstrate the location of a site through metal-detecting survey alone. For that reason, it may not be valid to argue from the lack of battle archaeology that a particular area is not part of the battlefield, as has been suggested at Agincourt (1415) (Sutherland 2009).

English battlefields from before 1461 have yet to produce any artefact scatters, despite several investigations – in large part because most artefacts deposited were of ferrous metal (Pollard and Oliver 2002, 52). Only when one reaches the prehistoric period does clear evidence reappear, in the form of highly stable flint artefacts such as arrowheads. From the Neolithic there are substantial scatters of flint arrowheads on several sites, while scatters of stone slingshots on several hillforts date to the Iron Age. The slingshots may once have been accompanied by scatters of iron arrowheads, but these are likely to have decayed in the intervening millennia. Their best chance of survival is incorporation into stratified deposits, as has occurred with ferrous ballista bolts from several sites of the Roman period.

Ascertaining whether battlefields from 1066 to the 1450s contain battle archaeology is a key issue, which can be addressed through a programme of carefully targeted research on several battlefields. These should be well-preserved sites where the documentary record, constricted terrain, or other evidence leaves little doubt as to the location. Examples include Hastings (1066) and Northallerton (1138). This work should be complemented by intensive resurvey of late 15th- and 16th-century battlefields where, unlike Towton, little battle archaeology has yet been removed. Here the lead projectiles may provide a framework within which more typical medieval military material resulting from archery and hand to hand action can be sought. These sites include Bosworth, Flodden, and Barnet (1471), where the presence of lead round shot has been demonstrated. Northampton (1460) is another candidate where at least some artillery seems to have been fired in the battle (National Army Museum 1995l). The battlefield at Northampton may already have been identified in the parkland beside Delapre Abbey, if 'battle dyke' is the ditch of the Lancastrian camp which was the focus of the action (Hall 1980).

Previous collecting

Aside from those found on prehistoric sites, most battle-related artefacts are of metal and thus normally retrieved using metal detectors. Survey methodology has evolved significantly over the last decade, and work undertaken some years ago will not meet the standards expected today. Only a few sites in England have seen intensive archaeological metal-detecting survey across most of the battlefield. At Towton this has been of an unstructured 'random' form, more typical of non-archaeological investigations. The only systematic archaeological surveys on this scale so far completed in England have been at Edgehill and Bosworth – both undertaken in non-ferrous mode. Survey work has recently started at Flodden (C Burgess pers comm) and is planned on other sites, including Roundway Down (1643). Small-scale intensive sampling, some in all-metal mode, has also been undertaken on other sites, such as Shrewsbury and Sedgemoor (Pollard and Oliver 2002).

The greatest problem with data from archaeological surveys of battlefields is the lack of consistency in sampling. Without such consistency it is very difficult to compare results between surveys on different sites, or to integrate data from different surveys on the same site. This is clearly seen in the four different pieces of development-led fieldwork undertaken in recent years at Pinkie (1547) in East Lothian, Scotland (Foard 2008f). To address the problem, standards need to be agreed and best practice then disseminated to both curators and contractors.

A large amount of material has been recovered from some battlefields by a few detectorists who have embarked on independent surveys without the benefit of archaeological expertise. An undefined amount of material has also been removed, typically without record, by treasure hunters. 'Collecting' and 'collector' are used here as neutral terms for all non-archaeological recovery of objects from battlefields. The objectives and methods followed by collectors vary enormously. At one extreme collectors may make a record of find locations to see what pattern they make across the landscape, in an attempt to understand the battle – this was the reason for the collecting at Naseby. Others report finds to the Portable Antiquities Scheme with a general location to the site, but lack interest in the information that distribution patterns can provide. Some are simply intent on assembling private collections or amassing material for sale on eBay. While most collectors are law abiding and work with landowner permission, there are a small number – the 'nighthawks' – who work illegally on protected sites.[14]

Collecting can provide useful information, especially if there has been some attempt at recording find locations. Work on a handful of sites, including Naseby, Marston Moor, and Towton, from the late 1970s through to the late 1990s, played a large part in demonstrating the archaeological potential of our battlefields. Despite this, it must be recognised that artefact removal outside the framework of a well-designed archaeological survey will typically destroy valuable information. At best, collectors' records have tended to be sketch plots to an Ordnance Survey map base, and usually made later, from memory – sometimes long after the event. The unreliability of such data can be seen from comparison of the archaeological GPS plot of Paul Roberts' detecting finds, made on one day at Marston Moor, with that collector's sketch plan of all finds from years of collection, including that day (Fig 2.11).[15] The discrepancy between the two distributions suggests that the sketch plan misrepresents the true pattern, reinforcing concern over the discrepancies between Roberts' plan and the sketch plan compiled by Newman from his field-walking survey of the bullet scatter in the late 1970s (Foard 2007a). While the quality of evidence may vary between different collectors, the Marston Moor example demonstrates the care that must be taken when such sketch plans are employed.

The identification of types of artefact or calibre of bullet on sketch plans is often very basic, if given at all. While amateur collectors can be highly knowledgeable on some classes of metal artefact there is no way to revisit their classification, because in the past finds were not normally separately bagged and located. In other cases collectors have dispersed the material, as appears to have happened with many of the finds from Marston Moor. Calibre classification alone is suspect, given the complexity of the calibre graphs discussed below (see Figs 7.39–7.40 and 7.42–7.44).

Storage of finds also poses a problem. Bullet assemblages are often stored together in large containers, leading to damage through abrasion which in turn generates lead carbonate dust that poses significant health risks. Attempts to limit chemical decay through the control of humidity are usually not made.

There are exceptions to these generalisations. At Edgehill in the late 1970s, Captain Grant investigated a small part of the battlefield using metal detecting. Not only did he produce a 1:2500 scale map of find locations, he also recorded his survey transects and intensive survey areas, noting the time spent detecting in each area (Foard 2008c). The finds were not individually numbered, however, and their present whereabouts is unknown. Another potentially significant assemblage is that collected in the 1970s and 1980s at Cheriton (1644). It is possible that this work was systematic, detailed and well recorded, but it is difficult to validate the claim as the published data comprise the finds from just one field (Bonsall 2000; 2008).[16]

Where such collection was undertaken ten or fifteen years ago it cannot be criticised, as nowhere in Europe was there then archaeological best practice to follow. Today such collection should not be considered acceptable. As we have seen, in the absence of systematic methods of recovery, recording, and analysis, the data provided by collectors can be misleading. Even more importantly, the haphazard removal of finds in large number distorts the distribution of surviving material compared to the original distribution, so compromising future systematic survey.

In recent years some collectors have begun to use navigation grade GPS to record the position of each artefact.[17] However, at Marston Moor in 2000 and more recently at Newburn we have found collectors abandoning the practice as too time-consuming, probably because the principal interest of many collectors is in the objects rather than in the information that accurately recorded spatial patterning can provide (Foard 2010b). Even where collectors now provide fairly accurate information to the Portable Antiquities Scheme (PAS) there may still be

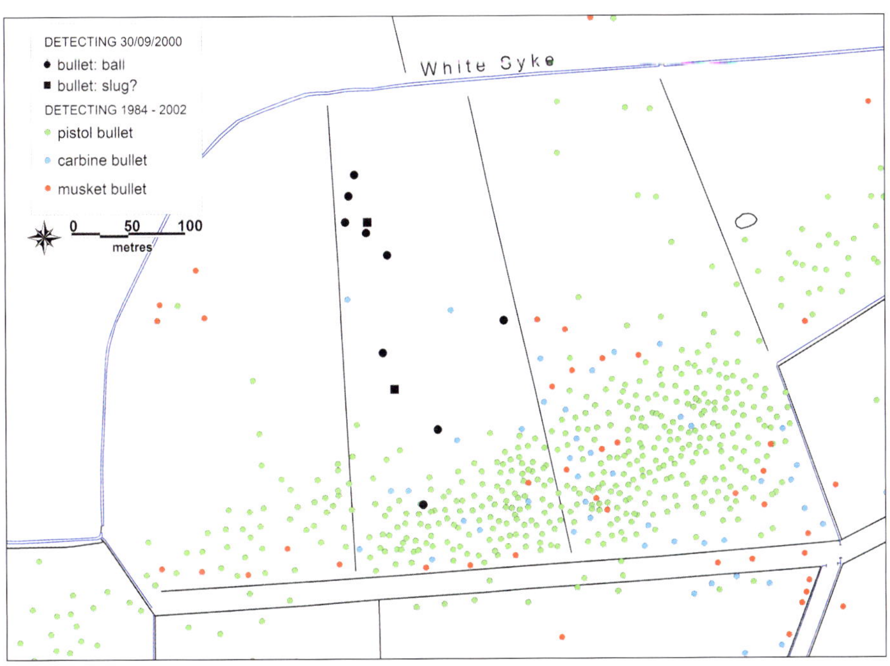

Fig 2.11 There is a major discrepancy at Marston Moor (1644) between the archaeological record of metal-detecting find locations made on one day using GPS, and the sketch mapping of this and the rest of Roberts' 18 years of collecting on the site

concerns over accuracy and consistency. More alarmingly, some collectors may provide intentionally inaccurate information to conceal the true location of the site from other detectorists. Even recording by a finds specialist may not always recognise the true significance of a battle-related find; for example, two lead round shot, a Burgundian jetton, and a belt fitting found by a collector at Barnet (1471) may indicate the exact location of that major battle. Although the form and calibre of the round shot are comparable with those from Bosworth and Flodden (discussed below), the PAS database identifies them as probably of the 17th or 18th century. It also places them in locations other than those subsequently described by the finder to the Battlefields Trust (see Fig 5.3). While the former location might make sense if the currently favoured deployments for the armies were moved slightly north-eastwards, the locations given to the Battlefields Trust fit better with an alternative site some distance to the north-west.

What is needed, wherever practicable, is the integration of reliable collectors into archaeological surveys. The progress made at Towton is an example; up to 1997 the finds made there by Simon Richardson were added to a sketch map with an unspecified accuracy level. Subsequently the sketch mapping was made onto a large-scale Ordnance Survey map base. By 2002, following the lessons learned from work with GPS at Marston Moor (see Fig 2.11), recording using GPS was instituted at Towton and the data were subsequently digitally mapped by Sutherland, though using Penmap software rather than true GIS. The collection method, however, continued to be determined by the detectorist, and thus remained unsystematic, while no record was made of survey intensity or extent. The distortions that can be introduced by non-systematic work are demonstrated below for Sedgemoor (see Figs 7.10–7.12).

Systematic survey methods

Two main methods have been employed to produce consistent data in battlefield survey. The first uses a grid which is accurately laid out and recorded. Each square is systematically surveyed by a detectorist, following one orientation of the grid, to give full surface coverage. Each find is then separately bagged and its location accurately recorded for later analysis in GIS. This method was applied, using a 20m grid, in the late 1990s to produce high-resolution distribution patterns in the survey of the Grafton Regis siege site (1643) (see Fig 7.38). A similar method was applied in the survey which sampled part of the battlefield at Culloden (1746) (Pollard 2009, 142). For more complete recovery of artefacts each square can be re-detected at 90 degrees to the original survey, thus taking account of problems posed for a detector by the angle at which objects lie within the ground. However, the grid method is very time-consuming and so is best used where the aim is 100% coverage of limited areas of a battlefield.

The alternative method uses a series of regularly spaced parallel transects for each field – an approach first applied in the Little Bighorn survey (Scott *et al* 1989). It is effective where the intention is to cover a large part or all of a battlefield by systematically sampling less than 100% of the surface area. The intensity can, however, be increased to match that of the grid-based survey. The method described here is that developed for Edgehill in 2004–07 and subsequently applied in the Bosworth survey of 2005–10 (Fig 2.12). The first step is to accurately lay out baselines using ranging poles and a cross-sight (Foard 2008c, 207–11), ideally setting them *c* 20m from either end of the field. They are measured out using two reels with nylon ropes several hundred metres long and tagged in different colours at 10m and 2.5m intervals. Coloured flags are then positioned on each baseline to identify every transect. Each transect is marked by a series of at least four flags of the same colour, the third and fourth flags being sighted-in by eye at the field boundaries with reference to the flags on the baselines. If the field is long, or has uneven terrain which interrupts the line of sight, then the baselines may be differently positioned and intermediate flags added, again by sighting along each transect. The flag colours for adjacent transects are rotated in sequence through red, yellow, red, yellow, green to aid discrimination. The detectorist then keeps exactly to his line while detecting by ensuring that the flags in front along the transect are always aligned (Fig 2.13). Given that the sweep of a detector is *c* 2m, depending on the exact technique of the detectorist, a 10m spacing of transects gives a *c* 15–20% sample of the surface area. A navigation grade GPS unit attached to each detector uses the 'tracking' option to record the position of the detector every fifteen seconds during the survey. This shows which transect was covered by each detectorist and their speed of forward movement. This in turn enables the intensity of survey by each individual to be accurately determined, for the speed

Fig 2.12 Lead-composite round shot 97mm in diameter being retrieved at Bosworth in 2009. Battle-related artefacts, even round shot, normally lie within the topsoil. Uniquely, this artefact was found at the bottom of the topsoil – at *c* 300mm depth – half-embedded in the subsoil. It is unclear whether this is simply an effect of its high mass, or if on first bounce it hit at an unusually high angle or struck ridge and furrow side-on, driving it into the subsoil. The navigation grade GPS, used for all recording at this stage of the survey, can also be seen

of coverage will affect the density of the finds recovered and thus the patterning on the final distribution maps. Consistency within the team is encouraged but there will always be some variation. Such data are essential if we are to calibrate and compare the intensity of survey by different teams on the same or different sites.

Recovery of finds is undertaken by the individual detectorist, who records the locations for each object using the 'waypoint' option on the navigation grade GPS and writes his initials and the waypoint number on the finds bag. Waypoints are also recorded at the beginning and end of each transect, so there is a clear record of the transect from which each find came – information which is essential to the resampling of the data at a later date. The level of accuracy noted on the GPS unit normally varies between *c* 2m and *c* 10m, depending on satellite positions and the on-site masking caused by factors such as relief and tree cover. Tracking and waypoint data are later uploaded into GIS for integration with data on each find, enabling digital mapping and analysis of distributional patterns.

The recording method was improved in the later stages of the Bosworth survey by the supplementing of the navigation grade GPS with a sub-metre accuracy GPS unit (Trimble GeoExplorer 2008 series) with Terrasync software employing differential GPS (DGPS) to increase accuracy). This unit was used to make a more accurate record of each transect and each find location in the following manner: after normal bagging and recording by the detectorist, using the navigation grade GPS, the find was pin-flagged to the findspot. At the end of each survey session each bagged find was then collected and its location recorded using DGPS.

At Edgehill 10m spaced transects were used to undertake 5km^2 of detecting, covering most of the surviving area of the battlefield in 432 man days. It would have been impractical to use a grid method comparable to that employed at Culloden because 6100 man days would have been required to cover the same area. The 10m intensity survey appears to be just adequate to provide an overview of a 17th-century battle, assuming a forward detecting speed of no more than 12m per minute, a team comprising detectorists experienced in battlefield survey, and the use of high-specification detectors such as the Minelab Explorer. Such sampling intensity allows variations in the density and type of bullet to be distinguished, with, for example, a hailshot scatter generally being represented by two or three bullets (see Figs 7.21–7.22). However, resurvey using 2.5m spaced transects was required at Edgehill to recover finer detail in key areas; in addition, one artillery hailshot scatter was resurveyed at 1m spacing for yet higher resolution.

It is important to minimise and record the biases in systematic survey that can impact on recovery rates. These include sampling intensity, the equipment used, experience in using it, and conditions on the day. One of the important aspects of recording to a high standard is to be able to recognise where such biases exist and thus to define the limitations of the data set. Fieldwork on Sedgemoor battlefield provides valuable insight into the biases that can arise. The greatest variable is the type of detector, together with the technique and experience of the detectorist (see Fig 7.10). One factor here is the extent of ground coverage by the detector, which is determined by attributes of the coil, the width and speed with which the detectorist swings the detector, and the speed at which he walks when scanning. Variation in detecting conditions is another factor: extremes of soil moisture appear to have a significant effect on recovery rates, and crop conditions can affect ground coverage, especially where newly cut stubble or other conditions of high crop density or height are present, reducing the width of swing to a narrower sampling area. Therefore, a standardised record should be made of cropping, ground, and weather conditions for every day's survey on every field.

The nature of the battle archaeology, particularly the size of an object, will also affect recovery rates. For example, on 17th-century sites there is a sample bias against small calibre bullets because of the cone-shaped form of the detecting signal, which tapers with

Fig 2.13 Systematic metal-detecting survey underway on Bosworth battlefield in 2010. The swing of the detector enables each detectorist to sample a corridor *c* 2m wide along transects spaced at 2.5m intervals, each marked by different-coloured flags. This spacing ensures no overlap, which might otherwise confuse recovery rates

depth, and because of the lower intensity of signal produced by smaller objects. The depths from which artefacts are recovered are not normally measured during surveys of ploughed land but experimental detecting has confirmed that there is a bias towards the recovery of larger calibre bullets at greater depth. In arable or temporary pasture, because the bullets have been mixed through the soil column within recent years, the bias is less acute, but in permanent pasture, where bullets will have migrated to the bottom of the topsoil, no small calibre bullets may be recovered even though they are in fact present (Foard 2008c). The amount of 'background noise' – the non-battle metal artefacts in the ground – is also of significance. Where the survey is being conducted in non-ferrous mode then extraneous 'junk' tends not to be a major problem except occasionally in proximity to modern farms or other settlement. If the key artefacts are ferrous then major problems do arise because of the presence in the topsoil of large numbers of, mainly more recent, iron artefacts such as nails and fragments from farm machinery. In such cases the speed of coverage slows dramatically, and can render intensive large-scale survey impractical.

For the survey of the late 15th-century battlefield at Bosworth transects at 10m spacing were used for reconnaissance survey because a vast area was to be covered (Foard and Curry in prep). This was considered adequate to identify a density of artefact scatter similar to that at Towton – then the only guide as to the character of 15th-century battle archaeology – but it did not prove to be of sufficient intensity to differentiate the far thinner scatter of battle archaeology finally recognised at Bosworth from the background noise. Subsequent resurvey has shown that at least three round shot were missed in the 10m survey before the first round shot was finally recovered. This 4:1 recovery rate is a significant ratio because resurvey was undertaken on 2.5m spaced transects and so gave four times the intensity of coverage (see Fig 5.10).

Survey on 2.5m spaced transects proved effective in revealing a pattern of battle archaeology at Bosworth and is thus recommended as the minimum intensity for future surveys of contemporary sites. Given the available resources and the limitations of time imposed by the agricultural regime this was the highest intensity possible in the Bosworth survey. In 2009–10 a little over 1km^2 of detecting was completed at 2.5m with the aim of defining the overall extent and pattern of the scatter, although the full extent of the round shot distribution has probably not yet been established. It is also likely that some round shot were missed between transects, though in the limited areas where resurvey was undertaken at 90 degrees to the original 2.5m survey no additional round shot were found. Given the low density of the battle-related artefact scatter on a site like Bosworth more intensive coverage may be needed, however, to resolve a clear pattern in the artefact scatter – if one exists. This is particularly true for the round shot, where one is looking for regularity in the distribution of overshots in firing from a given battle array; missing just a few objects might fragment the overall pattern.

The strength of transect surveys, if multiples or divisions of 2.5m are always used, is that the intensity can be tailored to the objectives of the survey and the nature of the battle archaeology without compromising comparability. This is a major consideration given that comparability between data sets from different surveys is a priority. Comparison with data sets from other transect surveys, even if conducted at different intensity (spacing), is always possible because the data sets can be resampled in GIS. Thus, for example, every fourth transect of a 2.5m survey can be selected to facilitate comparison to a 10m survey. In addition, of course, one needs tracking data and information on the survey conditions to enable other significant variations to be taken into account.

The Bosworth and Edgehill surveys were undertaken in non-ferrous mode to enable rapid survey. This is essential where an overall pattern is required from a large area, and is acceptable because most of the identifiable battle-related artefacts from the majority of battlefields of the late 15th to the 17th century may be expected to be of non-ferrous metal. As just noted, surveying in all-metal mode is far more time-consuming because there are vast quantities of ferrous junk in most fields in England. Small-scale sampling at Bosworth suggests that surveying in all-metal mode can lead to a 40-fold increase in the number of artefacts to be dug. Battle-related ferrous artefacts can add significantly to the understanding of a site: on a 17th-century battlefield identifiable ferrous artefacts, present in small numbers, might include gun parts or grenade fragments as well as buckles and other fitments (Bonsall 2008). Unfortunately, identification poses many problems because ferrous artefacts are frequently in poor condition and their form is often not diagnostic as to period. In exceptional circumstances, as with the Towton arrowheads, ferrous artefacts can represent key evidence for a battle, although they may survive only in very restricted areas on a few sites (see

Fig 5.5). Thus, the most effective approach may be to undertake a base survey in non-ferrous mode and then to resurvey selected areas in all-metal mode. If, however, the survey is being undertaken as recording action prior to destruction of a part of a battlefield then survey of the whole area at high intensity and in all-metal mode will often be essential.

Mass graves

The other significant element of battle archaeology is the graves of those killed in action. There are 106 records of burial sites on the Database, 80 of which are from separate fields of conflict. Those sites with multiple recorded locations are almost all major battlefields,[18] the largest number being that for Edgehill, where seven sites are suggested as a result of detailed research. At Newbury I and II the numbers of potential grave sites reflect the unusually high level of enhancement of battle-related information on the Historic Environment Record (HER). However, most of the records on these and other sites are known only from antiquarian reports and many may prove to be spurious.

Only one mass grave in England has been subject to substantial modern excavation (Fig 2.14). This was in Towton village, and even there it was a rescue excavation undertaken in difficult circumstances, without adequate time or resources and involving a feature which had already been partially destroyed by construction (Sutherland 2000b). At East Stoke rescue recording was undertaken on a small part of a mass grave which is almost certainly related to the 1487 battle of Stoke Field, but this has not been published (Nottinghamshire HER).

Not all burials showing weapon trauma are necessarily related to battles. At Heronbridge, outside Chester, a series of individual inhumations showing such trauma gave a radiocarbon date compatible with the early 7th-century battle of Chester (Mason 2006) but the form of the individual burials is very different to that normally seen on a battlefield, unless the graves are of those who died later of their wounds. For this and other reasons the association with the battle of Chester is perhaps not as secure as it might at first appear. Other excavations of individual and mass graves have taken place in Civil War garrisons, including that from All Saints in Fishergate in York and a cemetery in Abingdon, Oxfordshire, but such burials are probably all related to sieges.

The condition of mass graves is likely to vary enormously. A few seem to have survived as earthworks into the 19th century, such as the site said to be from the 1138 battle at Northallerton, which was known as the Scot Pits (see pp 59–61). These earthworks seem to have survived until ploughed up in the 19th century, probably after 1839, when the tithe map shows that the land was still pasture. Levelling by cultivation sometimes occurred much closer in time to the events themselves; at Naseby, for example, remains were being ploughed up within a decade of the battle. Even more destructive will have been the removal of bodies to consecrated ground, which is known to have occurred on a few medieval battlefields in the decades following the battle. This is the case at Towton, where the major graves at the centre of the battlefield were cleared in the 15th century and the remains removed to Saxton churchyard. Test pits dug recently on the original grave site revealed little beyond a scatter of the smaller bones (Sutherland pers comm). As with other charnel deposits, the skulls and long bones will have been the main parts collected and reburied. Some grave sites may have been disturbed by antiquarian or other digging on the site, as reported at Sedgemoor in the late 19th century (Fig 2.15).

The mass grave at Towton has shown the insight that can result from a well-recorded full excavation followed by palaeo-pathological analysis. The results argue for a systematic programme of investigation of battlefield mass graves which would allow study of such themes as the effectiveness of armour and weapons of different periods (Jones 2010, ch 5). If an undisturbed mass grave could be excavated in the heart of a medieval battlefield the distribution of ferrous arrowheads and of trauma on the bodies might also allow us to see the relative significance of archery compared to 'handstrokes'. In later centuries the effectiveness of gunshots might similarly be assessed.

What the graves will rarely provide, however, are examples of the arms and equipment in use, since bodies normally appear to have been stripped prior to burial, as is clearly depicted on the margin of the Bayeux Tapestry. Only in exceptional circumstances, for example at Wisby in Sweden, will the dead have been buried in their armour and clothes (Thordeman 1939). Thus, the evidence in graves will normally be limited to skeletal remains, any projectiles that were embedded in the bodies when they were buried, and artefacts introduced accidentally in the backfill.

While it could be argued that human remains should be left undisturbed in the field as a mark of respect for those who fell in battle, in reality the dead

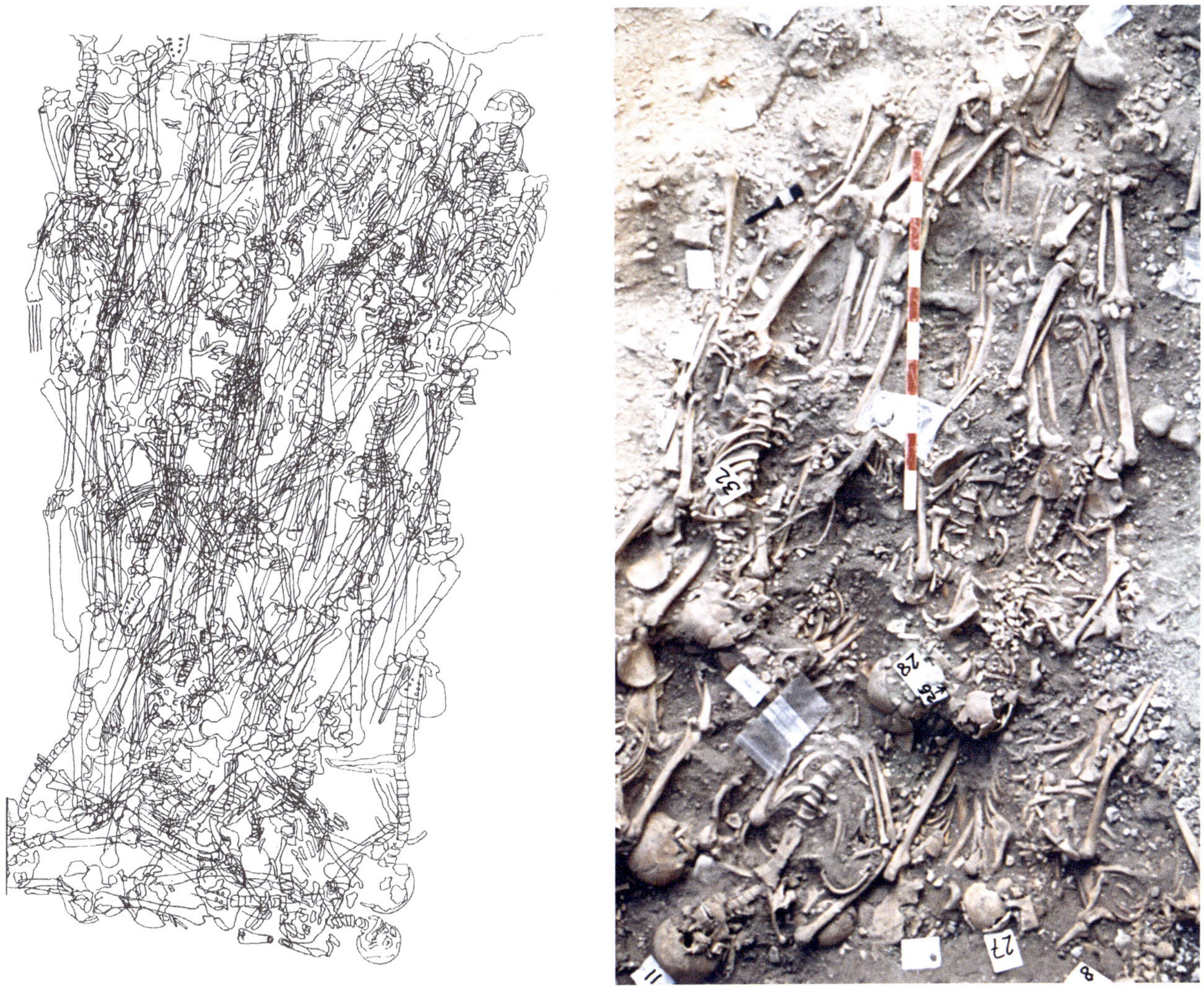

Fig 2.14 Drawing and photograph of the overlapping bodies in the mass grave of 1461 in Towton village, excavated in 1996 (© T Sutherland)

Fig 2.15 A mass grave on Sedgemoor (1685) as depicted in an engraving in the 1890s, soon after it had been dug into to 'satisfy vulgar curiosity'. It is an example of how even the best-located graves noted in early reports can prove remarkably difficult to locate today (Barrett 1896)

are rarely safe where they lie. Such remains are very vulnerable to the impact of modern agriculture, as recent discoveries of teeth and bone fragments in the topsoil at Towton have shown (Sutherland 2009). Identification of mass graves is thus a priority for conservation as well as research purposes.

Identifying burial sites is likely to prove very difficult, and thus it will be necessary to target sites where there is already some idea as to the location of the graves. Northallerton (1138) may be an ideal site for such work, as here the 'Scot Pits' field names should assist in locating the graves in the heart of the action (see Fig 3.16). If these graves survive it may be possible to recognise a high level of arrow trauma among the Galwegian troops, who fought on one flank of the Scottish army: the documents say that these troops were not armoured and so were cut down by the arrows from the English archers. There might thus be a difference in the nature of trauma on the bodies of the better-protected Scottish troops on the other flank.

Mass graves will exist on most battlefields – a concentration is normally to be expected where the main engagement began, because where there were high densities of bodies they were usually buried close to where they fell. Thus, eye-witnesses of the preparations for burial at Edgehill (1642) saw the bodies pulled together in a series of huge piles in the area where the two armies had first clashed. While the numbers of dead vary greatly from battle to battle, they will typically be in the thousands: at Edgehill the most reliable accounts indicate a number over 3000 (Foard 2008c, 203–4). For medieval battles far more fanciful numbers, in the tens of thousands, are sometimes quoted in primary accounts.

While many soldiers might be killed where the main clash occurred, losses were often greatest during a rout, as the battle formations broke up and troops became more vulnerable. Some mass graves, therefore, will lie far from the initial action. Some will have been dug where there was high mortality in a small area, such as at a pinch point that made it possible for troops to reform and attempt to stand and fight once more. More often it will be where such terrain restricted escape, allowing disordered fleeing troops to be caught and cut down. Thus, at Stoke Field (1487) the proven mass grave and the other supposed burial sites – suggested by antiquaries – lie close to where the ancient enclosures of East Stoke village will have restricted the flight of the rebel forces (Fig 2.16). There may be a similar explanation for the mass graves reported in the 19th century on the western edge of the medieval town at Lewes, which lie close to where routed troops from the 1264 battle may have encountered an area of settlement enclosures (Carpenter 1987; National Army Museum 1995i). In such circumstances, Burne's use of the mass grave as an indicator for the location of the main action may not always be as clear-cut as has been assumed (Burne 1950).

Bodies from a rout will frequently have had to be collected together from a wide area, most likely in carts which would have allowed them to be taken to a churchyard for burial. This might explain the bodies excavated in the mass grave in the village of Towton, which lay more than a kilometre from the centre of the battlefield. This practice is also well documented for the major battle at Pinkie (East Lothian, Scotland) in 1547. Patten, an English eye-witness to the battle who returned along the main line of the Scottish rout eight days later, saw many rotting corpses still unburied, but reported that many more had already been interred in Inveresk churchyard. Another report notes that it took two days to find enough carts to collect up the Scottish dead for burial, while even a month after the action there were still some bodies not yet buried (Patten 1548).[19]

In churchyards both close to and far from the action one might also expect to find individual or mass graves of men who later died of their wounds (Foard 1995, 309–19). The individual satellite burials around the mass grave in Towton village may fall into this category (Sutherland 2009, 112). Also to be expected in a few churchyards are disarticulated bones in a mass grave representing bodies removed decades after the battle for reburial in consecrated ground, such as the remains from Bosworth (1485) battlefield, which were translated to the chantry in Dadlington chapel in the early 16th century.

As already indicated, there are major problems with the reliability of most of our existing records of mass grave sites. A few reports of discoveries date from a time close to the battles themselves: Naseby (1645) has been noted (Foard 1995, 354–6), while at Hastings (1066) a 12th-century entry in the chronicle of Battle Abbey reports the discovery of a mass grave, although there is no indication as to where it was found (Searle 1980). At Shrewsbury (1403) a 15th-century description is much more specific, stating that the mass grave lay within the ditched enclosure where the battle chapel stands (National Army Museum 1995n). The majority of reported burial sites show only a tenuous link with the battle to which they are supposed to belong. Most are undated burials found in the 19th century or before, and a few can now be shown to

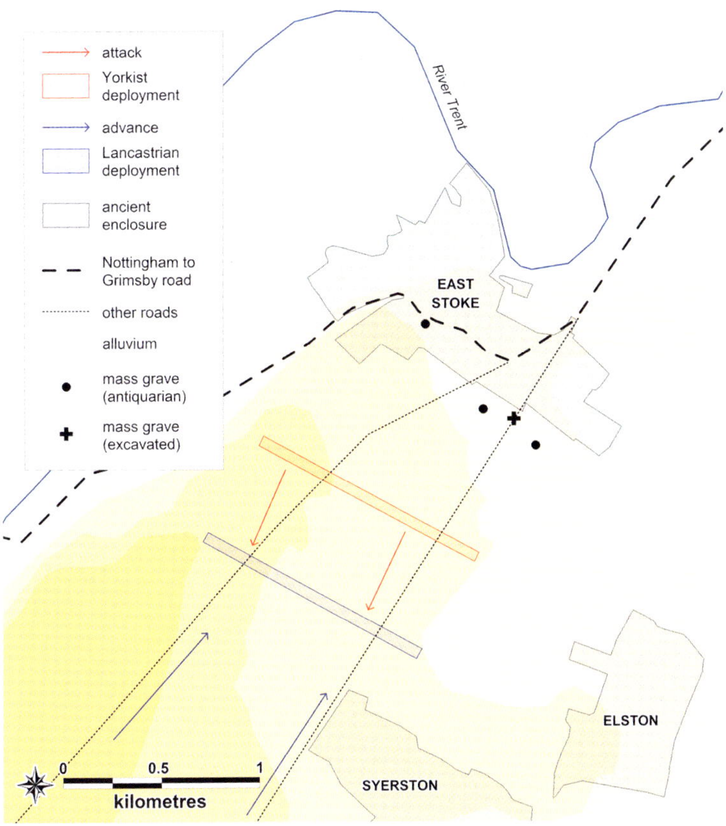

Fig 2.16 Map of the battlefield at East Stoke (1487) showing mass grave locations. One is certain, having been confirmed by modern investigation. The others are from antiquarian reports. Their location may result from fleeing Yorkist troops being slowed down as they tried to negotiate the narrow passes where the roads crossed the enclosures of East Stoke village[20]

belong to ordinary cemeteries of other periods. The most obvious examples of clearly spurious associations are those where the battle is now known to have been fought elsewhere, as with the burials and swords said to have been found close to the chapel at Heavenfield (AD 633) (see Fig 3.9).[21]

Even where a battle is securely located there can still be problems with early reports of burial sites. Thus at Towton a number of supposedly battle related burial sites have been shown, through systematic investigation including geophysics, to be spurious (Sutherland 2000a). Even when the burials may relate to the battle in question, they may have been over-interpreted. For example, Leadman claimed that burials discovered during drainage works on Marston Moor in the 19th century lay in White Syke Close and thus represented the last stand of the Earl of Newcastle's regiment (Leadman 1891) but as Newman has convincingly demonstrated, this identification was incorrect (Newman 1979). There are just a few exceptions where antiquarian work does appear to have provided secure evidence, as with Fitzgerald's excavations at Naseby. Other probably genuine battlefield mass graves are from Lewes (1264), where at least four were found during 19th-century development; three of these, in one location, were said to contain some 500 bodies (National Army Museum 1995i).

Other sites are identified solely by traditions as to where the dead were buried. Where these traditions are recorded early then they may be valid, especially where the report is reasonably close in time to the battle itself, so that a secure continuity of oral history is likely. Thus at Edgehill several sites where bodies are said to have been buried are first reported in the 1720s, within about 80 years of the battle, though exact locations are not given until the 19th century (see Fig 7.15).

Battle graves are hard to find mainly because they seem rarely to have been marked by anything more than an earthen mound that usually has long since been levelled by ploughing. Moreover, they are very small compared to the extent of a battlefield. One of the largest European mass graves so far fully excavated is from Wisby (1361) in Sweden: although it contained some 800 individuals it covered only *c* 72m^2 (Thordeman 1939). Within a battlefield which may cover as much as 10km^2, such a feature will be hard to locate unless there is evidence which enables narrowing of focus of investigation to just a few hectares.

Towton demonstrates these difficulties, which are encountered even when tradition has provided a reasonably accurate location and an artefact scatter indicates the area of heaviest fighting. In the late 1990s Sutherland spent several years there carrying out investigations, mainly using magnetometry and resistivity, aimed at locating the burial pits in the heart of the battlefield. While he was able to dismiss most of the antiquarian reports, he failed to find any trace of pits on the main traditional site at the centre of the action, even though they are reported in relatively early and remarkably specific records. This led him to question their very existence and to suggest that most bodies had been simply left in the open at Towton, and after many other medieval battles (Sutherland 2002). Not until small fragments of human bone were found on the surface of the plough soil during metal detecting did targeted geophysics and trial trenching finally identify the remains of the mass graves in the traditional location (Sutherland 2009).

A few specific references to intentional non-burial of the dead do exist, as at *Ashingdon* in 1016 and Stamford Bridge in 1066. Yet a mass grave has been found even at the Good Friday battle at Uppsala (1520) in Sweden, where sources state that the Swedish bodies were left for dogs and wolves in the marshes and swamps where they fell; but the nature of the skeletal remains is indeed consistent with the bodies having being left in water for five to six months before burial (Syse 2002). Such delays could be attributed to the relative isolation of the site from settlement or to the non-agricultural nature of the land. In contrast, references to the dead on English battlefields are overwhelmingly to their burial. This is probably because, in England's intensively exploited landscapes, the clearance of bodies will have been essential in most cases for practical agricultural and health-related reasons, if not on religious grounds.

In the past mass graves have, in almost every case, been identified by chance. What is needed now is an effective methodology to locate them, which may be achieved through research on several well-preserved and securely located medieval and later mass graves such as those at East Stoke, Naseby, and Northallerton. These graves and their environs should be explored with a range of techniques: in addition to geophysical survey and study of the artefacts scatters, there is need to seek a chemical signature for this site type. In particular, the potential of calcium phosphate should be trialled because it is a chemical that is, in theory, stable in soil; it was used with apparent success to identify a pony kill site on the 19th-century Washita battlefield (Oklahoma, USA), though even here the testing was possible only because tradition placed the kill site within a 10-acre area (*c* 4ha). In exceptional circumstances such work might even suggest where graves existed in the past but have been destroyed by subsequent cultivation (Neff 2002).

Management of this aspect of battle archaeology, even where the sites of graves are well known, is currently as ineffectual as is that of artefact scatters. In some circumstances it will be appropriate for Registered areas to be extended to encompass the sites – as is the case, for example, with remaining burials in Towton village – but even then their management needs would not necessarily be better addressed. Neither of the securely located grave sites at Towton are yet protected as Scheduled Ancient Monuments, while that on Stoke Field is scheduled only because it lies adjacent to medieval settlement remains. The failure to give such sites statutory protection is the more surprising because mass graves, unlike unstratified artefact scatters, are man-made features and so eligible for scheduling.

Yet, as we have seen, the first step for the majority of battlefields must be the formulation of an effective methodology to locate the grave sites themselves and to establish their condition, their depth, and therefore their vulnerability to agriculture. Only with such knowledge will it be possible to apply statutory protection or measures to modify the agricultural regime to assist their survival.

Towards integrated study

Once battle archaeology has been mapped, the integration of the data set with the existing reading of documented events, already set within the reconstructed terrain, will rarely be simple. It will be necessary first to revisit the original written accounts, for the archaeology often casts new light on details they contain. Thus at Naseby a single account mentioned dead scattered for two miles (3.2km) on the royalist side, and then more beyond this from the rout. This information had been largely ignored by historians because it did not make sense within the accepted interpretation of the battle. The significance of the account was transformed, however, when it was seen closely to match the physical evidence. The detail of wording in other accounts also took on new meaning once the bullet scatter had been mapped (Foard 1995, 275 and 285–6).

Such interplay between battle archaeology and other data can also reveal gaps in understanding which call for further research on the terrain, more intensive resurvey of elements of the battle archaeology, or suggest the need for experimental research.

For example, within the area of infantry action at Edgehill small quantities of hailshot – bullets fired as large groups from artillery, normally when working in close infantry support – were recognised. Analysis, supported by results of experimental firing, showed the hailshot to be key evidence which might allow the initial position of the defending parliamentarian army to be pinpointed. As a result a new phase of more intensive survey was undertaken in this zone to recover as many hailshot bullets as possible and so clarify their distribution. This provided evidence for the orientation of the artillery fire and thus the location of the guns which, in 17th-century battles, were typically deployed between the infantry brigades.

When all data are integrated it should be possible to arrive at a more secure placing of events within the contemporary landscape. This is crucial for understanding the battle for, as military commanders have long known, 'a large part of a victory depends on the actual place in which the battle is fought' (Vegetius III.13). With such knowledge it is possible to reassess the battle, considering issues such as the effectiveness of commanders in exploiting the opportunities the ground provided.

Physical evidence from the battlefield may offer more, such as details of the equipping of the armies, and once we have exemplar studies from different periods and countries, in Europe and beyond, this evidence will contribute to the exploration of wider themes. There is thus a possibility of revealing the true chronology of the changing technology of war: when, where and how gunpowder weapons were introduced to the battlefield, as well as showing the intensity of the fire they were able to lay down. For earlier centuries the potential is largely unproven, but battle archaeology may in due course be able to contribute to themes such as the development of increasingly heavy armour in response to the use of the crossbow and the couched lance (Jones 2010, 93–6).

Notes

1. This database consists of two GIS tables in MapInfo: UK Fields of Conflict and UKFoC Feature; and one bibliographic file in Endnote: UKFoC Bibliography. The data structure is broadly that detailed in the appendix to Foard and Partida 2005.
2. The HERs provided copies of records relating to battles and sieges. Several had no significant actions in their area or no records relating to fields of conflict. Only York did not provide feedback.
3. The sources differed significantly from those used for Scotland and hence direct comparison of this aspect was not possible.
4. Microsoft Virtual Earth and Google Maps, accessed in January 2008.
5. For Hastings the numbers include all visitors to Battle Abbey and Battlefield (information from Andrew Brown, English Heritage). For Bosworth numbers are for paying visitors to the exhibition, whereas some 100,000 visits are reported to the country park as a whole (information from Richard Mackinder, Leicestershire County Council).
6. For a survey of preservation and interpretation in the USA see http://www.cr.nps.gov/hps/abpp/, accessed 9 April 2011.
7. 'Come over Culloden Muir – reflections on the field of battle', Burns' Journal of his tour in the Highlands, Aug–Sept 1787: http://burnsscotland.com/database/record.php?usi=000-000-497-815-C, accessed 9 April 2011.
8. Ruined monastery: Hastings. Collegiate church: Shrewsbury. Chapel: Wakefield, Heavenfield. Destroyed chapel: Bosworth, Towton, Barnet, Evesham. Funerary monuments: Edgehill (2), Stow, Towton, Willoughby on the Wold. Plaques: Boroughbridge, Cropredy, Dyrham, Fulford, Hopton Heath, Lostwithiel, Maldon, Northampton, Norwich, Winceby, Worcester. Stones: Hedgley Moor, Geteryne, Homildon Hill, Flodden (2). Monuments: Adwalton Moor, Alnwick, Barnet, Bloody Field, Blore Heath, Bosworth (2), Bovey Tracey, Chalgrove, Cheriton, Edgehill (2), Evesham (2), Flodden, Halidon Hill, Heavenfield, Lansdown, Lostwithiel, Marston Moor, Mortimer's Cross, Naseby (2), Newbury I, Northallerton, Otterburn, Sedgemoor, Stamford Bridge, Stoke Field, Stow on the Wold (2), Stratton, Tewkesbury, Towton, Wakefield, Wigan, Worcester.
9. *Gentleman's Magazine*, December 1746, p 640 and Plate VIII.
10. For the present research MapInfo has been used.
11. An enhancement of the principle detailed by Burne, but taking account of the practical limitations and potentials of the technology and tactics of the period (Foard 2008, 23).
12. English Heritage has funded landscape characterisation in various counties. http://www.english-heritage.org.uk/professional/research/landscapes-and-areas/characterisation/historic-landscape-character/ Accessed 9 April 2011.

13. Detecting at Shrewsbury by Simon Richardson, prior to construction of the battlefield trail, and then by the Bosworth survey team in 2007 at both Shrewsbury and Flodden, for comparative data to Bosworth, failed to recover substantial battle archaeology in key locations across the Registered areas.
14. These issues, including monitoring of eBay for sales of battlefield items, are the subject of detailed research by Natasha Fergusson at the University of Glasgow.
15. Roberts' data digitised from a sketch plan on an Ordnance Survey 1:2500 scale map base, published on a CD which accompanied the book by Newman and Roberts (2003). GPS recording was by G Foard with the assistance of T Sutherland on 30 September 2000. GPS accuracy was *c* 40m, as this was prior to implementation of WAAS in Europe and while degradation of signal accuracy was still taking place.
16. Fieldwork by McGovern and McGovern. Data from one field were published in Bonsall 2008. This suggests there may be high-quality battlefield-wide data, but the finds and records remain inaccessible in private hands.
17. Examples are at Naseby (information from Peter Burton); and Tywardreath, Cornwall (information from Steve Hartgroves, Cornwall CC).
18. Edgehill: 7; Newbury I: 6; Flodden, Newbury II and Stoke Field: 4; Lewes: 3; Marston Moor, Sedgemoor, Stokesay and Towton: 2.
19. Also *Treasurer's Accounts*, ix, 121 and 129, quoted in Fergusson 1963.
20. The mapping and discussion of Stoke Field is based on analysis by Foard in 2004, available: http://www.battlefieldstrust.com/resource-centre/warsoftheroses/battleview.asp?BattleFieldId=42 Accessed 9 April 2011. That study identified various inconsistencies between the primary accounts and the battlefield as currently interpreted. The Nottingham–Grimsby road is mapped from Ogilby 1675, plate 78.
21. Northumberland HER.

3

ENGLISH BATTLEFIELDS: FROM PREHISTORY TO 1454

The Database contains 1102 English sites.[1] While this provides a reasonable overview of the battlefields, the evidence for sieges, skirmishes, and raids is far less complete. Of the battlefield total, only 37 sites appear to be spurious: these derive mainly from dubious archaeological discoveries in the 19th century or before, together with a few based purely on place-name evidence. Of the 1065 likely to be genuine, most have just one recorded site, but for 39 there are alternative sites, revealing the degree of uncertainty that exists about the location of even some of the most important battles: 29 have two candidate sites, 6 have three, while Hexham (1464) has four, *Ethandun* (AD 878) and Ashdown (AD 871) have six, and *Brunanburh* (AD 937) a remarkable total of seven.

Of the total, 321 are from before 1066 and 781 are later (Table 1). Just 102 of these are classified as battles, with a further 101 identified as possible battles (see Appendix I; Fig 3.1). Of the possible battles 79% are from before 1066, confirming the high level of uncertainty about all aspects of battlefields from this early period; in contrast, only two are from the 17th century. It is likely that some uncertain battles from the earlier periods will be reclassified as skirmishes, although the paucity of the written record for the actions before 1066 makes secure classification of these impossible. In contrast, for later centuries a small number of the skirmishes may justify reclassification as battles, re-emphasising the difficulty of defining the boundary between the two. The dominance of 17th-century sites in the classes of siege (243 of 383 sites) and skirmish (142 of 189 sites) is in part a result of bias in our enhancement of the Database. It also reflects the far greater detail available for military action during the Civil War compared to that for earlier periods. Despite this, all skirmishes, even those of the 17th century, are likely to be grossly under-represented on the Database.

It is important that fields of conflict are viewed in an international context, but in the absence of a database covering Europe as a whole, for most purposes we have been limited to comparison with Scotland only. Such comparison is valid for battles, as the

Table 1: Battles and other actions in England and Scotland grouped by period

	England			Scotland		
	All actions	Battles	Multiple sites	All actions	Battles	Multiple sites
Total records	1182	262		368	72	
Total actions	1102	203	28	345	56	
Roman (AD 43–410)	14	3	1	4	1	
Early medieval (AD 411–1065)	201	114	18	45	8	1
Later medieval (1066–1535)	285	33	5	109	23	2
Wars of Roses (1455–1487) (also included in later medieval)	32	15	4	-	-	-
Post-medieval (1535–1639)	38	7	2	55	7	1
Civil War (1640–1659)	436	29	2	26	10	1
Stuart rebellions (1660–)	23	1	0	26	7	1

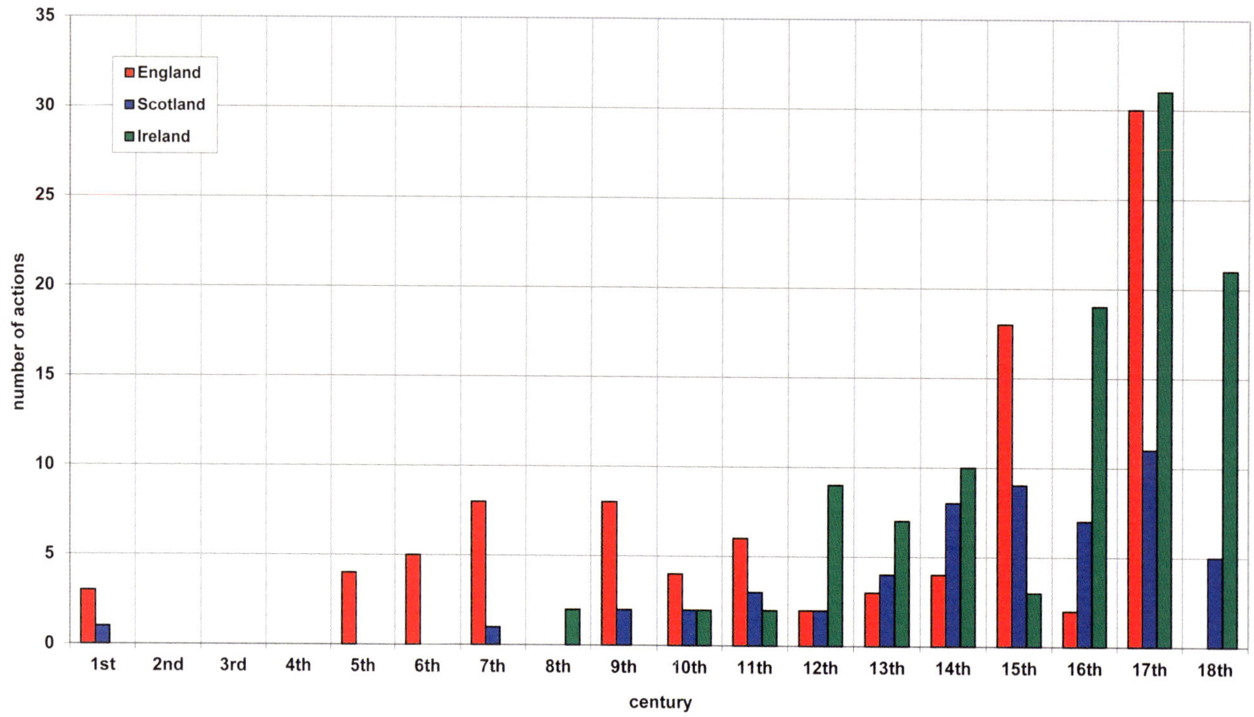

Fig 3.1 Graph showing the number of battles by century in England, Scotland and the Republic of Ireland[2]

enhancement of the Database for these was similar for both countries. It is not, however, useful for sieges, which were systematically added to the Database for England only. Where the battles are graphed to display the chronological distribution, additional information has been added for the Republic of Ireland which, though not classified according to identical criteria, is likely to be closely comparable.

The scale of the battles varies enormously. In terms of numbers engaged, Marston Moor, with about 45,000 men in five armies, was probably the largest. The numbers fall progressively until 5000 is reached, below which problems of classification become acute. It has been decided not to quote figures for numbers engaged in medieval battles because of the uncertainty that arises from the often unrealistic and inconsistent claims made in the primary sources. One can also assess battles in terms of the extent of the battlefield, but this is even more problematic – in part simply because of the difficulty of defining battlefield extent, but also because in some battles the action will have moved across the landscape to a far greater degree than in others. A further complication is that the frontage of armies when deployed in battle array was determined not only by the numbers engaged but also by the tactics employed. These varied between periods, leading to substantial differences in frontage. For example, very deep or even square formations were in use in the 16th century while in the 17th century, in contrast, very shallow arrays were employed, with deployments just eight, more often six and occasionally even three ranks deep (Prestwich 1996, 315–23; Roberts 2010). Thus a 17th-century battlefield may be expected to be far broader in frontage than a 16th-century one, even when similar numbers were engaged. The issue is further complicated for the later medieval period because there is uncertainty as to the nature of deployments and hence the size of the battlefields on which they were drawn up.

When the distribution of sites is viewed nationally some degree of patterning is visible (Fig 3.2). For example, a concentration of battles is noticeable along the Anglo-Scottish border but, significantly, where the actions extend away from the border they congregate on the east rather than the west. This reflects the ease of access between the two countries along the eastern as opposed to the western route. Much of the patterning is linked to topographical factors: there is an absence of battles in the mountainous areas, especially the Pennines and Cumbrian mountains of northern England, and also in some other zones, such as the Fens of eastern England and the woodland of the Weald of Kent and Sussex. Other patterning becomes visible only when the distributions are broken down chronologically.

Many of the battles are from periods in which warfare was of restricted scope and intensity. Thus, during the Wars of the Roses (1455–87) most battles

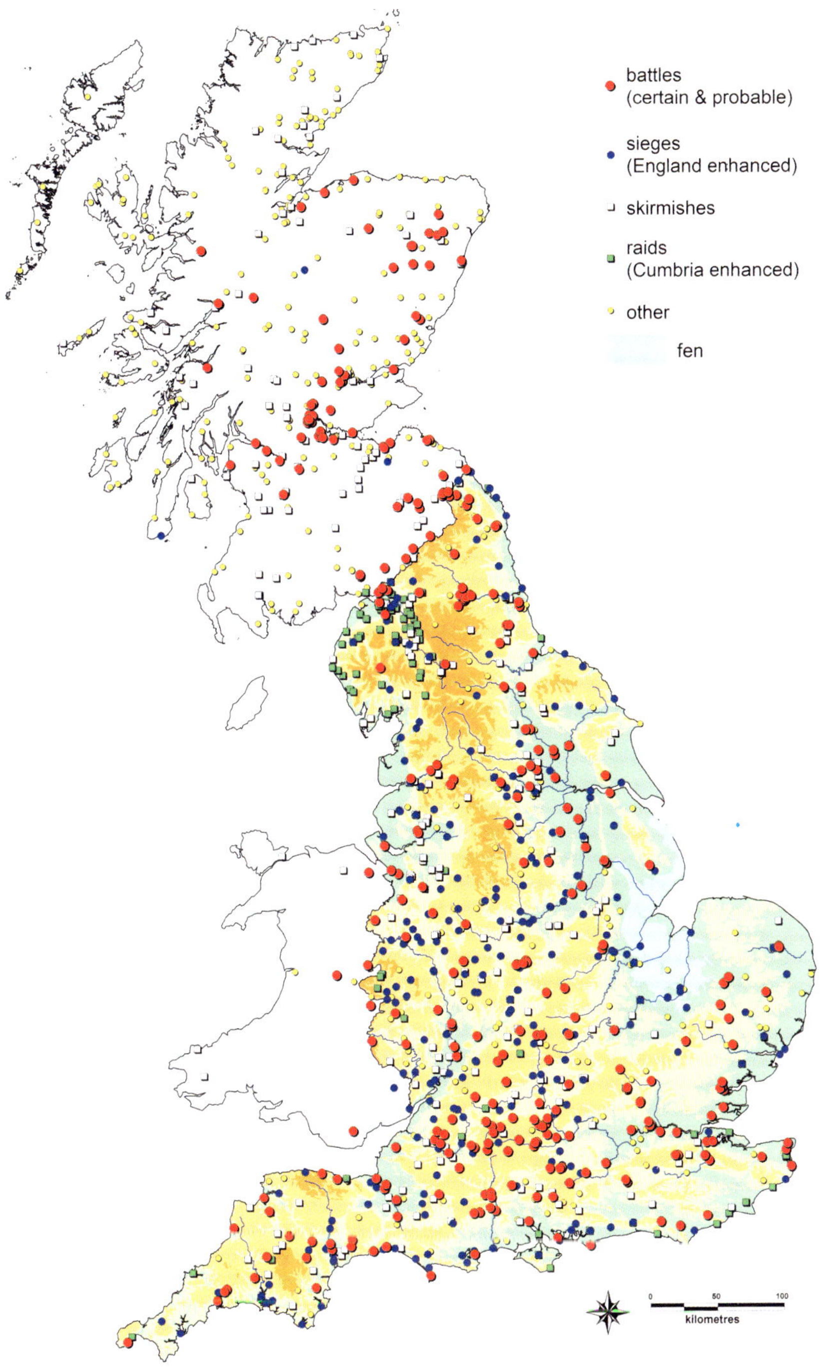

Fig 3.2 Map of all fields of conflict on the Database in England and Scotland classified by type. Alternative sites for battles are included where they have been suggested. Information for Wales is incomplete

were fought as episodes within short, sharp campaigns separated by long periods of peace. Similarly, the events of the de Montfort rebellion (1263–65) were restricted to short campaigns in which a relatively small number of garrisons were involved. There were a few periods when warfare was more intense, of which the clearest is the Civil War of the 17th century (Kenyon and Ohlmeyer 1998), but which also include the civil war of Stephen and Matilda in the 12th century (Bradbury 1998) and the phase of the Wars of the Roses when garrisons in the north-east controlled a broad territory and held out for a long period (Haigh 1995, 69–77).

Of different character are the two marcher zones, which, to some degree, were almost always on a war footing. Along the Welsh border this situation largely ceased after the conquest of Wales by Edward I, but on the Scottish border conflict continued to the end of the 16th century, with periods of heightened tension leading to action of varying scale on both sides of the border. Only sites on the English side are discussed here, but full understanding of the evidence calls for a detailed cross-border study. In these two zones, as with the Civil War, there is potential for the integration of the study of battles with an investigation of wider conflict. This would involve an examination of

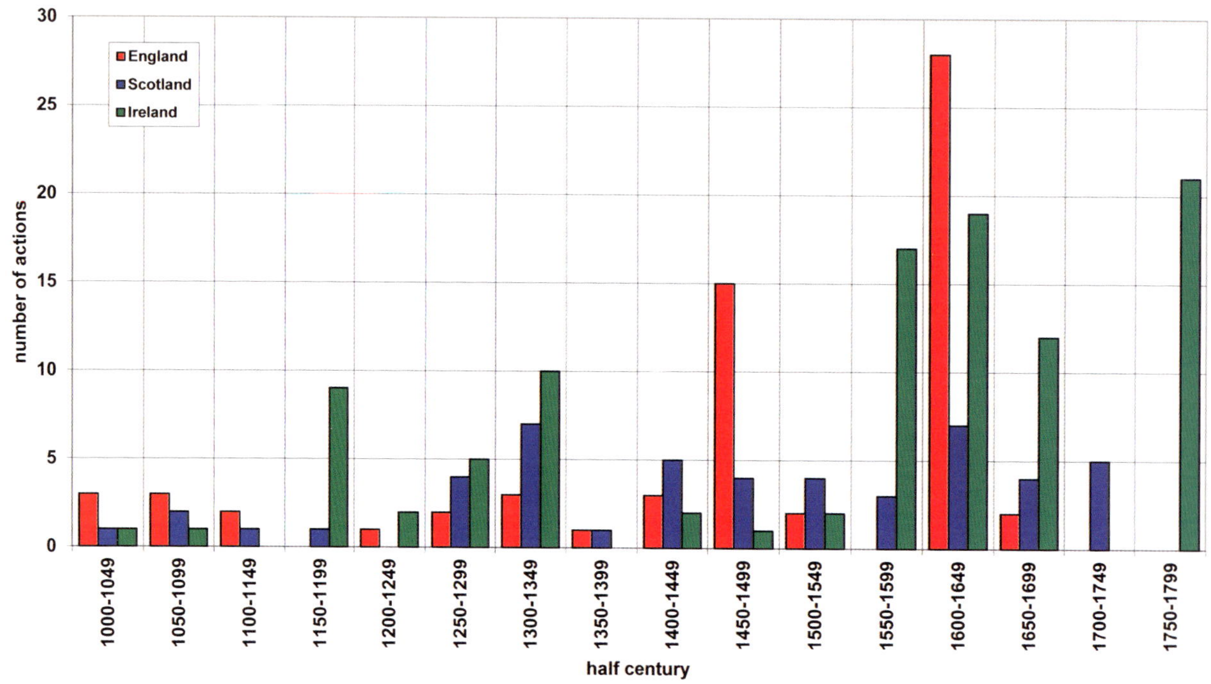

Fig 3.3 Graph of battles in England, Scotland and the Republic of Ireland by half century between 1000 and 1799

sieges, skirmishes, and raids. It would also require the study of the development of fortifications and even roads that will have modified the strategic and tactical context. These wider themes are touched upon here in discussion of later medieval battles, but it is with the Civil War that we have taken the opportunity to explore more fully the range of conflict sites.

Over the previous millennium the number of actions apparently declines as one moves back in time, particularly if the unverified sites are excluded. To a degree this reflects the decrease in quantity and quality of primary documentation for earlier centuries. Before 1066 this became a significant problem. The decline also seems to reflect the generally accepted view that, compared to sieges and lesser actions, battle in the Middle Ages was very much a matter of last resort. The most distinctive peaks in this type of action are the Wars of the Roses in the second half of the 15th century and the Civil War in the mid-17th century (see Fig 3.1).

England's fields of conflict can be usefully divided into six main chronological phases, based on their broad archaeological and documentary potential. Between the Neolithic and the late Iron Age sites are known only through the archaeological record and, at present, all appear to be essentially sieges, while a handful of battles are documented in the Roman period. Between the 5th and early 11th century, increasing numbers of battles and other actions appear in the documentary record, but rarely, if ever, in sufficient detail to enable their exact location to be identified. The only exceptions are actions against fortified sites, of which a handful are known. Hastings (1066) is the first battle with both detailed documentation and an accurately located site. Thereafter, the general locations of many late medieval battles are known but, partly because of the limitations of the original accounts, few have yet been securely placed in the landscape. At present, only for actions from the later 15th century can the full range of archaeological and documentary evidence be exploited. Potential is further enhanced in the 17th century, where we consistently see the large-scale use of firearms that deposit vast quantities of lead projectiles, and the documentary record often includes detailed first-hand accounts.

Thus in England, at present, only battlefields of the last millennium appear amenable to archaeological investigation. These battlefields are relatively rare compared with most other types of archaeological site and, as the graph in Fig 3.3 shows, their chronological spread is very uneven. With such a small number of sites in some periods, the addition of even one or two sites to the list of battles could be significant. Equally, if any prove to be very poorly preserved this may have a large impact on the scope for research in that period. As Fig 3.3 also shows, the different countries underwent major phases of conflict at different times. Hence, to gain a broad picture of the evolution of warfare it will be necessary to study a larger sample of well-preserved sites of each period than any one country can provide.

Such an international approach was demonstrated a century ago by military historians such as Delbruck and Oman (Delbruck 1923; Oman 1898), and is valid because warfare developed as part of a broad European tradition. It is also true that the evolution of warfare varied between different countries in both chronology and character, sometimes quite significantly. For this reason it is important also to compare and contrast experience in different countries, and to look at the armies of any one country wherever they were fighting. A battle fought by an English army in, say, France during the Hundred Years War might look very different to one fought in Ireland, where the terrain was different and the enemy wished to avoid open battle. Different again would be a battle fought in a civil war, where the two sides had almost identical arms, equipment, and tactics.

Prehistoric and Roman warfare

Warfare in the prehistoric period is a specialised research area which is normally treated separately from the study of later battlefields because the evidence and the investigation techniques employed are so different (Carman 1997). No systematic data collection or analysis for this period has been attempted here, therefore, and only five prehistoric sites were revealed in the search of the Historic Environment Records. As many defensive sites of this period have left a substantial and distinctive archaeological signature, the greatest potential appears to lie with the identification of actions against fixed positions rather than open battles, with the most obvious evidence likely to be in the form of groups of inhumation burials showing weapon trauma. Hitherto the discovery of such remains has usually been by chance, as was the case with the Bronze Age burials from Tormarton (Mercer 1981; 2006; Osgood 2005).

As with later battlefields, it is likely that secure evidence of military action will be in the form of projectile distributions. Flint arrowheads and stone slingshots have been found in significant quantities on several defensive sites that were attacked in the Neolithic and Iron Age, respectively, and it is possible that concentrations might be revealed by fieldwalking on arable land where defensive sites have been ploughed flat. Where sites remain as earthworks the evidence will be difficult to recover, requiring extensive excavation to do so. The most impressive evidence for the Neolithic is from Crickley Hill, where a large spread of flint arrowheads has been mapped. Discussion about this pattern has dwelled on the distribution of flint arrowheads alone (Mercer 1999), but ideally such scatters should also be compared to the 'background noise' – the distribution of other non-battle flint artefacts.

These projectiles rarely, if ever, provide evidence which confirms whether or not they had been loosed in action. This is a problem for siege sites of all dates, where substantial numbers of projectiles are likely to have been deposited by mechanisms other than military combat. A tentative differentiation has been made at the Iron Age hillfort of Danebury between slingshots intended for hunting birds and those intended for battle. However, there is no analysis of slingshot patterning across the site because, it is suggested, most of those retrieved were from the collapse and redeposition of stockpiles maintained in readiness for action, rather than from actual fighting (Cunliffe 1984). It might yet be possible to tease out combat evidence from the Danebury assemblage, but such analysis may need to be part of a wider consideration of the nature of projectile distribution patterns. A comparison between the patterning seen on prehistoric sites and that revealed on battlefields of the second millennium AD might enable general principles to be identified.

In the Bronze Age the recovery of copper alloy artefacts after an action was presumably a high priority because of their value and potential for re-use, but the robust nature of copper alloy means that those that were left behind should survive in the ground and be retrievable through systematic metal detecting. In contrast, the numbers of surviving ferrous artefacts, such as projectile points from the Iron Age, is likely to be low. Where the soil has a high pH then stratified artefacts may survive, but the survival of those that lay in the topsoil is unlikely to be good.

With the arrival of written records, information on open battles becomes available for the first time. Britain's only examples from the prehistoric period are the accounts of Caesar's campaigns in 55 and 54 BC, which record military actions of various scales (*De Bello Gallico*, 4.20–37, 5.2–24). None of the actions described can be securely located, although suggestions have been made (Johnson 1917).

The written record for battle in Roman Britain is sparse and irregular, and few of the major military actions are likely to have been recorded in the sources that survive. We are, for example, dependent upon the eulogy written by Tacitus for his father-in-law Agricola for two of the most important battles of the period in Britain: Boudicca's defeat and Mons Graupius *(Life of Agricola*, 16, 29–37). In England only three significant engagements can be reasonably identified as battles: Medway and Thames in AD 43 and Boudicca's defeat in AD 61 (Webster and Dudley 1973; Webster 1993). There are two documented Roman battles elsewhere in Britain: Mons Graupius, Agricola's major victory of AD 84 in Scotland, and Caratacus's defeat in AD 51, for which Cefn Carnedd in Wales is just one suggested site (Webster 1981; Fraser 2005). None of these actions is securely located, however, despite much effort on the part of many authors, and the various locations that have been suggested for the Roman invasion landing of AD 43 are excluded here, as none is convincing.

A brief examination of the battle in which Boudicca was defeated demonstrates the difficulties that have to be overcome in identifying Roman battlefields in Britain (Webster 1993; Marix Evans 2007). Four of the sites with the most strongly argued cases are mapped here, but there is no secure evidence to prefer these or any of the others (Fig 3.4). The primary source is Tacitus, writing some 50 years after the events he describes; he was thus not an eye witness, although he may have had report of the event from Agricola, his father-in-law, who was serving in the army in Britannia in the year of Boudicca's defeat. It would appear that Suetonius, the Roman commander, had to withdraw the majority of his troops from a campaign in Wales to deal with Boudicca's rebels, who were active in the south-east, where they sacked *Camalodunum* (Colchester) and *Verulamium* (St Albans). Since the majority of Suetonius's forces appear to have had to march back towards London it is believed by many that a site along Watling Street is most likely for the encounter; this is further narrowed to somewhere between the West Midlands and St Albans, but there is nothing in the original source to show that either of these assumptions is correct.

> Suetonius had the 14th legion and a detachment from the 20th, and auxiliaries from the nearest (allies), some 10,000 troops in total. He decided to fight without further delay. He selected a place in a narrow defile enclosed at the rear by a forest. This guaranteed that the enemy could not attack except from the front; and the front was an open plain which removed any apprehension of ambush. He therefore drew up the legionaries on close ranks with the light armed auxiliaries on either side; the massed ranks of cavalry stood on the wings. On the other hand the British forces were moving this way and that in groups of various sizes, and in numbers never before seen. So confident were they, that they had brought their wives to witness their victory, and placed them on wagons positioned around the extreme edge of the battlefield.
>
> (Tacitus, *Annals* 14.31–6)

This is topographically vague, and when our very limited knowledge of land use at the time and land-use change is considered the difficulties look insurmountable. An examination of just one suggested site, near Paulerspury in Northamptonshire, where Watling Street runs through Whittlewood Forest (Marix Evans 2007), illustrates the problems. The site appears originally to have been suggested because of the presence of a large undated cemetery in close proximity to Watling Street. The small side valley here, opening into the valley of the Tove, might accord with the terrain described by Tacitus, although in the immediate environs several other small valleys also cross Watling Street. Our knowledge of the extent of woodland is also problematic, even though this region has been subject to archaeological investigation and historic landscape mapping (Cooper 2006; Jones and Page 2006; Partida *et al* in prep). Woodland coverage when this area was part of the medieval royal forest of Whittlewood is to some degree understood, with the woods to the west of the Tove valley at that time lying almost wholly on the boulder-clay-capped plateau. Although medieval woodland did not extend close to Watling Street, in the earlier medieval period it may have lain across much of this boulder clay. If this was the case it would have been largely the result of woodland regeneration in the post-Roman period, because aerial survey and pottery scatters show that clearance of the clays for agriculture was well advanced by the end of the Iron Age. Indeed, several Iron Age sites are known on the boulder clay adjacent to the suggested battlefield, so it is likely that by AD 61 woodland had been cleared well away from Watling Street. Casting further doubt on the probability of this site being that of Boudicca's defeat are the burials in the cemetery and associated finds, which have now been dated to the early Middle Ages (Northants HER). Small-scale metal-detecting survey, not surprisingly, failed to produce any supporting evidence (J Kliene pers comm).

We need to know far more about the nature of the archaeology of Roman battles before we can determine

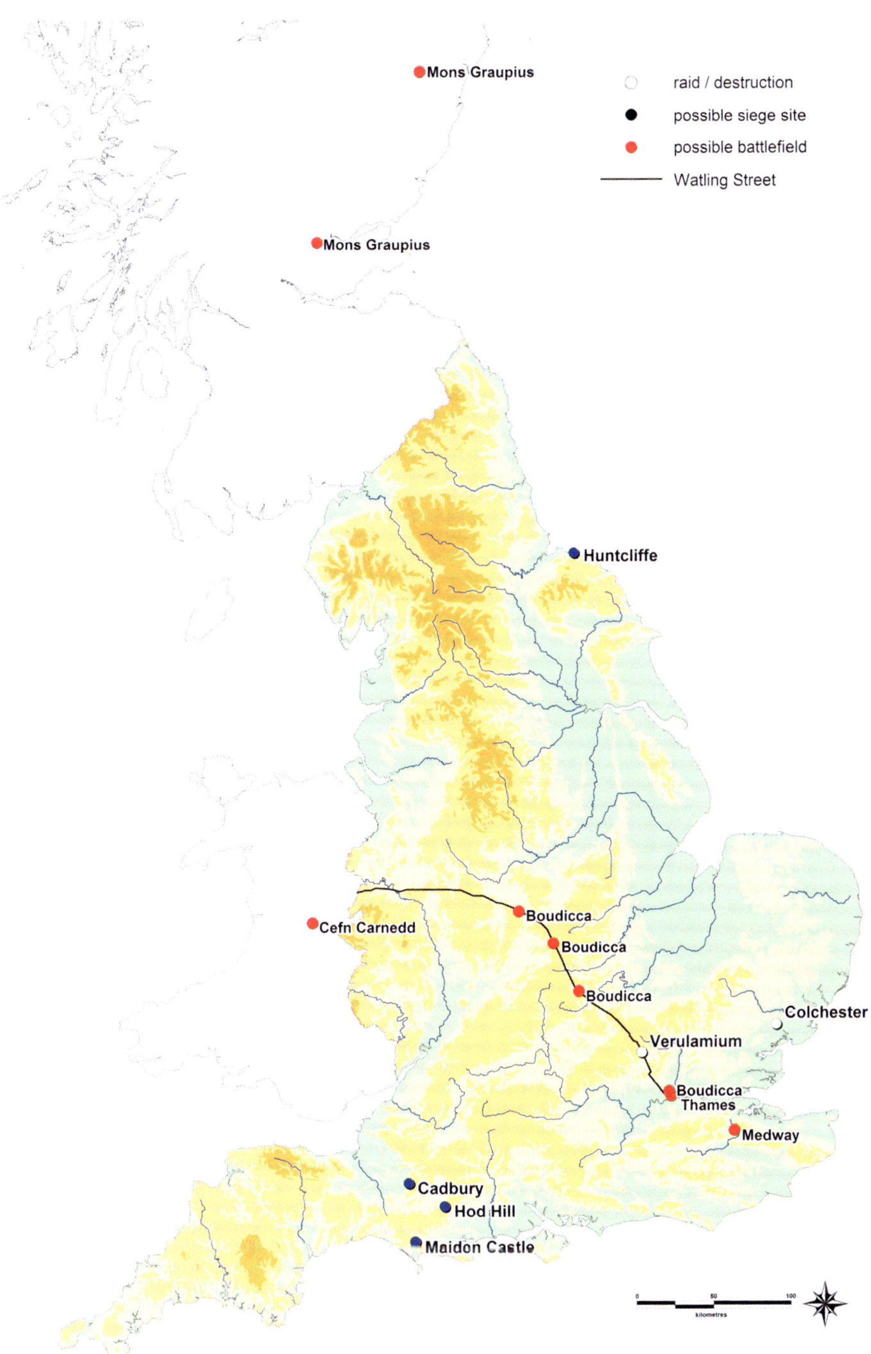

Fig 3.4 Fields of conflict in Roman Britain, including four alternative sites for the Boudicca battle

what their signatures may look like. The greatest problem is likely to be distinguishing battle-related scatters from the background noise of artefacts deposited over several centuries of Roman-period occupation and agriculture. Evidence from Germany, however, shows that recognisable battle archaeology from the Roman period does exist. A find of a mass grave of 40 men and 30 horses was reported from Krefeld-Gellep (Coulston 2001), while the best-known and most extensively explored site is that at Kalkriese, near Osnabruck. This was probably where the Roman army under Varus was destroyed in AD 9 while on campaign well beyond the frontier (Harnecker 2004; Wilbers-Rost 2007). The broader site has been known from finds of coins and other material since the 19th century, and modern investigation followed the collection of exceptional finds during metal detecting in the area (Clunn *et al* 1999). A broad distribution of Roman coins and other distinctive artefacts extending across some 10–20km have been recovered as chance finds, in casual collecting and through systematic metal detecting. They are interpreted as representing the destruction of the legion over a period of several days as it marched westwards. The best-preserved area of this scatter, towards the western end at Kalkriese, has been examined through large-scale excavation over a number of years. Here the deposits are exceptionally well preserved and represent a deeply buried battlefield surface protected by more than a metre of medieval and later deposits of turf brought in over a long period to improve the fertility of the soil. The finds appear to be associated with – and in places possibly buried by the decay of – a Germanic fortification argued by some to represent a stronghold used against the Roman forces. With all this said, it must be noted that almost no projectiles have been recovered from the core area and that the assemblage is, it could be argued, more typical of what might be expected from the destruction of a baggage train than from an open battle between armies deployed in battle array. The wide and impressive range of finds is now displayed at Kalkriese in a purpose-built visitor centre on the battlefield, a small part of which is accessible to and interpreted for the public.

Kalkriese is important because it shows what a battle of the Roman period might look like archaeologically, although the site appears atypical in a number of ways. Firstly, because it is believed to represent the near-total destruction of a legion a wide range of distinctively military artefacts will have been deposited in large numbers. Secondly, because the battle was fought outside the Roman Empire most of the artefacts carried by legionaries – not just military items but also 'domestic' artefacts – were relatively rare if not unique in the area. As a result they are easily distinguished from other contemporary Roman material, which might have reached the area in small quantities through trade or plunder. In contrast, the Germanic forces are near-invisible. This is not simply because they were the victorious force and hence their losses were fewer, but could also be because the vast majority of artefacts that they lost during the action may not be distinguishable from other artefacts deposited in a non-military context at an earlier or later date.

The late Roman battlefield at Harzhorn, also in Germany, provides a very different picture (Geschwinde *et al* 2009; Geschwinde *et al* 2011; Günther Moosbauer pers comm). Here battle archaeology was discovered by chance in highly constricted terrain, where an important pass crosses the Harzhorn ridge close to the Harz Mountains. Over a thousand battle-related artefacts have been recovered in varying density along the pass. Of these, just a handful are of copper alloy or other non-ferrous metals. The vast majority, including 130 bolt heads, 41 arrowheads and items from personal equipment and fittings from carts, are ferrous. They cluster in groups along the pass, but, while some of the gaps and variations in density seem genuinely original and significant, elsewhere the absence of finds has a very different explanation. Preservation conditions are exceptional, with even the projectiles points having meaningful patterns of orientation because they come from a woodland context on steep ground where no cultivation has taken place since the battle. The ferrous artefact scatter ceases almost completely where, all along the pass, medieval strip fields extend up to the steep ground. Had this been a wholly ploughed site it seems likely that there would have been just a handful of non-ferrous artefacts surviving and the site might never have been recognised as a battlefield, even though, like Kalkriese, it lies more than 100km beyond the Roman frontier. Of the Germanic enemy there was almost no trace in the artefact record. The paucity of non-ferrous finds compared with Kalkriese may be in part because the Roman force survived the engagement and perhaps also because these were auxiliaries and thus equipped differently from a legionary force.

Kalkriese and Hartzhorn provide extraordinary information on the character of deposits that may have existed on parts of other battlefields. Yet their exceptional nature means that neither can be a model for archaeology likely to survive on Roman battlefields in Britain. While northern Scotland in AD 81 might be sufficiently beyond the frontier to meet one criterion, Mons Graupius did not see the destruction of the Roman army and so there will not be corresponding artefact loss as seen at Kalkriese. Artefacts from the native forces, even if lost in substantial numbers, may not stand out from the background noise, at least in type, although they might do so in terms of density. For battlefields in England, it would appear that none of the conditions at Kalkriese may apply. Only in exceptional conditions, such as those seen at Harzhorn, might there be a chance of recovering meaningful battle archaeology.

It is, therefore, to sieges that we must look, because the locations of fortified sites are well known. What can be achieved by widescale recording of artefact scatters, in this case of lead slingshot, is demonstrated from investigation of the attack in 348 BC on Olynthos, Greece (Lee 2001). No systematic attempt has been made here to collect data relating to sieges or raids that led to the destruction of settlements, but several examples have been noted, including possible conquest-period sieges of the hillforts at Hod Hill and Maiden Castle and a possible siege or massacre deposit of *c* AD 60 at Cadbury hillfort. In addition, there are the raids of AD 60–61 on Colchester and *Verulamium*.

The other key identifier of Roman-period warfare may be the chance discovery of a mass grave in which the bodies show clear evidence of weapon trauma, as seen in the excavations at the late Roman signal station at Huntcliffe (Hind 2005). HER responses to our enquiries yielded several other locations with such evidence, including the site with mutilated bodies from Whittlesey (Cambridgeshire), but this and most others lack any secure associations with military action. Two HERs also provided records of artefact collections which had been interpreted as possibly indicating battle sites, but both appear spurious and have been excluded.

Early medieval warfare: AD 411–1065

There are 232 early medieval records on the Database for England. Of these, 29 appear to be sieges, all but two from the 9th to 11th centuries; at least two are assassinations; and a further 49 are impossible to classify or are spurious. Of the remaining 154 sites at least 20 relate to battles with more than one possible location, including *Brunanburh*, with seven alternatives, *Ethandun* and Ashdown, with six, and *Assandun*, with three (Fig 3.5).

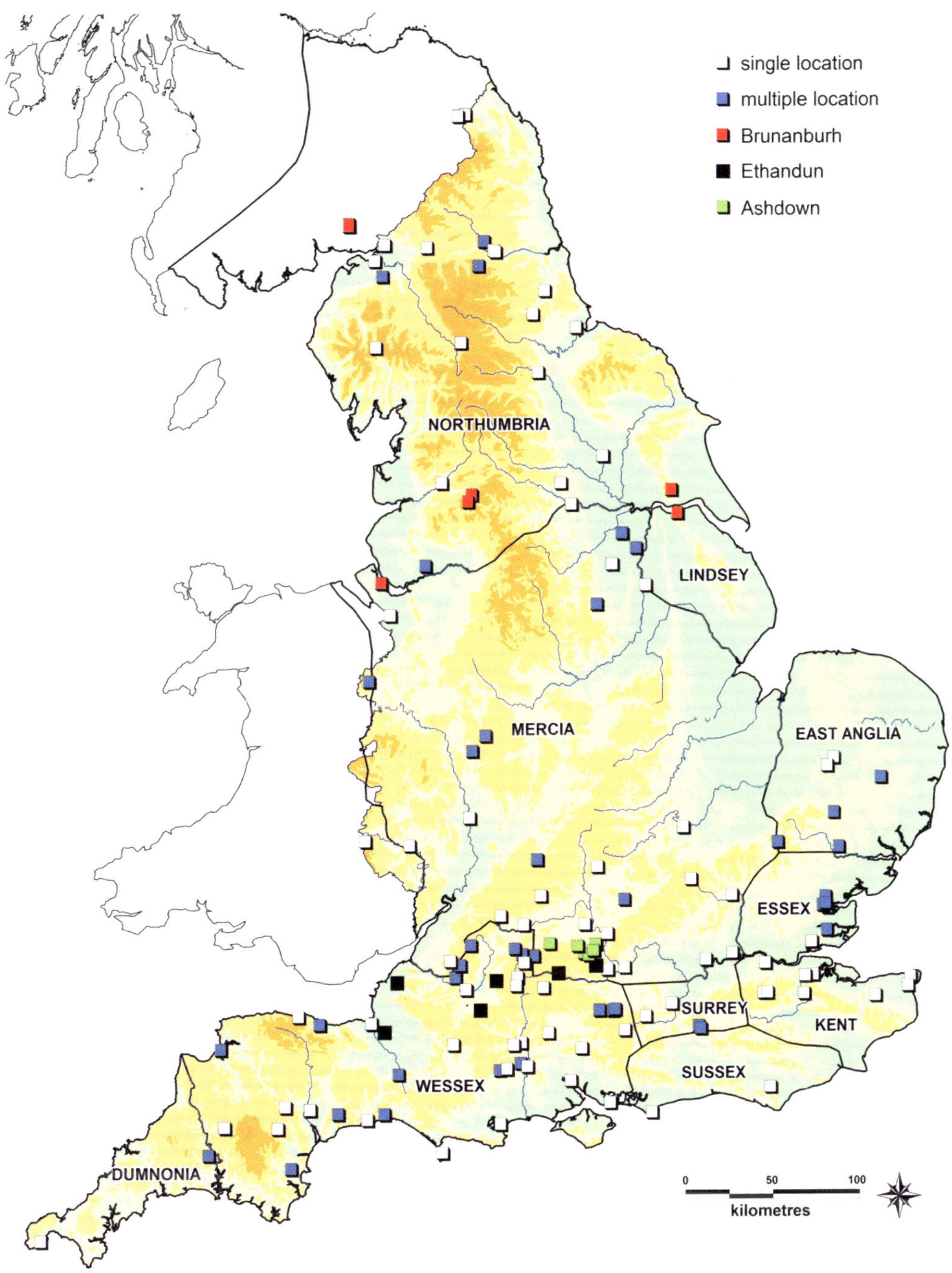

Fig 3.5 Map of early medieval battles, indicating alternative sites where they exist, shown in relation to approximate territorial boundaries. Boundaries are from Hill 1981, 31, and Cunliffe *et al* 2001, 58

The alternative sites of some actions with more than one possible location, such as Maldon (AD 991), lie within a relatively small area. Others, in contrast, are widely separated. *Brunanburh* (AD 937) is the most extreme case, with alternatives spread right across northern England and into southern Scotland, although place-name analysis now indicates that the site probably lay in the Wirral (Higham 1997). Such an isolated location might initially appear improbable for such a major battle, but it could perhaps relate to the deployment of an Anglo-Saxon army to control the major road between the strategically significant city of Chester and an important early port at Meols on the tip of the peninsula.

Although 114 battles or possible battles have just one recorded site, these are often locationally insecure. Such uncertainty is a result of the sparse evidence in the primary written sources, with many reported in just one source, the *Anglo-Saxon Chronicle*. We may know who the combatants in many actions were, but the actions' outcomes may be unclear and the nature of the fighting uncertain. In most cases all we have to locate the site is the name of the battle. In the case of Luton (AD 913) the place-name association with the modern settlement is accepted, but there is no evidence as to where the battlefield may lie in the surrounding territory. Other battles, including some which had been thought to have been identified, remain unlocated. The battle of *Bedcanford* (AD 571), for example, used to be placed at Bedford, but place-name scholars no longer accept this identification of the name.

Most battles are, like Luton, located sufficiently accurately by their names to allow analysis on a national scale, and some of the biases introduced by our sources are immediately apparent once the sites are mapped at this level (Fig 3.6). For example, the concentration of battles in Wessex in part reflects the focus of interest of the compilers of the *Anglo-Saxon Chronicle*. Indeed, until the 9th century even something as basic as the overall distribution of early medieval battles must be viewed with caution because the compilation of the *Anglo-Saxon Chronicle* itself did not begin until the 890s. Although the *Chronicle* drew from earlier annals and other sources that have not survived, there is a low degree of confidence in the detail for the 5th–7th centuries.

Despite these limitations, some general conclusions may be drawn from a comparison of the early medieval distribution with other data sets. For example, comparison with the network of Roman roads suggests some degree of association at a strategic level (see Fig 3.10). Similarly, there appear to be concentrations of battles along some boundaries between Anglo-Saxon kingdoms (see Fig 3.5), though one must bear in mind the level of uncertainty over these boundaries and the

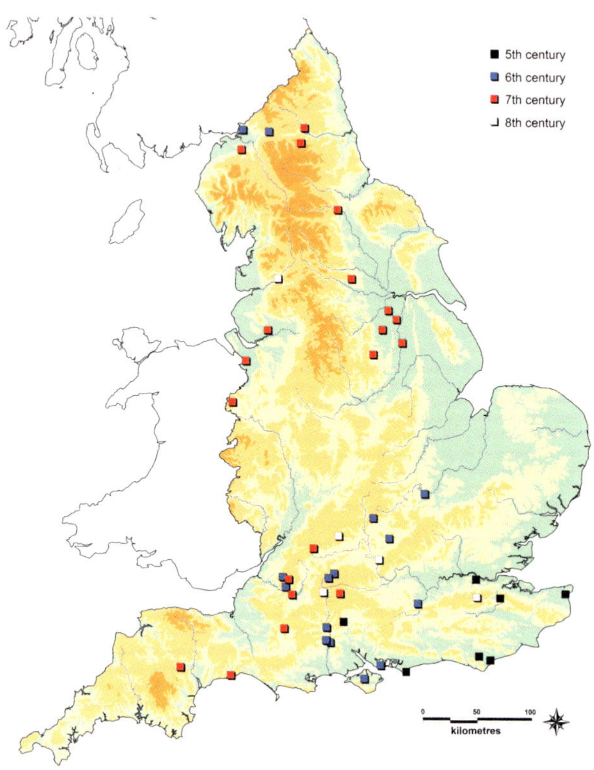

Fig 3.6 Map showing the distribution of battles and sieges of the 5th to 8th centuries in England

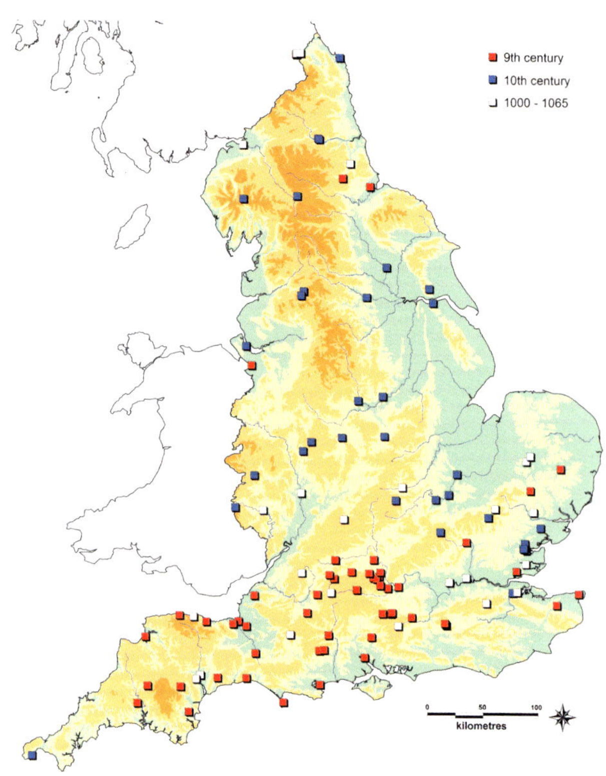

Fig 3.7 Map showing the distribution of battles and sieges of the 9th to 11th centuries (up to 1065) in England

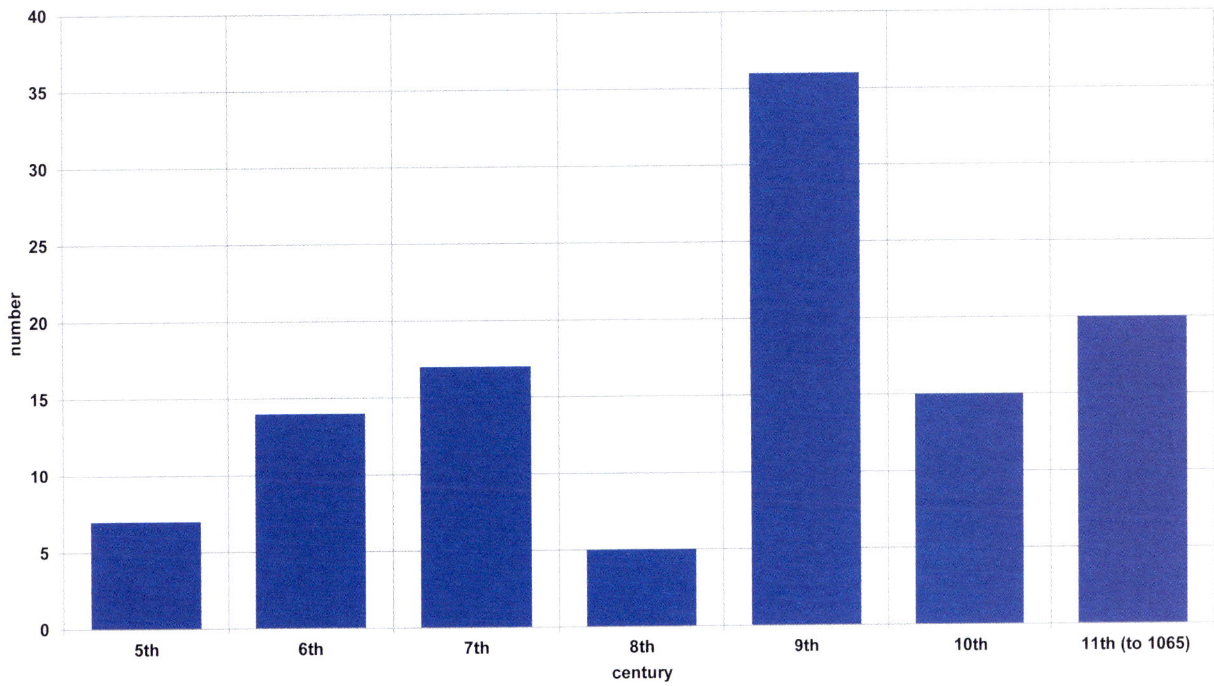

Fig 3.8 Graph of early medieval battles in England by century

degree to which they changed over time (Wood 2008). This analysis can be extended to patterning by chronology, where conclusions may be drawn about the spread of warfare across the country in different periods (Figs 3.7 and 3.8). Thus, for example, the 10th-century campaign of re-conquest from the Danes is clearly visible in central and northern England.

Unfortunately, none of this assists in the identification of the actual sites of the battles. Until we are able to locate early medieval battlefields with confidence, a research strategy to investigate them archaeologically remains out of reach. There are only two early medieval battlefields which, at first sight, seem to have secure sites – Maldon (the only example from before 1066 to have been Registered) and Heavenfield. Yet even for these, uncertainties remain.

Maldon

The *Anglo-Saxon Chronicle* states that a battle took place in AD 991 near Maldon. This must be Maldon in Essex, because the English commander was Brihtnoth, Ealdorman of Essex, and earlier plundering by the Viking force with which he engaged took place at Ipswich, 48km to the north-east. The position of the battlefield has been interpreted from topographical evidence provided in the broadly contemporary poem *The Battle of Maldon* (Laborde 1925, 161–73; Keynes 1991; Cooper 1993). The key facts are that the Viking force landed at, or marched to, a position on one side of a tidal section of the Blackwater river, or a channel within its estuary, which was then called Panta. It was high tide when they first faced the Anglo-Saxon forces across the channel. Although it was too deep to cross at that time, the channel was sufficiently narrow for the opposing forces to negotiate by shouting across the water. When the tide fell the Viking troops were allowed to cross, passing in a westerly direction across a *brycg* – a causeway or ford – after which they deployed and the two armies fought.

Three main candidates for the site have been proposed. One lies immediately north of Maldon at the place now known as Heybridge, today completely built up as a suburb of Maldon (Freeman 1869). The Viking force was suggested as having crossed the Blackwater river north-eastward, from just outside the Maldon defences, to attack the East Saxon army gathered on the north-east bank. The case for this site has been rejected, in part because it does not appear to meet the criteria relating to the tides and in part because the poem makes no reference to Maldon town, which would have been immediately to the back of the Viking force (Burne 1952). The second candidate is Osea Island, which lies in the north of the estuary and is connected to the mainland by a causeway. But, even when subsequent sea level rise is taken into account, the 1km distance between the island and the mainland is too great to fit the events in the poem (National Army Museum 1995j). The strongest candidate is immediately opposite Northey Island, in the Blackwater estuary just to the east of the town of Maldon. This interpretation is supported by detailed geological study of the area (Petty and Petty 1976; 1993) which has shown that in the 10th century the site would have fitted closely the descriptions in the poem, including the way in which the rising tide flows around both sides of the island to meet at the causeway (Laborde 1925). While today the distance from mainland to island might be considered too great for a shouted exchange, the land here has been sinking since the last glaciation and sea level has risen by about 1.8m (6 feet) since the 10th century. As a result there are now saltings where there was dry land at the time of the battle, with a channel no more than *c* 110m wide. The adjacent land was dry pasture, dipping gently to a steep river bank. In AD 991 the causeway would have been covered by 1.8–2.4m of water at high tide, while silts similar to those seen today would have made crossing the channel impossible except via the causeway. According to the poem, moreoever, there was a wood nearby, for one Englishman let his hawk fly to the wood before he advanced to battle, while others fled there after Brihtnoth's death, and the parishes to the west of Northey Island have woodland-related names: Woodham, Hazeleigh, and Purleigh (Dodgson 1991). However, no reconstruction of the distribution of woodland in this area in the medieval period has apparently been attempted, so it is unclear how closely the woodland might have extended towards the battlefield, or indeed when it may have existed. The Northey Island interpretation has also been challenged (Bessinger 1963), although today the strength of the circumstantial evidence is strong. The problem is that there is no definitive evidence in support of the Northey Island site because the topographical detail in the primary source is not specific. So, unless or until archaeological evidence for the battle is recovered, the exact site of the battle of Maldon remains in doubt.

Heavenfield or Denisesburn

Heavenfield is an example of an early medieval battlefield which was once believed to have been securely identified, but in fact remains unlocated. This battle, a celebrated encounter in the early 630s between the Northumbrian king Oswald and the Welsh leader Cædwalla, was often said to have taken place at Heavenfield. Bede described the place, 'called in English Hefenfeld and in Latin Caelistis Campus', as being on the north side of 'the wall with which the Romans once girded the whole of Britain from sea to sea' (HE iii 2). The site lies immediately to the north of Hadrian's Wall and a short distance east of Chesters fort, and is beside a turret where entry was presumably possible through the Wall into an area surrounded on the north and west by falling ground (Fig 3.9). The site is marked by a late medieval chapel which may be the successor to an early 8th-century commemorative church recorded by Bede. He further tells of an annual journey to the site by the brethren of Hexham Abbey to keep vigil and sing psalms for the good of Oswald's soul (HE iii 2).

If Heavenfield were the battle site then it would certainly be a candidate for intensive archaeological survey. In fact, re-examination of the sources shows that Heavenfield and the battle were in different places, which Bede himself makes clear.[3] The name of the battle in at least two sources is *Catscaul*; this means 'the battle within the wall', suggesting that it took place to the south of the Wall (Raine, I, xi, ff., cited in Plummer, II, 122–3). Heavenfield, which lies immediately north of the wall, appears simply to have been the site of Oswald's camp the night before the battle. According to Bede and Adomnan, Oswald moved from here to launch a dawn attack on Cædwalla's camp.[4] The Tudor antiquary Leland, working from an older tradition, may provide a clue to where the battlefield lay when he says: 'There is a fame that Oswald won the betelle at Halydene, a 2 miles est from St. Oswalde's asche' (*Itinerary* 2 vii 58). Plummer identifies Halydene with Hallington, but this is north of the Wall and so can be discounted (Plummer, II, 123). It seems more likely that Halton, 6.4km (4 miles) east of Heavenfield, is meant by Leland, or the adjacent Roman fort of Onnum, which lay where Dere Street crossed the Wall.

The battle concluded with the death of Cædwalla and the destruction of his force at *Denisesburn* (HE iii 2). Bede gave it its English name, 'the brook of the *Denise*',[5] and *Denisesburn* probably equates with Rowley Water, which is south of the Tyne.[6] The Rowley Burn today is just a tributary of the Devil's Water, some 6km south-west of Corbridge. Close to the head of the burn there was a farm called Rowley Head on Armstrong's 18th-century map of Northumberland. The Ordnance Survey first edition six-inch mapping gives Devil's Water for the stream that runs into the Tyne next to Corbridge, as does

Armstrong's map. The identification is also supported by the place-name Dilston, which has a 'devil' derivation according to the English Place Names Society, though Mills gives 'dark stream' (Mills 2003).

There is nothing to suggest why an army in flight would be anywhere near the Rowley Burn, as we know it today, unless we are missing a key piece of the Roman or medieval road pattern. If the battlefield lay at Halton then Cædwalla must have fled south down the Roman road through Corbridge, but was caught on the far side of the Tyne at *Denisesburn*. Yet if the battle had been fought at Halton, or the nearby fort of Onnum, then why was it not named after them or even after Corbridge – the (later) parochial area within which they lay? If it had been fought close to Corbridge then, again, why did it not take that name, as did several later battles?

The confusion of the place called Heavenfield with the site of the battle is probably explained by three linked factors. One was the devotional emphasis given to the victory very soon afterwards. This was sustained through the later Middle Ages, when Heavenfield was the destination of an annual procession, the scene of 'innumerable miracles of healing', a pilgrim destination, and the site of a commemorative church. In the 16th century Leland recorded that 'men there aboute yet finde smaule wod crossis in the grounde' (*Itinerary* V 61). The second factor is the symbolism of the setting up of the cross. Bede and Adomnan gave prominence to Heavenfield because, as far as Bede knew, no symbol of the Christian faith had previously been erected anywhere in Bernicia (HE iii 2). The moment of the cross-raising and the army's fall to prayer was thus a national turning point. Third, in Bede's thinking, Heavenfield was where the battle was actually won, even though its events occurred elsewhere.

As the much later case of Bosworth (1485) shows, it is not unusual for the reputed site of a battle to move several kilometres across the landscape. At Bosworth, too, the site was intimately linked with a foundation myth – that of the Tudor dynasty – although the reasons for Bosworth's wandering were more prosaic (Foard and Curry in prep).

Locating early medieval battlefields

Heavenfield is clearly not a battle that can yet be located with sufficient closeness to enable field investigation. At present, apart perhaps from Maldon, neither can any other important early medieval battle

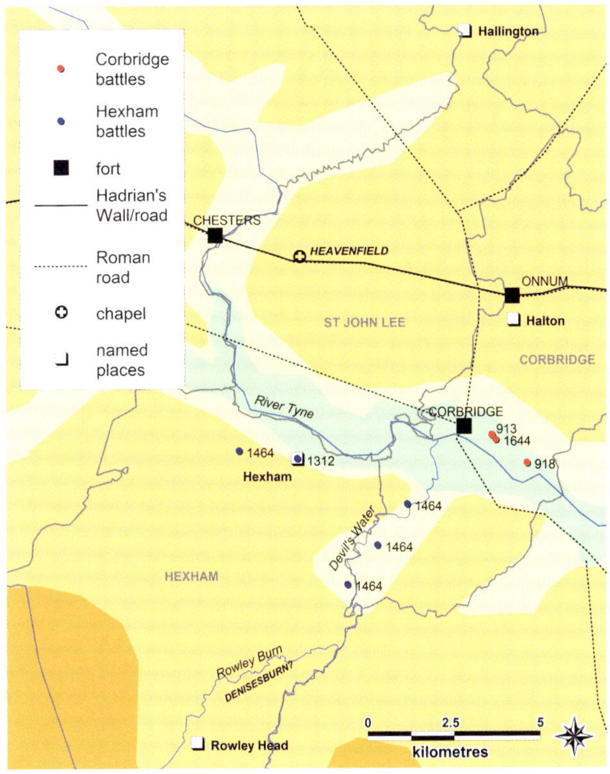

Fig 3.9 Map showing the context for the battle of Heavenfield or Denisesburn, including key elements of the Roman and medieval landscape. Also shown are later battlefields, including the four alternative sites for the 1464 battle of Hexham. Parish boundaries are from Kain and Oliver 2001 and Roman features from Ordnance Survey 2001

in England. The various battle plans one sees published for the period, such as Burne's plans of Ashdown, Deorham and *Ethandun*, which show deployments set in the landscape, are mere conjecture (Burne 1950; 1952). One might worry, therefore, that, unless there is a chance discovery, say of a securely dated mass grave showing distinctive weapon trauma, there is little chance of archaeology identifying early medieval battlefields. But this may be too pessimistic.

Commemoration might provide one avenue by which actively to seek some battlefields. Most obvious are the few battles where a memorial chapel was constructed to commemorate a victory or remember the dead – as with the 1016 battle of *Assandun*, though in this case the location of the chapel itself is uncertain (Rodwell 1993). Yet, as Heavenfield shows, even if the site of the chapel is securely located it need not stand on the battlefield (Fig 3.9).

While mass graves seem most likely to be found by chance, there may be clues as to their location from antiquarian reports and place-names. However, the case of Chester, discussed above (p 30), has shown that, even when there is modern excavation and scientific dating, the claims of links to a battle can be challenged.

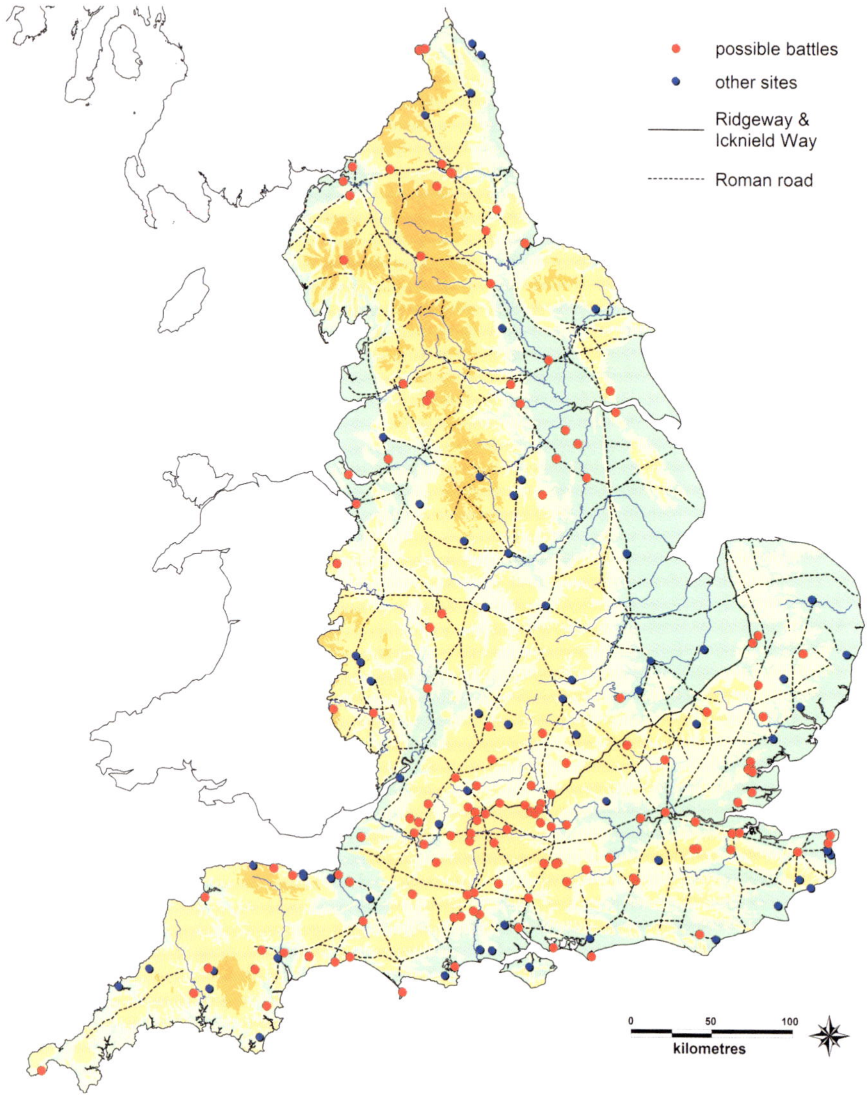

Fig 3.10 Map of early medieval fields of conflict in England, viewed against Roman and other early roads. Roads from Ordnance Survey 2001; Ordnance Survey 2005

Antiquarian reports of battle graves will be yet more suspect, and many probably relate to normal cemeteries of other periods. Such discoveries sometimes themselves gave rise to local names that might now be taken as place-name evidence supporting a link to a battle. For instance, Bloodmoor Hill (Gisleham, Suffolk) is a name now known to have been bestowed following the opening of an Anglo-Saxon barrow in 1758, and probably relates to the discovery of early Anglo-Saxon burials with weapons (Newman 1996). A few place-name attributions may prove genuine. Battle Wood in Stoke Lyne (Oxfordshire) may be such a case; Stenton established that the 12th-century name of a wood there was *Fethelee*: this he linked to the battle of Fethanleag of AD 584 (Stenton 1947, 29; *Trans Royal Hist Soc*, 4th Ser, **22**, 19–20).

Suggestions have also been made of links between finds of artefacts and battle sites. There is a report of archaeological finds from the Fleet Valley, London, which have been linked to the battle of London in 1066 (Mills 1996). Even the recently discovered Staffordshire Hoard has been proposed by some to be booty related to a battle, but until we establish the true character of early medieval battle archaeology from an assemblage that can be securely linked to a known battle then assessment of otherwise unexplained finds will remain speculative. By analogy with later sites, what is needed is understanding of distinctive spatial patterning from larger numbers of finds.

At present we know little about the types of artefact that are likely to have been lost during an early medieval battle. We can take it as given that the size, form and material of the weapons and equipment will have had an influence upon what was deposited and what has survived. Iron spears are likely to have formed a substantial proportion of the projectiles used. However, since such spears will have been far easier than arrows to retrieve for re-use, few may have been left. Moreover, spears, arrows, and many other artefacts will have been of ferrous metal which will not normally have survived in the topsoil for more than a thousand years. Such items may only survive where part of a battlefield's surface has been buried beneath alluvium, was waterlogged, or was left uncultivated for long periods. In contrast, objects of copper alloy and lead are far more likely to have survived but may have been deposited in such small numbers that no meaningful pattern can be discerned.

Recent interdisciplinary work on civil defence in Anglo-Saxon Wessex may offer an alternative way forward, through a study of the strategic and tactical aspects of the landscape.[7] Potential strands of evidence include the nature of the action, that is, whether it was a set-piece battle, raid or skirmish; the detail of the communication network, including roads, signalling systems, and mustering points; the topography, including geology, relief, and land use; and other monuments such as fortifications, burial sites, and meeting-places. If probable locations for encounters can be identified through the location and consideration of such features, then approaches discussed above might be put into effect.

Two main forms of action can be discerned from primary sources. One is the swift raid into enemy territory to inflict damage and capture booty; this appears to have been the most common. A second is the large set-piece battle, where the purpose was to force the opponent into submission, signified by the giving of hostages and tribute. The difficulty of gathering large forces together and coordinating confrontations may mean that landform was highly significant for the second category. There are indications in sources that places of assembly played a key role, whether for the gathering of allied forces or in the identification of a place to meet hostile forces. The entire process, from first summons through local and regional mobilisation to final arrival at the battlefield, demanded complex organisation and a pre-existing network of assembly places. The origins of the hundredal system are unclear, but it is possible that the mobilisation of a later Anglo-Saxon army took advantage of existing administrative structures. Forces would gather first at local moots, and then regional meeting-places, before assembling with the rest of the *fyrd* at a predetermined spot. The meeting at *Swinbeorg*, mentioned in Alfred's will, is traditionally taken to refer to a mustering at the assembly place of Swanborough hundred (Wiltshire) prior to the Battle of Ashdown in AD 871. In AD 878, before the battle of Edington, Alfred stopped first at *Ecgbryhtesstane* ('Egbert's Stone') on the borders of Somerset, Dorset, and Wiltshire. This was perhaps an established mustering point possibly at Iley Oak, the meeting-place of the hundreds of Warminster and Heytesbury. The battle site itself is believed to lie near the probable meeting-place of the hundred of Whorwellsdown, in the vicinity of Cresswell Down Farm.

The essential feature of all meeting-places, whether for mustering, diplomacy, or battle, was accessibility. Often this meant proximity to major roads or waterways, but it could also mean a site on a territorial border. The names of numerous meeting-places give topographical information which may sometimes suggest the location of battlefields. Halsall suggests that the limited number of campaigning routes and the basic nature of early medieval scouting made the selection of a battlefield a question of convenience as much as tactical choice (Fig 3.10). He notes that 22 of the 26 broadly located battlefields of the period *c* AD 600 to *c* 850 were near river-crossings or significant landmarks (Halsall 2003, 156). Halsall also points to examples of armies stationing themselves at legal or administrative centres perhaps as a form of challenge.

Distinctive topographical features may thus help to pinpoint battlefields. The large number of later Anglo-Saxon military engagements with place-names in *ford* – Fulford, Stamford Bridge, Brentford, Thetford, Hereford, Castleford – point to the tactical significance of river-crossings, a consideration which can also be seen throughout later centuries. In addition, it is notable that many battles between *c* AD 850 and 1066 were fought in close proximity to Anglo-Saxon fortified sites, Viking encampments, or prehistoric monuments – examples include Wilton, Maldon, Hereford, Cynuit/Congresbury, Thetford, and Reading. Many of these might be expected to have been focal points for the mustering of troops, and they were also, of course, notable landmarks and therefore perhaps useful for armies attempting to locate one another. For purposes of mustering and engagement accessibility would ideally be combined with ease of identification, especially when the *fyrd* was operating outside its own shire. Shire meeting-places marked by distinctive landscape features may be identifiable through fieldwork. Similarly, the location of several battles involving the 'seizure of ships' are constrained by topographical factors, including terrestrial and submarine contours, harbours, and navigable waterways; these too may be amenable to archaeological analysis.

In sum, different types of evidence may assist in identifying the general area in which an early medieval battle was fought. Such analysis could probably be aided by comparative study of the context of well-located later battles to determine whether general principles can be isolated and, if so, which are the most useful. However, as is clear from analysis of later battles, the choice of a specific site on which to fight will in most cases have been determined by the tactical opportunities and threats posed by the terrain. Identifying where in a general area troops are likely to have deployed will thus hang upon the principle of inherent historic military probability – the application of which will prove far easier in some contexts than others, as the later case of Towton (1461) demonstrates (see Fig 5.4). A first step might be to review a series of different battles to find one or more with highly constricted terrain. Even then, all that can be established will be one or more hypotheses, which will then need to be tested through a search for battle archaeology. Which returns us to the point that the nature of battle archaeology of the period still awaits characterisation.

There are two ways to address this problem. The first is to work backwards from Hastings, which appears the most accurately located battle from this period (see Fig 3.14). If we can establish the character of the battle archaeology at Hastings then it may be possible to predict what, if anything, can reasonably be expected on earlier battlefields. The second is to seek one or more actions which took the form of an attack on a defended site, the location of which can be identified with some confidence, such as a Roman fort or a known *burh*. The investigation of such sites might yield direct information as to the character of the battle archaeology of these earlier centuries. However, as with later fortified sites, it is also possible that the signature of battle archaeology may be lost against a background scatter of artefacts deriving from occupation.

From all this, one thing seems clear: in the absence of an unexpected discovery of a mass grave, establishing the viability of archaeological investigation of early medieval battlefields will be a long and complex task.

Later medieval warfare: 1066–1454

There are 31 battles from the later medieval period on the Database for England (Fig 3.11). A further seventeen are possible battles where the scale or nature of the action is unclear. The possibles vary from events such as Bramham Moor (1408) and Fornham St Genevieve (1173), where further research is likely to confirm that they were battles, to those such as Clitheroe (1138), where the primary sources give little more than a vague reference.

Our intensive sampling of Cumbrian sources suggests that the sites of lesser actions are far more common than the Database currently indicates. The present study has not attempted to conduct a national search for such lesser actions or to recover more detailed information on the location and character of those which have been included; most will prove even more difficult to locate than major battles because the documentary and physical evidence is usually less substantial. The present analysis focuses instead upon the 31 certain battles, yet even for some of these the evidence is so poor that the sites may never be identified.

The period has been defined from 1066 because Hastings, fought in that year, is the first battle in England to be well located and for which detailed near-contemporary accounts exist. As things stand, only from this point can we begin to make a meaningful assessment of individual battlefields. In following centuries the written records tend to improve, although before the 17th century only a handful match the detail available for Hastings. While the sites of many later medieval battles are identifiable in general terms, accurate placing of the action is another matter, as for most there are few sources and rarely are they first-hand accounts, instead usually being written at a distance, in both time and space from the events they record. Their weakness is most clearly seen in the numbers of troops they claim were engaged or killed: medieval chronicles regularly specify armies that are far greater than are seen in even the largest of early modern battles; and, most significantly, that are also far larger than the better-documented medieval English armies that fought on the continent (Curry 2005). The numbers of dead reported for Towton actually exceed the numbers engaged at Naseby!

Another problem lies in the limited topographical detail that sources provide. Even what they do give is frequently challenged by historians, who argue that it may be elaboration drawn from descriptions of earlier battles or from military manuals such as Vegetius. In some cases this may be true, but, as work at Bosworth has shown, such detail can prove remarkably accurate. The apparent similarities between early accounts of different battles may often simply reflect the high degree of continuity from classical times to the 17th century in the tactical responses of commanders to the opportunities and problems provided by terrain. Detailed eyewitness accounts of early modern battles such as Edgehill and Naseby corroborate this. There

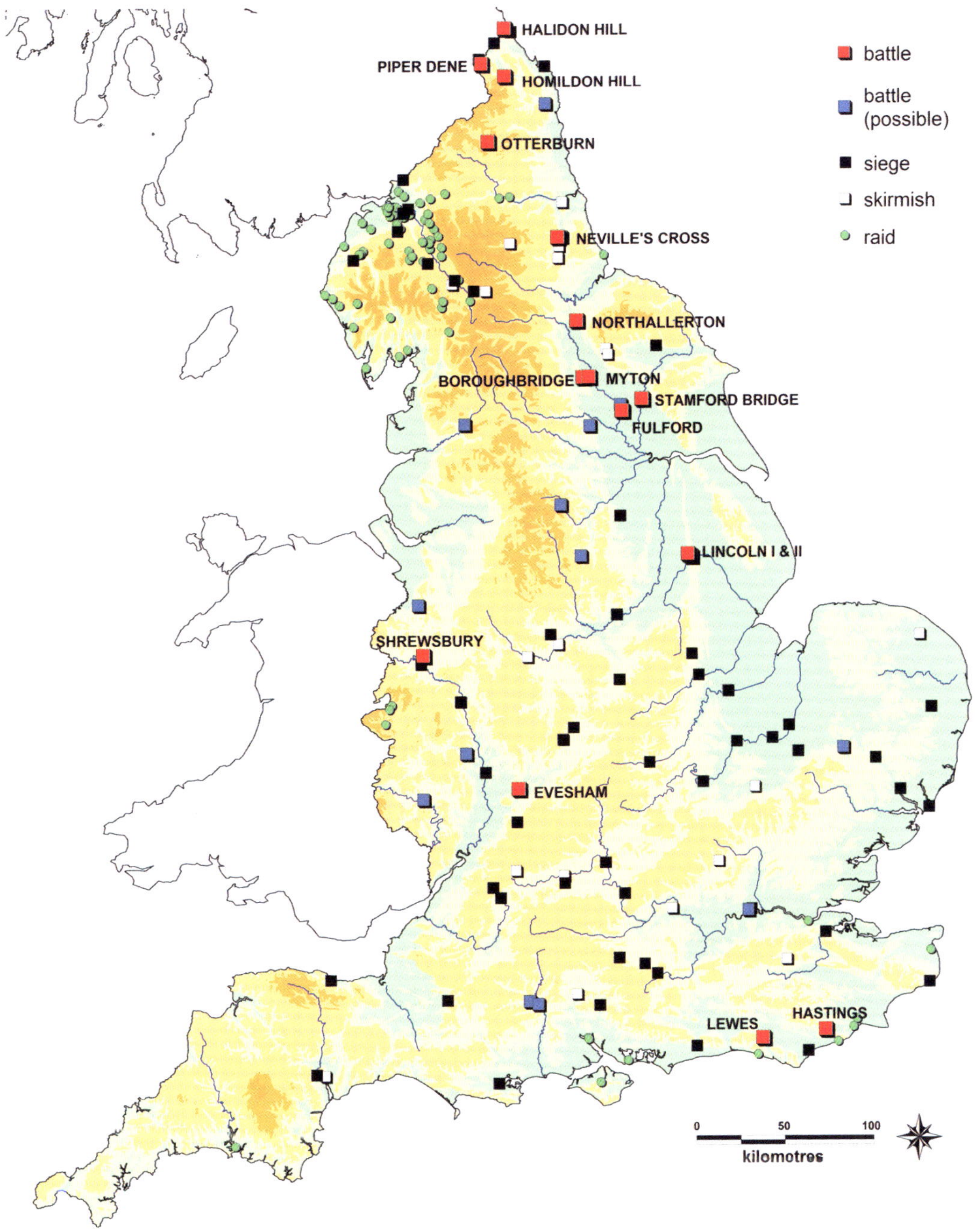

Fig 3.11 Map of fields of conflict in England between 1066 and 1454

may thus be grounds for thinking that the sparse topographical detail in accounts of some late medieval battles nonetheless provides useful evidence about location.

Later medieval battles can be divided into four main groups. First are the three great actions of 1066: Fulford, Stamford Bridge, and Hastings. Next there are the battles which relate to civil wars, including those of Stephen and Matilda (Lincoln I, 1141), and of Simon de Montfort (Lewes, 1264 and Evesham, 1265), and the battles of Boroughbridge (1322) and Shrewsbury (1403). Thirdly there are the seven Anglo-Scottish battles: Northallerton (1138); Myton (1319); Halidon Hill (1333); Neville's Cross (1346); Otterburn (1388); Homildon Hill (1402); and Piper Dene (1435). These all lie along the eastern corridor through Northumberland, and run as far south as Myton (1319), just 20km from York. Lastly, fifteen battles date from just 32 years in the late 15th century – a period of discontinuous warfare now known as the Wars of the Roses (1455–87) which was dominated by brief periods of intense action and by battles rather than sieges. These battles, the only medieval battlefields yet to have produced battle archaeology, are discussed in detail in Chapter 5.

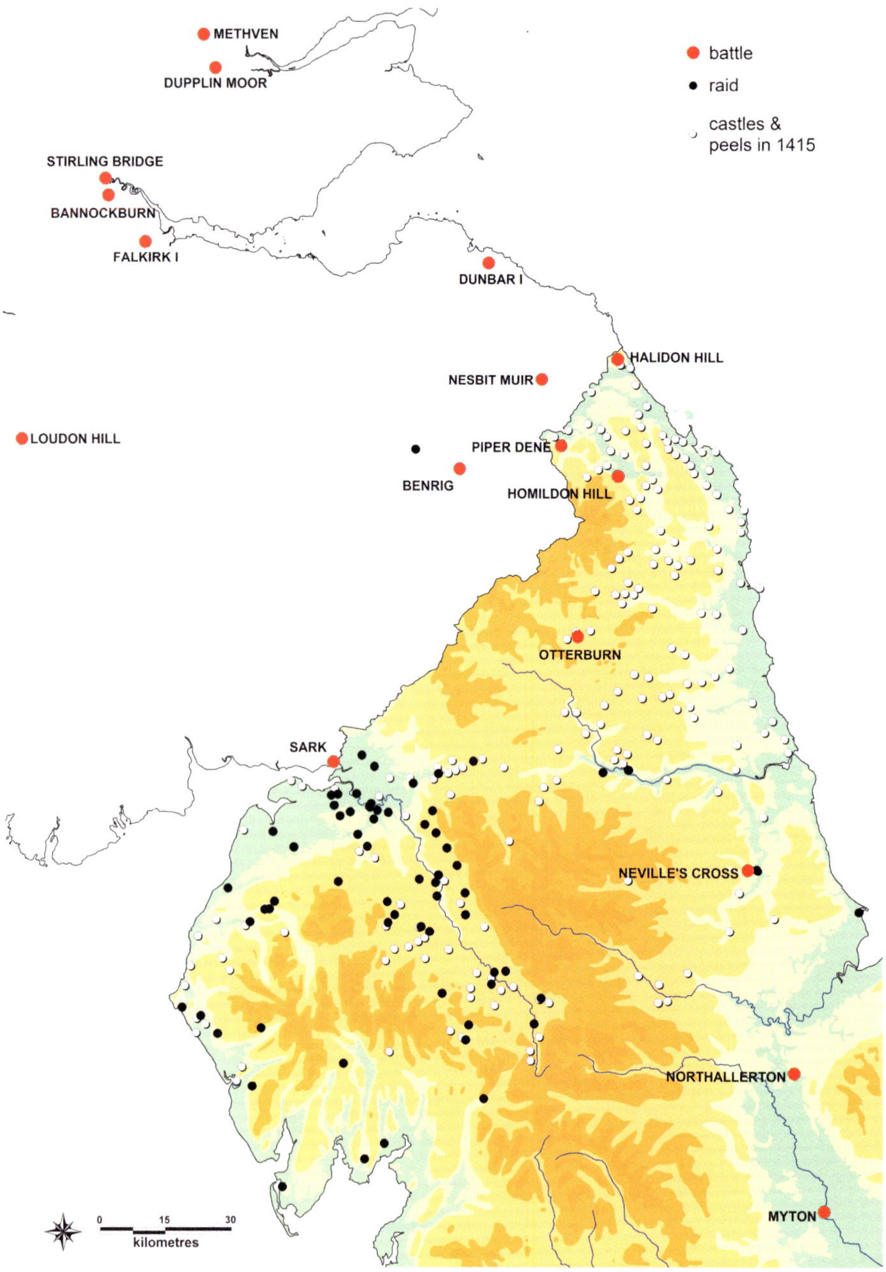

Fig 3.12 Map of later medieval warfare on the Anglo-Scottish frontier. The modern national boundary is shown here because, for short periods, some areas of England were under Scottish control and *vice versa*. Fortified sites from the early 15th century are depicted in England only. The large number of raids shown in Cumbria results from specific data enhancement for that area – a similar pattern should be expected both in Northumberland and north of the border

The Anglo-Scottish frontier perhaps needs to be considered in more detail because of its greater volume of evidence for actions below the level of the full battle. It also demonstrates the need to work at an international level, in this case integrating evidence of actions fought by English armies in Scotland and by Scottish armies in England.

This region was heavily fortified throughout the later medieval period. There were major defensive sites at Carlisle, Berwick, and Newcastle; other great castles, such as Norham, Bamburgh, and Prudhoe; a vast number of lesser defended pele towers; and, bastle-houses, the smallest defensive sites (Rowland 1994). Conflict here was similarly on a number of levels (Fig 3.12). At the lowest level was the raid. Raids extended from localised cattle rustling through to a few very large military incursions. They are under-represented in our data. Some impression of the true density of the larger raids is revealed in our more detailed sampling of Cumbrian sources. A similar pattern may be expected across Northumberland, extending southward into adjacent counties at a lower density. In the period of Scottish ascendancy after Bannockburn there were extensive raids deep into England, which in 1318 extended almost as far south as York and Preston (Cunliffe *et al* 2001, 90–1). Larger incursions could end in substantial engagement. The battle at Otterburn (1388), for example, occurred where a Scottish force was engaged during retreat along one of only a handful of major cross-border routes. Some long-distance sorties ended in major battles, such as Neville's Cross and Myton. Major incursions could also involve substantial

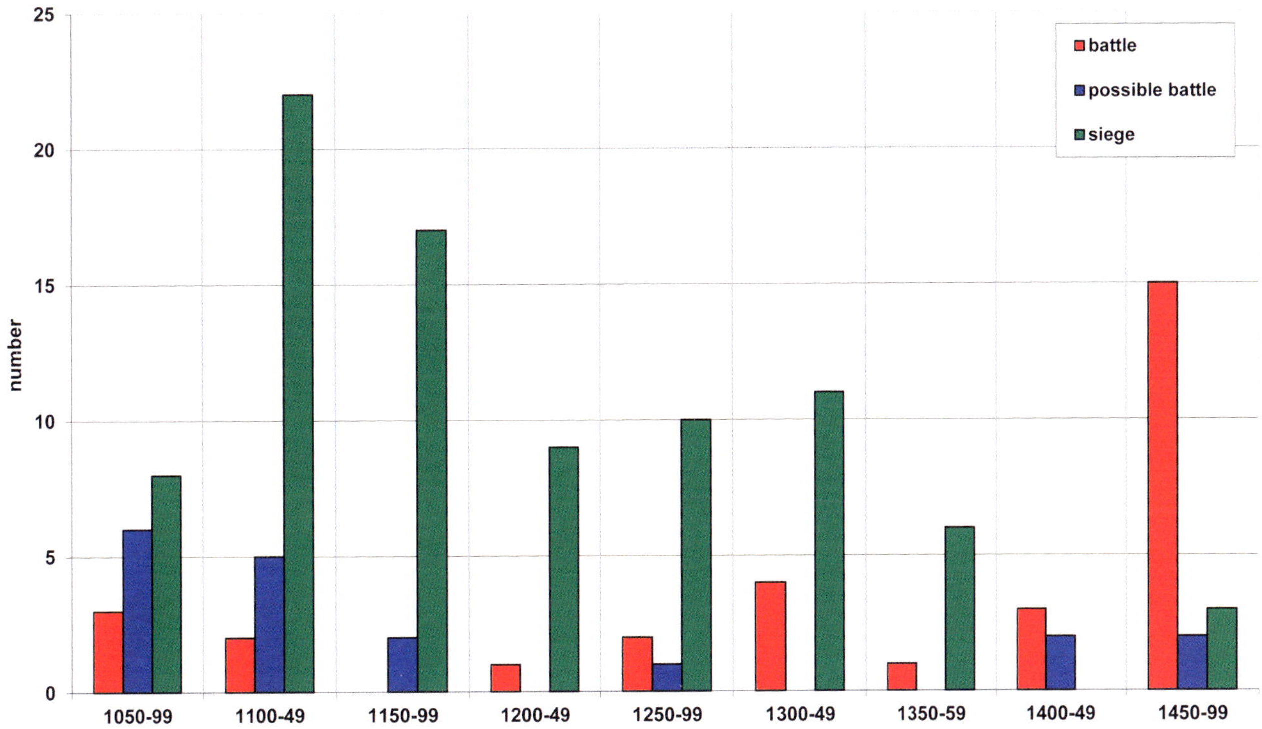

Fig 3.13 Graph of later medieval battles and sieges in England by half century

sieges. While the possibility of the Scots taking control of the border regions was real enough, with Carlisle and Berwick changing hands several times, it was only the English invasions of Scotland, particularly under Edward I, which seem to have had potential for large-scale conquest. This is, in part, a matter of geography. While castles such as Stirling – in the heartland of Scottish power in the lowland regions – lay less than 150km from Berwick or Carlisle, such a distance would not bring a Scottish army even to the gates of York.

Despite the incomplete nature of our data for sieges, siege warfare can be seen to have been far more common than open battle. Only during the Wars of the Roses were battles predominant. This means that concentration on battles alone will give only a partial view of warfare in the period. However, artefact scatters for later medieval sieges are probably both more ephemeral and rare than are those from the early modern period; while impact scars made by siege engines such as the mangonel or trebuchet may survive on defensive walls, no example has been identified in our very cursory assessment. Large calibre stone balls believed to be from the siege of Kenilworth castle in 1266 are displayed on-site, but there are no extensive impact scars on fabric of the period. This is a topic which would justify further investigation to establish whether there is evidence of projectile scatters, impact scars, or both.

There are relatively few battles from before 1455 (Fig 3.13). If one then takes into account the changing character of warfare over time, the sample available for study in each period reduces dramatically. Thus it is only at Fulford and Stamford Bridge, in 1066, that one sees both armies, Anglo-Saxon and Scandinavian, fighting on foot. This contrasts with Hastings, where the same tactic was employed by Harold's army but was set against the integrated infantry and cavalry tactics of the Normans. Seventy-two years later, at Northallerton (1138), northern English and Scottish armies fought largely on foot, with just a small body of cavalry used for specific tactical purposes. The Scots were defeated in part because they had many unarmoured troops, who suffered substantial losses in the face of an arrow-storm from English archers supported by well-armoured men at arms – presaging famous English victories two centuries later during the Hundred Years War.

By the following century, as seen at Lewes (1264) and Evesham (1265), mounted attack by heavy cavalry was the key battle tactic. It was, however, an approach that failed disastrously against a Scottish army using infantry tactics in 1314 at Bannockburn (Stirling, Scotland). A similar failure was also seen in a civil war in England, at Boroughbridge in 1322. Here a small rebel force dominated by heavy cavalry was defeated by a royal army from the northern border. The latter, like their more usual Scottish adversaries, used an infantry formation protected by spears. Such defeats led to a dramatic shift in tactics by English armies, seen first at Dupplin Moor (Scotland, 1332) and then to even greater effect at Halidon Hill (1333). These battles saw Scottish forces decimated by the large-scale use of the warbow, with the archers supported by men at arms fighting on foot. Over the following century such tactics would make English armies feared across Europe, with victories at battles in France such as Crécy in 1346 and Agincourt in 1415 (Strickland and Hardy 2005). Assessments of the character of the arrows (as evidenced from artefact scatter) and their effectiveness (as revealed by trauma on the bodies) from battlefields like Northallerton and Halidon might cast light on changes in use of the warbow between the 12th and 14th centuries.

Even if all our later medieval battlefields were accurately located and well preserved they would still be a small sample. Comparison of evidence in primary sources with the terrain of currently accepted sites raises doubts about the exact whereabouts of several of them. For example, at Halidon Hill topographical details in the written accounts do not seem to accord with the hilltop terrain of the presently favoured site. The English army was deployed to stop Scottish forces from relieving the besieged Scottish garrison at Berwick. In this context it would have been strange if no attempt had been made to control the Great North Road, which even in 1333 is likely to have lain close to the coast – almost a kilometre to the east of the Registered battlefield. Such a location may also be supported by another account, which describes certain troops as being deployed on the wing near the sea. Perhaps the traditional site of the battle migrated to the hilltop in later centuries by virtue of the prominence of the hill in the surrounding landscape (National Army Museum 1995h; Foard 2010b).

With all doubts allowed for, some battlefields do appear to be securely located, because, for example, there is more topographic detail in the primary accounts or the terrain is constricted, thus allowing few, if any, alternative locations. There may also be features established soon after the event that commemorate the battle. An example is Evesham, where in 1265 Simon de Montfort was defeated by Prince Edward (later Edward I).

Evesham

D C Cox provides the most authoritative discussion of the historic terrain at Evesham, although not all of the topographical features from the accounts have yet been identified on the ground (Cox 1988; National Army Museum 1995f; Ramsay 1908; Burne 1950); there has been 20th-century development in the area, but a substantial part of the presumed battlefield still remains undeveloped. The terrain is highly constricted because the town and Greenhill, where the battle was fought, are bounded on three sides by the river Avon. In the medieval period a single bridge, on the south, carried a road across the river which then passed through the town before ascending northwards up Greenhill and on towards Alcester. Near the highest point, at the parish boundary, it crossed the Salt Street, which ran west to Worcester and east to cross the Avon via Offenham Bridge. Meadows lay along the narrow flood plain of the Avon, while open fields may have covered much of the remaining area (Cox 1988). In the absence of a detailed survey such as those by David Hall at Towton and Bosworth (see Figs 5.5 and 5.7), it is unclear how extensive the open fields actually were at this time. However, Cox has argued that Greenhill may have been common pasture in the 13th century, while the Lanercost Chronicle says de Montfort was killed in Godescroft, a name indicating enclosed fields. If such details can be securely placed in the landscape they will be critical to our understanding.

James Ramsay's interpretation places de Montfort's army in battle array on the ridge where the Obelisk monument now stands, in the grounds of the Abbey Manor House in the north-west of the area (Ramsay 1908, 243). The arguments for dismissing this interpretation were presented by Alfred Burne, who has the royal forces approaching from the north-east over Offenham Bridge (Burne 1950, 53–63). More recent interpretations suggest that the royal forces split and approached from several different directions; the Evesham Chronicle says that, near Siveldestone, Edward divided his forces into three divisions and ascended the hill. Cox's research indicates that Siveldestone is Siflaed's stone, a marker on the late Saxon boundary of Evesham, which lay a short distance to the west of Offenham Bridge.

Various authors depict de Montfort's forces deployed immediately to the south of Battle Well and Edward's army a little to the north, an interpretation that draws upon a tradition dating close in time to the battle itself (Brooks 2005; Burne 1950; Carpenter 1987; National Army Museum 1995f). Battle Well, said to be the site where de Montfort died, was first recorded in 1272–73 as a spring where miracles had taken place. It subsequently appears on the late

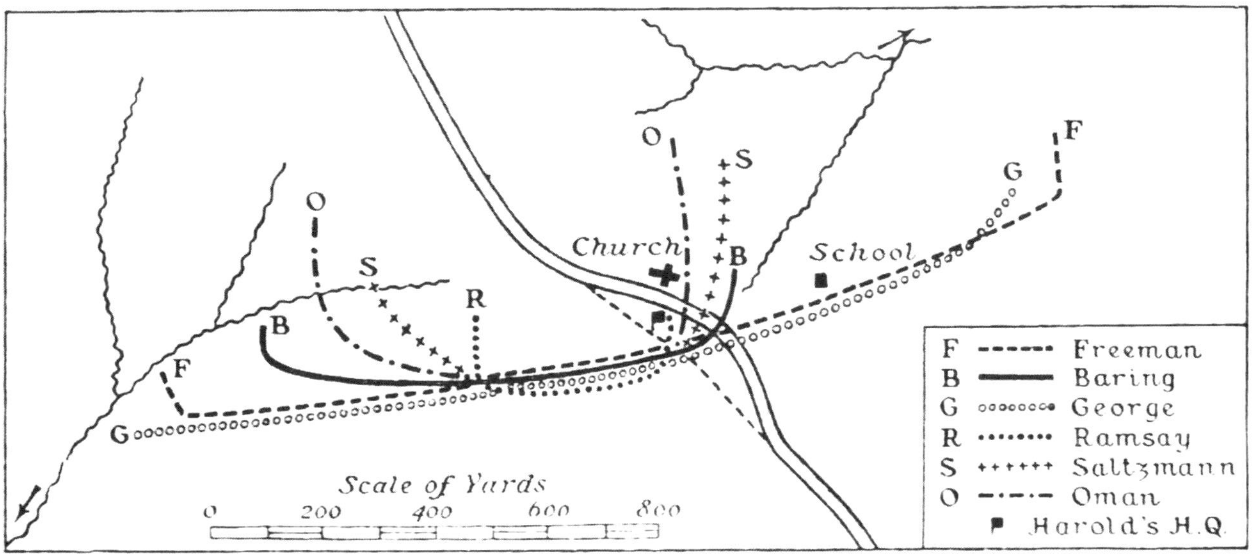

Fig 3.14 Map of alternative battle deployments at Hastings, as suggested by six different authors (Burne 1950)

19th-century Ordnance Survey first edition six-inch map and the map of Evesham of 1827, at which time buildings stood immediately to its south; the site can be traced back to the 15th century. A newly discovered account of the battle seems to imply that it was de Montfort who deployed first, and thus that he chose the ground, for he viewed the enemy advancing up onto Greenhill. A deployment immediately to the south of the Battle Well would make sense in tactical terms, enabling him to use the small side valley in which the well lies to provide some protection for his left flank while his main body sat astride the road (Cox 1988).

The analysis by Cox has transformed our understanding of the battle, and the broad character and location of the action now seem to be clear. It is thus one of the few battles before 1455 to be located with reasonable security. There is further topographical detail in the accounts which might give even greater accuracy, if they can be correctly placed.

Even when it appears that a battlefield has been identified, questions remain. The interpretation of later medieval battlefields depends a great deal upon two things: the numbers of troops present and the tactical deployments that were used. It is from this information that the width of the frontages, and hence of the battlefield, can be determined. The principal military manual in use by commanders in the later medieval period was by Vegetius, written *c* AD 400. This manual was reworked by several medieval authors, including Pisan, with a translation finally published in English in 1489 (Pisan 1489). It remained in use partly because many of the things it discussed, such as the space taken by individual infantrymen when deployed in battle array, were of enduring relevance. Unfortunately, neither the revisions made to the text of Vegetius nor the original accounts of individual battles provides clear definition of the tactical formations in use (Strickland and Hardy 2005). The implications of spacing and formation were clearly articulated by Burne in connection with Hastings, with his presentation of a plan showing the many different interpretations that have been suggested for the Anglo-Saxon deployment in the battle (Fig 3.14). It is an issue that has still not been resolved.

Fulford (1066) is the only English battlefield from this period that has so far been subjected to extensive archaeological investigation. Given current knowledge of the historic terrain, only one location for the battle seems to make tactical sense: a site where a major road running south from York crosses the stream at the south end of the village of Gate Fulford, now a suburb on the southern edge of the city. Various archaeological investigations, both independent and development-led, have recently been undertaken in response to a development threat. The former involved an extensive metal-detecting survey, as yet unpublished, which is said to have yielded evidence for early metalworking that has been suggested as evidence for the battle (Jones 2011). However, nothing comparable has been reported on any other early battlefield.

The failure to find artefactual evidence in any way comparable to that discussed below for Towton, or even a thinner scatter of non-projectile artefacts such as that seen at Bosworth, raises basic questions. Is the lack of finds a result of the methodology, or because the site is elsewhere, or simply because battles of this period left little in the way of distinctive metal artefacts that are likely to survive in the topsoil until the present? If the character of the archaeology of battlefields of the 11th to the mid-14th centuries is to be established there are two approaches that can be followed. The first is to work backwards from the battlefields of the Wars of the Roses for which, as discussed below, archaeological evidence has now been demonstrated. Battlefields from the mid-14th century onwards might yield a similar pattern of finds because, as in the late 15th century, most cavalry dismounted to fight, leading to intensive hand to hand fighting by high-status troops. In contrast, the heavy cavalry charge of the 13th century, as seen at Evesham, may have left less in the way of artefactual evidence. Further back again, in the 11th and earlier 12th centuries, the majority of action seems, once more, to have been on foot. The second approach, therefore, would be to investigate early exemplar sites that appear well located, well preserved, and reasonably well documented. Hastings is one obvious candidate. Stamford Bridge may be another.

Stamford Bridge

In September 1066 the Norse king Harald Sigurdsson, later known as Hardrada, landed in Yorkshire to challenge for the English throne. After a bloody but successful engagement at Fulford on 20 September, he received the surrender of York. In response, the new English king, Harold, marched north to confront Hardrada, who had drawn off 11km eastward to Stamford Bridge to receive hostages. Harold's army approached Stamford Bridge from the west on 25 September, their rapid advance taking the invaders by surprise.

Such little information as exists for the battle derives principally from much later sagas, the detail of which is suspect (DeVries 1999). It is said that Hardrada deployed his main force on the eastern side of the river, but with some troops positioned at the river crossing to delay Harold. Once the crossing was taken it appears that the ensuing action was fierce and bloody, though not necessarily prolonged. The English had superior numbers and quickly gained the upper hand. Unable to maintain their battle array, the invaders were broken into small bands that were quickly surrounded, and Hardrada was killed.

The initial action for control of the ford and bridge over the Derwent was long thought to have been where the north–south Roman road crossed the river, adjacent to the later village. The present crossing is not on the medieval site, as a new stone bridge was built in 1727 about 90m downstream to the west (Brooks 1956, 17–18). However, when the Derwent was low in *c* 1880 and again in *c* 1950 the remains from the early bridge are said to have been visible (Leadman 1891, 13; Burne 1950).

The location for the first stage of the battle must now be reviewed in the light of new evidence. Aerial archaeology has revealed two other Roman roads (Fig 3.15) that were associated with a nucleated Roman settlement and ran westward to a second river crossing 1.5km downstream from the modern bridge (Roe 2009; Bewley *et al* 2003; Lawton 1997; 1999). This second crossing was probably a bridge. Hence, if the river was too deep to be forded here, the alignment would have been lost after the Roman period, leaving the single shallow crossing of the first Roman road – the stone ford of the name Stamford. The medieval open-field furlongs do not seem to respect the east–west Roman alignment, tending to support the idea that this road had gone out of use by the medieval period. However, until this is proven, the possibility that Harold used the southern crossing cannot be ruled out. If this does prove to be the case then it may lead to the definition of a different battlefield.

Mike Griffiths has questioned the validity of the Registered area, which is centred on an area called the 'Battle Flats' to the south-east of the town. Griffiths also disputes the narrative of action for control of the river crossing (Griffiths 1997). The latter argument is countered by Kelly DeVries, who draws upon a wider range of sources (DeVries 1999). Even so, doubts about the Registered area are not easily answered; original sources say little to support the area that had been delineated.

In 1998 a development-led excavation in the north-west corner of the Registered area found no evidence of the battle. This absence has been cited in support of the case that Battle Flat was not part of the battlefield (Roe 2009). However, such bald claims need careful assessment in the light of what we have learned from recent methodological progress. For instance, the report makes no mention of an intensive metal-detecting survey before the excavation or in spits as the topsoil was machined away. Nor does it report a detecting survey of the remnant furrows which were

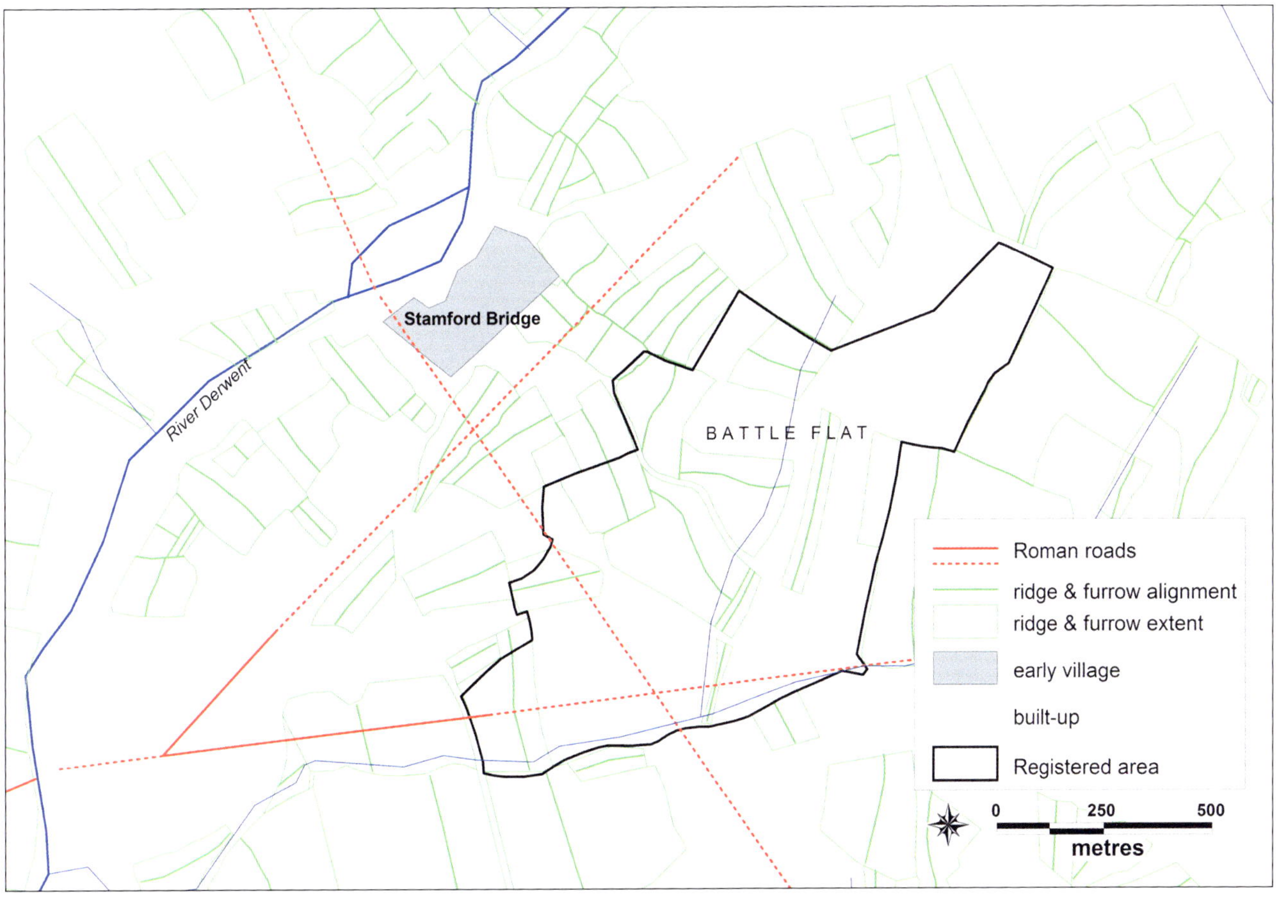

Fig 3.15 The Registered battlefield at Stamford Bridge (1066), shown in relation to Roman roads and the extent and orientation of ridge and furrow recorded from aerial photographs[8]
(© English Heritage / Crown copyright 2012. Ordnance Survey Licence number 100024900)

revealed after topsoil stripping, even though these could be an ideal reservoir for the survival of battle artefacts, as discussed below for Towton. Without such survey, undertaken by an experienced team, a claim based on negative evidence is not acceptable.

With all this said, there is still no evidence to support the current location. Moreover, almost the whole area between Battle Flat and the ford has been lost to development – an area large enough in which to lose a whole battlefield. For these reasons, Stamford Bridge is not an ideal site on which to seek evidence for the character of pre-15th-century battle archaeology.

Northallerton

A more suitable candidate may be the battle at Northallerton (1138), more often known as the Battle of the Standard. This battlefield shows how the difficulties of placing the events of a later medieval battle in its contemporary landscape might be overcome.

No significant topographical detail is to be found in the battle accounts. The site has been located by the battle name and more particularly by local tradition about where the Scottish dead were buried. The graves can be closely positioned using field names (Fig 3.16). In 1839 three fields called Scot Pits lay immediately north of Scot Pits Lane. 'Pit' was a common medieval term for grave. A map of 1765 relates the name only to the western two fields, the easternmost field being 'properly called Little Moor'.[9] Immediately to the south-east of Scot Pits the early maps also give the field name Standard Leeze. The term 'leys' typically refers to strips within the open-field systems that have been put down to permanent pasture, usually in the early modern period. In addition, the rising ground to the north is called Standard Hill.

In the later 17th century, Dugdale wrote of the battle: 'the Ground whereon it was fought, lying about 3km distant from North Alverton [Northallerton] (on the right hand the Road, leading thence towards Durham) is to this day called Standard Hill, having in it divers hollow places still known by the name of the Scots Pits' (Dugdale 1675, 1, 62). In the mid-18th century it was said that a few 'trenches' called 'The

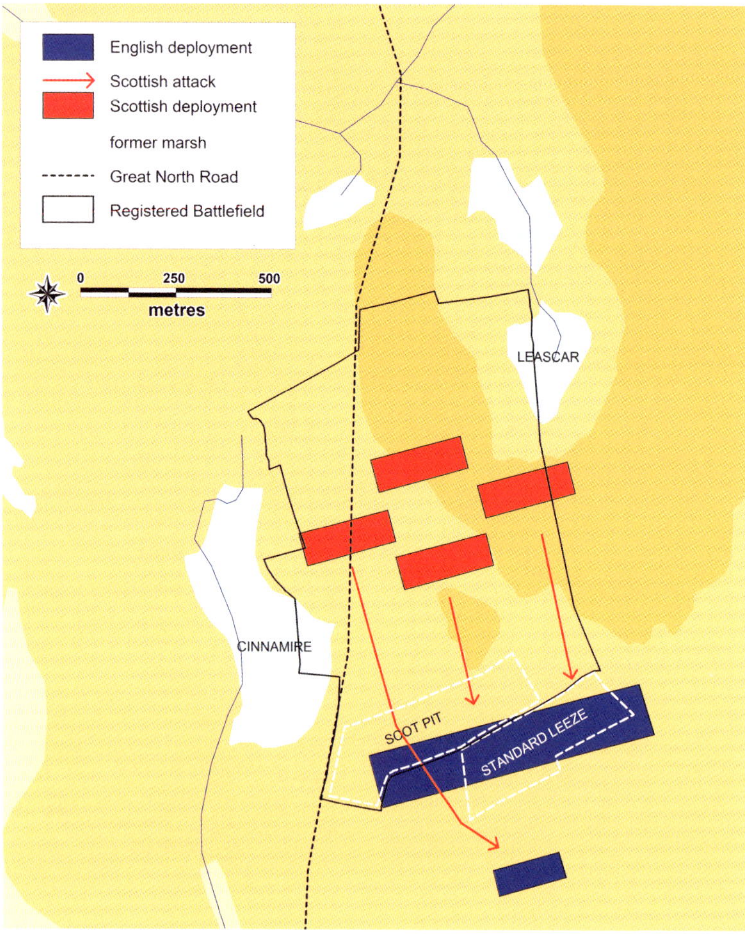

Fig 3.16 Map showing a conjectural reconstruction of deployments and terrain for the battle of Northallerton (1138), based on the historic map, field name, geological, and antiquarian evidence discussed in the text

Scots Pits' were still to be seen (Gale 1781). By the early 19th century ploughing had apparently destroyed all the earthwork evidence but Leadman, writing in 1891, says that within living memory the 'bones of men and horses have been found' at Scotpits Lane (Leadman 1891, 24).

A reconstruction of the historic terrain at Northallerton is difficult because of the early date of the battle. The principal elements are the relief, the road network, and probable areas of former marsh identified here from the association of mire and carr field names with the extent of alluvial and lacustrine deposits on the geological mapping. Running through the area is the Great North Road, which is shown on Matthew Paris's map of *c* 1250 passing northwards through Northallerton to Durham (Paris and Luard 1884). The earliest depiction of its exact route appears in Ogilby's *Britannia* (Ogilby 1675).

Traces of ridge and furrow have been noted, on the ground and from aerial survey, in a small part of the battlefield. Furlongs are also indicated by the 'ley' field names that are associated with long narrow enclosures probably representing piecemeal enclosure of small bundles of strips. This suggests that much, although perhaps not all, of the area was given over in the medieval period to the furlongs of an open-field system. The type of survey undertaken by David Hall at Towton (see Fig 5.5) might enable the mapping of the full system, which could be complemented by large-scale geophysical survey to reveal the fine detail of the pattern from remnant furrows surviving beneath the modern plough soil. The potential of such evidence has been revealed by similar work in the Vale of Pickering (Powlesland 2008; Powlesland and Lyall 2006). Even if the pattern was recovered, it would not necessarily demonstrate the character of the landscape at the time of the battle, because furlong patterns often reached their full extent as much as a century later (Hall forthcoming). Without exceptional written sources it would be impossible to distinguish which furlongs, if any, existed here in 1138 and what part of the battlefield then remained as moor – the early land use implied by the Little Moor field name.

Even without such refinement, our basic terrain reconstruction suggests a tactical context within which to place the deployments and action. The English army marched from the south and chose the ground. They are likely to have deployed in such as way as to control the major road, to stop the Scottish advance southward. In this area, around Standard Hill, there was formerly a mire on the west of the road and a carr on the east. If the English had deployed adjacent to Cinnamire – seemingly the larger of the formerly boggy areas – it would have provided protection against an outflanking Scottish attack on the English left. Such an interpretation is also compatible with the location of Scot Pits. Where mass graves are known or suspected they are often, though not always, located at the point where two armies first clashed. If this was the case at Northallerton then, as it was the English army which stood to take the Scottish attack, so the English deployment may have lain just a little to the south of the Scot Pits. Interestingly, this would place the English army in the area of the 'leys' field names.

It is on this evidence, albeit from a preliminary study of the battle and the terrain, that we have produced our reconstruction of the battle deployments. If it has any validity then it would extend the battlefield south of the Registered area. It also highlights the need to consider the inclusion of carr and mire within the boundary, both for their tactical significance and because they might contain relevant palaeo-environmental data. Indeed, if there are still waterlogged deposits in these areas there is a chance that exceptional well-preserved artefacts from the battle might lie within them (Foard 2010b).

Uncertainties clearly remain, but the combined evidence provides a powerful case for Northallerton as a principal target, alongside Hastings, for research into the character of the battle archaeology of the 11th to 14th centuries. Such an investigation would include geophysical and geochemical survey, to find mass graves, and metal-detecting survey to seek battle-related artefact scatters. If the mass graves are located, then, in the light of Towton, where the scatter of arrowheads centres on mass graves at the heart of the battlefield, this would focus the search for ferrous arrowheads.

Notes

1. The ancillary features database contains 354 records, including locations of modern excavation of burials, field survey of artefacts scatters, and dubious early finds, through to memorial chapels and monuments associated with a battle.
2. Scottish research reported in Foard and Partida 2005. The Irish data are based on the initial list of battles assessed for inclusion on the Register of Irish battlefields.
3. The leading source is HE iii 1–3. Writing in the earlier 8th century, Bede describes the raising of a cross by Oswald's soldiers on the eve of the battle, around which the entire army knelt in prayer. Next morning Oswald's force made a dawn attack on Cædwalla's army, which was destroyed at a place called *Deniseburn*. Other references to the battle site occur in *Historia Brittonum* 64; *Annales Cambriae*, s.a. 631; Adomnan, I 1, 14–15. The name of the battle in both *Annales Cambriae*, 631, and Nennius, § 63, is 'bellum Catscaul': Plummer, II, 121.
4. HE iii 1 gives no hint of the distance that Oswald's force travelled to engage with Cædwalla, but his use of the word *superveniente* (translating as something like 'coming upon' or 'overtaking') clearly indicates movement from one place to another.
5. *qui lingua Anglorum Denisesburna, id east Riuus Denisi, vocatur*, HE iii 2.
6. Plummer, II, 123: *Denisesburn* is identified by a charter edited by Raine, Appendix iv.
7. This section paraphrases relevant sections of Baker *et al*, forthcoming. We are extremely grateful for their contribution.
8. Roman roads and ridge and furrow from the National Mapping Programme data in the National Monuments Record.
9. Tithe map of Brompton in 1839 North Yorkshire Record Office Mic 2237; map of 1765 'an old plan of Mr Crosfields Estate' NYRO ZEK 1/10.Z

4

Gunpowder weapons on the battlefield

From the late 15th to the mid-19th centuries, millions of lead bullets were deposited by Europeans in battles across the world. Fired either singly from handguns or in large groups as hailshot from artillery, the mundane bullet, often dropped into the 'junk' box by collectors, offers a unique perspective on one of the most important cultural developments of the last millennium. Together with its rarer but larger cousin, the round shot fired from artillery, the bullet is the archaeological signature of firepower. By studying bullets we can advance understanding not just of battles but of the very development and application of gunpowder weapons themselves.

Projectiles – bullets, round shot, arrowheads, crossbow bolts – were deposited in patterns of type and density that varied according to the nature and scale of the fighting. Distributions of projectiles should thus be more representative of the action and more easily interpreted than those of other battle-related artefacts. This assumes that the factors affecting their subsequent survival or disappearance are understood. Such issues are touched upon here, but discussed in detail in Chapter 8.

To date, of all projectile types only those of lead have been shown to survive consistently and in sufficient numbers to allow analysis of battlefield-wide patterning. This is why a discussion of such evidence at this point is both possible and necessary. It is first important to explain why a comparable analysis of arrowheads and other artefacts cannot be provided. The warbow was of great importance to English armies of the 14th and 15th centuries – more so, perhaps, than was the crossbow to continental armies. Following the introduction of handguns to the battlefield, in English armies the bow remained in regular use alongside them well into the second half of the 16th century. By the 17th century the bow had gone out of serious military use in England, even if its advocates can be found right through to the Civil War. The last deployment of significant numbers of archers on a British battlefield appears to have been in Scotland during the Civil War, in Highland battles such as Auldearn (1645) (MacBain and Kennedy 1892, 49–57).

While arrows were shot in their tens of thousands during large medieval battles, arrowheads are not common battlefield finds. In part this is because retrieval of arrows, during or immediately after a battle, was often practicable. Unless intense fighting had occurred where they had fallen, thus breaking the shafts protruding from the ground, arrows could be salvaged and used again. However, the principal reason is that they were made of iron. In the wet environments of northern Europe, iron usually decays in the topsoil over timescales of 500 years or more. Special preservation conditions seem to be necessary for their survival on English battlefields. For these reasons the distribution of arrowheads across a site, if they survive at all, will reflect the varying influences of factors such as post-battle recovery and preservation as much as the intensity of their use.

To date, arrowheads have been archaeologically recovered in significant number on only one European battlefield, Towton (1461). A small number have also been found in survey on the 1361 battlefield of Gotland (Sweden), while others from excavation at Holme Castle (Gloucestershire) may derive from the 1471 battle of Tewkesbury (Starley and Cubitt 2006; Knarrstrom 2009). The wider evidence for the battlefield at Tewkesbury was recently assessed by Border Archaeology (2010). The Towton assemblage has yet to be fully analysed and published, and the factors leading to its survival have not been fully determined. Until that has been done it is not possible to generalise about the significance of these artefacts as battlefield finds, or to consider adequately what conditions on other battlefields might lead to their survival.

Related problems surround non-projectile finds from battlefields of the 15th to 17th centuries. Although some evidence has been presented for Cheriton (Bonsall 2008), there is not, as yet, a comprehensive published study from any site. Such a study will need to consider how battle-related finds can be confidently distinguished from the background noise; the relationship of the finds to the types and status of troops and their equipping; the ways in which the objects are likely to have been deposited during or after the action; and how representative their distribution may be of particular aspects of the fighting and subsequent clearance. Where the deposited objects were of copper alloy or, more rarely, of lead, silver, or gold, they survive well in the ground. What is unknown is what proportion of the original artefact distribution they represent, for ferrous items in the topsoil will probably have decayed or disintegrated. Thousands of such copper alloy artefacts have been recovered at Towton. On other battlefields, from Bosworth (1485) to Sedgemoor (1685), they appear far fewer. It is not known why such variation in density occurs between sites, although issues relating to ground conditions on the day, the intensity of the fighting, and the nature of the forces engaged will all have played a part. For these reasons, detailed consideration of the character and meaning of non-projectile find distributions is not yet possible.

The early use of guns

Gunpowder and gunpowder weapons were first developed in China, from where the technology was transferred to Europe, apparently via India and the Middle East. From the second half of the 13th century there are recipes for gunpowder manufacture in Europe, although the earliest weapons are not recorded until the early 14th century.[1] There is good evidence, both written and graphic, from the 14th and 15th centuries for the use of large numbers of guns in sieges, where cumbersome artillery pieces did not need to be moved quickly or frequently (Porter 2000, 54–61; Nicholson 2004, esp ch 4).

The introduction of guns to the battlefield was a more tentative process – probably because here they initially proved less effective. While there was time to deploy them in the initial battle array, all but the very smallest would have been difficult to move in the often fast-flowing action that followed. If guns were placed in prepared defensive positions to protect them from rapid attacks, the enemy often simply made an outflanking move and assaulted the position from another direction, before the guns could be repositioned. Even where artillery pieces and handguns were deployed in large numbers, they rarely had a decisive impact on the outcome of field engagements: this would require further technological advances in the second half of the 15th century. As refinements continued, these weapons seem finally to have taken on a decisive, battle-winning role in the first half of the 16th century – a transformation often associated with the French campaigns in Italy and, most specifically, the battle of Pavia in 1525 (Hall 1997).

A siege train of gunpowder artillery pieces was taken with the English army which fought in France in 1346, though the claim in one source that several of these cannon were used in the battle of Crécy is disputed. By 1382 we find the Flemish forces at Beverhoutsveld (Belgium) deploying 200 small two- or four-wheeled carts each mounted with several small guns. At Aljubarotta (Portugal) in 1385 at least sixteen light artillery pieces were used by the Castillians against the Portuguese. At Castagnaro (Italy) in 1397 large numbers of wagon-mounted guns were used, each firing a stone said to be about the diameter of a hen's egg. The Hussite Wars of the 1420s in Bohemia saw another development – the use of wagon 'fortresses'. These comprised a collection of wagons containing guns and, between them, handcannons and mounted guns protected by large shields known as pavises (Hall 1997, 45–55). More specifically relevant for English armies is the French success in the later stages of the Hundred Years War which is in part attributed to the effective application of more advanced artillery in sieges. It was a process which culminated in 1435 at Castillon (Gascony, France) in the final defeat of an English army in the field during the War, when they came under intense artillery fire from fixed guns in the French camp.

Given the scale of use of guns in certain continental battles of the late 14th and earlier 15th century, one must ask whether similar artillery were used on any English battlefields. However, of the nine battles in England during this period – from Halidon Hill in 1333 to Piper Dene in 1435 – only Shrewsbury (1403) has seen even small-scale archaeological survey. Hence, the current absence of relevant finds may not be significant. There is apparently no documentary evidence to suggest the use of guns in any earlier battles. The first reference we have identified to the use of artillery in a field engagement in England is from 1450, when the King's Master of Ordnance brought guns to the 'battle' against Jack Cade's rebels at Sevenoaks on 18 June (Ramsay 1892, 2, 128). Investigation of English sites from before 1450 for evidence of gunpowder projectiles would thus be speculative.

The most effective archaeological strategy may be to first target continental battlefields, where their use is well documented, in order to establish the character of the archaeological record.

Technological advances through the 15th century seem to have included improvements in gunpowder, the introduction of cast-iron projectiles, and developments in the casting of bronze gun barrels – although these and later cast-iron barrels would not finally replace wrought-iron stave-built barrels until late in the 16th century. The character of the guns has been most fully defined for the arsenal of the dukes of Burgundy. Throughout the century this contained handguns and a bewildering array of artillery, both large and small. Ammunition for the former was almost solely lead ball. For the latter it was mainly of stone or, less often, of iron – initially wrought iron but later cast iron – and of lead (Smith and DeVries 2005).

Large numbers of artillery as well as handguns were deployed in European battles of the second half of the 15th century, such as those in 1476 at Grandson and Murten in Switzerland. A number of Burgundian artillery pieces were captured by the Swiss in these actions. Some of them still survive, and suggest that the smaller field pieces already had carriages which in many respects were similar to later artillery, making them highly mobile on the battlefield. This was probably a key development, as earlier artillery, even those mounted on wagons – which continued to be used – had been cumbersome and difficult to deploy and move (Machiavelli 1521, 90–91, 96–7). The first appearance of such carriages with limbers may have been as early as the 1460s (Hall 1997, 107–14). By the later 15th century English kings and their military commanders seem to have adopted gunpowder artillery as enthusiastically as their counterparts in any other country (Grummit 2008); for example, in 1456, at the beginning of the Wars of the Roses, we see the crown ordering 60 field guns (Wiedemer 1967, 166–7). Such investment was not simply because of the psychological impact made by such weapons; the guns also enabled a commander to strike the enemy at a far greater distance than the warbow. Thus, at Bosworth the artillery of Richard III opened fire on Henry Tudor's forces at a range of a quarter league – at least 600m – which is more than double the range of the warbow.

There were also changes which may have been critical for the effective application of handguns to the battlefield. The earliest handguns had been relatively cumbersome and inefficient 'handcannon', typically fired from the waist. These were usually fired manually, rather than with a trigger mechanism. In the second half of the 15th century they were progressively replaced by the normally shoulder-fired 'arquebus'. These new weapons had a similar basic form to later muskets, including a wooden stock and a trigger controlling a matchlock firing mechanism, although surviving examples show that they were of a larger bore (McLachlan 2010). These guns also show that there was no simple division between handguns and artillery. The larger bores are from guns of intermediate types, similar in form to handguns but larger and heavier, so fired from a rest, a wall, or a wagon. At the upper end of the range they also seem to overlap with the bore of true artillery. Advances continued in the following century, culminating for hand-held firearms, by mid-century, with the introduction by the Spanish of the musket. With some modification, this was to become the dominant infantry firearm for the next 300 years, until rifled weapons began to be produced in large numbers.

Given the apparent scale of use of artillery on continental battlefields in the 14th and 15th centuries it is surprising that more physical evidence has not been forthcoming. Some round shot has been collected from battlefields such as Grandson, but the general pattern of discovery has been sparse. This may largely reflect a lack of systematic survey. English battlefields of this period have just begun to yield significant archaeological evidence: in 2008, only four round shot had been found on England's 15th-century battlefields, while today there are 39.[2]

From 1455 to 1487, during the Wars of the Roses, there were fifteen battles. Most were major engagements and it is to be expected that the forces involved in them would where possible have employed the full range of available field guns. It is possible that these 32 years spanned a critical period in the development of artillery which led to more effective and mobile field pieces. There may already be a hint of this in the archaeological record: after more than two decades of intensive metal detecting, Towton (1461) has produced just two small calibre round shot, compatible with either handguns or the intermediate mounted types; in contrast, 34 round shot of a wide range of calibres, up to the bore of the largest mobile field guns in use in later centuries, have been recovered from Bosworth (1485) – a battlefield discovered only in 2009. The battlefields of the Wars of the Roses may, therefore, represent an important resource for the archaeological study of this transition. The documentary record, though limited, identifies various battlefields where artillery were used, and the testing of early sites such as Blore Heath (1456) is required to see if they repeat the picture from Towton, and that of later sites, such as Barnet (1471), to see if they mirror Bosworth.

The application of handguns to the battlefield by English armies followed a significantly different trajectory from that of other major European powers, such as the Burgundians, who as we have seen were already using them in large numbers by the 1470s. Handguns were in large-scale use in major English garrisons throughout the 15th century and apparently also saw wider ownership in later-15th-century England – the most extensive written evidence coming from Calais, which, until it fell in 1558, was England's main garrison on an international frontier and had the greatest concentration of military hardware (Grummitt 2008; 2010). Despite this ubiquity, however, handguns appear to have seen only limited use by English armies on the battlefield. The warbow had the advantage of a high rate of fire compared to the crossbow, which was in general use on the continent, meaning that the warbow could continue in effective use for far longer. There appear to have been just two battles where handguns were used in large numbers during the Wars of the Roses: Barnet in 1471 and St Albans in 1461 – where substantial numbers of mercenary handgunners were engaged. Thus England may provide little evidence for the evolution of handguns and their application to the battlefield. However, the sites must still be tested to confirm that the impression provided by the documentary record is indeed correct. The evidence so far recovered from Bosworth suggests that it is.

It is to the small number of 16th-century battlefields in England that we must look to see the growing use of handguns. They did not form a major part of the supply of the English army taken to France in 1513, and later in the century Henry VIII seems to have depended principally upon foreign mercenary handgunners (Cruickshank 1990, 60–74). English commanders first sought to exploit what they saw as the complementary strengths of handgun and bow, and by mid-century both the key English military manual (Audley) and documentary evidence from the battle of Pinkie show that they were deploying the bow and handgun in equal numbers. Handguns were also, by now, in use by some mounted troops, though the latter were far fewer in number than the heavy cavalry armed with a lance. Thus by the mid-16th century the handgun had taken its place on English battlefields alongside the artillery, although to put this in perspective, at Pinkie there were still fewer than 1000 handguns in an English army near 20,000 strong (Patten 1548).

By the time of the Civil Wars the picture was totally transformed. Artillery was now providing close infantry support; ideally two-thirds of the infantry carried muskets; the cavalry typically carried pistols and/or carbines; and dragoons carried a musket, sometimes of a slightly larger bore (Blackmore 1990). In the 1640s the intensity of fire that could be laid down had become a key determinant of success in battle.

The increase in the number of infantry carrying firearms was accompanied by changes in the depth of deployments. This was in part to enable more effective use of the firearms and also, perhaps, in response to the destructive effect of artillery on deep formations. The numbers of ranks were reduced progressively, from the sometimes very deep, even square, formations of the mid-16th century to ten, then to eight and finally to six deep in the 1640s. This was also a response to small changes in the technology of guns and in loading and firing procedures. These tactical changes will be reflected in the numbers and distribution of bullets on the battlefield: the earlier the period, the fewer the numbers of bullets likely to have been fired in a battle and hence the sparser the distributions – where they exist. Changes in the width of the frontages and in the placement of the artillery within the battle arrays should also be reflected in the distribution of bullets and round shot across the battlefield.

Projectiles

Lead has always been the principal, indeed almost the sole, material for small arms bullets.[3] As discussed below, it is a relatively stable metal, and as a result bullets can survive in topsoil for centuries in relatively good condition in a variety of ground conditions.

Where bullets were deposited in very high densities, then recovery after the action might be a possibility. Such densities are most likely to have occurred on siege sites. Thus, in the American Civil War large quantities were collected, particularly when lead oxidisation had turned the bullets whiter, so permitting easier identification. Such collection for reuse was an organised affair in the Confederate armies, as noted at the sieges of Petersburg and Atlanta (C Haecker pers comm). No comparable evidence has yet been found in England in the 17th century, although artillery rounds were collected for payment on siege sites in Ireland in this period. A later problem will have been collection for sale as souvenirs, a practice reported in England in the 19th century, when rounds were collected by ploughmen and sold to tourists (Foard 1995). Following behind the plough with their eye to the ground, they were using essentially the same fieldwalking technique by which Newman recovered bullets in his survey of Marston Moor battlefield in the 1970s (see Fig 8.12). Given how rare the visual discovery of bullets is compared with the recovery rate with a detector, the numbers so recovered are likely to have been small compared to the total number in the ground. Thus, where battlefields have not been seriously affected by modern collectors, it is likely that distributions of early modern bullets capable of providing information on the location, intensity, and character of fighting (Meller 2009) will survive in the topsoil.

Given these factors, where a site has not been severely depleted by collectors, archaeology is well placed to provide direct evidence on the use of guns in a way that it is unlikely ever to do for the bow. It may provide new information on the origins, development, and battlefield application of firepower, demonstrating the changing scale and character of the use of small arms and artillery. Comparison between battles of different dates, in different countries, and involving different armies should, in the long term, enable us to chart these changes in a way that the documentary record alone cannot do.

Round shot

While some of the earliest artillery pieces fired a special form of arrow, these were soon replaced by spherical projectiles of lead, stone, or iron. While stone and iron may have been the dominant materials for artillery rounds in the 15th century, a significant proportion of the ammunition, especially for the smaller pieces, was of lead, either in solid form or as a composite of lead with iron dice, stone pebbles, or flint shards. Burgundian documents record in 1476–77 the 'making of 2,000 plommées, 6 f. and purchase of 600 livres of iron to make cubes to put in plommées', and, in 1473–74, 'Item 200 lead plommées, some of which have iron inside, for the said serpentines, the said plommées weighing 505 livres.' Significantly, the Burgundian records suggest that composite rounds were much more expensive to make than solid metal round shot (Douglas Smith and DeVries 2005, 253–4). There is some comparable detail for the English army taken to France in 1475, which had 45 serpentines for use in the field. Among other materials, these were supplied with 2000 round shot weighing in all 3500lb (Holmer 1977, 79, 220). If these were all solid lead then it suggests an average mass of 794g and diameter of 51mm, though composite rounds may have been included.

Iron round shot were initially of wrought iron, but had probably been replaced by cast iron by the end of the 15th century. Despite being of ferrous metal, these wrought- and cast-iron projectiles are likely to survive in the topsoil in many contexts, though they will normally have suffered significant surface decay. Round shot of stone may be expected to survive in very good condition, but will be difficult to recover efficiently in systematic survey. Lead round shot were also a significant component of magazines for use by field artillery, especially during the later 15th and 16th centuries. In the 17th century solid lead was still used for the smallest bores of artillery; by this time stone had all but disappeared from use, with the vast majority of round shot being of cast iron. As with bullets, the survival of lead round shot on most battlefields will be good and recovery easy, although the relatively small numbers of artefacts concerned means that the distribution patterns will be highly vulnerable to the impact of collectors.

The earliest round shot so far recovered from an English battlefield appear to be the two small calibre balls, noted above, from Towton (1461). These are of *c* 22mm and *c* 30mm; the smaller is of solid lead, the other of lead composite containing an iron die. Towton is also exceptional in having produced two small fragments of barrels from bronze guns, again both of small bore (Sutherland 2011). The regular failure of gun barrels, probably as a result of inferior casting techniques for bronze, is well recorded for this early period. Thus, such finds are probably far more likely at this time than in later centuries, although a fragment of a cast-iron artillery barrel has also been reported from the 1644 battle of Cheriton (Bonsall 2008).

Solid lead round shot of larger calibre have been collected from Barnet (1471), where primary sources state that an artillery exchange took place before the battle. Of these, one weighs 538.4g and has a diameter of 46.2mm and the second weighs 362.6g (40.3mm); the third has a diameter of 40.7mm. Since no record has been identified of Civil War action in the area, and round shot of lead are not common finds, it is

Fig 4.1 A composite round shot, consisting of a die of iron cast-about with lead, recovered in the 2007 survey of Flodden battlefield (1513). The full size of the die is masked by the lead. To the right a major impact has compressed the ball. Maximum diameter *c* 47mm

Fig 4.2 Three-dimensional laser scanning of a solid lead round shot from Bosworth in collaboration with ISIS Innovation, Harwell

likely that all three derive from the battle of Barnet. The Bosworth assemblage contains both solid lead rounds as well as most types of composite round shot (flint shard, stone pebble and iron dice), ranging in calibre from 21mm to 97mm, with almost all the larger rounds being composite. The absence from Bosworth of cast-iron balls cast-about with lead may be because cast iron was not then in use for projectiles in England. Interestingly, the few round shot so far recovered from later battlefields are all either of solid lead or are composites with iron dice. All three round shot from Flodden are lead composite with iron dice (Fig 4.1), as are two from Pinkie, where the third is solid lead (Foard and Curry in prep). The warship *Mary Rose*, which sank in 1545, provided a large assemblage of unfired round shot for English artillery.

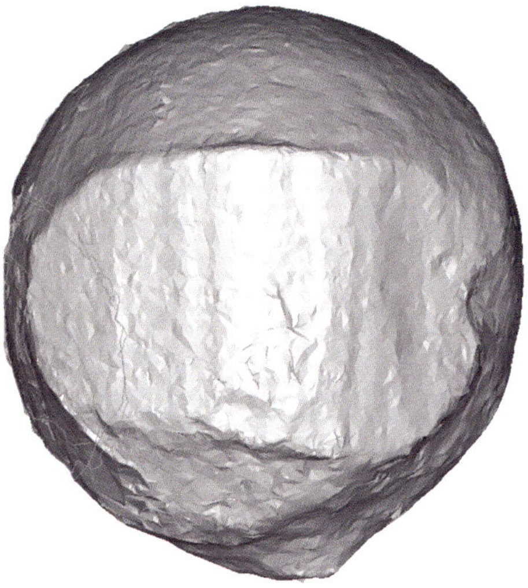

Fig 4.3 Image from a three-dimensional laser scan of a lead round shot from Bosworth (ISIS Neutron and Muon Source/ Science and Technology Facility Council)

While the larger calibres are of iron or stone, the smaller calibres are almost all composite, mainly with iron dice but also including other types (Hildred forthcoming).

The composition of the round shot and the firing and impact evidence left on the lead has yet to be fully explored. In addition to the full application of the analytical method previously developed for small arms rounds (Foard 2008c), scientific research has begun on the Bosworth assemblage. This includes investigation of composition using neutron tomography to reveal internal form (Cross 2011). Three-dimensional laser scanning has also been piloted for the recording of the geometry and broad surface attributes of the projectiles (Figs 4.2 and 4.3), and is complemented by high-resolution imaging for the recording of the finer detail of surface striations and melting (Foard and Curry in prep) (Fig 4.4).

This analysis has in turn been complemented by firing experiments in collaboration with Dr Derek Allsop of Cranfield University. These have confirmed and extended the interpretations of firing and impact evidence first developed through the study of small arms rounds, as well as giving some indication of the final range of the guns. Fired point blank using modern gunpowder in a modern 60mm smooth barrel, lead round shot achieved a range of up to 1.2km after bounce and roll. Firing experiments were also undertaken using a reproduction gutter-built wrought-iron breech-loading artillery piece; the distinctive signature left on the lead round shot from these firings suggest that it may, in some cases, be possible to distinguish round shot fired from a stave or gutter-built wrought-iron barrel as opposed to one of cast iron or bronze. It may even prove possible, depending on the nature of the compression and melting on the lower hemisphere of the ball, to suggest whether it was fired from a muzzle- or a breech-loading gun (Foard and Curry in prep).

As we have said, iron round shot were initially of wrought iron, but by the late 15th century this was being replaced by cast iron. Both types are present in the assemblage preserved in La Neuveville in Switzerland which, along with the guns, are said to be part of the booty from the 1476 battle of Murten (Foard and Walton in prep). Iron, though having a lower mass than lead, is approximately three times the density of stone and gives a projectile able, on impact, to deliver far greater kinetic energy than could stone. It was thus much more effective for smaller-bore artillery (Hall 1997, 93–4).

Cast-iron spheres, both for later artillery and from industrial and other uses, are quite common finds, and problems can accordingly arise with the dating of cast-iron round shot. In contrast, identifications of lead and

Fig 4.4 A small calibre round shot of solid lead from Bosworth, showing a distinct area of 'banding' with superimposed striations. The banding is a flattened area where the ball was compressed to the sides of the bore of the gun barrel by the pressures generated on firing. The striations were presumably created as it rubbed along the inner face of the barrel. Superimposed on the band and extending across the rest of the ball are one deep and one shallow rotational impact mark. These long grooves may be created when a ball contacts a small stone on one of its many bounces as it travels down range. The lack of melting on the lower hemisphere suggests this ball was fired either with a wad or (if fired from a breech-loading gun) a wooden tampion between it and the gunpowder. Maximum diameter *c* 35mm

especially lead composite round shot as battle-related will normally be secure. In part this is because lead spheres were rarely used for non-military purposes, but also because they were less frequently used as projectiles in later centuries. Although solid lead round shot continued in use in the Civil War in England, particularly for the smallest artillery pieces, its use had by then reduced in favour of cast iron. Composite round shot, on the other hand, had gone out of use almost completely by the late 16th century, when the last examples with iron dice are listed in the Tower (Blackmore 1976). They were occasionally used in the 17th century, as finds of small calibre round shot containing pebbles from a mass grave on the 1636 battlefield of Wittstock in Germany have shown (Eickhoff *et al* 2011). The explanation given for these was a shortage of lead. Instructions for the manufacture of lead composite round shot containing stone shards, intended to reduce the mass of the ball by a specified amount, are also given in at least one English military manual (Nye 1647, ch 30). However, there is, as yet, no report of such a lead composite round from a Civil War battlefield in England, and nor do they seem to appear in the lists of munitions supplied during the war (eg Roy 1964; 1975).

While the recovery of lead, lead composite and (at least in all-metal survey) iron round shot should not pose a significant problem in battlefield survey, the situation for stone is very different. As yet we have no clear idea as to how common round shot of stone (as opposed to lead and iron) were on 14th- and 15th-century European battlefields. To establish whether such projectiles can be recovered, what is needed is systematic fieldwalking to complement a metal-detecting survey on a European battlefield where sources suggest that many stone round shot were used. If this approach proves unsuccessful then it may be necessary to await advances in technology whereby such projectiles can be found at depth using ground-penetrating radar or some other prospecting method.

Hailshot

Beginning probably in the early 17th century with the reorganisation of the Dutch army, there was apparently far closer integration of light artillery into battle formations in the early modern period. The largest gun used in this way was typically a *saker* (*c* 6 pounder). Writing in the early 16th century, Machiavelli also identifies the saker as his ideal field piece (1521, 90–7). Where heavier guns, such as the demi-culverin, were used on the battlefield in the 17th century it was normally in fixed batteries. Despite the large-scale use of artillery to fire iron or lead round shot at a distance, these projectiles are relatively uncommon finds in surveys of 17th-century battlefields. There is, as yet, no distribution pattern to compare with the round shot scatter of 1485 at Bosworth.

While round shot was typically used to engage the enemy at long range, for close-quarter action the normal munition was hailshot, which is more usually described in later centuries as case shot or canister. The term hailshot is used here because in this early period it could be fired not only in wooden cases or metal canisters, but also in bags of canvas or even loose. By the 17th century these munitions typically comprised large numbers of lead bullets, often of musket calibre. Hailshot was also sometimes described as 'murdering shot' and could comprise iron dice, pebbles or flint

Fig 4.5 Small, irregularly shaped dice of iron from the wreck of the *Mary Rose* (1545). These projectiles were intended for use as hailshot, fired loose from a small artillery piece known as a hailshot piece (Reproduced by permission of the *Mary Rose* Trust). Width of die far right *c* 15mm

shards instead of lead bullets. The character of iron dice, for use in 'murderers', is seen in evidence from the *Mary Rose* (Hildred forthcoming) (Fig 4.5). The term grape shot is sometimes incorrectly used for these munitions; grape usually comprised a series of larger balls of iron, often mounted on a wooden spindle, and seems typically to have been principally a naval munition (Blackmore 1976, 193), although there is evidence for its use in field actions. Thus, on Monmouth battlefield (1778) in the USA munitions containing iron grape shot weighing three ounces (85g) were used (Sivilich and Sivilich 2011).

When hailshot first came into use and what form it took are unclear, although dates as early as 1400 are claimed for Germany (McLachlan 2010, 50). Also uncertain is when the transition to lead bullets as the typical projectile occurred. In England hailshot is reported in 16th-century documentary sources and is found on wrecks; the army taken to France in 1513 by Henry VIII appears to have been supplied with hailshot of lead (Cruickshank 1990, 72). It is also listed in the 1547 inventory of royal possessions taken after Henry's death (Starkey *et al* 1998).

Fig 4.6 A lead bullet from Edgehill (1642), which shows the distinctive evidence of having been fired as hailshot from an artillery piece. On firing, the lead ball has been compressed against the other bullets to create a surface of polygonal facets. This is the typical signature seen on lead balls fired in this way, though often the faceting is far more confused by melting, caused by hot gases passing through the munition during firing. Maximum diameter *c* 19mm

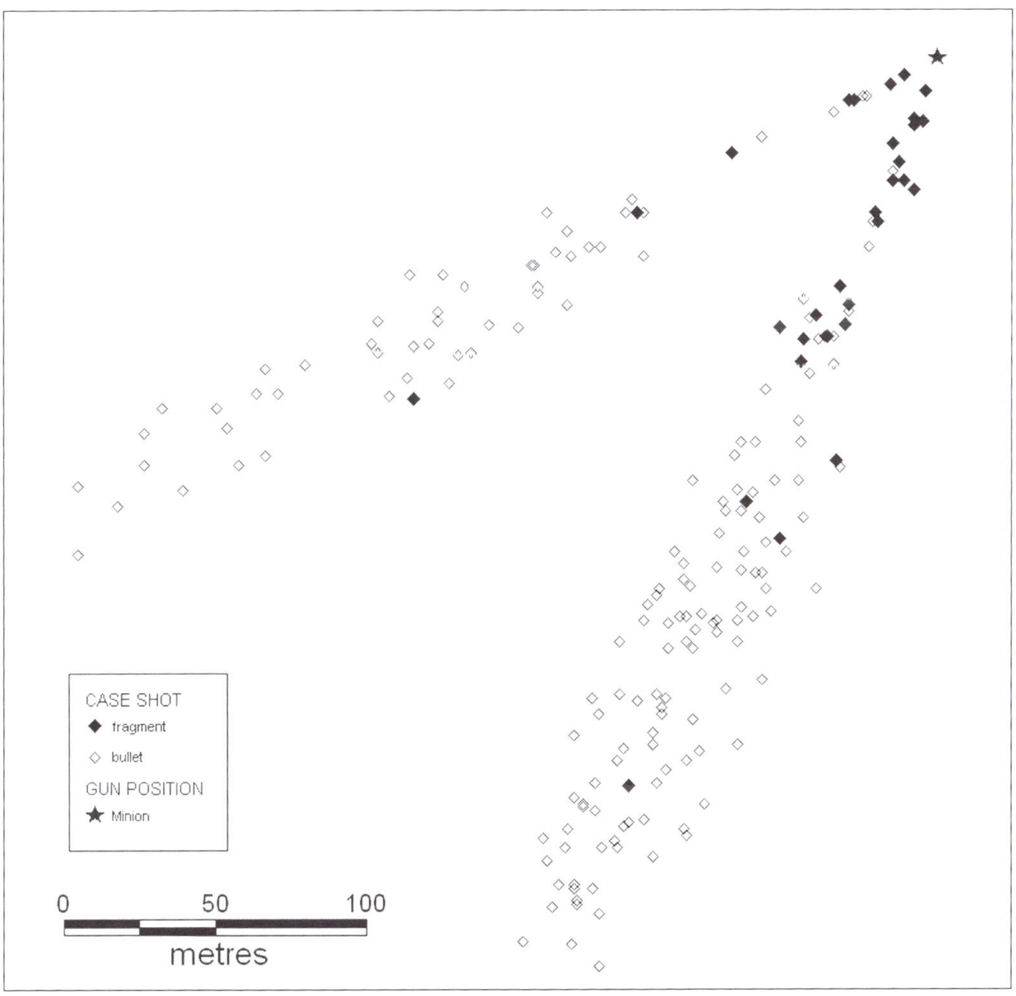

Fig 4.7 Distribution of bullets recovered from the experimental firing of hailshot, fired on two different alignments from a barrel with the bore of a minion (Allsop and Foard 2008)

The absence of evidence for hailshot from 15th- or 16th-century battlefields may simply be because, at this date, iron dice or stone were the more typical components. Iron dice may not have survived in the topsoil or only in such decayed condition that the original function is not recognisable, while the recovery of stone pebbles or flint shards used for this purpose will only be possible, if at all, on sites where these are not naturally present in the topsoil. Their recovery would also require fieldwalking survey, a method applied only infrequently to battlefield survey. Where lead bullets were used for hailshot, however, a clear archaeological signature is to be expected. For the Civil War the character and significance of its battlefield use can be considered in detail through both the written and archaeological records (Edwards 2000; Foard 2008c). Lead bullets fired as hailshot from artillery tend to show distinctive firing evidence in the form of polygonal facets, although the clarity of the evidence varies (Fig 4.6). These features have been reproduced in firing experiments, which have also demonstrated the probable final range and spread achieved with such munitions. When fired point blank in a wooden box of 82mm diameter from a minion, using modern gunpowder, a linear spread some 50m wide and extending a little over 300m from the gun position was produced (Fig 4.7). This provides an initial baseline for the interpretation of battlefield scatters, although the evidence needs to be refined by a more extensive series of firing experiments using guns of varying bore and gunpowder reproducing properties of that used in the 17th century (Allsop and Foard 2008).

Small arms

The 4000 lead bullets or 'pellets' for handguns supplied for the army taken to France by Edward IV in 1475 weighed in all 700lb (Holmer 1977, 220). This suggests an average bullet weight of 79g and diameter of 24mm. Limited studies of surviving early handguns suggest that they have bores extending from 18mm up to 35mm (McLachlan 2010; Kempers 1983). Once windage of *c* 2mm is taken into account, to allow the ball to be introduced into the barrel, the projectile calibre will range from 16mm to 33mm. As previously mentioned, the upper part of this range encompasses a transition to the intermediate type of mounted guns, where it may also overlap with the lowest bores of true artillery. On the basis of this very limited analysis the English battlefield evidence can be reviewed. The two rounds from Towton, at 20mm and 30mm, may prove to relate to a handgun and a mounted gun. At Bosworth there are two rounds probably from handguns and one which may be from a mounted gun.

Small arms were clearly present in English armies of the period, as seen from the 100 hook guns and 150 handguns supplied for Edward IV's campaign in France in 1475 (Holmer 1977, 215). The paucity of rounds from such guns in battlefield survey presumably reflects the continued dominance, in the field, of the warbow in English armies. The only exceptions may be the second battle of St Albans (1461) and Barnet (1471), where large numbers of foreign mercenary handgunners were present (Burley *et al* 2007; National Army Museum 1995b). While it could be argued that it was the presence of the foreign mercenaries that led to the report of handguns in those two battles, rather than the exceptional nature of their use, this seems unlikely. The issue of whether handguns were in more general use on English battlefields may only be finally resolved through archaeological investigation of battlefields of the period, in England and on the continent, where these weapons were certainly used, to establish the calibre of the guns. Survey will not be possible at St Albans, as that battlefield has been almost completely destroyed by development and mineral extraction (P Burley pers comm), but at Barnet the battlefield may have survived reasonably intact; the potential for its investigation is discussed below.

During the 16th century evidence becomes clearer. Documentary sources related to weapons captured suggest that handguns may have been used in significant numbers, at least by Scottish forces. In the battle at Flodden (1513) and at Solway Moss (1542) the weapons captured from the Scots included many handguns (National Army Museum 1995g; National Army Museum 1995o). Given that these early references are of weapons captured, the failure of the accounts to mention English forces using handguns need not mean that they did not do so. However, the first definite documentary evidence for large-scale use of handguns on the battlefield by English armies seems to be from Ancrum Moor (1545) in the Scottish borders (Foard 2007c), and then at Pinkie (1547) in East Lothian, Scotland (Foard 2007b).

A potential problem affects the archaeological evidence. Several English battlefields of the later 15th and early 16th centuries, including Towton, Bosworth, and Flodden, have produced small numbers of small

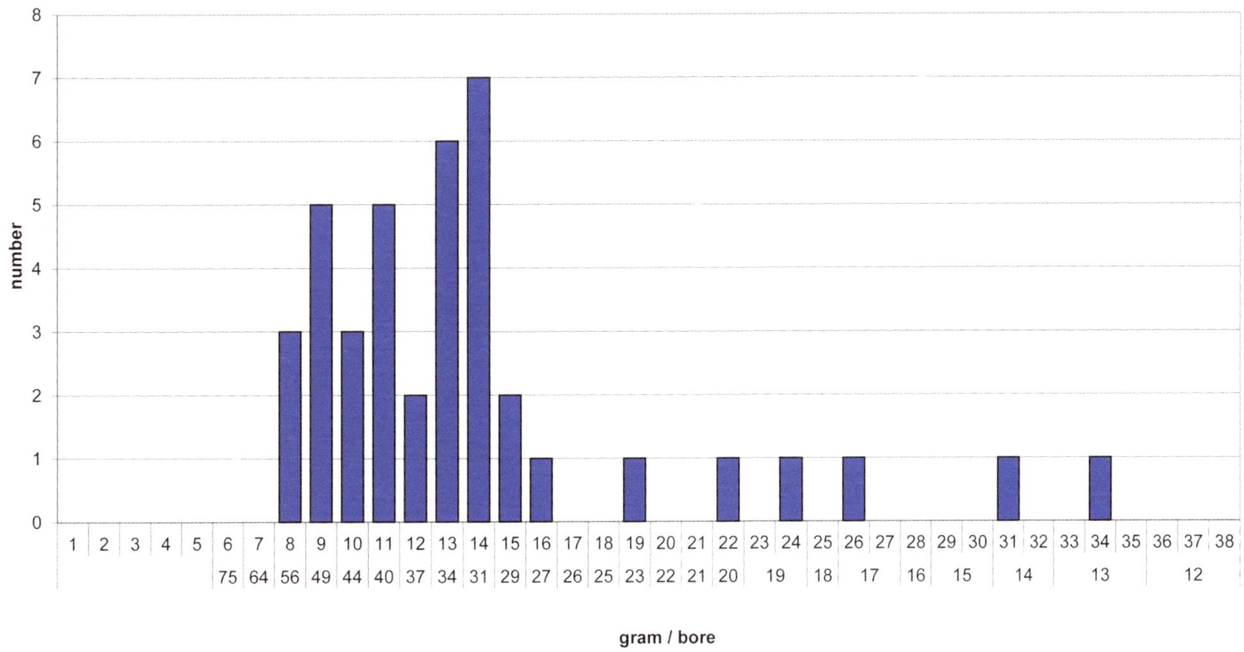

Fig 4.8 Graph showing the calibre of lead ball of below 20mm from the Towton Battlefield Survey. These bullets appear to represent background noise from later sporting activity. Calibre is shown in grams and in bore (bullets to the pound of lead)[4]

calibre lead bullets – well below the calibres discussed above for early guns and comparable to the background noise of sporting activity seen in other parts of the English landscape (Foard 2008c) (Fig 4.8). However, the calibres are compatible with 16th-century handguns. While such small-bore guns will not have been present at Towton, it is unclear when they did come into use, and they cannot be dismissed for 16th-century battlefields. At Bosworth analysis of the small calibre bullets is complicated by the presence on the 1485 battlefield of a cavalry skirmish of the 17th century. In this skirmish both carbines and pistols firing bullets which lie within the same broad calibre range as the arquebus – in so far as that is currently understood – are likely to have been used.

In the absence of battlefield finds from the 16th century we must look to the assemblage from the *Mary Rose* to establish the character and calibre of small arms bullets used by English armies in the mid-16th century. This assemblage gives a snapshot of the transition from bow to bullet, with hundreds of projectiles for small arms and artillery preserved alongside the more famous longbows (Walker and Hildred 2000; Hildred forthcoming): in addition to round shot and hailshot for artillery, the *Mary Rose*'s magazine, according to her inventory, originally contained more than 1000 lead bullets for small arms, only 6 per cent of which have so far been retrieved from the wreck. Given the small size of the sample, and the fact that the bullets came from various locations within the ship, it is a question whether they are representative of the calibres in overall use on the vessel and by English armies of the period.[5]

Examination of the lead bullets from the *Mary Rose* demonstrates that they were manufactured in a similar way to those of the 17th century (Fig 4.9). The one potentially distinctive attribute of some is the presence of multiple cuts caused during sprue removal. This is a feature which has not yet been recognised on later material, but may ultimately prove irrelevant to the dating of bullets; it is likely that it will only be from analysis of the calibre of a battlefield assemblage as a whole that 16th-century bullets may be distinguished from background noise. In the graph which compares the *Mary Rose* bullets with those recovered from Pinkie the exact positions of peaks and gaps seem to show a degree of correlation (Foard 2008d; Foard 2008f; Foard 2008e) (Fig 4.10). If we take into account the calibre shift – seen especially in larger calibre bullets as a result of loss of lead through melting during firing – then the correlation is even closer. In both cases, however, the samples are far too small to provide secure evidence. The investigation of several battlefields of the later 15th and 16th centuries where handguns were used is needed to reveal the calibre signatures. This is arguably the single most important area of research required to advance the study of 16th-century battlefields in England. If a clear picture of the calibre of bullets in use can be obtained it may be possible to correlate this with surviving handguns from the period.

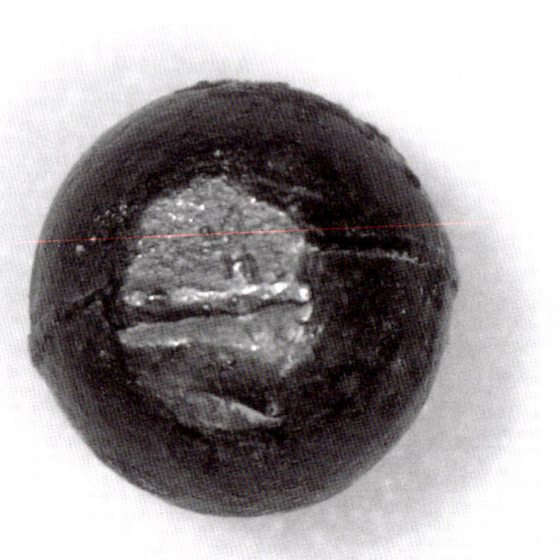

Fig 4.9 A lead bullet from the *Mary Rose* intended for use in a hand gun. To right and left is the mould ridge, created because the two halves of the mould were ill-fitting, allowing lead to leak slightly along the join. To the fore is the sprue snip, a flattish area with a central bar, where nippers have cut down slightly into the sphere when removing the lead sprue – a protrusion from the bullet representing the hole through which molten lead was poured into the mould (Reproduced by permission of the *Mary Rose* Trust). Maximum diameter *c* 19mm

From the 17th century onwards both written and archaeological evidence is more detailed and has been the subject of more extensive research (Sivilich 2007; Foard 2008c; Allsop and Foard 2008). As a result, the calibre of bullets can, with caveats, be related to different weapon types and thus to the type of troops that fired them.

The calibre for all solid lead bullets, except the non-spherical slug, is most effectively defined from its mass. For an assemblage this can be presented in graph form. Calibre is best understood from unfired bullet assemblages, as weight loss resulting from firing and impact may blur the pattern. Garrisons provide one context within which such material may be recovered, as many were occupied only briefly and some may be expected to have destruction phases, providing exceptional sealed assemblages of Civil War date. It is possible that the remains of the magazine may survive on a few sites. This seems to have been the case with the 1691 garrison of Ballymore in Ireland, whence more than 2000 unfired bullets provide detail about the calibres in use by the Jacobite force occupying the garrison (Fig 4.11).

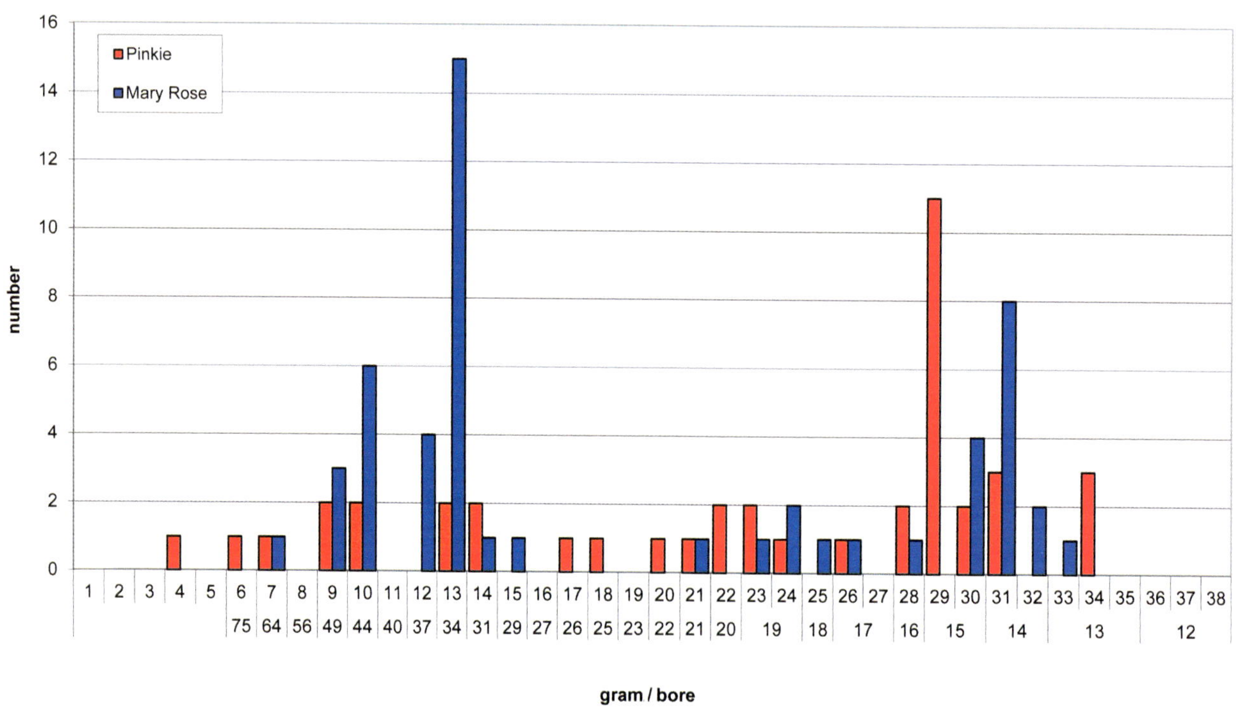

Fig 4.10 Graph comparing the calibre of lead ball from the probable area of the battlefield at Pinkie (1547) with unfired lead ball from the *Mary Rose* (wrecked 1545). Calibre is shown in grams and in bore (bullets to the pound of lead)

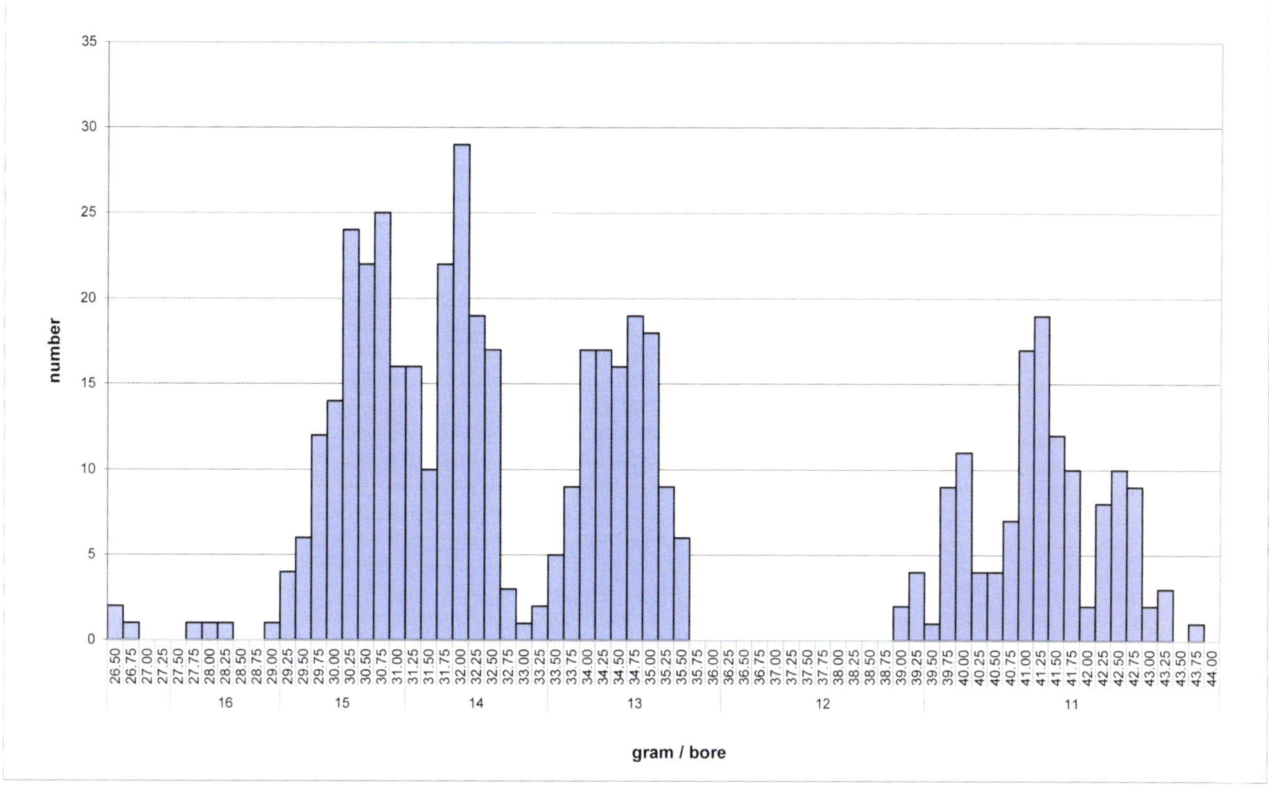

Fig 4.11 Graph of the calibre of unfired lead ball from the 1691 siege site at Ballymore in the Republic of Ireland. The graph reveals several distinct musket calibres in use by the Jacobite forces (Foard 2008c)

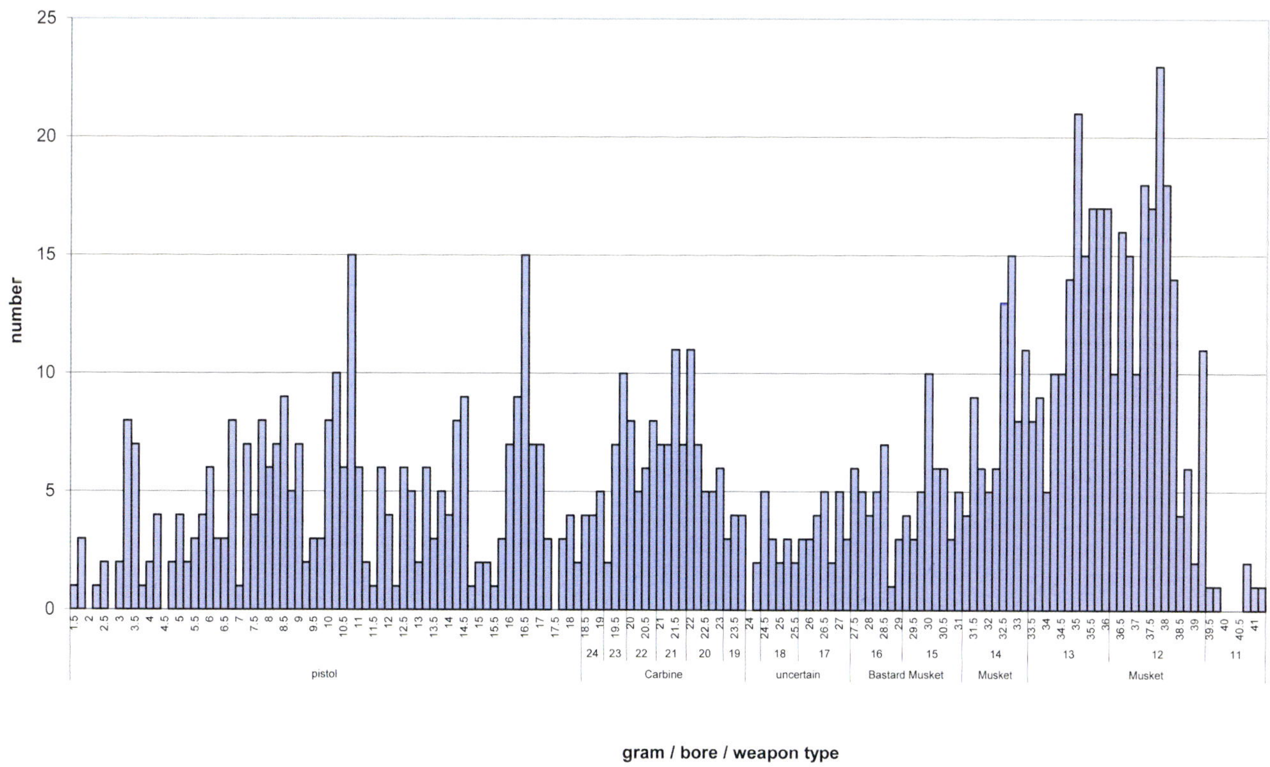

Fig 4.12 Graph of the calibre of lead ball from the Edgehill survey (2004–07), showing numbers of bullets by mass, bore (bullets to the pound of lead) and probable weapon type. While broad groupings are visible, the picture is far more confused than that seen for the unfired Ballymore assemblage

Of even greater importance for the characterisation of 17th-century munitions are well-dated sealed assemblages from European shipwrecks around the world. The value of these data have already been demonstrated from the limited study of several examples; what is now required is for significant data from all excavated wrecks to be brought together in a single study. Such a study would provide baseline data on the calibres and character of munitions in use by different European armies from the 16th century onwards – an essential reference point for the archaeological study of early modern warfare.

Returning to the battlefield, the difficulties involved in identifying the calibres in use are demonstrated by the graph from Edgehill, which is far more complex than that of unfired bullets from Ballymore (Fig 4.12). Here, as in most battlefield assemblages, the pattern is complicated by weight reduction from firing and from the more extreme impact damage, while intermixing of the bullets from both armies may introduce more variation. Complicating the assemblage further are the guns that were used at Edgehill, which had been assembled from a wide range of different magazines, including many old and outdated weapons (Foard 2008c).

Fig 4.13 Unfired lead ball showing detail of manufacture. To the fore is the raised remnant of the sprue, which here has been cut slightly above the surface of the sphere. The snip shows the distinctive central bar that results from the use of nippers. To top and bottom of the image are the faint trace of a ridge running around the ball, representing the join between the two halves of the mould. Maximum diameter *c* 17mm

Fig 4.14 Images comparing a bullet recovered from Edgehill (left) with one which has been fired experimentally (right). Across the centre of each is a band where, under pressure during firing, the bullet appears to have expanded to fit the barrel. The experimentally fired bullet shows minor striations on the band, presumably made by irregularities in the bore as it travelled down the smooth-bore barrel. On the Edgehill bullet corrosion has obscured any such marks. The lower hemisphere (below) shows melting, because no wadding was used and thus the bullet rested on the gunpowder. The upper hemisphere (top) shows the original bullet surface, which remains unaltered by firing. Maximum diameter *c* 18mm

Fig 4.15 Image comparing the lower hemisphere of the same bullets as in Figure 4.14. Radial movement of the melted lead from the centre of the hemisphere, carried by the gases expanding around the lead ball, is clearly visible on both. Maximum diameter *c* 18mm

Fig 4.16 A lead ball of musket calibre from Edgehill which has distorted on impact with a hard, smooth surface. Experimental filing suggests this, like most impact marks on battlefield bullets, is probably the result of hitting a small pebble when the bullet bounced after missing its target. Diameter *c* 19mm

Fig 4.17 A lead slug from Edgehill. This is a distinctive type of ammunition, typically created by hammering a larger calibre lead ball to fit a smaller-bore weapon – usually from musket down to carbine or pistol calibre. Length *c* 30mm

As we have seen for round shot, lead bullets often take a signature when they are fired. Such marks enable us to see whether a given projectile has been fired or not (Figs 4.13–4.16). However, in general, the smaller the projectile the less clear is the evidence. Pistol calibres are the most difficult to analyse because of the low charge used and the low mass of the bullet. In order to isolate evidence of use for such projectiles, it is first important to distinguish those attributes of form and surface detail that derive from manufacture (Fig 4.17).

Future research

A programme of scientific analysis, supported by experimental firing and other work, is now required to provide a general foundation of statistically valid data on the issues discussed above. Only with such research will a sophisticated interpretation of bullets and round shot be established, in turn enabling the potential of battlefield evidence to be realised (Figs 4.18 and 4.19). Pilot work has already been undertaken in collaboration with Cranfield University (Eyers 2006; Harkins 2010; Miller 2010). These experiments will enable original bullets and round shot to be compared to those produced under known conditions, and can also be extended by the application of modern ballistics and forensics techniques, enabling assessment of such issues as the range and effectiveness of the guns. Results from this work will complement evidence from written sources. Thus, for example, according to Bellone in 1587, the point blank range of a falconet was 381m (250 paces or 1250 feet) and the extreme range 4572m (3000 paces, 15,000 feet) (Arnold 2001, 31). However, neither he nor any later authors provide the information needed to interpret the archaeological distributions, which represent the final range, where the artefact comes to rest after bounce and roll.

Such research must be underpinned by an understanding of surviving early guns and related matériel, including developments in gunpowder manufacture and firing practices. The principal data for this will come from the study of military manuals and 'firework books' from the 15th to 17th centuries, and can be complemented by evidence from scientific analysis of the incorporation and chemical composition of gunpowder residues. Small quantities of residue may be present on the bore of gun barrel fragments recovered from battlefields, as noted at Towton. Far more is present in the breech and breech chambers of some surviving guns, such as those from the 1476 battles of Grandson and Murten in Switzerland (Foard and Walton in prep). Other information, for example on obturators (wads and wooden tampions) and on some containers for hailshot which were of organic materials, will need to come from the study of wreck assemblages.

For firing experiments, such information is needed to enable the effective reproduction of guns, propellants, projectiles, and obturators. The experimental data on muzzle velocity and on bounce and roll in different ground conditions can also be used to develop a physics engine within a computer modelling programme to explore the trajectory and final resting place of projectiles when fired on different battlefields. This will enable exploration of the effects of individual variables, such as charge and elevation, in different terrain contexts, on a scale not achievable through live-firing experiments. In this way it should be possible to arrive at more developed interpretations of the patterns presented by the scatters of bullets and round shot recovered in battlefield surveys.

Fig 4.18 Experimental firing of a bench-mounted 12 bore barrel undertaken in collaboration with Cranfield University and the Royal Armouries. Here the bullet velocity was accurately measured as it passed down range and there was soft capture of the projectile, so preserving the firing evidence uncontaminated by impact effects

Fig 4.19 Experimental firing by Miller at Ashdown in 2007. A bench-mounted 12 bore barrel was fired using modern powder and the velocity of the bullets was tracked using Doppler radar. The series of paper sheets, set at standard intervals, recorded the deviation of the ball as it passed down range. The impact marks from subsequent bounces and the final resting places of the bullets were also recorded, to establish the degree to which bounce and roll determined the final range (Miller 2010)

Notes

1. A concise although largely unreferenced summary of the development of the technology of gunpowder weapons in Europe is given in McLachlan 2010, though the principal focus is upon early hand-held firearms; a more detailed study is provided in Hall 1997.
2. Towton 1461: 2 in 2011 (1 in 2008); Barnet 1471: 3 (3); Bosworth 1485: 34 (0). For the 16th century there are just 3, from Flodden.
3. This discussion draws heavily upon Foard 2008c and Foard and Curry in prep.
4. Analysis by G Foard on bullets from the Towton Battlefield Project provided for analysis by Simon Richardson.
5. Information from A Hildred. Calibre and character detail are from the author's analysis of the assemblage.

5

The Wars of the Roses: 1455–87

Fifteen battles were fought in England between 1455 and 1487 – the period now known as the Wars of the Roses (Fig 5.1). Two of them, Towton and Bosworth, are the earliest battles in the UK from which substantial battle archaeology has so far been retrieved, and therefore provide the first opportunity to address questions of tactics from a relatively secure understanding of how the events played out within the historic terrain. As we have seen, the Wars of the Roses also provide the earliest sites in England where documentary and archaeological evidence demonstrate the application of gunpowder weapons to the battlefield.

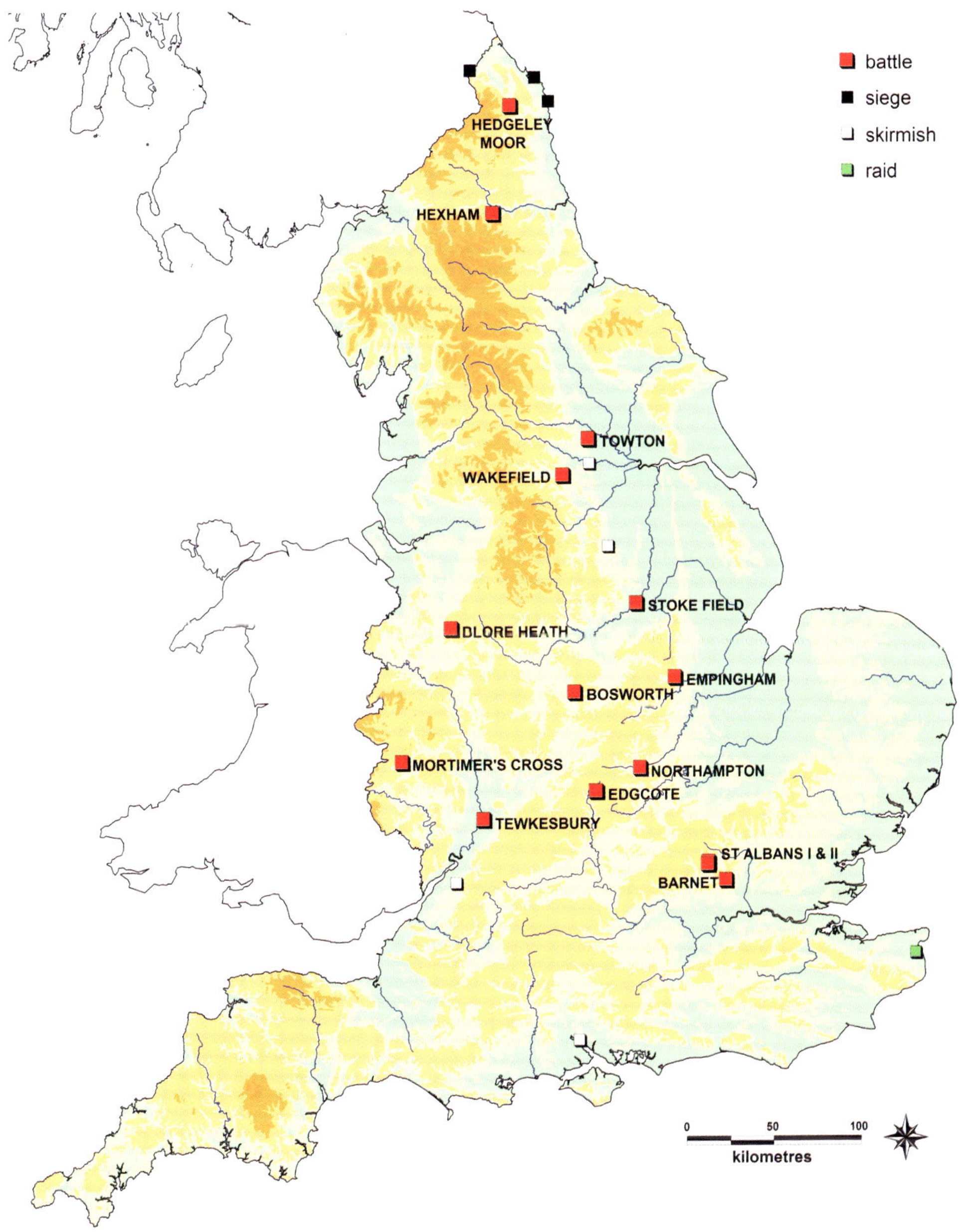

Fig 5.1 Map of fields of conflict in England from the Wars of the Roses (1455–87)

Fig 5.2 The battle of Edgcote (1469) named as the battle of Danesmore on Speed's 1612 map of the county of Northamptonshire

Before the battle archaeology can be explored, however, the sites must be located, and for the late 15th century this is often a major challenge. At Hexham, for example, the battle fought in 1464 has at least four contending sites in the environs of the town (see Fig 3.9). As with most battles of preceding centuries, the written sources provide limited topographical information, and the best evidence we have for some is simply the battle name and a tradition regarding the location of the action. The problem can be further illustrated by the battle of Edgcote, fought in Northamptonshire in 1469, which was excluded from the Register because the site was not securely located (Haigh 1997; National Army Museum 1995e).[1] It is described by contemporary sources as the battle of Edgcote, one of which says that it was fought on the land of a certain Clarell who, according to Baker, was at that time the lord of the manor of Edgcote (Baker 1822, 500). Several late 16th- and early 17th-century sources, however, call it the battle of Danesmoor (Fig 5.2). That Danesmoor lay in Edgcote parish in the 15th century is shown by those sources which call the settlement 'Hegecote seu Danysmore' (Gover *et al* 1933), while on Eayre's county map of 1791 and Bryant's of 1826 Danesmoor is crudely depicted as the area of the Cherwell valley in the north-east part of the parish running up to Trafford bridge. Baker is very specific:

> Danesmore (for so it was certainly called as long since as 1469) or Dunsmore (as the Countrey People now frequently call it) [is] a pretty spacious Valley on the South of Edgcote ... The spot now called Danesmoor is a small plantation of a few acres, but the name at this period had doubtless a much more extended application.

There is no land between the Cherwell and the spinney which would seem to accord with the description of moor, for the reconstruction of the open-field system by David Hall shows ridge and furrow covering all this area. In contrast, the upper reaches of the side valley, to the south of the spinney, fit very well with the description of a moor (Partida *et al* in prep). The topography of this side valley also fits depictions of the terrain in the primary accounts of the battle, which described the action being fought in an area between three hills. As at Bosworth, survey of the battle archaeology is likely to be the only way in which the site will be securely located.

Given such uncertainties, even where a battlefield is believed to have been destroyed, reassessment is important to confirm that the location concerned is the correct one. In the case of St Albans II, fought in 1461, reassessment has confirmed the identification, although when assessed for the Register it was considered that the battlefield was too badly damaged to justify inclusion. This action is notable for the presence of continental handgunners in significant numbers. Given the site's potential to contribute to the understanding of the early use of handguns in England, a rapid desk-based assessment of the likely survival of battle archaeology has been conducted here. While much of the action took place within the urban area of St Albans itself, part was on Bernard's Heath on the north-eastern edge of the town, where the Yorkist forces were driven back north-eastwards towards Sandridge and Nomansland Common (Haigh 1995, 46–54; Burley *et al* 2007). The extent of Bernard's Heath was taken from the 1805–06 Ordnance Surveyor's Drawings and the likely extent of the urban area of St Albans was plotted from Hare's 1634 map, all of which information was transcribed to the 1883 Ordnance Survey first edition six-inch map base. Comparison with modern mapping showed that the greater part of Bernard's Heath, as it survived in the early 19th century, had been unaffected by development. However, a more detailed study undertaken on the historic landscape of the St Albans area and particularly Bernard's Heath tells a different story (P Burley and H Watson pers comm): this shows the heath to have been more extensive prior to enclosure in the 1670s, spreading north-eastward from the 19th-century area. Most of this area is now covered by housing. Their research has also demonstrated that quarrying had extended over most if not all of the surviving area of the former heath (P Burley pers comm; Hunn 1991; Reynolds 2000). There is no realistic possibility of the recovery of bullets or round shot in the redeposited topsoil owing to the nature of the 20th-century restoration of this land. The clay extraction had been achieved by the digging of holes about 6m across and 3m deep and the dumping of the spoil beside the hole, and the first serious remedial work, undertaken in 1909, brought the spoil from the excavation of a nearby water reservoir and tipped it on top of domestic refuse to bring the surface to a level finish. The only area of undisturbed ground where battle archaeology might be found is to the north, where a prehistoric earthwork known as the Beech Bottom survives. It has been suggested that the place where this earthwork was crossed by the railway cutting is the location of the 19th-century discovery of a mass grave which supposedly contained artefacts of the 15th century (Burley *et al* 2007; H Watson and P Burley pers comm). This aside, it is clear that the research potential of the St Albans battlefield has been lost, and the decision to exclude it from the Register is confirmed.

Barnet

The travels of the battlefield of Barnet, as revealed by recent research, led to a very different conclusion. On 13 April 1471 a Lancastrian army of perhaps 15,000 troops, under the Earl of Warwick, took up position on the north side of High Barnet. Edward VI arrived from the City of London that evening with a force of perhaps 10,000–12,000. In the dark he deployed to the south of the Lancastrians, in a marshy valley very close to Warwick's army. Warwick then launched an artillery bombardment, but this passed over the heads of the Yorkist troops because of the lie of the land. In deep mist the next morning the two armies advanced, but the Yorkist left had deployed short of the Lancastrian right, whilst their right wing extended past the Lancastrian left. The Lancastrians quickly took advantage on their right flank, the troops under the Earl of Oxford pushing back the enemy troops they faced and driving them from the field. The Yorkists, similarly, fared better on their right flank, where they successfully pushed back the Lancastrian left. The battle was fiercest in the centre and it is here that the Lancastrians finally faltered as Edward launched his reserve, causing the enemy to break and flee.

The location of the battlefield is disputed; it was depicted on maps from the end of the 16th century through to the 19th century in an area to the north of Monken Hadley. Norden's map of Hertfordshire of 1598 shows, unusually for this period, the main road system and also seems very specific in locating the action. He places the two armies on either side of the road to Potters Bar just after it branched out north-eastward from the Great North Road (running north from London via St Albans) a little to the north of Barnet. Taylor's map of Middlesex in 1759 shows a similar location, which he appears to describe as Gladmore Heath. The monument to the battle was constructed in the late 18th century at the southern edge of this area and this location was accepted as the battlefield by Barrett and most other 19th-century authors (Barrett 1896). However, by 1898, when Charles Oman discussed the battle, the site had been shifted further to the south, onto the ground between Monken Hadley and the town of Barnet. This view was refined by Burne, providing the interpretation on which the Registration of the site was based in 1995 (Burne 1950; National Army Museum 1995b).

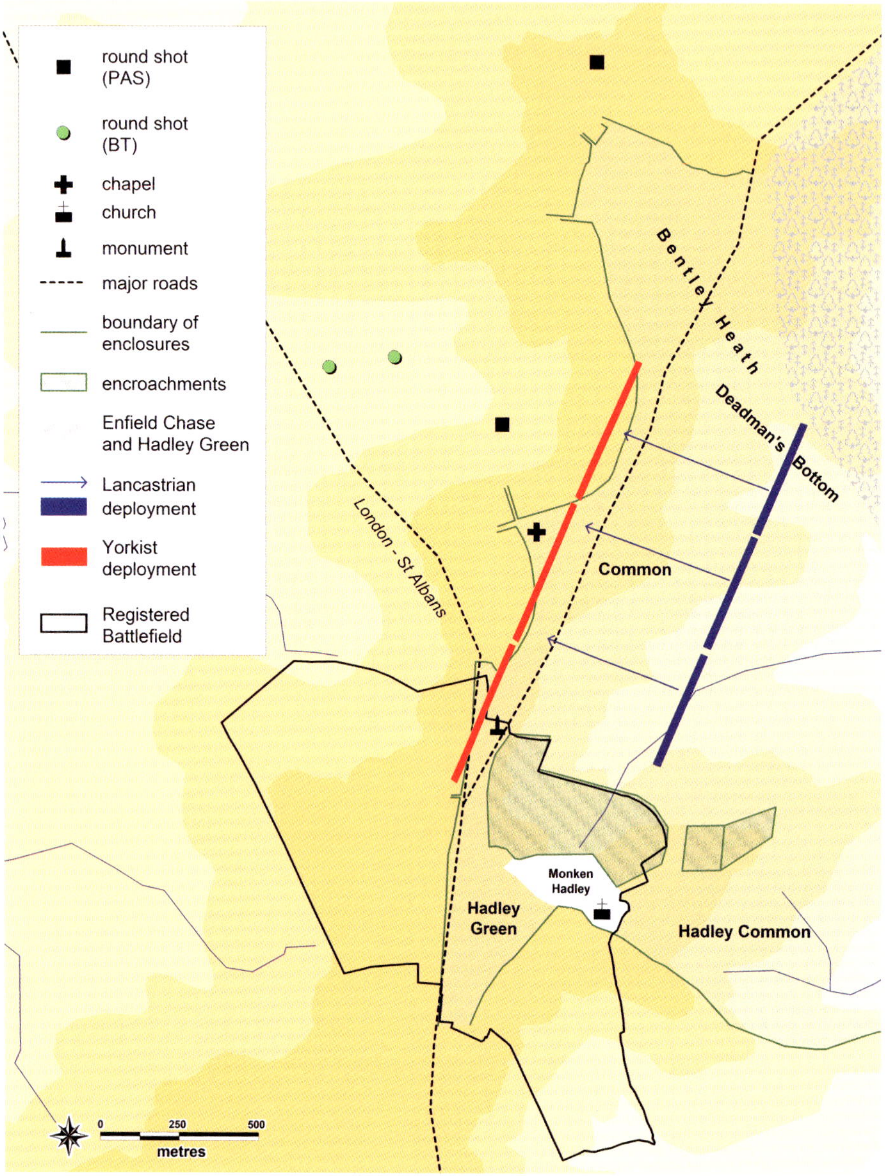

Fig 5.3 Map of Barnet (1471) battlefield, showing key elements of the historic terrain and possible deployments together with conflicting evidence for and interpretations of the location of the action[2]

Subsequent research by Warren has shown that the battle chapel at Barnet stood at the western edge of Enfield Chase, in an area known at enclosure in 1777 as South Mimms Common (Warren 2002). This site lies immediately north of Monken Hadley, exactly where the 16th- to 18th-century sources placed the battle. A simplified reconstruction of the historic landscape is presented here (Fig 5.3). The extent of Enfield Chase is defined from an un-implemented enclosure proposal map of 1656, with further detail on the pre-enclosure landscape taken from Rocque's county map of 1754. The combined evidence has been used to suggest the location of the deployments on the traditional site and adjacent to the chapel – a considerable distance to the north of the Registered area. The analysis has recently been confirmed and elaborated by more detailed documentary study of the wider historic landscape and re-analysis of the battle (Warren 2009). However, Warren's study is accompanied by only sketch mapping and there is still the need for accurate reworking of the evidence in digital form to a modern map base, which should be linked to further assessment of the documentary sources for the terrain and all the primary accounts for the battle itself.

Although this reassessment appears to provide a more secure location for the battlefield, the limited artefactual evidence poses difficulties. A number of cast-iron spheres of different sizes, several now in Barnet Museum, have been recovered from various locations in the Barnet area. They include at least one from Hadley Green, within the Registered area. It is possible, but unlikely, that cast-iron round shot were in use in English armies by 1471. Cursory examination of these artefacts in 2010 demonstrated that at least one of the spheres is actually a woman's shot for shot putt. The others may also have non-military origins, for there were various industrial and other uses for iron spheres in later centuries. The matter may only be resolved through scientific analysis of their composition.

Other finds, as discussed in Chapter 4, are more likely to be from the battle. These include three solid lead round shot of calibres similar to those from Bosworth, two of which were found by a collector, as well as a Burgundian jetton and a medieval purse bar, all now in Barnet Museum. The round shot are identified in the database of the Portable Antiquities Scheme (PAS) as being from the 17th or 18th century, even though no military action or training of that period is reported in the area to provide a context for their deposition. To further complicate matters, the quoted location on the database is at odds with the location given to the Battlefields Trust by the finder, which is a kilometre away in the small valley to the north-west of the chapel site (A Coulston pers comm). While the PAS location would be compatible with a battle frontage extending further north-east from our reconstruction, the other location might suggest that the battle was fought in the valley to the north-west of the chapel.

The matter can be resolved only by a systematic archaeological survey to seek a wider distribution of lead round shot and other artefacts, comparable to that from Bosworth (see Fig 5.9). The importance of such a study cannot be over-emphasised. It is not simply a matter of understanding the battle itself, nor of providing a round shot scatter to compare with Bosworth's, though both would be valuable. The key issue, rather, is that this is the only intact 15th-century battlefield in England where early handguns are known to have been used in large numbers.[3]

Towton

Towton is the most intensively studied English battlefield of the period. Fought on 29 March 1461, the action is claimed to have been the largest and bloodiest of the Wars of the Roses. The site contrasts with most other battlefields of the period in having a location which was apparently never forgotten. The topographical detail in the primary accounts is typically sparse but very specific, and shows the battle to have been fought on land between the villages of Towton and Saxton. This is an area with very constricted terrain, comprising a small plateau orientated north–south and bounded by steep scarps. The area is dissected from east to west by Towton Dale, providing only one logical location for the armies to have chosen to deploy and fought (Fig 5.4). The traditional site of the mass graves from the battle is identified on 18th-century maps and in earlier written records. Detailed interpretations of deployments and action set within this terrain were published in the 19th and 20th centuries, and studies of the battlefield, as well as archaeological work conducted since 1996, have confirmed and refined the traditional interpretation.

Until 2009 Towton was the only medieval battlefield in the UK to have produced substantial battle

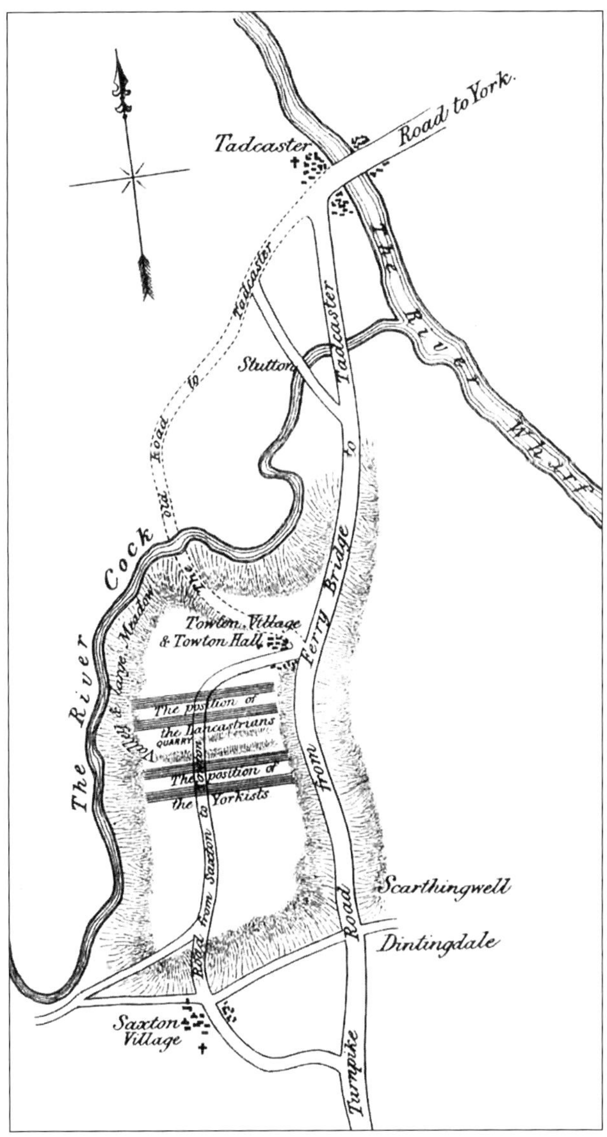

Fig 5.4 Towton (1461) battlefield as depicted in Brooke's sketch plan of 1857, showing the deployments on either side of Towton Dale within tightly constrained topography. Comparison with recent publications on the battle demonstrate how securely located the site has always been

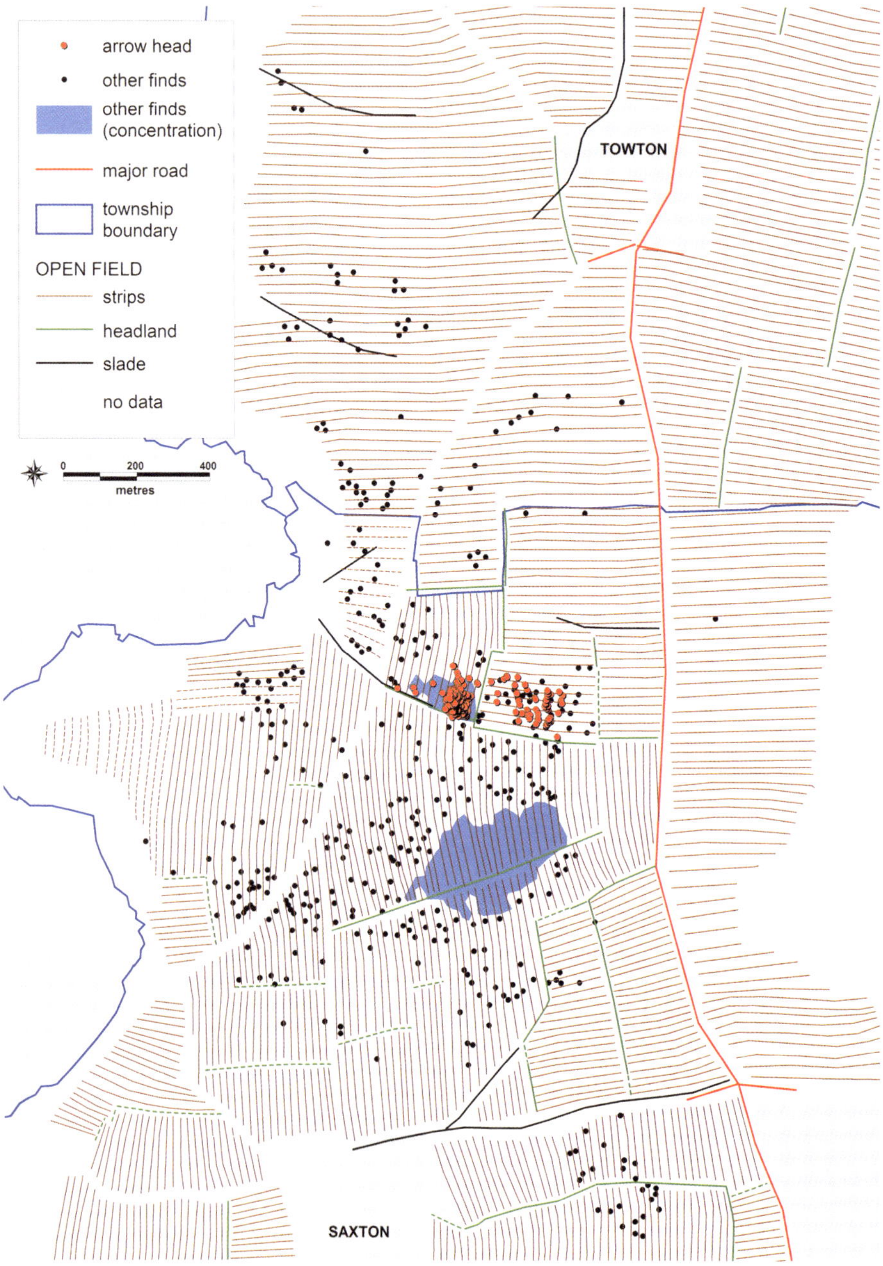

Fig 5.5 Map of Towton (1461) showing the artefact distribution, in so far as it has been published, against a background of the open-field furlong pattern as reconstructed by Hall[4]

archaeology. It thus appeared significant not merely in its own right but also as a guide to what evidence might be expected on other sites of the period. However, recent work at Bosworth, Flodden and elsewhere, discussed below, suggests that Towton may be exceptional in both the scale and character of its archaeology. The following discussion is based on the extensive series of interim statements on aspects of the battle archaeology: Sutherland 2000b; 2000c; 2005; 2009; Sutherland and Richardson 2007; Sutherland and Schmidt 2003.

Terrain is fundamental to the understanding of a battle. David Hall was accordingly commissioned for the present study to use his well-established methodology to reconstruct the open-field system of the relevant parts of Towton and Saxton townships (Hall 1995). Survey recorded headlands, slades, and the few fragments of surviving ridge and furrow, and included analysis of similar evidence on the 1940s RAF vertical air photographs and later aerial photography. This work was supported with information from the Ordnance Survey first edition six-inch mapping, the Saxton tithe map of 1848, and enclosure award of 1849 – all of which show a pattern of enclosure which to a high degree reflected the earlier open-field furlong pattern. A rapid search in the Borthwick Institute produced no terriers or related documents that would provide information on the medieval furlong names and land use, although relevant sources may exist in other archives.[5]

Hall's work shows that the greater part of both townships was under open-field cultivation by *c* 1300 (Fig 5.5), but without documentary evidence it is

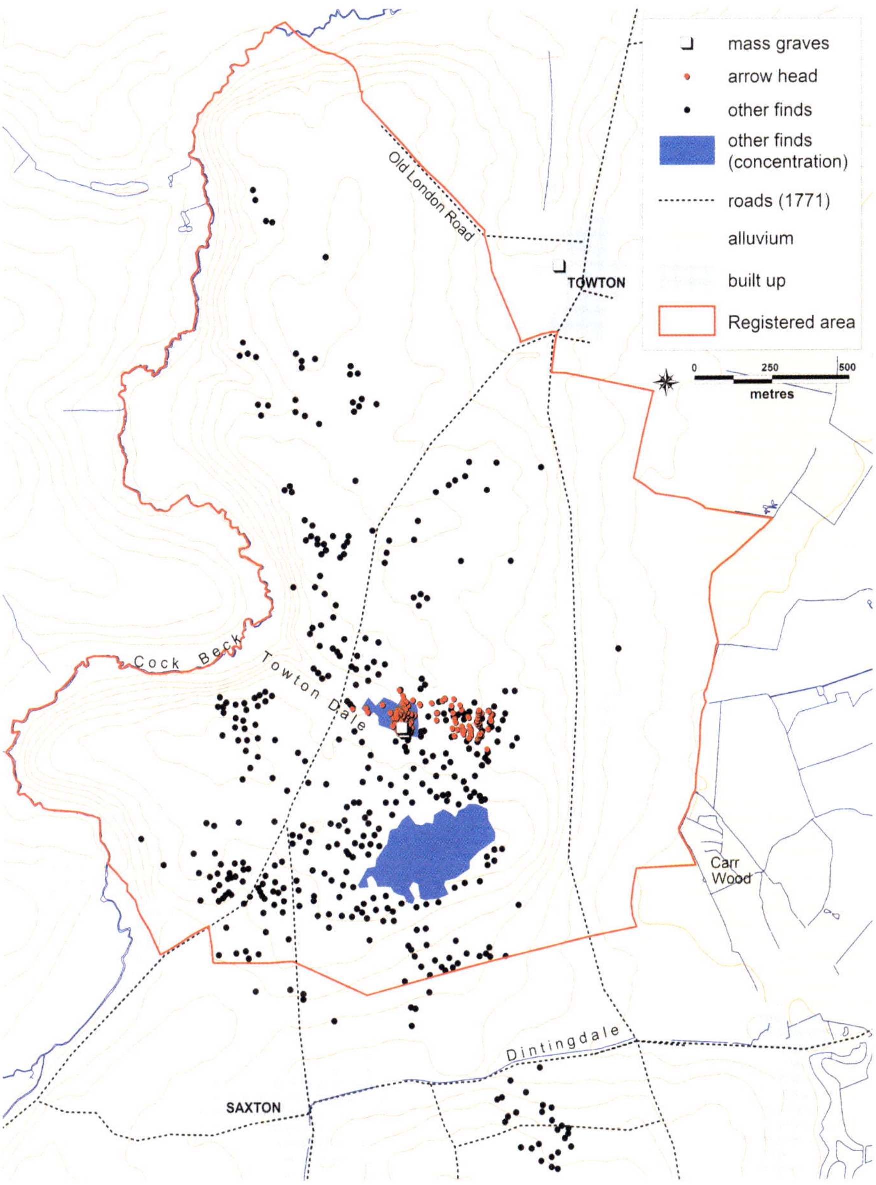

Fig 5.6 Map of Towton (1461) showing the published artefact scatter and proven mass grave sites in relation to relief (50m interval) and other aspects of terrain[6] (Reproduced by permission of Ordnance Survey on behalf of HMSO. © Crown copyright and database right 2012. All rights reserved. Ordnance Survey Licence no. 100024900)

impossible to say how much of this land, if any, might have reverted to pasture by 1461. On the eastern edge of the townships there is no evidence for open-field furlongs; rather, this zone, which coincides with silt and clay geology, is characterised by *carr* names, and small woods existed here in the 19th century. At least part of this ground was almost certainly boggy in the later Middle Ages, and possibly also partly covered by trees.[7] On the western periphery, likewise, there were no furlongs, in this case because the ground falls steeply into the dale of the Cock Beck and the deepest parts of Towton Dale. Some authors have suggested that the area on the south-western edge of the plateau, now called Castle Wood, was wooded in 1461. However, this land was not fully encompassed by the survey and the proposal still awaits testing.

Towton is the only later medieval battlefield in the UK where mass graves have been located using modern archaeological methods. The first to be examined lay in Towton village, close to the site of the medieval battle chapel and in the general area of the rout. This is 1.6km to the north of the initial engagement. The mass graves at the heart of the battlefield were located as a result of chance discovery of human remains on the surface. The presence of the graves was confirmed by closely targeted geophysics and then by test pitting. However, these graves are not intact, because some decades after the battle the remains were moved to the parish churchyard in Saxton. The transfer to Saxton rather than to the battle chapel in Towton may have been because these mass graves lay not in the chapelry of Towton but in Saxton itself. Hence, the mass grave and other burials found around Towton chapel may contain only those killed in that chapelry.

Almost the whole battlefield has been subject to metal detecting by Simon Richardson, at first independently but since 1997 as part of the Towton Battlefield Project. Until 2010 the detecting was non-systematic, and prior to 1997 the finds were plotted onto a rough sketch map of a small number of fields in the south of the battlefield. When the archaeological project began, in collaboration with Sutherland, the sketch recording was continued on a 1:2500 Ordnance Survey map with a numbering system which linked each separately bagged artefact to its location. Since 2002 locational recording has been carried out with a navigation grade GPS, which normally gives an accuracy of between 5m and 10m. It is understood that in 2010 the first systematic, transect-based survey work was begun at Towton (S Richardson pers comm).

Many other finds have been removed from the battlefield apparently without comparable recording. Two collectors are known to have carried out metal detecting on parts of the battlefield with landowner permission, as they have reported at least some material to the Portable Antiquities Scheme.[8] However, the PAS reports do not include a record of where they have detected or how intensively, and nor is there a comprehensive catalogue of what they have found and where. Other collectors are known to have metal detected without permission, but little or nothing is known about who they are or what they recovered. The degree to which the actions of collectors have distorted the distribution pattern or the overall character of the known assemblage is thus unclear.

This registered, Richardson's work has revealed a dense scatter of copper alloy artefacts which seems to indicate several stages of the battle, including the initial clash between the two armies and the Lancastrian rout, in which the troops moved northward past Towton village. In addition, a more restricted scatter of arrowheads has been recovered which may represent part of the great arrowstorm loosed into the Lancastrian lines by the Yorkist archers. No comparable scatter has been demonstrated on the southern, Yorkist, side of Towton Dale.

This is the only evidence on such a scale so far recovered anywhere in Europe. However, because systematic survey methods were not employed, there are apparently no data – at least no published data – on survey extent or intensity. As a result it is not yet possible to calculate recovery rates, in terms of man hours per artefact, for copper alloy artefacts or ferrous arrowheads in different parts of the battlefield. Without such data it is impossible to make direct comparisons with surveys on other battlefields. Nor has any comprehensive catalogue or mapping been made available of all the artefacts recovered by Richardson. Published distribution plans are incomplete and, apart from arrowheads, lack any breakdown into component types or classes of artefact. Only when such analysis is completed will it be possible to assess what the artefact assemblage actually represents in terms of the type and status of troops engaged in different parts of the battlefield.

Comparison with Bosworth and limited investigation on several other sites suggests that the Towton assemblage may be atypical in its density and character. This might, at least in part, result from the numbers of high-status individuals who were killed at Towton, a view supported by Richardson's belief that the majority of the copper alloy artefacts had relatively high-status owners (S Richardson pers comm). Equally, the density of finds may confirm the impression given by the primary sources of the exceptional intensity of the action (Boardman 2000; National Army Museum 1995q). In some ways, therefore, Towton may be an analogue to the Roman-period battlefield of Kalkriese in Germany (Chapter 3). There, the immensity of destruction led to an even larger and more unusual assemblage being deposited, with exceptional preservation conditions in one area allowing the recovery of a remarkable sequence of material. As we will see, comparable conditions may also have operated at Towton.

In an attempt to grasp the basic structure of the Towton scatter we have integrated data from two published plans and placed the combined evidence in a terrain context (Fig 5.6). One showed an unspecified proportion of the copper alloy artefacts that had been catalogued and mapped up to 2005; the other recorded all ferrous arrowheads recovered up to 2006 (Sutherland 2005; Sutherland and Richardson 2007).[9] While a clear pattern is revealed, the absence of a survey boundary makes it impossible to say whether the blank areas represent absence of artefacts or simply absence of survey. Similarly, a lack of data on survey intensity makes it impossible to determine the degree to which concentrations of artefacts reflect the original variations in density in the ground, as opposed to the intensity of survey.

Concentration on areas which produce large numbers of artefacts at the expense of those producing fewer appears to be a typical feature of non-systematic metal detecting. This may explain why unstructured collecting at Naseby (1645) produced little in the way of pistol or carbine calibre bullets from the cavalry action on the wings, whereas systematic archaeological survey at Edgehill (1642) produced clear but low-density evidence for such action (see Figs 8.13 and 7.21). The way in which increased intensity of survey in areas of higher density of artefacts can exaggerate that density can be demonstrated using the Edgehill data. The distribution from consistent survey on 10m transects (see Fig 7.14) shows a concentration in the core area of infantry action. That concentration is much over-emphasised when data from resurvey, at higher intensity and carried out only in the core area of infantry action, are added (see Fig 7.16). Given that distributional significance derives from relative densities of material it is inevitable that such biased data sets will compromise analysis.

It is likely that such reinforcement of the density in core areas relative to the periphery has occurred at Towton, so confusing the true patterning. A further problem is the lack of information to show how the battle archaeology has been differentiated from the background noise – that is, non-battle-related artefacts of medieval date. For example, one might have expected a halo of a higher density of background noise around the two medieval settlements, but, while traces of such a pattern are provided by the Bosworth survey, no such pattern is present in the Towton data. It is not clear whether these areas were not searched, or were searched at a lower intensity, or whether the background noise has somehow been filtered out of the data. These limitations reduce the confidence level of interpretations based on the published finds distribution. Thus, for example, the absence of material on the eastern part of the battlefield may be providing important information about the character of the deployments and the distribution of the action in the battle. However, it is not certain whether this difference does not simply reflect a lower intensity of metal detecting in this area.

With these caveats understood, the pattern so far published for Towton can be analysed in terms of the battle. It is improbable that the two armies would have deployed leaving their flanks unprotected, especially with a major road present on the east side of the field, for this would have left them vulnerable to an outflanking move. If the gap in the scatter on the east side of the battlefield is genuine then the most likely explanation is that this is where cavalry were deployed. A cavalry action on one flank appears in one of the later primary sources, in which Lancastrian forces are described as driving off and pursuing the Yorkist cavalry southward. Such a quick clash, if it actually occurred, is unlikely to have deposited a significant number of finds compared to the intense and sustained infantry engagement further west. Such a gap, or a very low density of finds compared to infantry action, may prove to be a normal signature for the battle archaeology of cavalry in all periods, for it has also been noted in the 17th-century battles at Naseby and Edgehill. In contrast, on the western side of Towton battlefield there is no such gap until the steep scarp down to the Cock Beck. This dramatic topographical feature would have provided the Lancastrians, who deployed first, with protection for their right flank, while to their fore the rapidly increasing depth of Towton Dale, as it runs westward from the Towton–Saxton road, would surely have precluded cavalry action on this wing.

Given the very low density of copper alloy artefacts on some other battlefields of the period, one might look to ferrous arrowheads to provide the key signature of medieval action on such sites. Throughout this period the iron arrowhead was certainly the dominant projectile. However, there are questions regarding the nature of such evidence. As we have said, arrows were used in their thousands in major battles, but it was practicable for them to be recovered for reuse both during and immediately after the action, unless they had been broken by action moving across the area. Thus at Towton the Yorkist archers are said to have stepped forward and retrieved many of the Lancastrian arrows which had fallen short because, unlike the Yorkist arrows, they were fired into the wind.[10] The pattern of artefact survival on a battlefield, therefore, may not fully reflect the true pattern of use. Another factor to be taken into account is the ground conditions at the time. Towton was fought partly during a snowstorm and the ground may have become very churned up in the intense infantry action, leading to many of the smaller artefacts being trodden into the topsoil. This is less likely to have occurred in some other battles, such as Bosworth, that were fought in summer or on pasture.

Far greater is the problem of post-depositional decay owing to the material from which the arrowheads were made – iron. In most soil conditions ferrous artefacts are very vulnerable to decay through oxidisation, which in turn makes them highly vulnerable to mechanical damage, especially where the ground is under sustained cultivation. These post-depositional factors need to be assessed so that their potential to distort recovery patterns, compared to the original pattern of deposition, can be understood. Towton shows that iron arrowheads can survive, but it appears that exceptional conditions of preservation in certain areas are determining the distribution pattern. While the copper alloy artefacts at Towton are spread over 200 hectares, the ferrous arrowheads extend across just 5 hectares. Indeed, it is yet more focused, with 111 arrowheads coming from just one hectare in the area of the proven mass grave. Soil analysis shows that Towton has a neutral soil pH, which would be conducive to the survival of ferrous artefacts.[11] This is not exceptional, however, being comparable to that seen at Bosworth (see below). Rather, it is the degree of aeration and mechanical damage caused by cultivation that is likely to have contributed to the destruction of arrowheads. Land-use records show that in the 1840s the land at the eastern end of the arrowhead scatter at Towton, like most of the other mapped land in Saxton, was under arable; by the 1930s almost all the battlefield was arable.[12] Thus, although the chemistry of the Towton soils is conducive to preservation, land use is likely to have created more aggressive conditions in the topsoil, which may have been further exacerbated by the apparently relatively free-draining nature of the soil.

It seems, therefore, that additional factors must be sought to explain why arrowheads have been recovered from just one small part of the battlefield. In this context it is probably significant that the arrowhead distribution lies on sloping ground, is closely related to two particular furlongs, and is in an area of apparent colluviation. The highly mobile nature of the soils at Towton was noted during the open-field survey and is also clearly seen in the substantial lynchet on the north–south headland immediately to the east of the mass grave location, which represents soil movement along the strips of the furlong to the east. Another similar scarp runs along the bottom of this section of Towton Dale (see Fig 8.6). Such colluvial deposits may have protected some arrowheads from the effects of cultivation. The geophysical survey shows remnant furrows from the open-field strips (Sutherland and Richardson 2007, 163) which may have formed yet another reservoir for arrowhead preservation beneath the topsoil, while the cut features of the mass graves and the remnants of the burial mounds may also have performed this function. If this is correct then the arrowhead distribution may, in part, reflect the distribution of unusual preservation conditions below the topsoil rather than the distribution of action. In turn, the recovery of these artefacts may have become possible because in recent years they have been incorporated into the topsoil by episodes of deep cultivation. For example, Sutherland reports at least one episode of deep ploughing, while the more regular use of the land to grow potatoes may also penetrate the deeper deposits. The extent of the arrowhead scatter may therefore also be partly determined by where the cultivation is and is not reaching any such reservoirs. If so, then the absence of arrowheads on the south side of Towton Dale might be attributable to the depth of colluviation here, rather than a lack of reservoirs to preserve arrowheads.

The complete absence of arrowheads elsewhere on the battlefield, despite a wide search by Richardson, reinforces the hypothesis of special conditions of preservation. As a result, the interpretation of the arrowhead scatter is fraught with difficulties in a way that bullet scatters are usually not. Those so far recovered might have been loosed by Yorkist archers from the southern crest of Towton Dale – about 300m away – and have lain preserved close to where they fell. Or, in the most extreme alternative interpretation, the arrowheads may derive largely from bodies collected together for burial from a wider zone; if so, the scatter may have little relationship to the actual area where the Yorkist arrows landed.

Once incorporated into the topsoil by cultivation, Richardson believes, the arrowheads have a very short life. This is based principally on the observation that where they are found at the surface later in the year, after months of frequent wetting and drying, they are typically in far worse condition than when recovered from below the surface or earlier in the year. All the arrowheads, but especially those more heavily decayed, are so heavily oxidised that very little solid metal remains. As a result they cannot be detected at a depth greater than *c* 150–180mm, with the deepest recovery being of the very largest and most intact arrowheads (S Richardson pers comm). The particular method of manufacture of the arrowheads, with braising used to fix tip and socket together, appears to be a major factor in their survival (Starley and Cubitt 2006), as without the braising they probably would decay even more quickly. If arrows from other periods were not manufactured in this way, does this mean that they are even less likely to survive?

When considering the potential for the recovery of non-projectile battle-related ferrous finds on other battlefields it is important to note that at Towton they comprise just five spurs and two spur rowels, all of which are in good condition because they are tinned (S Richardson pers comm). Where ferrous artefacts are preserved on other battlefields they too may be highly vulnerable to the effects of modern cultivation and possibly also chemical application, which can accelerate decay even in deeper reservoirs of finds. The need to establish where other such scatters may exist is thus urgent, for they may require positive management if they are to survive. However, any such work is likely to be effective only when we better understand the Towton assemblage, the factors that have led to the survival of the scatter, and the effectiveness of detecting methods in recovering the assemblage.

The final aspect of the Towton evidence is that relating to gunpowder weapons. As noted above, Towton has produced two small calibre lead and lead composite round shot, as well as fragments from two different exploded barrels of small bronze guns. Analysis using X-ray fluorescence (XRF) has shown that both barrels had fired lead or lead composite round shot (Sutherland 2011). It is improbable that only two guns were present on the battlefield and that both exploded. Indeed, the firing evidence on at least one of the round shot is comparable to that on fired rounds from other sites, suggesting it was deposited from normal firing, not when a gun exploded. Thus, one would have expected far more round shot to have been recovered during the Towton survey.[13]

The reasons for the paucity of round shot from Towton need to be considered, as it may indicate an aspect of battle archaeology that hitherto has been overlooked. The barrel fragments and round shot all come from the Lancastrian side of Towton Dale. The absence of other round shot might be because most of the rest of the rounds fired against Yorkist troops, which were deployed on the ridge on the south side of the Dale, overshot well beyond the area that was intensively searched. Alternatively, most rounds may have been of stone or even of wrought iron rather than lead, although the XRF evidence suggests lead is more likely, at least for smaller calibre rounds. Recovery of stone round shot, if feasible, would require intensive fieldwalking survey, which apparently has not yet been undertaken. Even iron rounds are unlikely to have been recovered because the vast majority of detecting across the battlefield, except where the arrowheads have been recovered, appears to have been in non-ferrous mode. A further possibility is that the de-stoning of the soil and potato riddling may have removed, displaced, or deeply buried large objects such as round shot. While Sutherland considers this unlikely, there is anecdotal evidence for this effect at Edgehill from the 1960s.[14]

Bosworth

The battle of Bosworth, fought on 21 August 1485, provides a contrast to Towton in a number of respects. Bosworth was originally known as the battle of Redemore. After the traditional location on Ambion Hill was questioned in 1985 a series of alternative sites was suggested for the battlefield (Foard and Curry in prep). These ranged over nearly 10km^2 of west Leicestershire with a further site, suggested by Michael Jones, some 6km away near Atherstone (Fig 5.7).

Between 2005 and 2010 a research project funded principally by the Heritage Lottery Fund as part of the rejuvenation of the Bosworth battlefield visitor centre applied the full range of techniques of battlefield archaeology in a search for the battlefield. This work built upon the important work already undertaken since 1985 (Foss 1998). The primary sources for the battle were analysed and the historic terrain was reconstructed for the five townships which encompassed the main alternative sites. Although re-analysis of the battle accounts within the context of the historic terrain failed to resolve the problem, it did enable most of the alternative sites to be dismissed as improbable, enabling survey for battle archaeology to be more closely focused.

Historical research demonstrated that in 1530 Redemore lay within or on the boundary of Dadlington township, confirming a link first identified by Peter Foss from a 13th-century document.[15] The other key evidence, first noted by Colin Richmond, was that the chantry established under Henry VIII in memory of the dead of Bosworth, to which the bones were to be moved, also lay in Dadlington. This in turn implied that at least some of the mass graves had been in that chapelry (Richmond 1985). Apart from the battle's names, the reference to a marsh in Polydore Virgil's account of the battle was the key topographical detail by which the battlefield might be located. He recorded that

> there was a marsh betwixt both hosts, which Henry of purpose left on the right hand, that it might serve his men instead of a fortress, by the doing thereof also he left the sun upon his back.

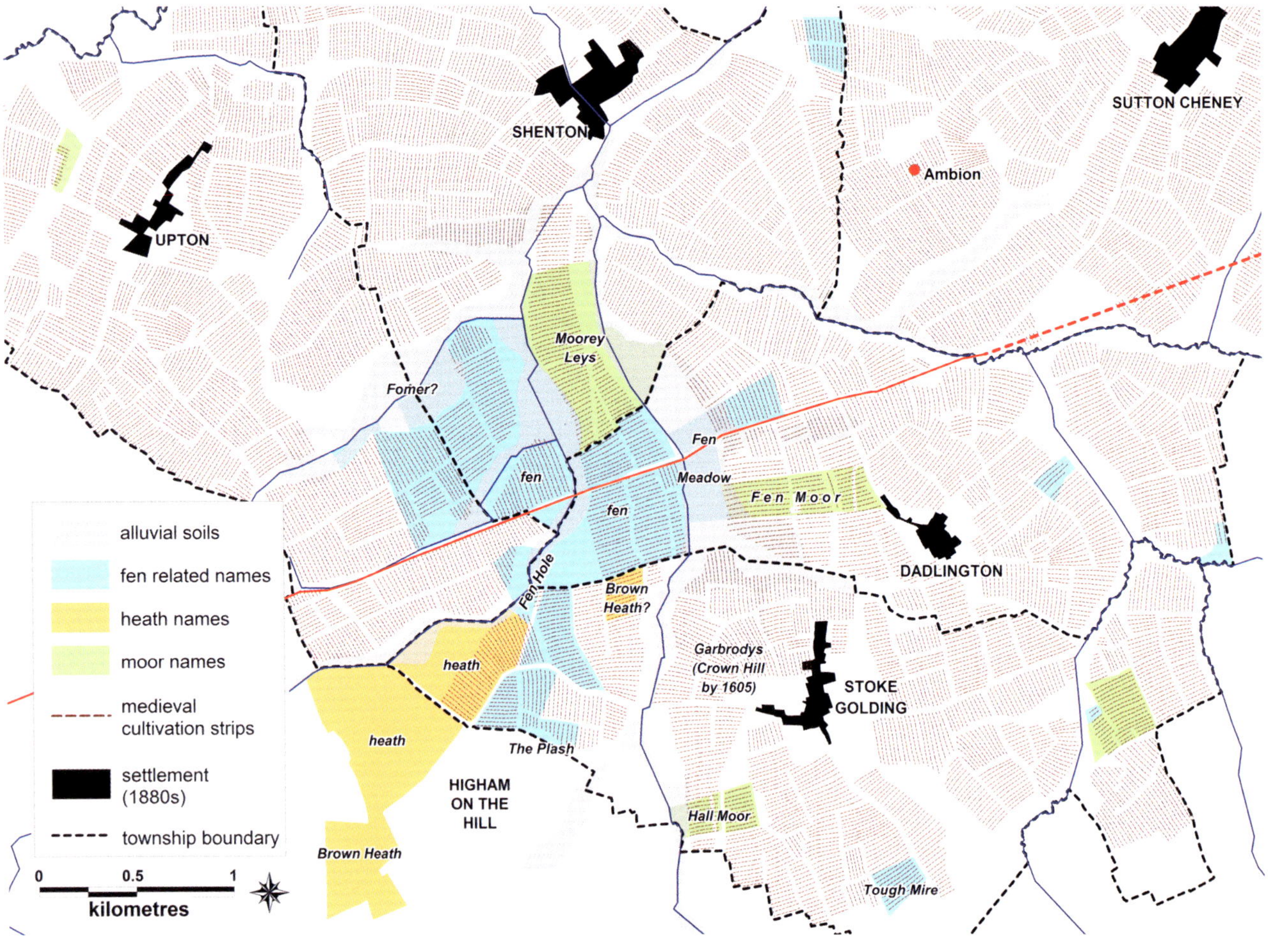

Fig 5.7 Map showing elements of the historic terrain of Bosworth (1485). The area covered encompasses the true site and three of the alternative sites previously suggested for the battle. The battle archaeology now indicates that the main action took place largely in the southern periphery of Upton township. The area lies to the west of Fen Hole and straddles the Roman road from Leicester to Atherstone (Foard and Curry in prep)

In the absence of a specific location for Redemore from the documents, it was necessary to fall back on the other key topographical detail and to establish where a marsh was and was not likely to have existed in Dadlington and its environs. Fortunately, wetland landscapes were not common in medieval Leicestershire and so the topographical circumstances that gave rise to them should have been relatively easy to identify. The post-medieval enclosed landscape, along with its field names, and the medieval open-field systems were thus mapped using a combination of documentary research and archaeological fieldwork, the latter showing the land that had and had not been covered by open-field furlongs. It was in the low-lying uncultivated ground, most of it formerly meadow, that marsh was to be expected. A soil survey was also undertaken to identify which soils had developed in a waterlogged context. These two data sets proved closely complementary, and showed that Ambion Hill, the accepted location of the battle since at least the 1770s, was covered by furlongs, while the narrow valley floors of the adjacent streams, where no furlongs existed, had no evidence for fen. There were, however, substantial areas further to the south-west where there was real potential for marsh.

Analysis of the field names showed a concentration of place-name evidence for former fen in one part of this latter zone. This lay on the western periphery of Dadlington and in adjoining areas of adjacent townships. Having identified this area it was possible to undertake a programme of intensive augering to locate peat deposits. Two were eventually found, both of which were linked to fen names. That in Fen Meadow was some 90m across, but radiocarbon dating showed that peat accumulation here had apparently halted in the 7th or 8th century AD. The other area, at Fen Hole, we had thought too small to have been tactically significant, but radiocarbon dating evidence did suggest that it was still open in the medieval period, making it the only likely candidate for Virgil's marsh.

In parallel with this terrain research, a systematic metal-detecting survey was undertaken in 2005–10. The strategy was initially based on interpretation of the Towton evidence, but applied the systematic survey methodology developed in the Edgehill survey, as discussed above (see Fig 2.13). The first stage involved detecting in non-ferrous mode on 10m transects, seeking a concentration of copper alloy artefacts comparable to that at Towton. More intensive work was not practicable because of the sheer extent of the area to be examined. However, given the density of the non-ferrous scatter seen at Towton, it was believed that this intensity of survey was adequate to locate the battlefield, and that, once located, it could then be investigated through more intensive resurvey. Previous non-systematic metal detecting around Ambion Hill and further north-east had covered several square kilometres. It had recovered a few finds, but there was no clear evidence of a concentration of battle-related material. Following an initial assessment of the combined evidence, fieldwork in the new project accordingly focused on the area suggested in Foss's analysis: in the western part of Dadlington and southern part of Shenton townships.

The first three and a half years of survey recovered only a small grouping of artefacts of later medieval date, though this did include several exceptional finds, most notably a late 15th-century silver heraldic badge in the shape of a bird. These came from an area called Green Hill in Dadlington and Shenton, in close proximity to the area where Foss had placed the battlefield. Unfortunately, intensive resurvey of sample areas here failed to produce a density of finds in any way comparable to that at Towton. By the end of 2008, after covering nearly $6km^2$, the detecting survey appeared to have failed. Evidence for the battle was found only in the very last stage of the survey, when its focus was shifted to fill a gap at the western periphery of the survey area, partly in response to the radiocarbon dating for the Fen Hole peat deposit. After the first find (a single lead round shot of 30mm diameter), survey on 2.5m spaced transects was initiated. Between March 2009 and December 2010 this intensive survey covered over $1km^2$ and recovered an extensive low-density scatter of lead and lead composite round shot (Fig 5.8). These projectiles, discussed briefly in Chapter 4, vary in calibre from 21mm to 97mm and all show evidence of firing; they can only relate to the use of artillery during the 1485 battle.

Surprisingly, the round shot scatter was accompanied by only a few other contemporary artefacts (Figs 5.9 and 5.10), although these do include several finds which demonstrate an association with the battle. Of particular note are a fragment from the guard of a high-status late 15th-century sword and, most remarkably, a silver gilt heraldic badge of a boar (Fig 5.11). This was Richard III's own symbol and, as it was silver gilt, it is likely to have been worn by a knight in the king's own retinue who may have ridden with the king in his last fateful charge. The badge was found adjacent to the former marsh at Fen Hole and it may not be too fanciful to consider a link with Molinet's contemporary account of

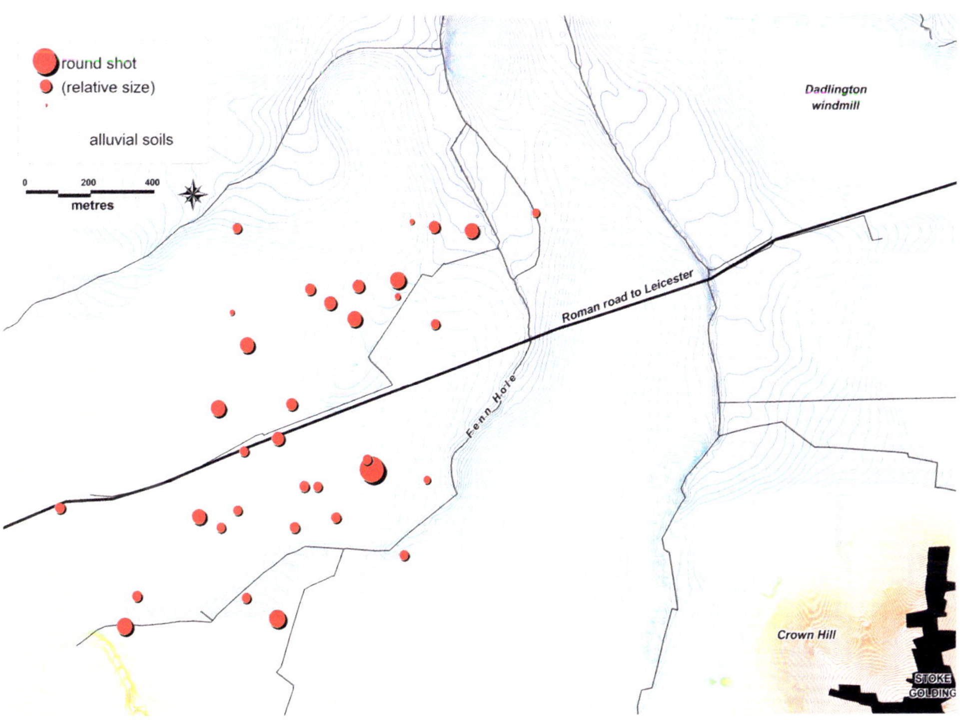

Fig 5.8 Map of Bosworth (1485) showing the distribution of round shot recovered before December 2010. Contours are shown at 0.1m intervals, to emphasise the fine detail of the relief and to show how Crown Hill dominates the area (Foard and Curry in prep) (dtm copyright Intermap Technologies Inc. 2007, provided by Getmapping PLC)

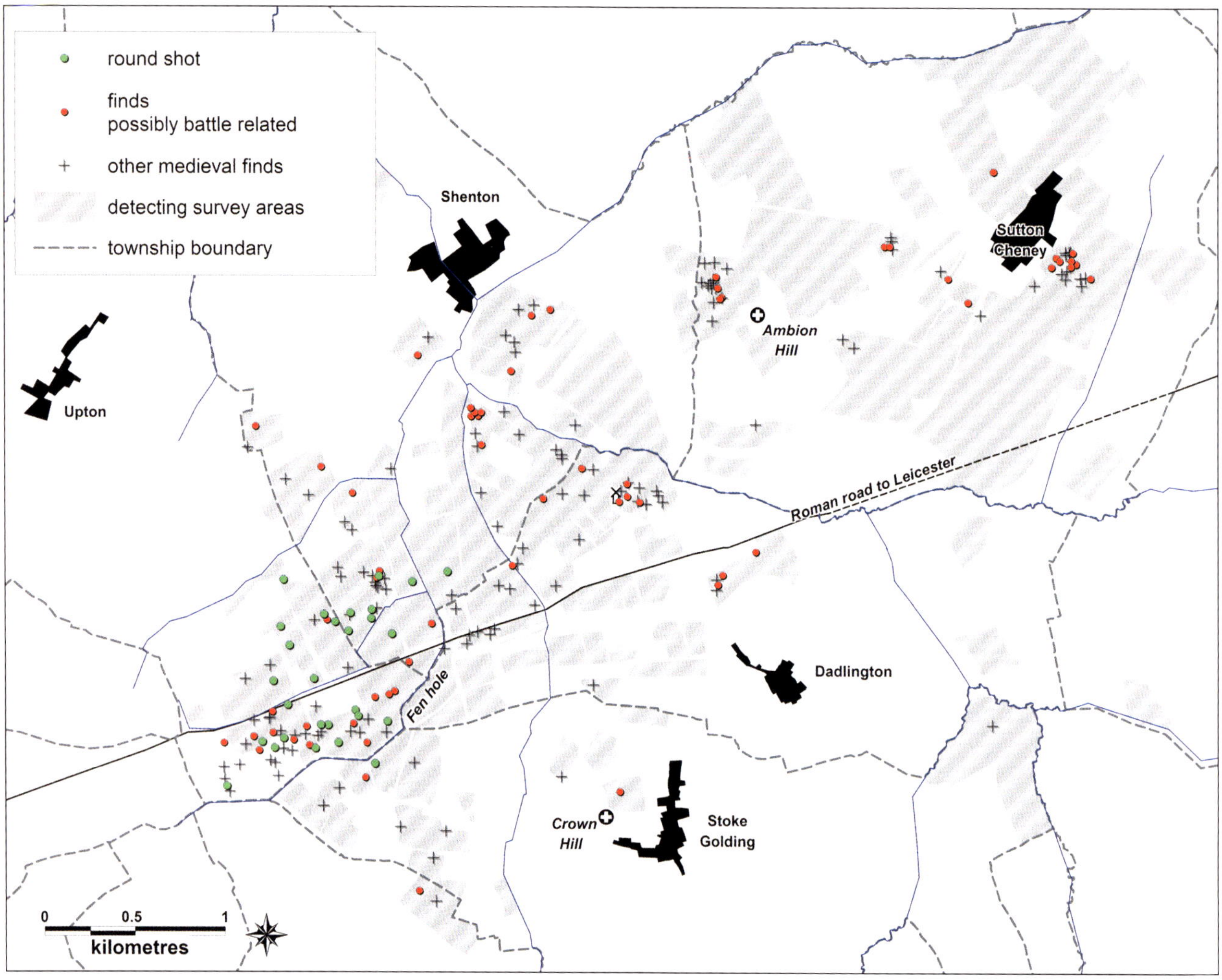

Fig 5.9 Map of Bosworth (1485) showing the extent of the scatter of medieval finds recorded up to January 2010 in relation to the area surveyed at varied intensities

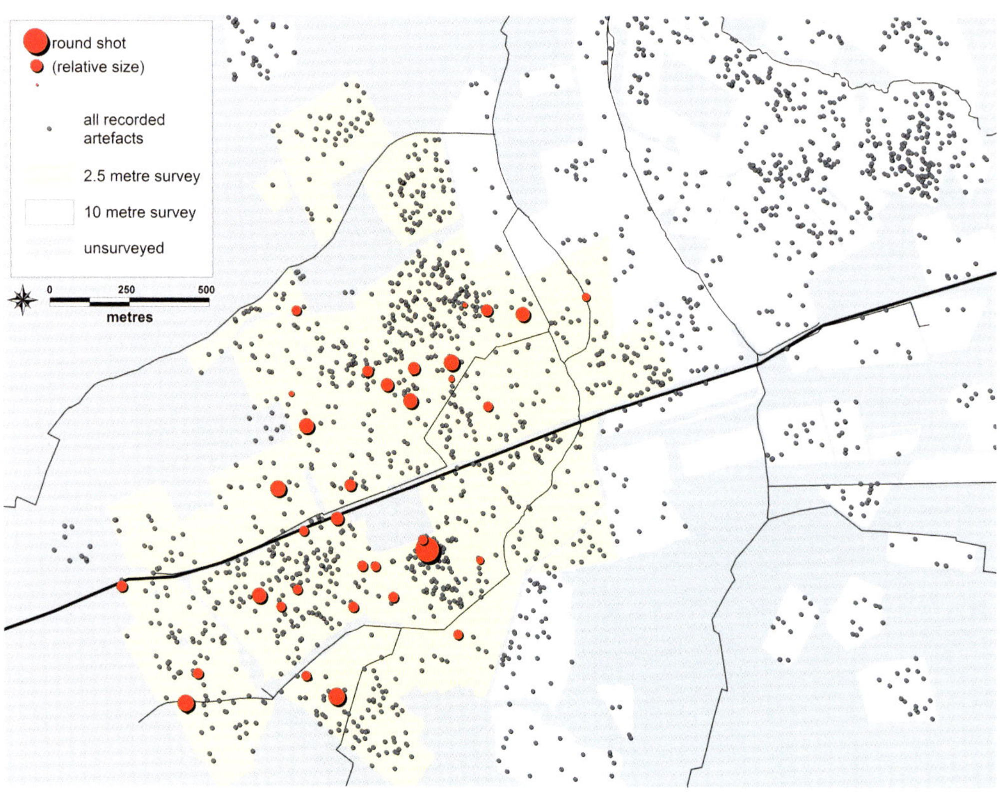

Fig 5.10 Map of Bosworth (1485) showing round shot with all other artefacts of all dates recovered before December 2010. Also indicated are the areas surveyed using 2.5m spaced transects, as opposed to those covered principally using 10m spaced transects

Fig 5.11 The silver gilt badge of a boar – Richard III's personal device – found close to Fen Hole on Bosworth battlefield. Length: 27mm

the battle, which reports that Richard had been killed when his horse became stuck in a mire.

When the types, the calibres, and the character of the firing evidence displayed by the round shot are taken into account some degree of patterning appears to exist in the scatter, which may be tentatively interpretated as faint linear groupings extending from north-west to south-east with distinct gaps between them. The more southerly of the central lines broadly correlates with the low-density non-projectile artefact scatter. This may reflect the main concentration of hand-to-hand action, with the outer lines of round shot possibly representing overshots. However, there are many uncertainties, not least that the scatter is in reality more complex than this, and reflects an overlapping set of firings from more than one pairing of battle arrays. Ideally, intensive systematic resurvey should be undertaken in an attempt to clarify the patterning by increasing the sample size.

In the absence of the artillery rounds, boar badge, and sword guard fragment the other finds would not have been sufficient to locate the battlefield securely. But it can also be said, with some confidence, that the 10m transect detecting survey would have identified a dense Towton-like scatter and a significant round shot scatter had either extended across the extensive area already surveyed further to the east. There is one other important caveat in interpreting the evidence: further 2.5m survey is needed to the north-west, west, and south-west to define the full extent of the round shot scatter and to ensure that no unexpected evidence lies here, beyond the existing survey boundaries.

The absence of any dense scatter of copper alloy artefacts seems to be repeated at Flodden, fought just 28 years after Bosworth. Here, in the heart of the battlefield, 20 man days of systematic detecting undertaken on 10m transects in 2007 recovered two lead composite round shot but no other artefacts that were certainly battle-related. At Shrewsbury (1403), where the battlefield church provides a clear focus, ten man days were undertaken without recovering any definitely battle-related finds. The results from this work, undertaken to provide comparative data for the Bosworth survey, mirror similar results from earlier detecting at both sites by Glasgow University (Pollard and Oliver 2002; 2003).

The search for arrowheads is more problematic. Detecting in all-metal mode was undertaken on small sample areas at Bosworth in 2010 but proved extremely time-consuming because of the vast quantity of ferrous junk that lies in most fields. Richardson reports that at Towton, in the core area of the arrowhead scatter, at least 40 pieces of modern rubbish are collected for every one arrowhead. Such survey is clearly only practicable over a small area. While further carefully targeted all-metal sampling is certainly appropriate at Bosworth as part of a coherent research programme working on the core area, the expenditure of vast amounts of time on wide-scale work, even if the soil pH on part of Bosworth's battlefield is comparable to that at Towton, would not be an efficient use of resources when the exact reasons for the survival of arrowheads at Towton are not understood.

Notes

1. The following is drawn from the discussion at http://www.battlefieldstrust.com/resource-centre/warsoftheroses/battleview.asp?BattleFieldId=13 Accessed 10 April 2011.
2. Roads from Norden's 1598 map of Hertfordshire and Ogilby 1675. Approximate extent of woodland as opposed to open ground in Enfield Chase, and of enclosures, is from Rocque's map of Middlesex of 1757 and from a map for the proposed Inclosure of Enfield Chase in 1656, at Hertfordshire Record Office.
3. The apparent absence of small arms rounds from previous collecting on the suspected site should not be taken as denoting their absence. This is because the significance of smaller calibre bullets is unlikely to have been recognised and so they may not have been reported. A group of poorly located bullets has been reported on Hadley Common, but this is well

over a kilometre to the south-east of the suspected site and they are likely to be of a later date (Foard 2006).

4. Major road from Ogilby 1675, plate 7. Saxton with Scarthingwell enclosure award and map, West Yorkshire Archives Service (Wakefield) QE 2/6. Tithe map and award, 1848, Borthwick TA163A. Ordnance Survey first edition six-inch mapping 1849. Artefact scatter from Sutherland 2005 and Sutherland and Richardson 2007.
5. Online search using A2A, British Library and National Archives indexes. Glebe terriers for Saxton in the Borthwick are an augmentation of Saxton with land in Collingham. Further records identified but not consulted include Court Rolls for Saxton 1463–65 and 1480, West Yorkshire Archives Service, Leeds: Gascoigne GC/M4/1.
6. Relief and water from Ordnance Survey Mastermap. Alluvium from British Geological Survey 1:50,000 scale mapping. Roads from Jeffery's map of Yorkshire, 1771. Battle archaeology as on previous map.
7. Saxton with Scarthingwell, tithe map, 1848, Borthwick TA163A; enclosure award and map, 1849, West Yorkshire Archives Service (Wakefield) QE 2/6; Ordnance Survey first edition six-inch map.
8. Information from the PAS officer for West Yorkshire.
9. There are no data on the distribution recovered since 2006 but Sutherland reports that the number of arrowheads has almost doubled from the 178 on the published plan.
10. The near-contemporary account by the Burgundian Jean de Waurin is controversial, but is corroborated by the 15th-century 'Brief Latin Chronicle'. National Army Museum 1995q.
11. Information from Rob Janaway. Further discussion of the taphonomic and other issues is given in Foard 2010b.
12. Saxton with Scarthingwell tithe map, 1848, Borthwick TA163A; Land Use Classification 1931–35.
13. Unpublished report by G Foard for the Towton Battlefield Project, 2009.
14. Information from Robert Leedham who was present during Peter Young's work at Edgehill in the 1960s.
15. Dadlington Court Roll: 30 May 1530, LRO 2D71/I/56. Foss 1998.

6

THE 16TH CENTURY

During the 16th century English armies took up the use of the pike in place of the much shorter bill, and the handgun in place of the bow. This transition is an important theme in the evolution of warfare, not least because the trajectory of technological and tactical change in English armies was so different from that seen in the armies of other major European powers. England is often viewed (unfairly, some would argue) as a backwater in which, through a high degree of inertia, the bow was retained against the international trend (Raymond 2007). Such a major divergence emphasises the importance of setting the battle archaeology from English sites within a European context.

There are, however, just six battlefields in England from this period through which these important changes can be studied. Furthermore, with the exception of Flodden, all these battles were fought in the 1540s, as were the ten 16th-century skirmishes recorded on the Database, most of which were related to regional rebellions rather than international warfare (Fig 6.1). This raises further questions. Were there significant differences between the composition and equipment of rebel forces and the armies raised to suppress them compared with those of the more permanent forces defending the frontier or the armies raised to fight major international actions?

Evidently, for data to complement the small sample of English sites we must look to battles fought by English armies abroad. Much of the Anglo-Scottish warfare in the 1540s, known as the 'Rough Wooing', took place in Scotland rather than England (Merriman 2000). While this phase includes only one major battle – that in 1547 at Pinkie in East Lothian – there were also several border raids that ended in battles, such as that in 1545 at Ancrum Moor in the Scottish Borders. In both these battles handguns were used in significant numbers by English forces (Foard 2007b; 2007c). Further evidence can be sought in Ireland, where

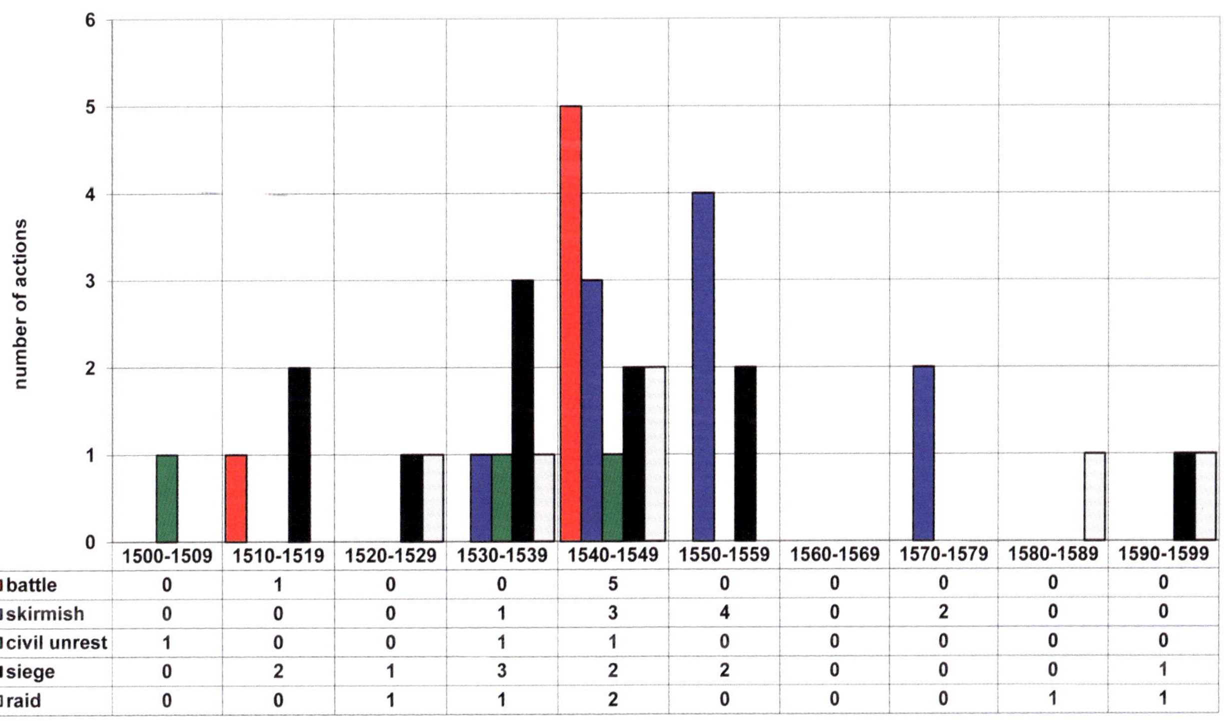

	1500-1509	1510-1519	1520-1529	1530-1539	1540-1549	1550-1559	1560-1569	1570-1579	1580-1589	1590-1599
battle	0	1	0	0	5	0	0	0	0	0
skirmish	0	0	0	1	3	4	0	2	0	0
civil unrest	1	0	0	1	1	0	0	0	0	0
siege	0	2	1	3	2	2	0	0	0	1
raid	0	0	1	1	2	0	0	0	1	1

Fig 6.1 Graph of all actions in 16th-century England. Sieges, skirmishes and especially raids are under-represented, probably by a wide margin

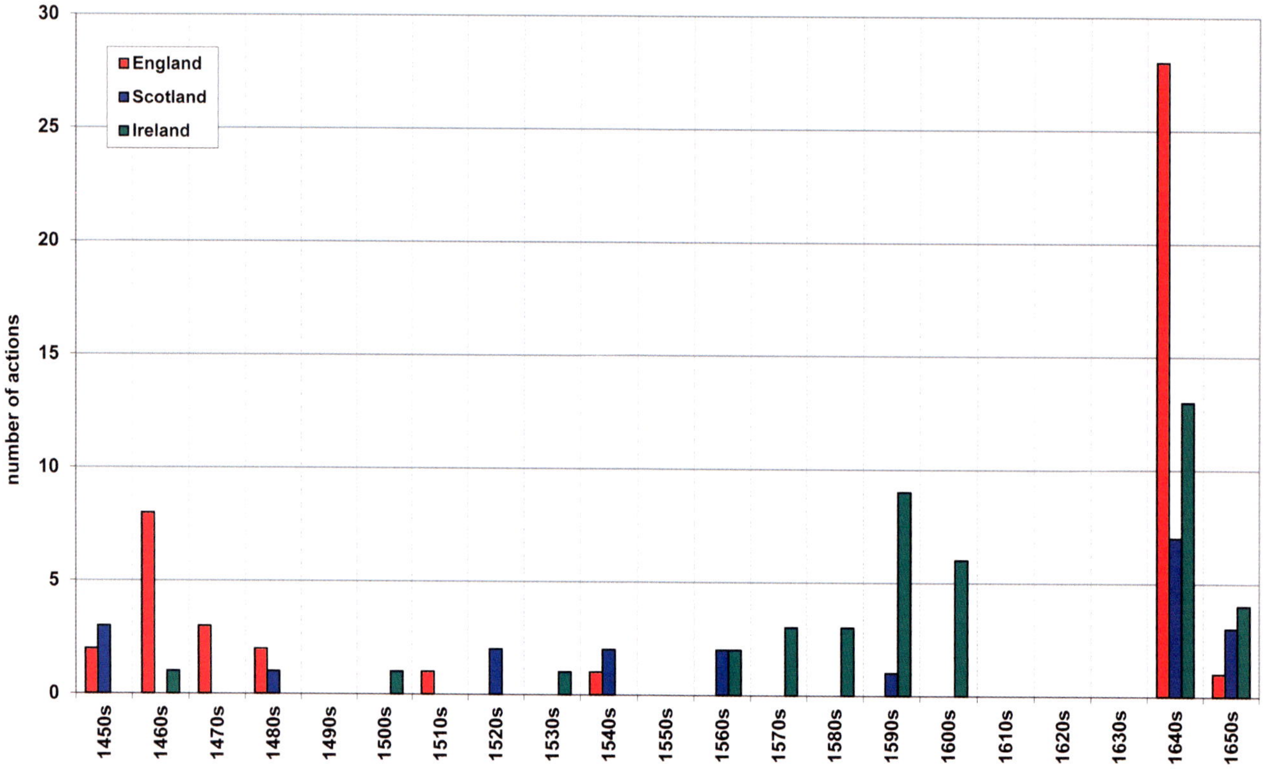

Fig 6.2 Graph of battles fought in England, Scotland and the Republic of Ireland, by decade, between 1450 and 1660

English armies were engaged in a series of battles which fill much of the gap in England between 1550 and 1640 (Fig 6.2).

As battles were rare in 16th-century England their sites have a particular importance to the study of battlefield archaeology and may justify more intensive study than the political or strategic importance of the action might imply. Investigation of these sites may be expected to reveal something of the calibres and types of gun in use and the scale and tactical context of their use. However, several problems need to be overcome before these aims can be achieved. Firstly, because handgunners made up a smaller proportion of the troops at this time bullets will be present in far smaller numbers than the tens of thousands characteristic of major battles of the 17th century. In addition, as discussed in Chapter 4, battle-related bullets may be difficult to resolve from the cumulative 'background noise' of very low-density bullet scatters left by sporting activity of the 16th to the 19th centuries (Figs 4.8–4.10). The introduction of cast-iron round shot, first alongside and finally largely replacing lead round shot, will also cause difficulties for the survey of the battlefields, because time-consuming all-metal survey will be required where long-range artillery fire is to be investigated. The degree to which hailshot for artillery was in the form of pebbles or iron dice as opposed to lead bullets may be a further challenge.

Despite such limitations, small arms bullets were fired in much greater number than artillery round shot and are less likely to have been recovered at the time than the much larger and more visible artillery rounds. In addition, they have a far shorter effective and final range. As we have seen, 60mm lead round shot experimentally fired point blank had a final range, after bounce and roll, of up to 1.2km. In contrast, small arms bullets of 12 bore, representing the more powerful 17th-century musket, have a final range of only about 300m when fired point blank (Allsop in Foard and Curry in prep; Miller 2010). Thus, bullet scatters may be expected to have a much closer association with the positions of both the troops who fired them and the enemy at whom they were fired. The denser scatter of artefacts, compared with that produced by round shot, is also likely to make for more robust distributional patterning.

As we have said, English armies continued to use the warbow side by side with gunpowder weapons through much of the 16th century. For this reason, 16th-century battlefields in England may offer unusual potential for the archaeological investigation of the bow in battle. If bullet and round shot distribution patterns can be recovered on battlefields where small arms were used in significant numbers and in known relationship to bows then the bullet distribution may

Fig 6.3 Part of a contemporary drawing depicting stages in the battle of Pinkie (East Lothian, Scotland), fought in 1547. Infantry and cavalry are shown deployed in very deep, square battle formations as they manoeuvred immediately before they engaged. The English are to the left and the Scots to the right. Close examination reveals that the three English infantry formations, or 'battles', each have a sleeve of archers on the far side and a sleeve of troops carrying hackbuts on the near side. This is exactly as specified in Audley's mid-16th-century military manual. The formations differ dramatically from those seen a century later at Naseby, when the frontages of battle formations were far wider (see Fig 1.3) (Ms. Eng. Misc. c. 13 (r). Reproduced by permission of The Bodleian Libraries, University of Oxford)

assist in targeting the search for arrowheads, as well as in interpreting the significance of arrowhead distributions on earlier battlefields, because the arrowhead and bullet scatters should correlate with the tactical formations used. At Pinkie, for example, a sleeve of handgunners was placed on one flank of the pike formation of each 'battle' and a sleeve of archers on the other (Fig 6.3). Similarly, the relationship of the round shot pattern to the bullet scatter may provide important information as to how, on earlier battlefields such as Bosworth, such round shot scatters should be interpreted in relation to deployment and action.

The approach generally adopted in the present study is that, at least in the short term, the investigation of skirmishes and raids should not be a priority. This is because much more information can be retrieved and more priorities addressed through the investigation of battles and, to a lesser degree, sieges. However, given the significance of the origins of firepower as a research theme, the lesser actions of the 16th century should have a higher priority. This may also partly compensate for the paucity of 16th-century battlefields in England, with some skirmishes perhaps able to deliver good archaeological evidence for the use of handguns. Another consideration is the potential of the lesser actions, particularly those from the various uprisings in mid-century, to demonstrate the degree to which firearms of particular types were by then in use in the militia.

The Scottish border

The greatest concentration of military action in 16th-century England was on its border with Scotland – at that time England's only land border, except for Calais, which was in English hands until 1558 (Fig 6.4). On both sides of the Anglo-Scottish frontier there were three Marches, military administrative territories which organised border protection through a series of garrisons. In England each had a major

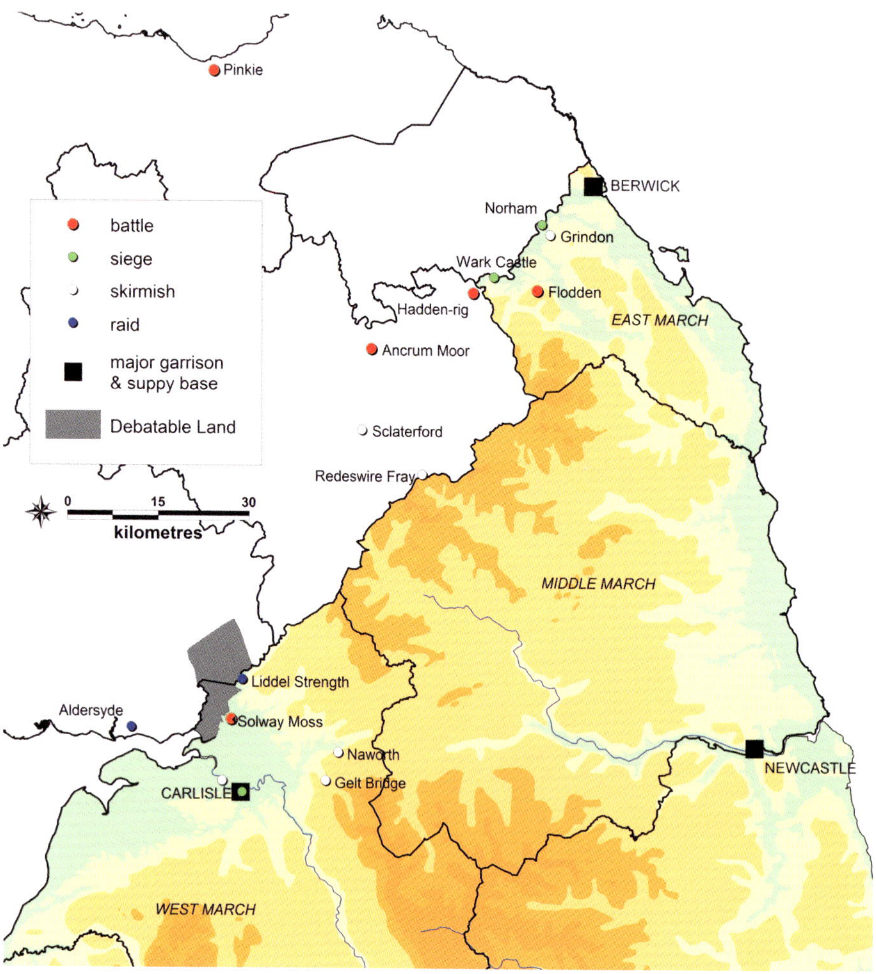

Fig 6.4 Map showing fields of conflict on the Anglo-Scottish border in the 16th century. The marches and debatable land are from McNeill and MacQueen 1996, 453, and Cunliffe *et al* 2001, 120

garrison: Carlisle in the West March; Berwick in the East March; and Newcastle, a key supply base with a major port, in the Middle March. In addition there were lesser garrisons and then, below them, a large number of defended houses, both large and small.[1] A number of garrisons were besieged and taken or destroyed during the period.

Raiding in the borders was often little more than local incursion to steal cattle, and was a way of life (Fraser 1974). However, while such minor actions lie beyond the scope of the present study, some raids, such as the 1537 Scottish attack on Muncaster in Cumbria, took on a more military aspect. These are probably under-represented on the Database, with only three identified for the 16th century in our more intensive pilot work on Cumbria. They could lead to significant engagements. An example is Grindon (1558), which is said to have taken place on Battle Moor, an area wholly undeveloped today. Another large raid through the debatable land – an area of some 110 square kilometres at the western end of the border, where neither country had undisputed control – precipitated the battle of Solway Moss in 1542. A further substantial skirmish took place at Gelt Bridge/Naworth in 1570, though there is uncertainty about the exact location.

While investigation of the sites of minor raids may yield little, study of the larger actions may provide a useful perspective on the character of warfare and the weapons in use by forces in the border region. The same is true of the small number of sieges against garrisons and other fortified sites along the border. Wark Castle (Northumberland), besieged in 1513 and 1523, is a Scheduled Ancient Monument where earthworks survive and a substantial part of the environs remain undeveloped. Liddel Strength (Cumbria), besieged in 1528 and 1583, is another Scheduled earthwork with a wholly undeveloped context. Both have potential for the recovery of artefact patterns arising from any fire fight. Other sieges include those which occurred as part of the Flodden campaign in 1513: at the important garrison of Carlisle, in the west, and at the castles of Norham and Etal, which lie close to the battlefield.

It is clear from work discussed below (Chapter 7) that for the 17th century siege sites have significant archaeological potential. No work has yet been undertaken, however, to establish whether this is also true of 16th-century examples in England. There ought to be artefacts scatters in the immediate environs of the sites, while in a few cases there may even be bullet or round shot impact scars on surviving structures. Such evidence is visible on the walls of Crichton Castle (East Lothian, Scotland), which also has a series of 16th-century gunports. Similar impact scars are seen on the nearby church. The site was besieged in 1559 and the scars may well be evidence for this attack. With this noted, recovering evidence of 16th-century sieges will not, in many cases, be straightforward. In places where multiple sieges have occurred the study will be complicated by the superimposition of artefact patterns from different events, while the surroundings of some siege sites are heavily developed: thus, at Carlisle the urban location probably means that little, if any, evidence survives outside the defences. However, if metal detectors are systematically used as part of the excavation method, it is possible that excavation will reveal evidence of bullet scatters.

The nature of warfare on the border means that the troops, their equipment and their tactical responses may have been somewhat different from that seen elsewhere in England. While the written record for Anglo-Scottish warfare in this region has been analysed (Phillips 1999), there is no wholly satisfactory account of the fields of conflict themselves. If these sites are to be managed effectively and their research potential realised then this needs to be remedied. An integrated regional study of the major battles, large skirmishes, sieges, and lesser raids may provide the best way forward. Around Berwick, in particular, the potential seems to exist for a major landscape-scale study integrating the physical and documentary evidence for Flodden with that for the various sieges, skirmishes, and raids. This would be best pursued in an Anglo-Scottish cross-border study, enabling the range of sites to include Ancrum Moor and Haddon Rig, together with skirmishes such as Sclaterford. Such a programme could logically be extended to include the Pinkie campaign and also to map fully the distribution of fortified sites in use in the period, to build up a coherent regional picture of the archaeology of border warfare in the 16th century.

The two Anglo-Scottish battles fought in England were Flodden and Solway Moss. Flodden (1513) involved some 40,000 English and Scottish troops and was of international scale and significance (National Army Museum 1995g). Artillery and probably also small arms were used, although, compared with the impact of the English archers, they were not critical in the outcome. Flodden, however, may not be wholly representative of the true state of development of English military practice in 1513. Henry VIII had taken the most important matériel to Calais for his campaign against the French. Flodden was accordingly fought by an army which probably lacked much of the most important new equipment (Cruickshank 1990). To date, three round shot have been recovered in archaeological survey there. Given that the site is largely undeveloped and has apparently not been seriously depleted by collectors, it offers a high potential for investigation (C Hallam-Baker pers comm).

Solway Moss (1542) was different in type and much smaller in scale. The English army there was dominated by light cavalry and severely outnumbered by the mainly infantry army of the Scots (National Army Museum 1995o). The terrain evidence in the primary accounts is too sparse to define closely the area of action, especially as the English cavalry seem to have engaged the Scots in loose order. It is likely, therefore, that the extent of the action will be determined only by a survey of battle archaeology, although, as in all periods, the cavalry action will be more difficult to locate and interpret than that of the infantry. The Scots had artillery and handguns in some quantity, but the primary sources do not provide details on their use, nor on the use of gunpowder weapons by the English force. The way in which the action was fought, with the rapid routing of the Scottish army, may mean there was, in fact, little opportunity for their use.

Given the likely nature of the battle archaeology it is unlikely that useful evidence would be recoverable during individual evaluations of proposed development sites. What is needed is a reconnaissance survey to establish whether battle archaeology can be located and, if so, what its character is and where it lies. In the absence of such work it will be impossible to quantify the threat posed by further development on the periphery of Longtown, which lies on the northern edge of the battlefield.

Rebellions, civil unrest, and naval raids

In other regions of England the 16th century was largely peaceful. In terms of international conflict there were just a handful of naval raids on south coast ports by the Spanish and French, such as the Spanish raid on Penzance and Newlyn in 1595. These raids appear to have been mainly urban in character and so

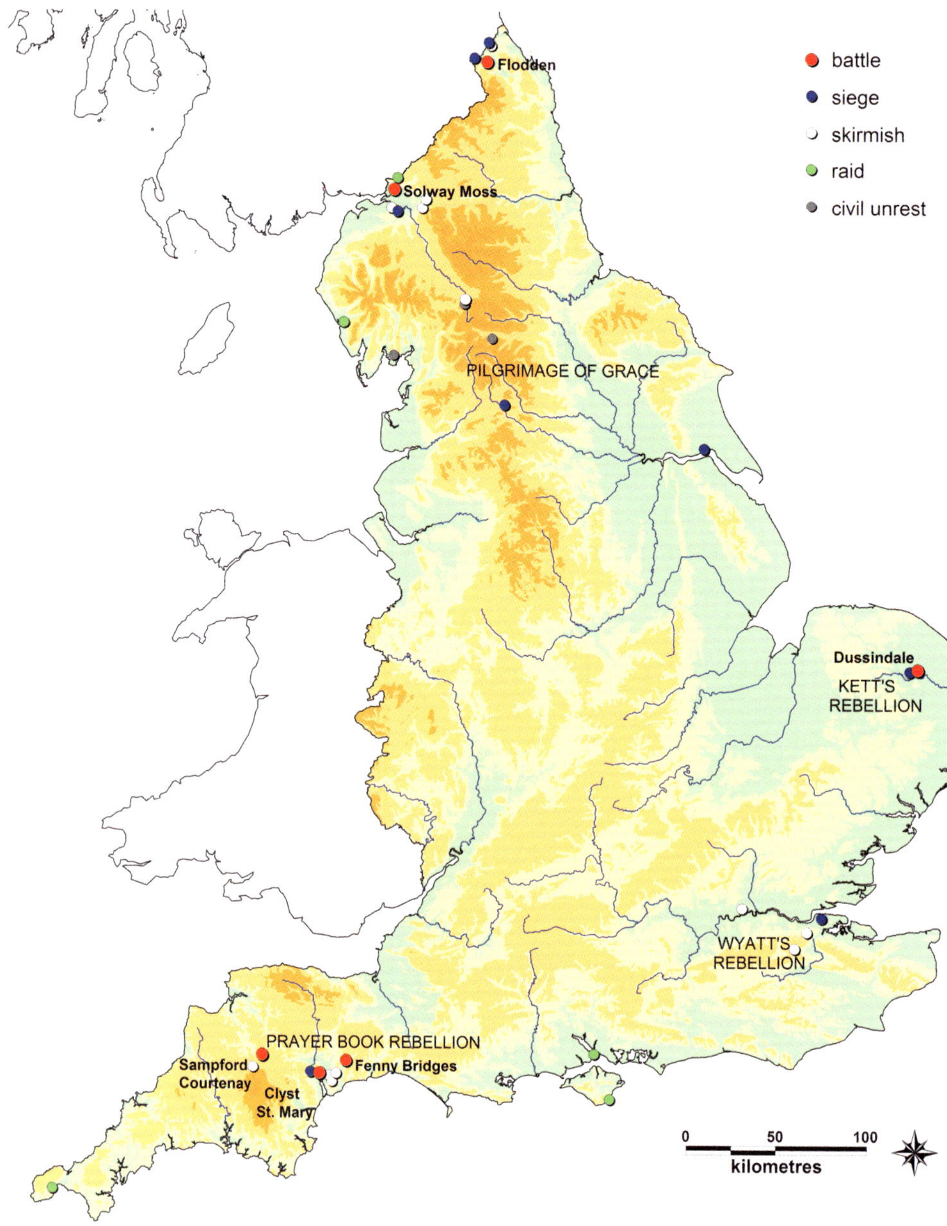

Fig 6.5 Map showing 16th-century fields of conflict in England, with battles and rebellions named

unlikely to yield significant battle archaeology. There were also some minor events of civil unrest, such as the resistance offered by the monks at Cartmel (Cumbria) to the dissolution of the priory in 1537 and private conflicts at Wharton in 1549 and in Ryedale. Again, at this stage none appears likely to have particular archaeological potential.

Of far greater significance are the mid-16th-century rebellions (Fig 6.5). These centred on religious grievances arising from the reformation of the church under Henry VIII and Edward VI, and then its brief restoration by Mary. The first was the Pilgrimage of Grace (1536–37), which included sieges of Carlisle, Hull, and Skipton castle in 1536, and a skirmish at Kirkby Stephen in 1537. Both Hull and Carlisle are probably now too heavily developed for significant archaeology from this period to survive; even if it does, it is likely to be confused by being overlaid by material deposited in other major actions in the 16th and 17th centuries.

Three other regional rebellions saw more substantial armed conflict. Wyatt's Rebellion, based in Kent in 1554, was part of a wider planned rebellion against the government of Mary. It resulted in skirmishes at Wrotham and Cobham, a siege at Cooling Castle, and a major street fight focusing around Temple Bar in London. While the latter was the most substantial action, it is unlikely to yield any significant evidence. The skirmish at Wrotham, which involved about 1000 combatants armed with firearms as well as bows, is more promising. A location in Black Sole field, on the western edge of the modern settlement, has been suggested, and here part of the ground remains undeveloped. Earlier, in 1549, there were two major armed insurrections, in Devon and Norfolk, against the religious changes imposed by the government of Edward VI. These are of particular interest because continental mercenaries, some of them handgunners, were deployed with the government forces. In addition, both rebel and government forces made use of artillery. On the rebel side it is to be expected that the core of the force and its equipment was provided by the local militias, and so it is possible that the archaeology of the battles may give some insight into the nature of the equipping of local militias in the period.

In Devon the Prayer Book Rebellion led to a siege of Exeter, several skirmishes, and three actions which may reasonably be classed as battles (Hodgkins 2008). Fenny Bridges, which was the smallest of these actions, began the main government response to the rebel uprising. Clyst St Mary and Clyst Heath were in effect one battle fought as two distinct actions on consecutive days as the royal forces moved to relieve Exeter. An action at Sampford Courtney ended the rebellion. The site of Clyst Heath was largely developed in the late 20th century and much, though not all, of the action at Clyst St Mary seems to lie beneath an expanded settlement. The exact site of the action at Fenny Bridges is in question, but it appears that part of the battlefield, particularly where troops fought for control of the bridge, remains largely intact. Without doubt, the best preserved site is Sampford Courtney, which is almost wholly open farmland – if the site is correctly identified. Here some 5000–10,000 men were engaged in an assault by government troops on a hilltop camp. The fighting appears to have included large-scale use of both artillery and handguns. Hence, if the site has not been damaged by collectors, it should have a very high potential.

The same year also saw Kett's Rebellion in Norfolk. This included an assault on Norwich by the rebels which involved skirmishing within Norwich itself, at St Andrew's Plain and Palace Gate. In this area in recent years 25 lead bullets were found by metal detecting in 16th-century garden soil in a small (4m × 4m) excavation. This was a very high density of bullets for the area examined, while association with other mid-16th-century artefacts suggest that it could relate to the 1549 action (Emery 2000). Unfortunately, the deposits were then stripped without significant investigation in preparation for full excavation of Anglo-Saxon deposits below. In the absence of published data on the bullet weights it is not possible to assess how the calibre of the assemblage relates to other assemblages from the period, but the lesson here is that, while in many urban settings there is little or no potential for significant archaeology of urban actions, on some sites useful data may exist and can be retrieved.

The major action of the Norfolk rebellion was on 27 August 1549, at Dussindale, to the east of the city on the eastern edge of Mousehold Heath. The site was lost for centuries, and was believed by some to have lain to the north of the city. However, terrain reconstruction by Carter has resulted in the suggestion of a new location (Carter 1984). While there is still the need for effective map regression to produce accurate mapping to a modern map base, Carter's identification is persuasive. The site lies to the east of the city, along a shallow north–south valley called Dussindale, after which the battle had been named. This dale was the first substantial feature travelling eastward across Mousehold Heath from the city. To the north were two enclosures called Lumners, while further enclosures lay to the south. If this is the correct site then Kett's rebel army will have deployed on a frontage of about a kilometre on the east side of the shallow dale, with the hedge in the dale bottom lying to their fore and with enclosures giving protection on both flanks. Despite this, a large government force destroyed the rebels in a battle in which 5000–10,000 troops were engaged; Neville's account suggests that 3500 were killed, but the number is more likely to be in the high hundreds (Champion 2001).

This action typifies the smaller battles of the period and the problems that they pose, for while a number of accounts do survive from the following decades, none accurately locates the action. The government forces numbered about 3500–4500 men who were largely experienced troops, including 1500 German 'lance knights' and Captain Drury's handgunners, as well as retinues of several prominent lords. The rebels were armed with bills and agricultural implements, but their force also included archers, who the primary sources show played a significant part. They may also have fielded as many as twenty captured guns commanded by a Master Gunner. The action thus saw the intensive use of both troops carrying handguns and archers, and there is also good reason to believe that the battle opened with a substantial artillery exchange. The latter will certainly have involved the use of round shot, including lead and lead composite projectiles, though it is unclear whether hailshot of some form was also fired at close quarters.

Over the last decade Dussindale has been one of the most threatened battlefields in England, as Norwich suburbs expand across the site. Despite the analysis by Carter in 1984, an evaluation of the site in 1995 displayed a lack of awareness that this may have been the battlefield;[2] and, despite metal detecting being included in the evaluation strategy, it was apparently decided to discriminate-out any finds of lead because priority was given to the investigation of much earlier settlement activity. Despite the development of battlefield archaeology in England in the 1990s no further evaluation involving an appropriate methodology of battlefield survey appears to have been undertaken, and nor by 2006 had Carter's site been added to the HER – when the battlefield was still shown under an existing housing estate to the west.

This lack of appropriate assessment and evaluation has not apparently been remedied even since the highlighting of the national importance of the site in our 2008 report. A subsequent field visit suggests that yet more undisturbed areas have been destroyed. The site is said to have been subject over many years to extensive metal detecting by a local detectorist who has reported no significant battle-related finds. However, detectorists normally dismiss low densities of lead bullets as irrelevant background noise – indeed, they may not have reported or even collected such material. Such collecting is certainly not an adequate alternative to systematic archaeological metal-detecting survey. While a substantial part of Carter's site has now been built over, sufficient probably remains for significant battle archaeology to be retrieved and the detail of the location of the battlefield to be resolved. A re-examination of all the evidence, together with systematic sampling for battle archaeology employing metal-detecting survey on 2.5m transects, is urgently required.

Notes

1. An example of the nature of the fortifications of the border zone is given in two plans of the area from Chollerton to Berwick, depicting castles and towers together with some notes on the defensive arrangements in Northumberland and Cumberland in *c* 1580. TNA, MPF 284.
2. Norfolk Archaeological Unit, Report 121.

7

THE 17TH CENTURY

In the late 16th and early 17th centuries England saw a period of relative peace. After the rebellions of 1549 and 1554 no battles were fought in England until Newburn Ford in 1640. In the interim there were some skirmishes, raids, and sieges on the Anglo-Scottish border, but even these halted late in the 16th century – a peace sealed in 1603 when England came under the rule of the Stuart kings of Scotland. Yet between the 1550s and the 1640s there had been significant changes in weapon technology and especially in tactics on the battlefields of continental Europe which appear on English battlefields in a highly developed form only in the 1640s (Roberts 2010).

There are over 400 English records on the Database for the 17th century. Almost all of them relate to the Civil Wars between crown and parliament from 1642 to 1651, when the kingdom was plunged into what was arguably the most intense period of warfare in its history (Fig 7.1). The Civil Wars in fact involved all three of Charles I's kingdoms – England and Wales, Ireland, and Scotland – each kingdom representing a distinct war theatre, with quite separate government and rebel forces engaged, although at certain stages troops were moved from one theatre to another. Thus, for example, in 1643 several regiments of troops were withdrawn from Ireland by the royalists to bolster their position in England, while in 1644 a large Scottish army entered the war in England as allies of, and funded, by the English parliament. While for practical reasons explained in the introduction our geographical scope is limited to England, ideally this warfare should be examined across national borders in the British Isles: ultimately, indeed, it has to be viewed in a wider context, for it is closely related to the Thirty Years War, which racked Europe in the first half of the

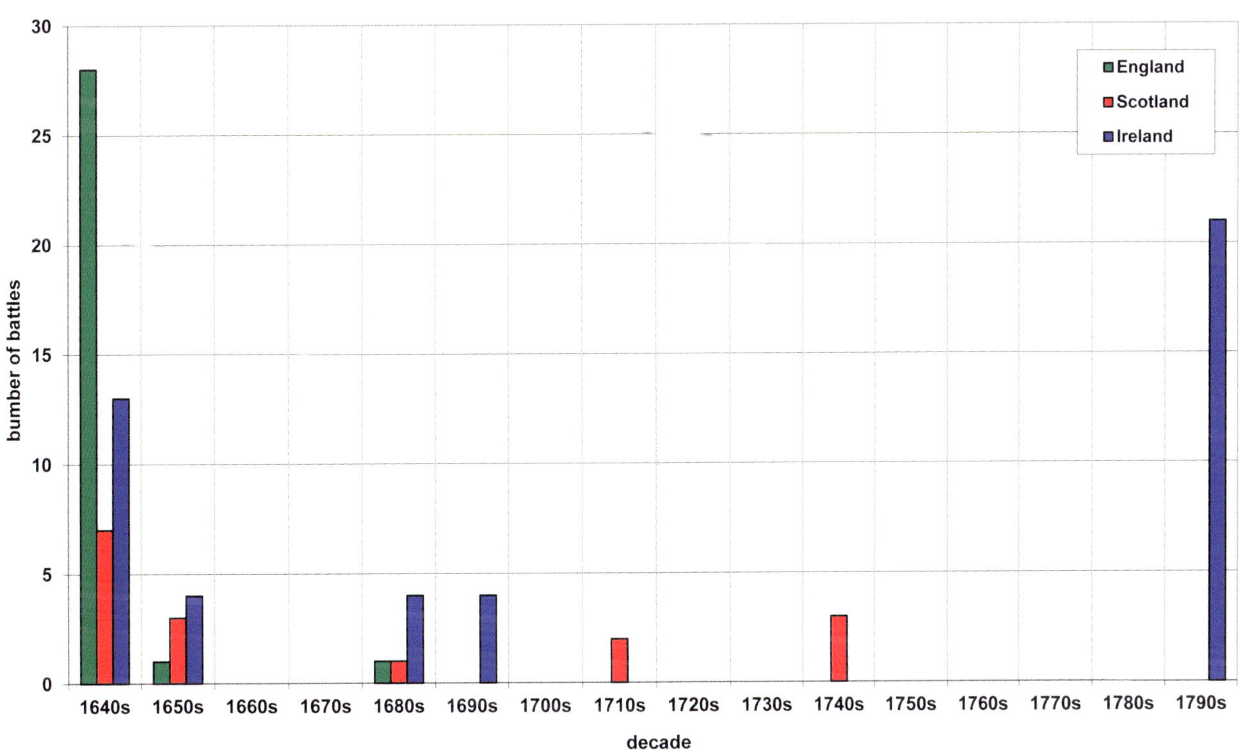

Fig 7.1 Graph of battles in England, Scotland and the Republic of Ireland between 1640 and 1799

century (Childs 2001). In England this period of warfare opened with a clash between Charles I and his Scottish subjects that led to the First and Second Bishops Wars, in the latter of which a Scottish army entered England in 1640, culminating in the battle of Newburn, to the west of Newcastle. Most of the fighting that followed belonged to the First Civil War (1642–46). The Second Civil War followed in 1648, and saw several battles and various sieges. The Third Civil War developed out of a pre-emptive strike by English forces into Scotland in 1650 designed to counter a campaign for control of England that was being planned by the son of Charles I from his Scottish kingdom. Despite Cromwell's dramatic success at Dunbar (East Lothian) in 1650, and victories in subsequent actions by his subordinates, a Jacobite invasion of England followed in 1651. However, the expected rising of royalists in England largely failed to materialise, and, as a result, this invasion ended in the destruction of the largely Scottish army at Worcester in one of the largest and most complex battles of the Civil Wars. The final years of the Republic were troubled by several small-scale royalist rebellions, the Penruddock Rising (1655) and the Booth Rising (1659), but these led only to minor skirmishes.

In the four decades following the restoration of Charles II in 1660 there were nine actions in England. Three were part of the Anglo-Dutch wars and involved naval landings around the Thames Estuary, on the Medway, and at Landguard and Sheerness forts in 1667. However, the main fighting in this period related to the Monmouth rebellion of 1685, an abortive attempt to overthrow the new Catholic king, James II. This campaign saw a series of skirmishes at Bridport, Keynsham, and Norton St Philip, and then the final destruction of the rebel army at Sedgemoor – the last battle to be fought on English soil. In military terms the events of the Glorious Revolution of 1688, which saw the successful overthrow of James II by a Dutch army under William of Orange, represent little more than a footnote to the Monmouth rebellion; because there was strong support in England for the removal of James there was only token resistance, in skirmishes at Reading and Wincanton.

There are just sixteen later sites recorded on the Database, all from the 18th century. The majority relate to the Jacobite risings in Scotland, which did impact on England, although the fighting which took place there would be best considered within a study of warfare in Scotland. In 1715, during the first Jacobite rebellion, a substantial army entered England via the west coast route: at Penrith they were faced by local levies that fled rather than engage them. Subsequently the rebel army was defeated in an urban action at Preston but, although some 6000 troops were involved, this was an urban street fight and is normally classified as a skirmish.

In 1745, during the second Jacobite uprising, another rebel army entered England following their victory at Prestonpans (East Lothian, Scotland). This force, of some 5000 men, again chose the western route. They first took the garrison of Carlisle and then continued south as far as Derby, where the massive scale of the government response forced them to retrace their steps. The Duke of Cumberland pursued the rebels with a detachment of cavalry, dragoons, and mounted infantry, and on 18 December he engaged them in a running skirmish around the village of Clifton and on Clifton Moor, on the upland pass north of Shap, Cumbria. Only about 50 troops were killed, during what was, in effect, a rearguard action which allowed the rebel army to escape into Scotland. Although these events cannot be classed as a battle they do form the last substantial action to take place on English soil. Clifton is also reasonably well documented, including a surviving Jacobite battle plan, and it may be expected to have left a significant archaeological signature.[1]

Clifton aside, for warfare of the 18th century in the British Isles it is to Scotland that one must look for the first half of the century, and thereafter it is to Ireland in the 1790s. The only other action in England was an American naval landing at Whitehaven in 1778, during the American War of Independence. Although four actions from the 19th century are recorded on the Database they were purely events of civil unrest, such as the Gordon Riots, which lie beyond the scope of the present study.

The Civil War period (hereafter referred to as 'the Civil War') differs from earlier periods of warfare in England not only in scale and intensity but also in the wealth of primary written sources; in the breadth of the scholarly analysis undertaken using this evidence; and in the survival of substantial physical evidence. The methodology for research into the battlefield archaeology of this period is well developed and has produced one of the largest bodies of physical evidence for early warfare in any country in Europe (Harrington 2004; Foard 2008c). In every respect this puts the Civil War on an international scale of importance as an example of warfare in the period when the full development of pike and shot tactics had been largely

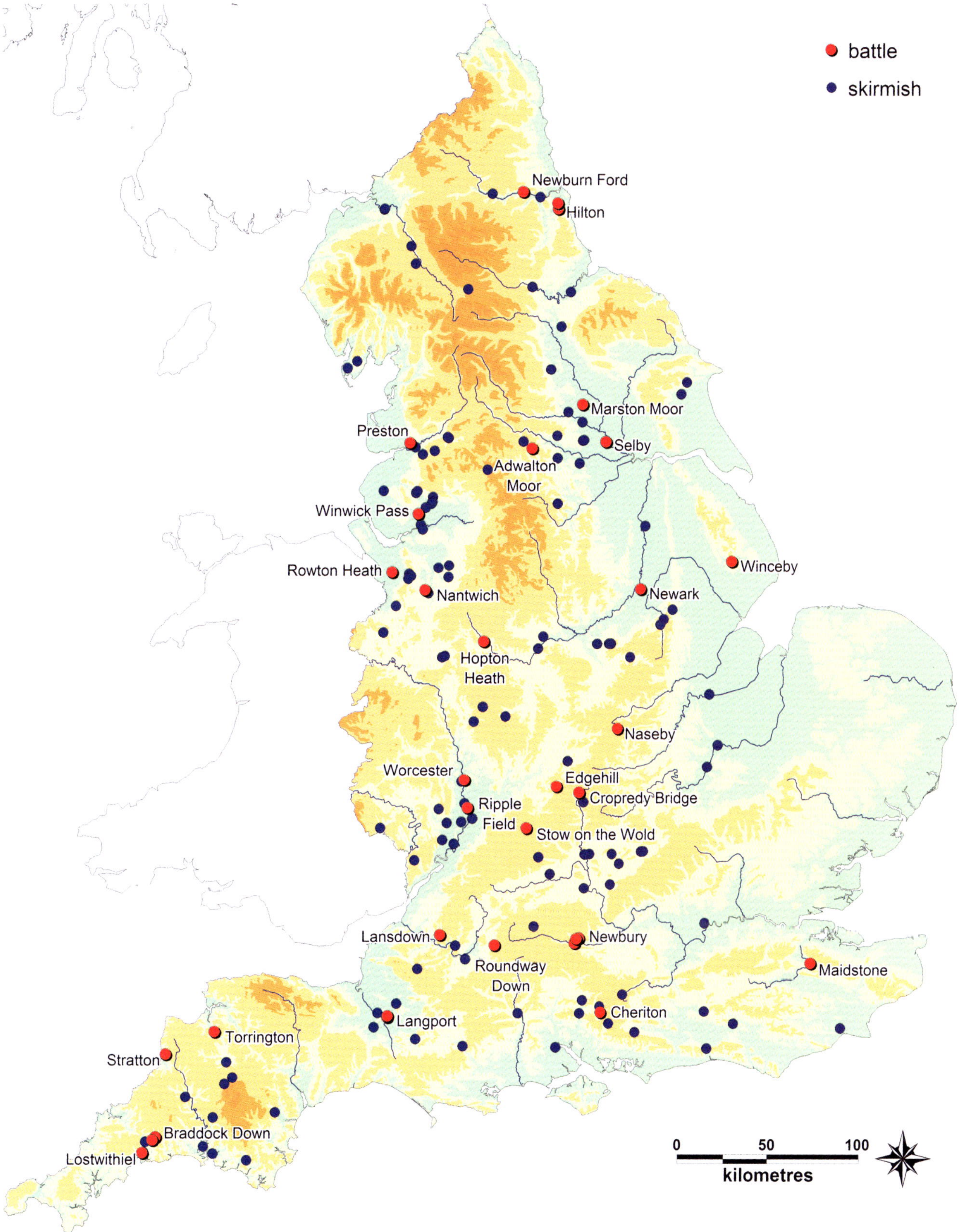

Fig 7.2 Map of battles (named) and skirmishes from the Civil Wars in England (1642–51). Also shown is the battle of Newburn from the Second Bishops War (1640). A few of the skirmishes, which are grossly under-represented in the data, may warrant re-classification as battles

achieved. Only limited changes in tactical deployments are seen between Edgehill in 1642 and Worcester in 1651. It was not until after the Civil War that the matchlock was phased out in favour of the flintlock and the hand grenade became a standard weapon. Otherwise, military practice and equipment appears to have changed relatively little between the 1640s and 1680s. Thus, at Sedgemoor the pike was still in use and matchlocks were still carried by one government regiment; the bayonet would not be used in action until Killiecrankie in Scotland in 1689. It is therefore reasonable to treat the Monmouth rebellion alongside the battles of the 1640s and 1650s.

No attempt has been made here to identify all the minor actions, but a pilot study was undertaken to establish the scale of information that could be rapidly retrieved. In addition to the more intensive work on all periods in Cumbria and West Yorkshire, discussed in Chapter 2, several of the county histories on the Civil War were also examined for sieges, skirmishes, and other minor military events. Four secondary works were used, most written in the later 19th or early 20th century, a period of intense interest in the history of the Civil War. Of these, Thomas-Stanford's 'Sussex' yielded four sieges and four skirmishes not already present on the Database and Bayley's 'Dorset' gave eight new sieges and three other minor actions, but Broxap's 'Lancashire' added no significant sites (Broxap 1910; Bayley 1910; Thomas-Stanford 1910). Such variation is partly explained by the fact that some Historic Environment Records have better listings of Civil War sites than others, while certain counties are better served by the national overviews which were used for the initial, national phase of enhancement. In addition, Shropshire was enhanced from a modern study of the war, followed by field visits with the emphasis on siege sites (Bracher and Emmett 2000).

Given that most counties or regions have one or more secondary works on the Civil War, a national review would be useful to collate the various lesser garrison and siege sites and many of the skirmishes that will have been missed in our search. This might also help to decide the scale of some of those actions which sit on the boundary between battle and skirmish. What is clear is that all the major battles, and probably all the major sieges, have been identified in the present study.

The Database lists 132 skirmishes. While a handful are based on local traditions and may be spurious, many genuine skirmishes have undoubtedly been missed in our research. Some distinct patterns seem to be visible in the mapping (Fig 7.2). The rarity of skirmishes in East Anglia is a genuine reflection of the level of military action: the area was securely held for parliament for almost the whole Civil War period. In contrast, the concentration in Cheshire and Lancashire may be as much a result of exceptional HER enhancement and greater representation in national works as it is a reflection of the true intensity of action compared to adjacent counties. It is likely that a more comprehensive study would give new insights into the variation in the scale and intensity of military action.

While a major enhancement of the Database to include skirmishes would be practicable, the higher priority for extensive work on both battles and sieges argues that at present the results would not appear to justify the resources required to do so. Nevertheless, recent work has shown that these lesser actions can produce insights. This is seen, for example, in the development-led investigation on the site of the 1642 'battle' of Aylesbury. The site has long been thought to lie beside Holman's Bridge, on the edge of Aylesbury, an assumption based on a vaguely reported 19th-century discovery of a mass grave. The recent fieldwork produced 24 lead bullets and four powder-box caps in addition to other possibly battle-related artefacts (Foard 2008b); clearly, this action involved at least some infantry. Engagements which involved only cavalry might be expected to produce less evidence, judging from that left by the cavalry action at Edgehill (see Fig 7.21). Battle archaeology from just such a cavalry skirmish may already have been incidentally recovered during the Bosworth (1485) survey discussed in Chapter 5. A single parliamentarian report of 1643 refers to a detachment of cavalry from Leicester intercepting royalist cavalry returning from 'tax collecting' in the Hinckley area. A slight concentration of small calibre bullets, together with at least two spur fragments, was recovered from the south-western part of the 1485 battlefield. On the northern periphery of the area there was also a low-density spread of silver coins, mainly of Elizabeth but also including several of James I and Charles I – something not seen elsewhere across the Bosworth survey. It is possible that these artefacts all relate to the Civil War cavalry skirmish, said in the contemporary account to have been fought on the very spot where Richard III was killed. Unfortunately, even with the 2.5m transect survey intensity used at Bosworth it is difficult to determine whether this bullet scatter is anything more than a faint increase in the background noise of early modern sporting activity. Another potential complication is the slight possibility that some of these bullets were fired from early small calibre handguns during the Bosworth battle itself (Foard and Curry in prep).

Such lesser actions are rarely well documented, but it is likely that their study will add to our understanding of warfare in the period. In order to gain a clearer idea of what may be achievable, systematic investigation is required across the whole of several well-preserved skirmish sites, both large and small, using the methodology which has been demonstrated in battlefield survey; ideally, there should be good documentary evidence for both the events and for the historic terrain. If such work shows that informative archaeological evidence does typically exist on such sites, then it may be appropriate for a representative sample of them to be conserved. This is particularly relevant given that the boundary of classification between battle and skirmish is rather arbitrary. Some substantial skirmishes, such as that fought in 1642 at Southam in Warwickshire, are likely to provide evidence comparable to that from smaller battles.

The problem of classification can be seen from a comparison of evidence for a range of battles and skirmishes. With actions involving more than 5000 troops there is little uncertainty, with the exceptions subject to clear explanation. Thus Modbury is classified as a skirmish because no substantial action occurred, despite the involvement of some 10,000 soldiers. Alton, with 6000 engaged, had the character of a skirmish similar to Preston II, with disbanded groups fighting through the town. In contrast, uncertainty regularly arises over actions involving 5000 or fewer troops. Hopton Heath (1643), for example, with just 2500 engaged, is a Registered battle, whereas Norton St Philip (1685), with 4500 involved, is usually categorised as a skirmish because of the nature and scale of the fighting. Two other actions with fewer than 5000 engaged (Powick Bridge and Chalgrove) were Registered despite being recognised as skirmishes. This shows that it was considered acceptable in 1995 for the Register to include skirmishes as well as battles, although a further four skirmishes that were assessed for the Register were dismissed. Even some actions where fewer than 2000 men were involved could be reconsidered. One example is Middlewich, which although a street fight is shown by a surviving battle plan to have involved the formal deployment of troops in battalions (Liddiard and McGuicken 2007).

Battles

In total, 29 actions have been classified here as battles. The level of detail which exists in the primary written sources for them means that almost all are located in general terms, Braddock Down being the only example with two alternative sites. At Cheriton a similar problem existed after an alternative site was proposed by Adair, but investigation of the battle archaeology has demonstrated that the traditional site is the correct one (Bonsall 2008).

The documentary record for the battles is often extensive, with numerous accounts that can be analysed for detailed understanding of the sequence of events. Such reports are often by eye-witnesses and so may be more reliable than most of the accounts we have for earlier battles. The quantity of information for some battles, indeed, poses problems of data handling, with extensive evidence for the armies and their equipping as well as the records of the action itself. Within the accounts there are also usually plenty of topographical clues that can assist in the accurate placing of events in the landscape, as long as the historic terrain can be effectively reconstructed in map form. This is often possible because our understanding of the historic landscape and the documentary record for individual landscapes of the regions of 17th-century England is generally better and more detailed than for earlier periods. Taken together with the topographical information in the primary accounts, terrain reconstruction can be very effective.

Investigation of the historic terrain is necessary not simply to place events in the landscape and to define the extent of the battlefield: it is also needed for better understanding of the battle itself. The nature of the terrain within which a battle was fought will often have had a key influence on the choice of ground, the tactics employed, and how events evolved. Indeed, commanders would manoeuvre in such a way as to force a battle in a specific type of landscape that best suited the composition and strengths of their forces. A good example is the Earl of Essex's approach to Newbury in 1643. The royalist army he faced was far stronger in cavalry, which would have the advantage in open ground, whereas his army was stronger in infantry and would have the advantage in hedged fields. Essex accordingly wanted to take advantage of the enclosed landscape to the south-west of the town, rather than fight in the more open landscape to the north.

Of the 29 battles from the period it has been possible to classify the terrain of 23 with some degree of confidence (see Appendix 3). Of these, thirteen were fought in a landscape which was largely open; four to six were fought in a mixed landscape of open and enclosed land; and a further four – Nantwich, Stratton, Newbury I, and Lostwithiel – were fought in a wholly or largely enclosed landscape. In almost every case where there were enclosures these were hedged. Only Stratton had boundaries comprising solely Cornish hedges (essentially stone-revetted banks), though several other battlefields, such as Lansdown, had one or more stone walls which played a role in the battle. Only one battle was fought primarily around fortified positions – that at Newburn, where two sconces controlled the river crossing.

Not surprisingly, given this bias towards fighting in open landscapes, most of the detailed studies of battlefield terrain and battle archaeology so far undertaken concern engagements fought on open-field land or moorland. This may introduce a bias into our understanding: there is, as yet, no detailed archaeological study of a battle in which hedged or walled enclosures were defended. Since the nature of battle archaeology on an enclosed landscape should vary from that in an open landscape, the investigation of a battlefield which was dominated by enclosures is clearly a priority. Given the small number of battlefields with this character, it is important that they are effectively managed to conserve the archaeology of both terrain and battle.

The principles of analysis using battle accounts alongside terrain reconstruction are demonstrated here through case studies of Braddock Down and Sedgemoor, both fought in a wholly or largely open landscape. Braddock Down shows what can be achieved with relatively limited documentary research, whereas the Sedgemoor study provides an example of the integration of documentary and archaeological evidence in mapping the historic terrain, both for the battlefield and for its immediate context. It then goes on to test this interpretation of the action by examining a sample of battle archaeology from the site.

Braddock Down

On 9 January 1643 a royalist army of *c* 5000 men defeated a parliamentarian army of *c* 4000 7km north-east of Lostwithiel in Cornwall. There were few royalist losses, but the parliamentarians suffered about 200 killed and 1500 captured, as well as losing their baggage train and several pieces of artillery. The battle secured Cornwall for the royalists and established the military reputation of Sir Ralph Hopton, the royalist commander.

The royalists camped the night before the battle at nearby Boconnoc. In the morning, on breaking camp, their vanguard of dragoons encountered enemy cavalry to the east. They discovered the parliamentarian army already deployed in battle array on Braddock Down – although a parliamentarian report claims it was they who were caught on the march by the royalists. Hopton quickly deployed his troops, with the infantry in the centre, supported by two artillery pieces and

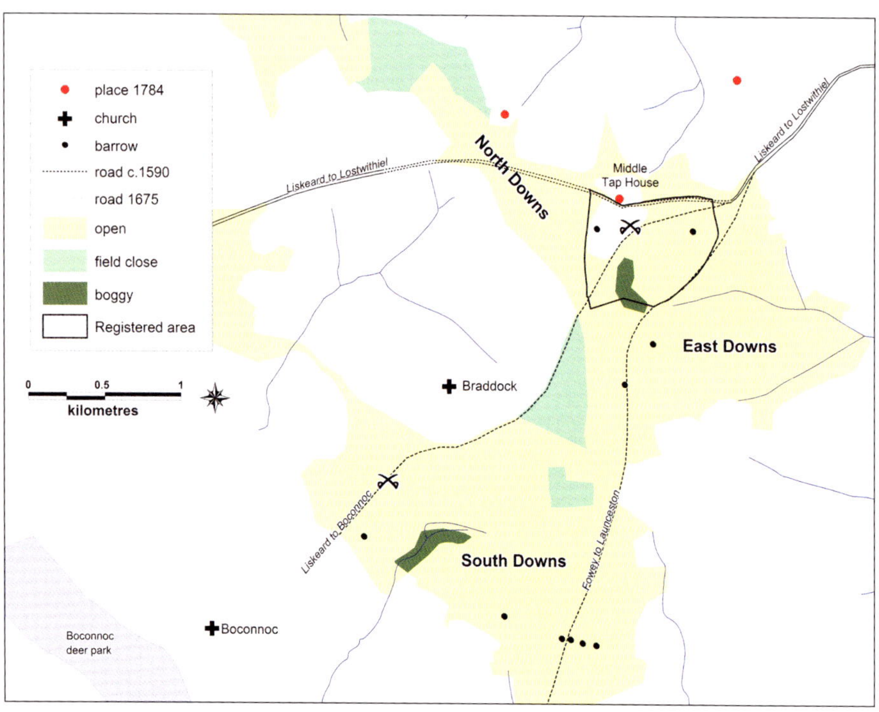

Fig 7.3 Map of the historic terrain of Braddock Down (1643), showing the traditional site to the south-west and the Registered battlefield to the north-east[2]

flanked by cavalry on both wings. A forlorn hope – a detachment of musketeers sent forward of the main body as a skirmishing unit – was placed in small enclosures closer towards the enemy. The two armies thus faced each other across a small valley. The action started with a prolonged fire-fight, neither side being willing to give up the advantage of their position. Eventually Hopton, after firing the two artillery pieces, led his entire army down into the valley and charged up the other side. The parliamentarians were overwhelmed almost immediately. Standing to fire only a single volley, they fled, deploying musketeers along the hedges on the road towards Liskeard to protect the retreat, but these were soon flushed out and the royalists continued the pursuit for almost 16km, into the town.

Braddock Down is one of the few Civil War battles where there is significant dispute over the exact location. Only one of the two alternative sites has been included within the Register boundary, even though there is no definitive evidence that this is the correct site. Detailed discussion of the battle is omitted by most battlefield guides and histories and, where it is addressed, most authors choose the traditional location, although Brooks presents both options (Burne and Young 1959; Brooks 2005; Kinross 1988). The traditional site, recorded in 1881 on the Ordnance Survey first edition six-inch map, lies between Boconnoc Park and Braddock church. The suggestion of an alternative site 2km to the north-east was made by a local historian after re-examination of primary sources and aspects of the historic terrain (Wilton 1985; 1992; National Army Museum 1995d). However, one thing that emerges both from the review of English battles in this study (eg with Barnet; Fig 5.3) and in work undertaken in Scotland (eg Bannockburn) is that the transfer of sites from their traditional locations is often unsatisfactory in outcome (Foard and Partida 2005).

The choice of open ground – reflected in the battle name of Braddock Down – follows a pattern regularly

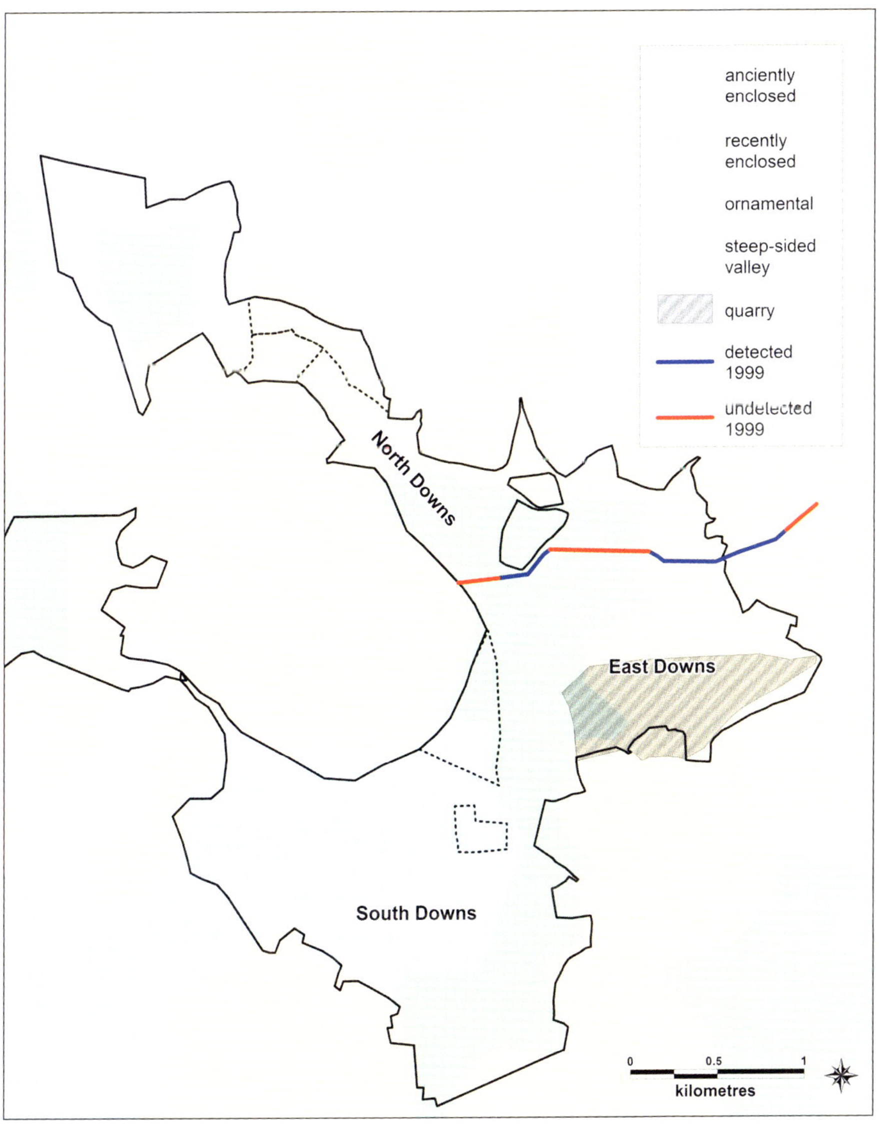

Fig 7.4 Map of Braddock Down (1643) showing open and enclosed areas from our terrain reconstruction (Fig 7.5), superimposed on the Landscape Characterisation mapping for Cornwall. Also depicted are the areas metal detected in the 1999 evaluation

observed in the anciently enclosed zones of Britain. Here, commanders often seem to have sought out open land, such as moorland or downs, in which standard 17th-century tactical formations could be most effectively applied. In one of the more detailed considerations of its type for the Register, the historic landscape and the main historic map sources for Braddock were reviewed in defining the Register boundary (CEI 1994; National Army Museum 1995d).[3] These sources were again discussed in a 1996 desk-based assessment prior to pipeline construction across the Registered battlefield (Buck 1996; Cole 1999). However, in neither case was a terrain reconstruction prepared. An initial attempt at such mapping is presented here; such work enables the sometimes disparate details from different sources to be brought together in a single coherent representation (Fig 7.3).

In reviewing the historic terrain we first examined the evidence provided in the landscape characterisation mapping for Cornwall (Cornwall County Council 1996). This provides generalised mapping that distinguishes anciently (pre-17th-century) and recently (17th–19th century) enclosed lands from other historic land-use types. Such information is available on a countywide scale for this and various other English counties as part of the English Heritage Historic Landscape Characterisation (HLC) programme, and provides a useful background against which to view the wider context of 17th-century warfare. However, while HLC gives a broad overview of historic landscape character, it does not provide a sufficiently fine-grained picture to enable analysis of battlefield terrain. The limitations can be seen by comparing the characterisation data for Braddock Down with our reconstruction of the historic terrain (Figs 7.3 and 7.4). The latter reveals ancient enclosures, common enclosed in the 19th century by parliamentary act, and field closes – that is, land enclosed at an early date but still commonable until rights were extinguished by parliamentary enclosure. It can be seen that the HLC classification merges different chronological elements with, for example, the ornamental component – essentially the designed landscape surrounding the country house at Boconnoc – obscuring the earlier pattern of ancient versus more recent enclosure. As a result, the accuracy of the HLC data appears low with, for example, key areas of common being misclassified as anciently enclosed and a small but potentially important area of ancient enclosure, at Middle Tap House, misclassified as recent. In addition, the field closes within the common are missed, despite good documentary evidence that the largest of these, lying between South and East Downs, was already in existence in the 16th century. The lesson is that battlefield investigation demands study at a scale greater than that for which HLC data were designed.

The historic landscape of Braddock Down is well documented, with a good sequence of historic maps running from the 16th to the 19th century. There is also an extensive written record for the Boconnoc estate from the 16th century onwards, which could not be exploited here but offers a high research potential. Gascoyne's county map of 1699 yields little, but that of 1748 by Martyn provides a valuable overview of enclosed versus open land at that date, with a level of detail only occasionally found in contemporary county maps. There is also more detailed local mapping. Few parliamentary enclosures took place in Cornwall, the majority of the open land being enclosed by agreement in the 15th–18th centuries, while in some areas enclosure is even more ancient. The extensive parliamentary enclosure of the Downs at Braddock, defined in a map and award of 1822, is thus relatively unusual for the region (Tate and Turner 1978, 82). Indeed, the enclosure was so late that the open downland was still able to be mapped on the Ordnance Surveyors' Drawings at two-inch scale in 1803. Enclosure maps, because of their very specific purpose, typically do not show the pre-enclosure roads and pre-enclosure field closes. However, both are shown on the Ordnance Surveyors' Drawings, which were intended to provide a representation of the militarily significant aspects of the landscape (Delano-Smith and Kain 1999). In addition, there is a detailed late 16th-century map of the southern part of the area, while in 1675 Ogilby shows the main post road across the Down. Of all the sources consulted for this assessment only the RAF vertical air photographs of the 1940s failed to produce any useful evidence.

The mapping presented here shows the extent of common still unenclosed in 1803 (Fig 7.4). Within that it distinguishes the field closes, at least one of which (to the east of Boconnoc church) is also depicted on the 16th-century map. The remaining areas were anciently enclosed, as defined on the enclosure map and broadly confirmed for the southern part of the battlefield by the 16th-century map. A small area of ancient enclosures surrounds Middle Tap House, to the north and south of the main Liskeard–Lostwithiel road. Ogilby's 1675 Itinerary does not show these enclosures, but does refer to the House itself, so there may already have been a small area of enclosures there at that time. However, given Ogilby's usual attention to such detail (Ogilby

1675, plate 69), it would have been surprising if they had existed on both sides of the road and yet remained unmapped. A large mound, interpreted as a Bronze Age burial mound, still survived in 1946 within the southern area of the Middle Tap House enclosures (Buck 1996). Contrary to the Register report's suggestion, this earthwork has little relevance to the reference to the placement of artillery on a barrow during the battle because at least ten barrows were recorded scattered across the downs in the 20th century, and many more appear on the 16th-century map.[4]

The road network will have been critical in determining the approach and flight of the parliamentarian army. The army's initial deployment, though not necessarily the principal deployment before the action, is said in one original account to have been at the place where the Liskeard road opened out into Braddock Down. The Register report describes the Liskeard road running through St Pinnock, but Ogilby clearly shows it on a more northerly course, joining the Launceston–Fowey road at East Tap House. The remaining road network is provided on the 1803 map, with roads in the southern half of the area largely confirmed by the 16th-century map. Another feature in the accounts which needs to be located on the battlefield is a small area of boggy ground. While the geological mapping provides no evidence of peat or even alluvial deposits across most of the area, the 1881 Ordnance Survey depicts a substantial boggy area immediately north of the Fowey–Liskeard road, to the south of Middle Tap House.

Having recovered the broad structure of the historic terrain it is possible to reconsider the detail presented in primary accounts of the battle and to review key arguments in the Register report. The parliamentarian account by Wrothe specified that they were attacked as they marched 'beside a dangerous bog and a very high hill'. This would seem to accord best with the road from Launceston to Fowey where, to the south-east of Middle Tap House, it crosses the boggy area depicted in 1881. The first encounter, therefore, seems most likely to be where the East Downs begin to narrow south-westward towards the South Downs. A royalist approach to the Downs from Boconnoc Park, where they were camped, will almost certainly have brought them across the traditional site of the battle on the South Downs.

Hopton states that the parliamentarians deployed on Braddock Down at the end of the lane coming out from Liskeard, while the royalists were on the west side of Braddock Down (Fig 7.5). At first sight this seems to fit well with the Registered site, but there were three separate downs. When the field closes are taken into account, and particularly those recorded in the 16th century on the East Common (South Downs), then it can be seen that the Liskeard–Boconnoc road would also enter the East Common through enclosed ground. Thus the descriptions could also be compatible with the traditional site.

The most specific of all topographical references is provided by Colonel Sir Bevil Grenville, one of the

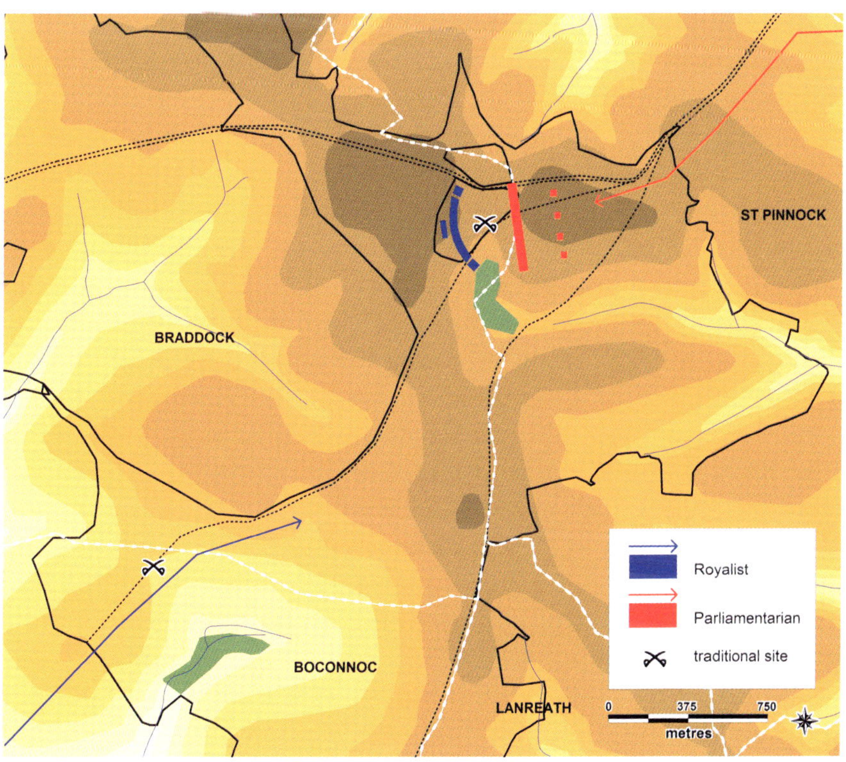

Fig 7.5 Map of Braddock Down (1643) showing deployments from the Register report and the traditional site of the battle. These are depicted against relief, key elements of terrain and (named and bounded in white) the early parishes

senior royalist officers who lived in this region. He states that the action took place on the heathland between Boconnoc and Braddock church, which fits perfectly with the traditional site. The Register analysis, following Wilton, presents a convoluted argument to accommodate this description with the modern re-interpretation of the battle site, arguing that Grenville mixed up Braddock church, which is close to and clearly visible from both sites, with St Pinnock church, which is over 2.5km to the east and largely out of sight of both alternative sites. They suggest that this error may have occurred because of the lack of clarity over the churches depicted on Speed's map, or in various published derivatives, to which Grenville probably had access.

Grenville then says that the parliamentarians deployed on a 'a pritty rising ground wch was in the way towards Liskeard'. The royalists, he says, were on another hill within musket shot of them – so the troops were perhaps some 250m apart. Symond's Diary states that on 7 August 1644, during the Lostwithiel campaign, Charles I's army camped on the site of the Braddock Down battle, on Pinnock or Broadoak [Braddock] Down, and then the next day advanced towards Boconnoc (National Army Museum 1995d). Though at first sight this might seem to be helpful, in fact there is again insufficient detail to be certain of the location.

Thus, even with detailed terrain reconstruction, it is impossible to be sure of the location of the battlefield. Unless new documentary evidence is found it will only be through a study of the battle archaeology that this problem will be finally resolved. There were at least three main elements to the action – a fire-fight; a rapid assault; and a destructive rout, including the clearance of parliamentarian musketeers from enclosures along the main road running towards Liskeard. The archaeological signatures of these three elements are likely to be spatially separate and distinctive.

Part of the Registered battlefield has been subject to an archaeological desk-based assessment, evaluation, and watching brief (Buck 1996; Cole 1999). A metal-detecting survey was conducted in advance of pipeline construction, but this was restricted to the Registered battlefield – incidentally, showing how influential the Registered boundary can be in governing the archaeological response to threats. The full 20m width of the planned pipeline was detected prior to topsoil stripping, but not all fields within the corridor were accessible. The survey, undertaken by metal detectorists under archaeological supervision, produced no Civil War-related artefacts. The subsequent watching brief during construction was conducted under difficult circumstances and, again, produced no significant results. The metal-detecting survey traced a transect through the two opposing deployments, as defined by English Heritage. While the absence of finds on the parliamentarian side is explained by the inaccessibility of the land for survey, the lack of finds from the area of the supposed royalist deployment does challenge the Register's interpretation. An absence of bullets from an area of cavalry action might be explicable, but the failure to find bullets from a substantial fire-fight between infantry is very difficult to explain. Even if the area had been under pasture for a century or more and the bullets had all migrated to the bottom of the topsoil the results from Edgehill demonstrate that at least some musket calibre bullets would be recovered by competent metal detecting. A systematic metal-detecting survey across a wide area encompassing both alternative sites is required to resolve the uncertainties.

Sedgemoor

In June 1685 the Duke of Monmouth mounted a rebellion in south-west England in an attempt to topple the new Catholic king, James II. It proved an abortive campaign and by 5 July the rebel army, about 3500 strong, lay cornered in Bridgewater, Somerset. That night Monmouth launched a last desperate assault on the camp of the royal army, marching by a circuitous route across the boggy wastes of King's Sedgemoor to attack from an unexpected direction. Unfortunately, the alarm was raised by a royal scout as the rebels attempted to cross the drain known as the Langmoor Rhyne. Then, in the darkness, their cavalry failed to locate the Upper Plungeon – a ford across a relatively shallow drainage ditch known as the Bussex Rhyne – which would have given access, between the enclosures, to the rear of the royal camp. After this failure most of the rebel cavalry seem to have fled the battlefield, although a small detachment did engage some royalist cavalry. Despite this major setback, Monmouth's infantry still marched up and deployed for an attack. However, the element of surprise was lost and they now faced royalist infantry who had already deployed. The inexperienced rebel troops could not be made to advance across the Bussex Rhyne to engage in hand to hand fighting; rather, they stood off and a fire-fight developed, which they could not hope to win against the far more experienced and better-equipped royal infantry. In open country, without cavalry support, the rebel foot proved

Fig 7.6 The battle of Sedgemoor (1685) within its contemporary terrain, as depicted on the third in a sequence of contemporary plans by Dummer, here showing the rebel army as it was routed (© Pepys Library, Magdelene College, Cambridge)

Fig 7.7 Aerial photograph from 1947 showing Sedgemoor battlefield. The Bussex Rhyne is clearly visible as an earthwork, prior to its levelling by modern cultivation. RAF VAP CPE/UK1924/3036and8 (© English Heritage NMR RAF Photography)

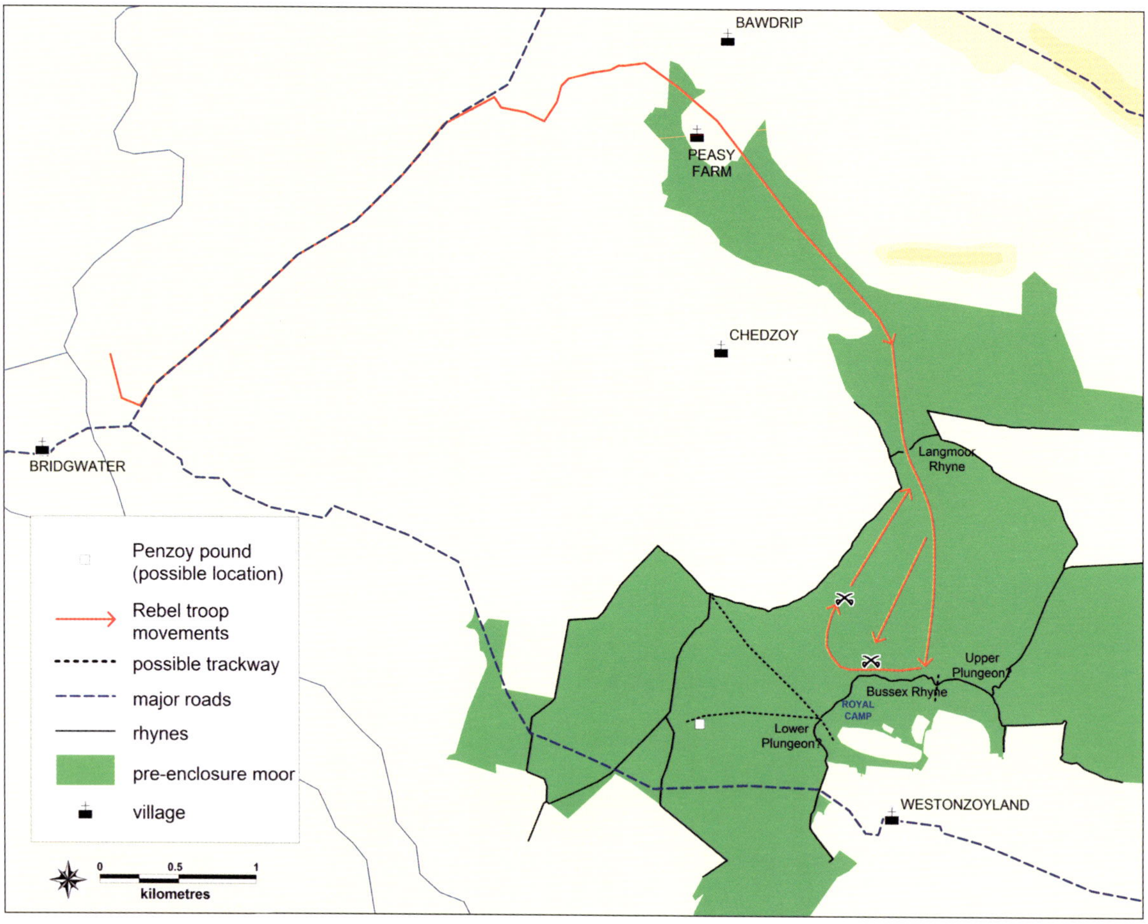

Fig 7.8 Map depicting the main terrain features of Sedgemoor (1685) and its wider context, showing the approach of the rebel army to the battlefield across the wastes of King's Sedgemoor (Foard 2003b)

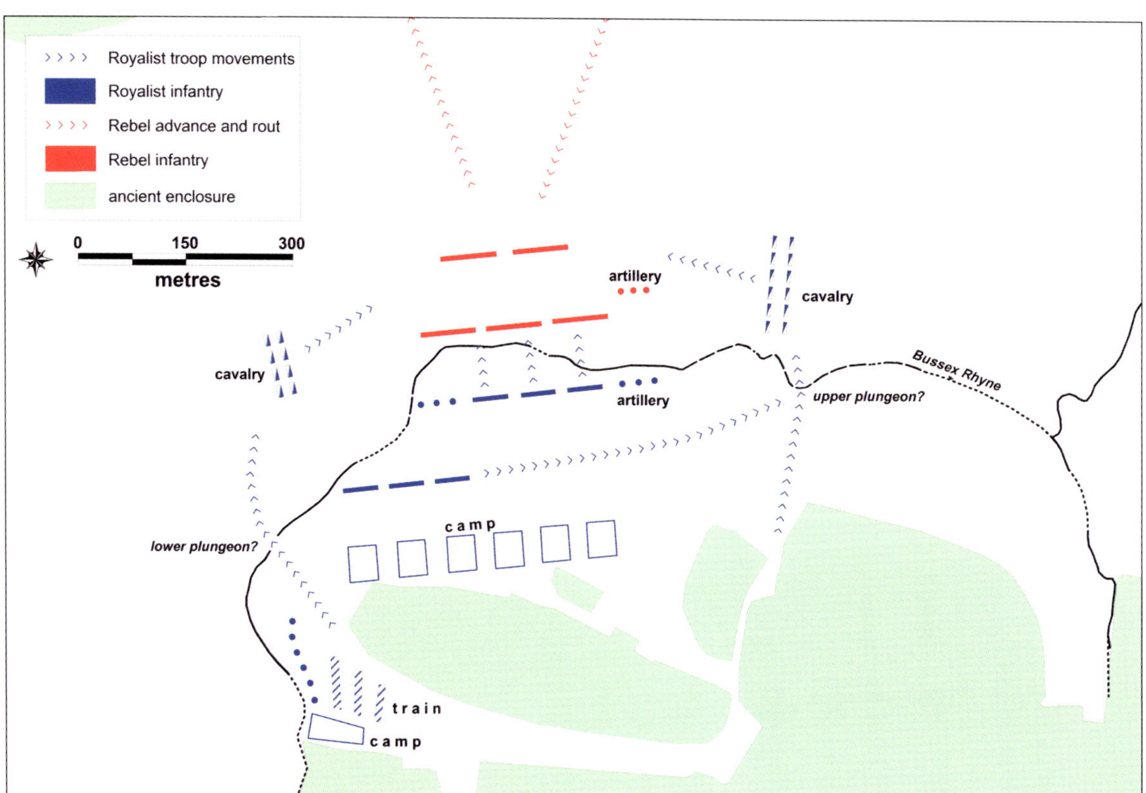

Fig 7.9 Map of Sedgemoor (1685) showing deployment and action within the reconstructed terrain (Foard 2003b)

an easy target. Once he had rallied all his troops from their quarters, the royal commander launched a joint cavalry and infantry attack which destroyed Monmouth's army (Chandler 1999).

Sedgemoor is arguably the best documented of all English battles. There are various detailed written accounts together with contemporary plans by both Dummer and Paschal (Chandler 1999; Young and Adair 1979, plate 13). However, its landscape is one that has been dramatically transformed, largely under an act of parliament of 1791 for drainage and enclosure of the moor. To place accurately the troops and action that are described in the primary sources calls for a detailed reconstruction of the historic terrain. Fortunately, excellent documentary and archaeological evidence is available, enabling a clear demonstration of the methodology of historic landscape reconstruction integrating both types of evidence (Foard 2003b) (Fig 7.6).

The analysis was made using a sequence of historic maps. As always in England, the Ordnance Survey first edition six-inch survey of the 1880s, registered in MapInfo to the modern Ordnance Survey Mastermap, provided the earliest accurate base map against which to work. There was also a sequence of three early maps of King's Sedgemoor: a late 18th-century pre-enclosure map; a drainage and enclosure map of 1795; and a tithe map of Westonzoyland from 1843. Relevant information from each earlier map was successively added, the later map providing the base for mapping from its predecessor, thus correcting for the geodetic inaccuracy of the early maps.[5] Where features were depicted on earlier maps but not later ones then earthwork evidence from the RAF 1947 vertical air photographs, rectified and registered in GIS, was used to position them accurately. This was most successful in locating the 'rhynes', or drainage dykes (Fig 7.7).[6]

The reconstructed plans show a section of King's Sedgemoor, a lowland moor of poorly drained alluvium, with adjacent anciently enclosed arable fields lying on the main islands of Chedzoy to the north-west and Zoy to the south. Westonzoyland lay at the north-west corner of Zoy. Dummer's battle plans show that small areas on the periphery of Chedzoy and of the mainland to the north-east had already been drained and enclosed as meadow by 1685. From Westonzoyland the main road led directly across the moor to Bridgewater. There was also a moorland route that crossed the Bussex Rhyne via the lower plungeon and passed by Penzoy Pound westward. A second track led from that plungeon to Chedzoy, entering the enclosures via Brinsell Gate. Another track crossed by the upper plungeon and went via Langmoor Stone, where it crossed the Langmoor Rhyne. From there it followed a thin tongue of moorland skirting Chedzoy to the east and north, ultimately joining lanes leading from the Bridgewater–Bristol/London road.

Taking the battle accounts and battle plans produced at the time, and using the troop numbers and principles of deployment in the military manuals, a detailed reconstruction of the approach of the rebel army to the battlefield and the deployment of both armies has been developed (Figs 7.8 and 7.9). This hypothesis was then tested by comparison with the pattern of battle archaeology, as provided to the HER by Barry Sagar, together with later investigation by Glasgow University, which itself took account of Sagar's information (Pollard and Oliver 2003, 126–77 and T Pollard pers comm), and subsequent limited archaeological survey carried out in 2007 in response to a threat from pipeline construction.[7] A more extensive data set, from collecting by John Pettet, is currently under analysis by Natasha Fergusson at the University of Glasgow, so the conclusions presented here remain provisional.

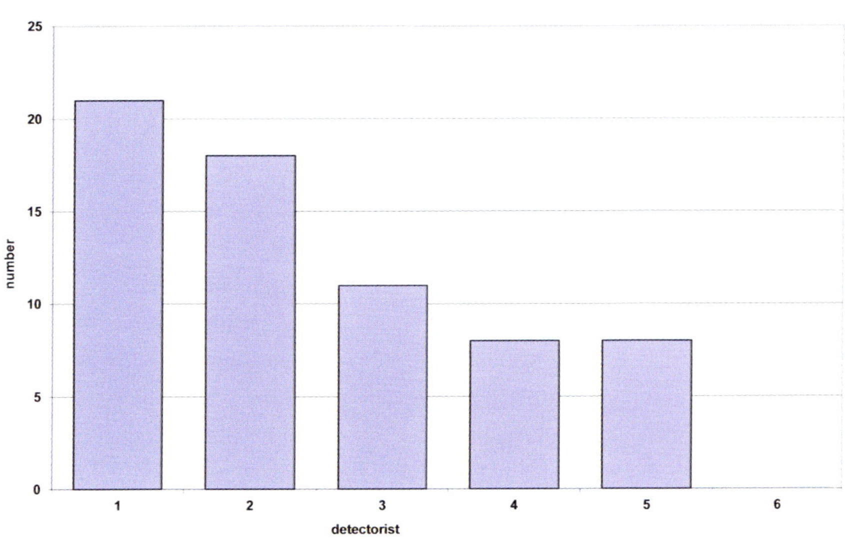

Fig 7.10 Graph comparing the rate of recovery of bullets by each detectorist during one day of survey at Sedgemoor in 2007. One detectorist recovered no bullets, while at the other extreme another recovered 21 bullets

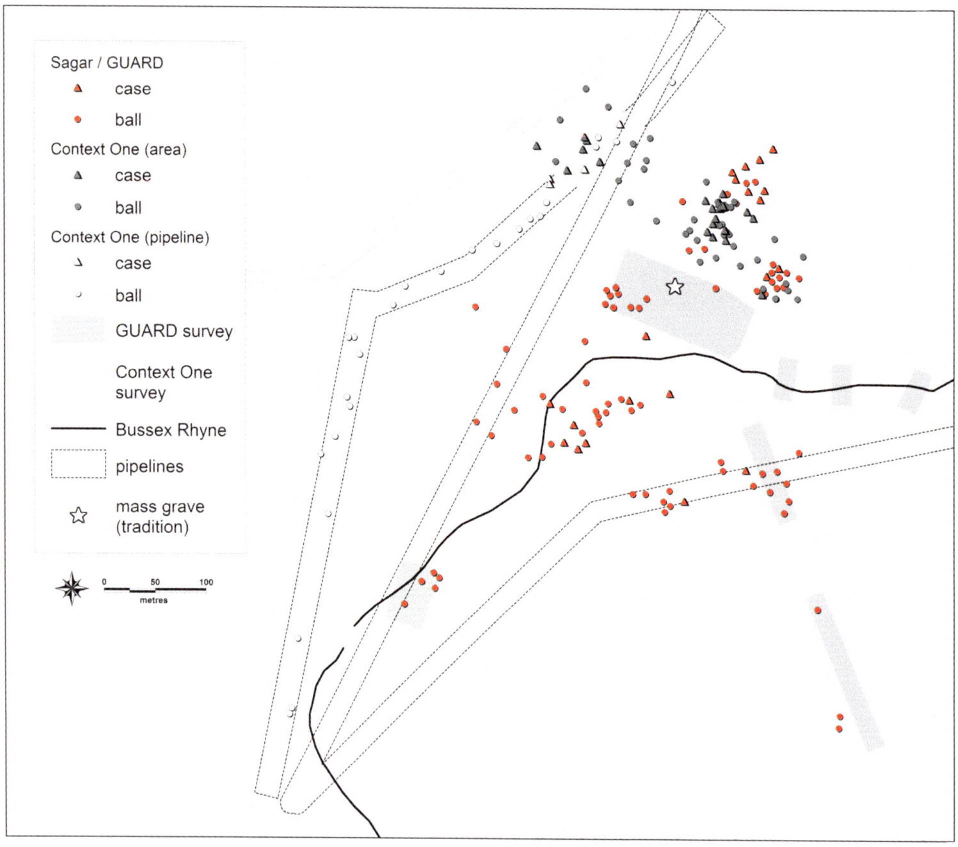

Fig 7.11 Map of Sedgemoor (1685) comparing bullet scatters from a detecting survey by Context One Archaeological Services, in 2007, with that from earlier survey by GUARD and collection by Sagar. Also shown is the extent of disturbance by two existing pipelines and by the new pipeline – construction of which required the 2007 survey prior to topsoil stripping[8]

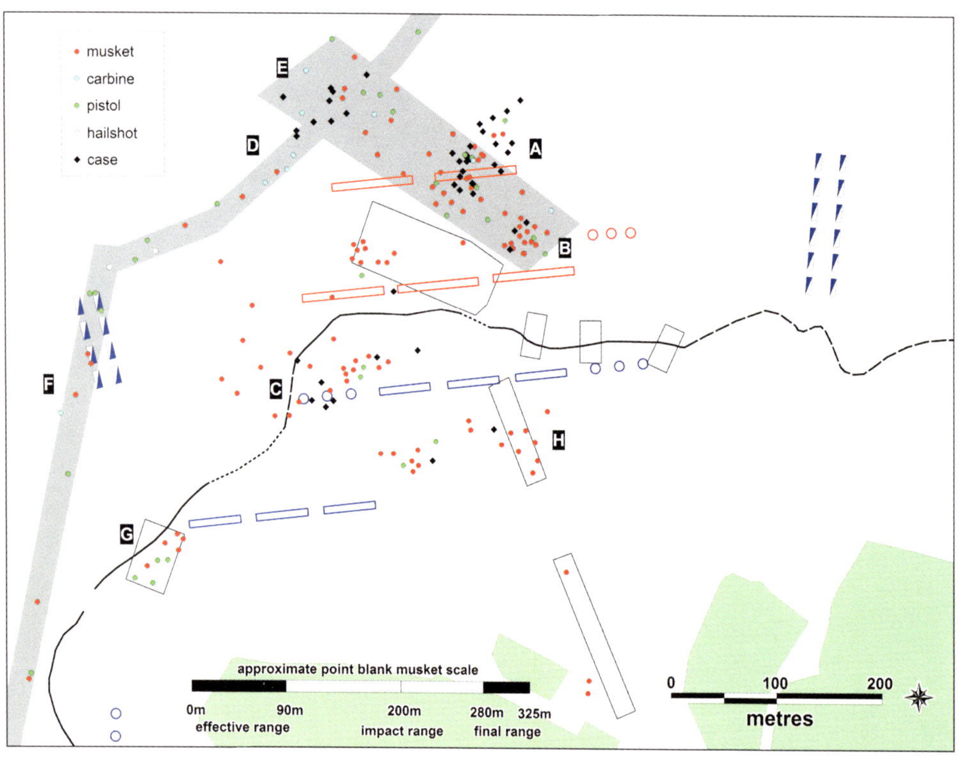

Fig 7.12 Map of Sedgemoor (1685) showing all battle archaeology (from Fig 7.11) in relation to the reconstruction of deployments and terrain (from Fig 7.9)

The 2007 survey was conducted on 2.5m spaced transects along the proposed route of the pipeline and on a single sample field to link the pipeline data to the wider context of the battlefield. It was undertaken with a team of six metal detectorists and followed the methodology applied at Edgehill, using navigation grade GPS to track each detectorist and centimetre-accurate survey grade GPS for recording of find locations. The dramatic variation in bullet recovery rates between detectorists demonstrates the biases that can arise in a systematic survey, and the need to take account of them. This is most likely to occur, as here, when a detecting team that is established for a short period is made up of detectorists with different levels of expertise and using different types of detector. This will have caused some distortion in the recovered pattern, although this was minimised by interspersing the transects surveyed by each detectorist (Fig 7.10).

The pre-2007 data set contains no information on survey extent or intensity. Comparison with the 2007 systematic survey suggests that the distribution pattern from the earlier collection is unrepresentative of the true pattern across the battlefield (Fig 7.11). The 2007 survey shows a far more extensive scatter, with discrete concentrations missed in the earlier work, although some elements of patterning do match. For example, the hailshot scatter recorded by Sagar is matched by that from the 2007 survey, but the latter extends the pattern and thus suggests new locations for artillery pieces. It also greatly extends the spread of battle archaeology to the north and west. Such bias in the evidence from collecting shows the care needed when interpreting sites using such data sets. In contrast, there is good correlation, in terms of both type and distribution of bullets, between the results of the 2007 pipeline survey and those from the survey of the sample field.

The plan combining all the battle archaeology broadly endorses the location of the action suggested by the documentary study, although it raises some questions of detail. The orientation of the hailshot scatters, which typically represent artillery fire in close infantry support, provides the first problem, particularly that at 'A' on Fig 7.12. It suggests that in one stage of the action the orientation of the deployments may have been rotated somewhat further in a clockwise direction than we have shown, for hailshot scatters might be expected to lie at right angles to the deployment. However, if enfiladed fire was involved, then 'A' could represent fire from the artillery on the left flank of the royal army's forward deployment (immediately to the right of 'C'). The furthest distance of this scatter from that suggested royal position is just under 300m, which is just within the range achieved in experimental hailshot firing (Allsop and Foard 2008). Such matters could probably be resolved by more extensive systematic survey aimed at identifying firing lines from the distribution of musket calibre bullets, which could then be compared to the orientation of hailshot scatters.

Though Sagar's work did distinguish artillery hailshot from other bullets, and pistol from musket calibres, there is no information on the criteria used in this classification and no other types, calibres, or evidence on use is presented. The main calibres from the 2007 data relating to pistol, carbine, and musket have been presented in plan form, together with the pistol and carbine bullets identified by Sagar. This demonstrates that the greater part of the scatter to the north-west side is in the form of pistol and carbine fire, representing cavalry action. It also includes very small calibre hailshot, which may have been fired from

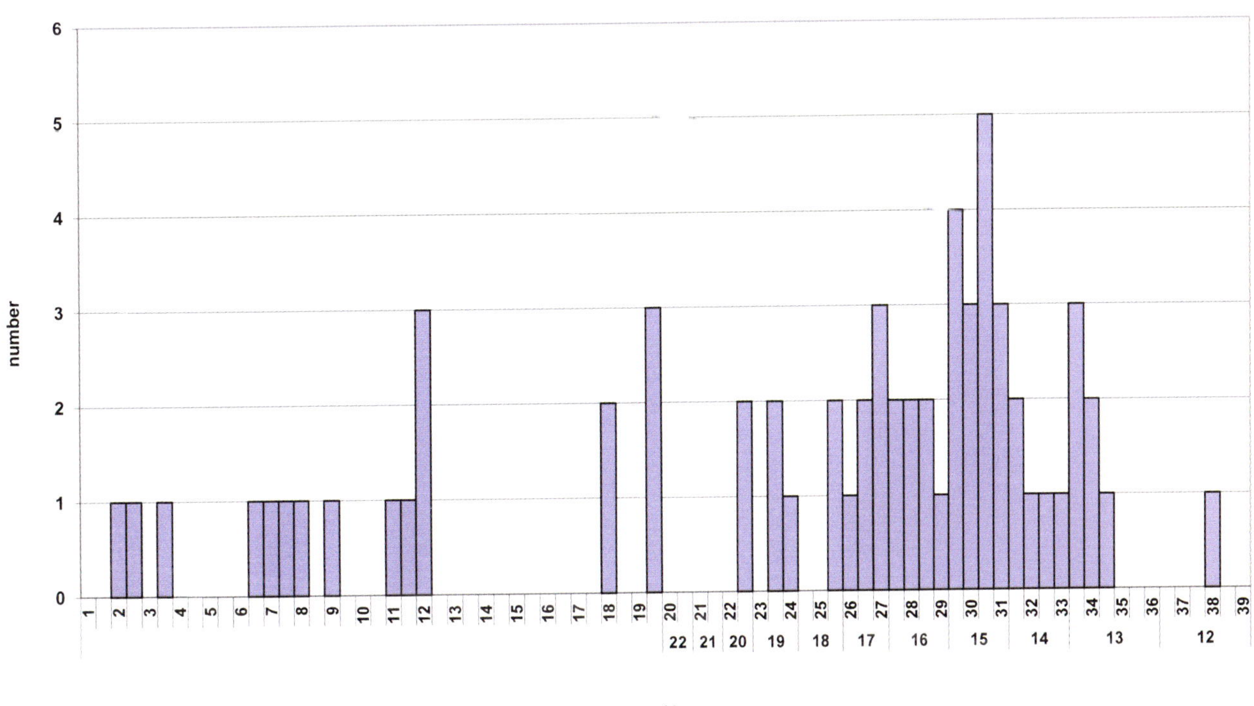

Fig 7.13 Graph of the calibre of bullets retrieved in the 2007 survey on Sedgemoor battlefield. Three possible musket calibres are suggested (centred on 27g, 30g and 34g), but the sample size is so small that the groupings may prove spurious when a larger assemblage of bullets is analysed

small arms as a multiple load together with a single carbine bullet (see Fig 8.7). This combined evidence accords reasonably well with the reconstruction of the royal cavalry's enveloping counter-attack on the rebel right flank.

In the centre there is a far higher density of musket calibres associated with the reconstructed rebel infantry deployment. The presence of a low proportion of pistol calibres within the infantry core may indicate cavalry sweeping through the rebel infantry position or, possibly, may relate to the very early stage of fighting, in which detachments of rebel and royal cavalry were engaged – or both. Such potential for superimposition of evidence is a recurring problem with scatters of battle archaeology and it is one that cannot easily be resolved. The point blank musket range scale tentatively constructed from the initial results of experimental firing (Miller 2010; Foard 2008c, 223–6) suggests that the musket scatters could be compatible with fire from the positions shown for the infantry in our reconstruction. However, the evidence is not sufficiently extensive or consistent to enable bullet overshot lines to be distinguished, which might then be related to deployments. Another problem encountered with the Sedgemoor data is the relatively low numbers of bullets showing impact damage. This is probably because in 1685 this was pasture on soft peat soils, so there were few impacts with stones on the ground when the bullets bounced. In this case it is necessary to examine the bullets to establish which have been fired and which may simply have been dropped. Until all the previously collected bullets are examined for such evidence, assuming that they can be located to individual find spots, such a patterning analysis is not practicable.

More detailed analysis was conducted on the 2007 bullets, using a calibre graph to identify groupings by weight in an attempt to distinguish individual classes of weapon (Fig 7.13). This reveals three peaks for musket which, when calibre shift due to weight loss in firing is taken into account, may broadly correspond with 16, 14 and 12 bore (Foard 2008c, 118). Also visible are five bullets of carbine calibre and three groupings of pistol calibres. Mapping of the distribution of the individual musket calibres suggested in the calibre graph may indicate a significant new pattern, with the 16 bore bullets all concentrated in the rebel position, whereas the 12 and 14 bore bullets are more widely distributed. This might indicate that the 16 bore bullets represent only royal musket fire while the 12 and 14 bore were used by both sides. However, given the small sample size, both the groupings in the graph and the patterns seen when they are mapped may prove illusory.

The case of Sedgemoor demonstrates how easy it is for field examination of a battlefield to miss the largely invisible past disturbance which may have distorted the distribution of evidence. It also shows how, with adequate evaluation, it may be possible to minimise further disturbance. The alignment of sewer pipelines was obtained for the purposes of this study from Wessex Water. While the routes of water mains were not released, as this is sensitive data, they expressed the opinion that although the mains do impinge upon the Registered area they 'occur in areas of previous disturbance which may limit their impact upon the battlefield'. There is no record of the width of the disturbed areas caused by existing sewer pipelines, but it is probably the case that *c* 0.3m of topsoil was removed over a 15–20m-wide working corridor, after which a construction trench *c* 2–3m wide was dug. For the present purpose a 20m-wide corridor spanning the recorded course of each pipeline has been mapped (see Fig 7.11). The two early sewer pipelines cross the centre of the main action, on either side of the Bussex Rhyne, and in this central zone, where most of the key action occurred, the pipelines have disturbed *c* 5% of the surface area. Had the 2008 scheme gone ahead as originally planned, the disturbance would have been increased to *c* 8%. Following evidence from terrain analysis and from an evaluation detecting survey of the proposed route, however, which demonstrated the wide extent of the battle archaeology in this central area, Wessex Water implemented a scheme of directional drilling. The only disturbance from this was the drill pits, thus limiting the impact to 0.5% of this core area.

It is not possible from this limited sampling exercise to assess the degree to which the old pipelines have disturbed the battle archaeology. This may only be determined, if at all, after systematic survey of the whole of the core area to determine whether there are any breaks in the patterning which correlate with the approximate pipeline corridors. The proximity of one pipeline to the apparent location of the lower plungeon, which was one of two crossing points of the Bussex Rhyne used by the royal army in their counter-attack, should also be noted. It is taken here to be the gap in the line of the rhyne on our plan. Had the pipeline been just 15m further to the north-west then it would have passed through the plungeon, destroying most of the information about its character compared to that rest of the Rhyne, which will be valuable in understanding its tactical importance.

Edgehill

While at Sedgemoor small-scale systematic survey was undertaken alongside non-archaeological collection of bullets, at Edgehill investigations on a battlefield-wide scale revealed the nature of bullet scatters. This study, undertaken for the Battlefields Trust between 2004 and 2007, represents the most extensive systematic archaeological investigation of a 17th-century battlefield so far undertaken in England.

On Sunday 23 October 1642 parliament's field army, commanded by the Earl of Essex, clashed with the army of Charles I in the first major action of the Civil War in England. Fought in the open fields between the villages of Radway and Kineton in Warwickshire, this battle was intended to decide the war. Although Edgehill is often viewed as indecisive, the king actually gained an important advantage as a result of this action as Essex failed to break through to his London base and, with his baggage train badly damaged, had to retreat to the security of the garrison at Warwick. This left Charles in command of the road to London – and control of the capital was the key to the war.

Edgehill was fought in open ground without prepared positions and involved no standing buildings. While there is some evidence to suggest the location of mass graves (see Fig 7.15) the objective of the investigation discussed here was to gain an understanding of the distribution of unstratified metal artefacts deposited during the action. The survey of surviving and accessible areas of the battlefield, involving some five square kilometres of metal detecting, took nearly three years of part-time work which comprised more than 3500 man hours of detecting on 10m spaced transects, all undertaken in non-ferrous mode. The use of all-metal mode would have been impractical, as can be seen by the speed of coverage achieved in the Culloden survey, which was undertaken in all-metal mode but examined just 2.4% of the area covered at Edgehill; if the Edgehill survey had been undertaken in all-metal mode, as at Culloden, it would have taken some 6100 man days compared to the 432 actually required. However, the analysis, made possible by the recovery of the bullet distribution across the whole of the surviving battlefield, more than justified the limitations imposed by non-ferrous survey. Moreover, the option still exists for resurvey of sample areas in all-metal mode to test the patterning of battle-related ferrous artefacts.

The lowest intensity of survey which still enabled meaningful patterning in the bullet distribution to be recovered was 10m spaced transects (Fig 7.14). With a detector sweep of 1.5–2.5m on each transect, depending on the technique of the detectorist, and with a forward prospecting speed of about 12m per minute ensuring near-complete surface coverage of each transect, the base survey represents a 15–20% sample of the surface area. After completion of the battlefield-wide survey, more intensive sampling using 2.5m spaced transects was undertaken to refine the detail of patterning in key areas (Figs 7.15 and 7.16).

In total, 3250 artefacts were collected and retained during the survey. Of these, 1096 are early modern lead bullets of a wide range of calibres and types. Only a handful of the other non-ferrous items are certainly of military origin, by far the largest group being the 29 powder-box caps and priming flask tops from musketeers' bandoliers. The number of non-bullet artefacts recovered that can with certainty be placed in the mid-17th century form a tiny percentage of the total assemblage (Figs 7.17–7.20), although further study of these artefacts, in comparison with material from other battlefields, may enable more information to be extracted. In contrast, the vast majority of lead bullets do relate to the battle, though the assemblage will have been contaminated by a small number of bullets from earlier and later sporting activity, almost all of less than musket calibre. The relatively low number of bullets recovered for each man hour expended is a result of the survey including such an extensive area of cavalry action and infantry rout, which tend to produce a low density of bullets. The greater part of the main infantry action, which typically provides a far higher density of bullets, had been destroyed by modern development or was largely inaccessible under woodland.

The bullets can be subdivided into three types: ball and slug for small arms and hailshot fired from artillery. The lead balls can be further subdivided into three main calibres, classified here as pistol <18g; carbine >=18g and <25g; musket >=25g, although the graph suggests that subsidiary calibres are present for both musket and pistol (see Fig 4.12). Using this basic classification there are 497 ball of musket calibre, 155 of carbine and 295 of pistol; 34 slugs of carbine or pistol calibre; and 127 balls fired as hailshot from artillery. The complexity seen in the graph may in part be due to variable weight loss caused by melting during firing, as discussed in Chapter 4. The other potential problem at Edgehill is the degree to which at this early stage of the war the armies were supplied with old equipment (Young 1967, 26).

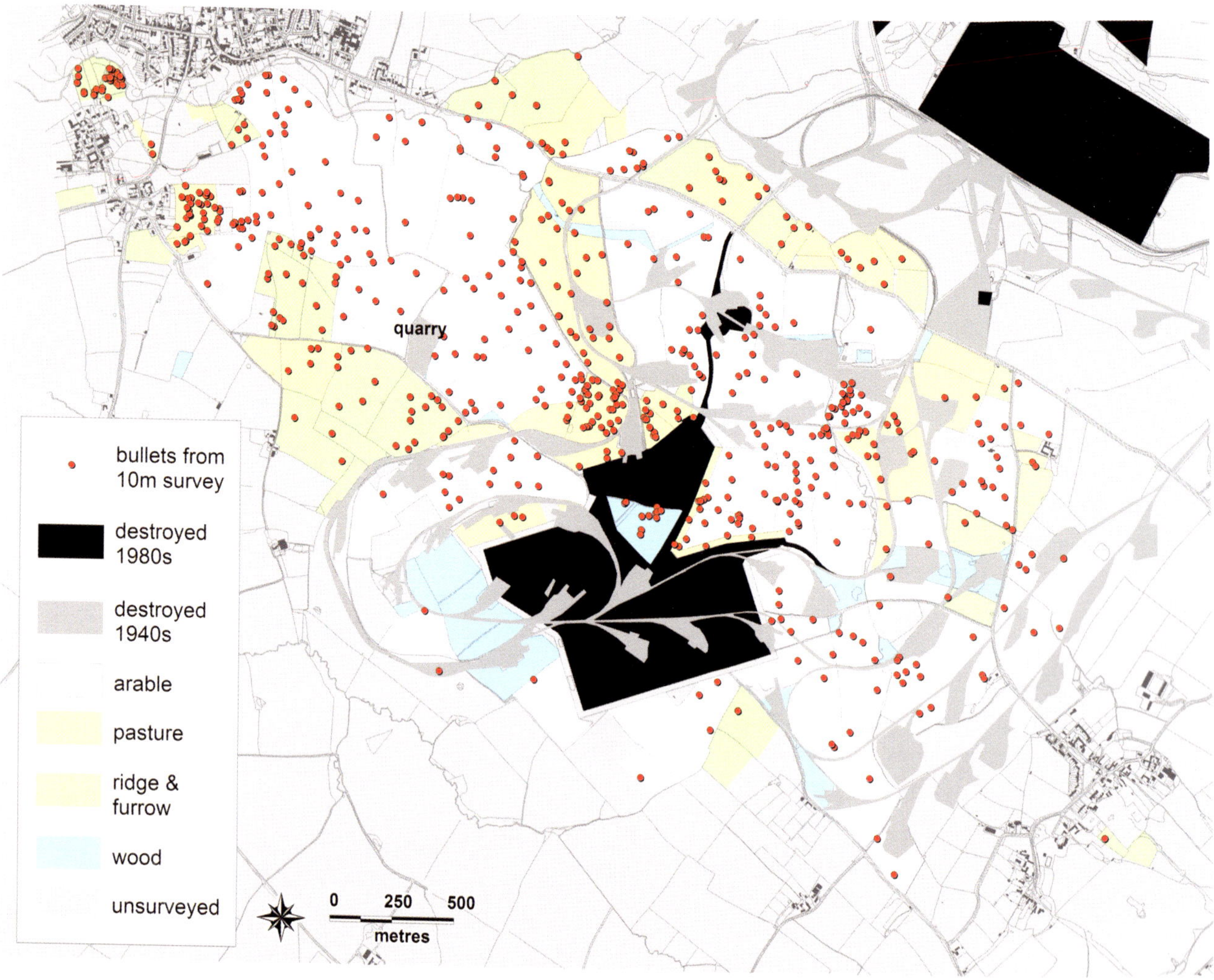

Fig 7.14 Map of Edgehill (1642), showing bullets from base survey (10m transects) set against a background of the state of development and land use in the survey area. The only woodland surveyed was that within the modern depot. The 1940s silos and rail lines were almost all removed in the 1980s, when the new depot was constructed (Foard 2008c) (Reproduced by permission of Ordnance Survey on behalf of HMSO. © Crown copyright and dataset right 2012. All rights reserved. Ordnance Survey Licence no. 100024900)

Fig 7.15 (facing page, top) Map of Edgehill (1642) showing bullets from the 10m transect base survey in 2004–07 and possible locations of mass graves. The traditional site where Captain Kingsmill (buried in Radway church) was killed by parliamentarian artillery fire is taken from the 1756 map of Radway (Foard 2008c)

Fig 7.16 (facing page, bottom) Map of Edgehill (1642) showing bullets from resurvey (at 10m and 2.5m) added to those from the 10m transect base survey. Comparison of this with Fig 7.15 reveals the impact of survey intensity on the density of distribution patterns (Foard 2008c)

The distribution of pistol, carbine, and musket calibres appears broadly representative of the intensity and character of fire-fights (Fig 7.21), and though not all fighting involved the use of firearms, the patterning may be expected to reflect the location, extent, and intensity of most of the action. Musket calibre bullets are concentrated in the centre of the battlefield, but they represent only part of the area of infantry action, much of which has been destroyed by modern development. The scatter of musket calibre bullets also extends north-westwards at low density, a pattern interpreted as the rout of parliamentarian infantry. The scatter increases again near Little Kineton, where it is mixed with a higher density of pistol bullets. This grouping is interpreted as the defeat of troops guarding the baggage train, positioned around Little Kineton, in the face of a royalist cavalry attack. The bandolier items also have a distinct distribution that appears to relate primarily to this area of infantry rout and defeat (see Fig 7.22). A further scatter of musket bullets, towards the east of the battlefield, appears to represent the final stages of the infantry action, when the royalists retreated in the face of a parliamentarian counter-attack. According to the battle accounts, this

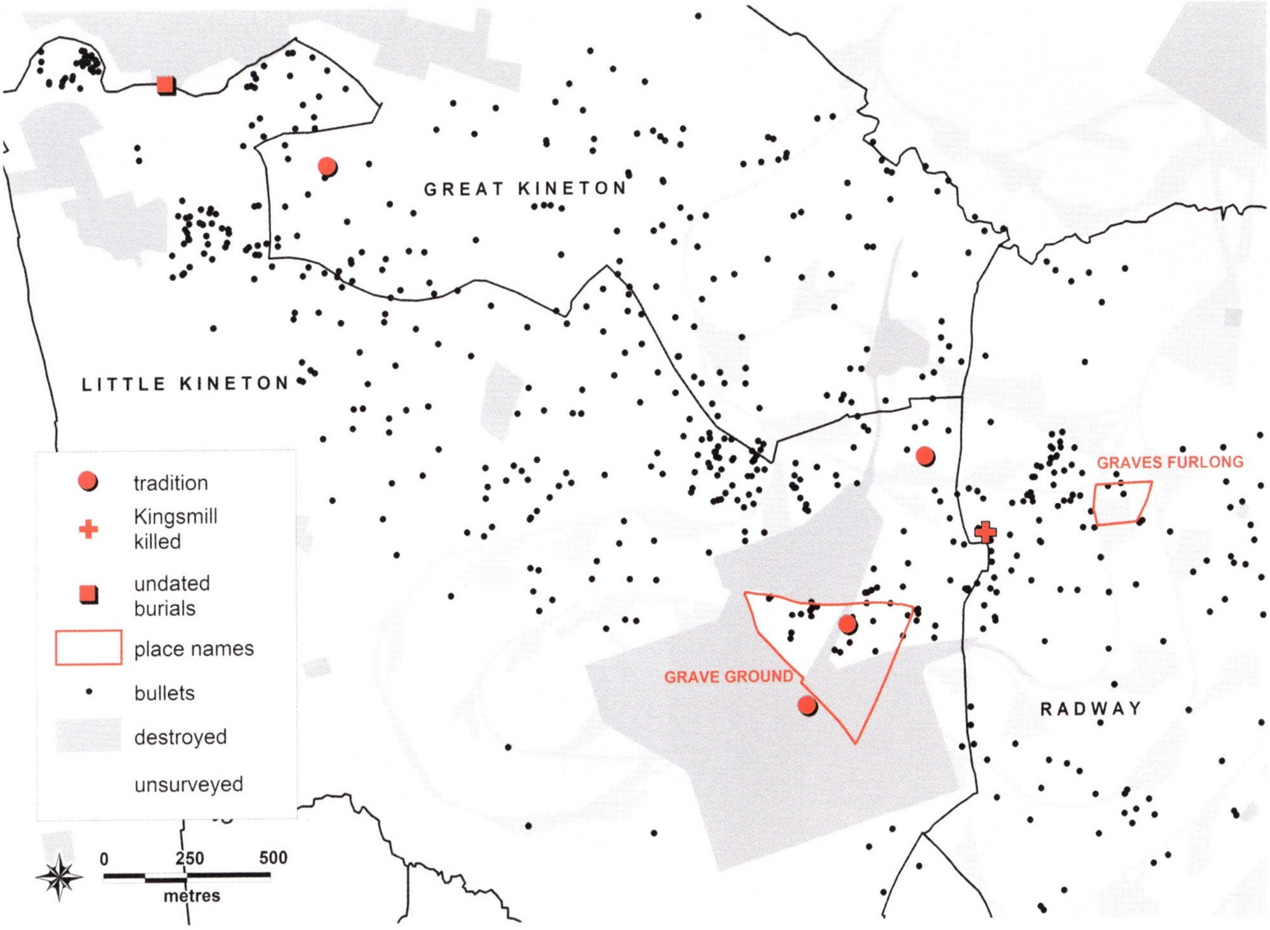
GREAT KINETON
LITTLE KINETON
RADWAY
GRAVES FURLONG
GRAVE GROUND
tradition
Kingsmill killed
undated burials
place names
bullets
destroyed
unsurveyed
0
250
500
metres

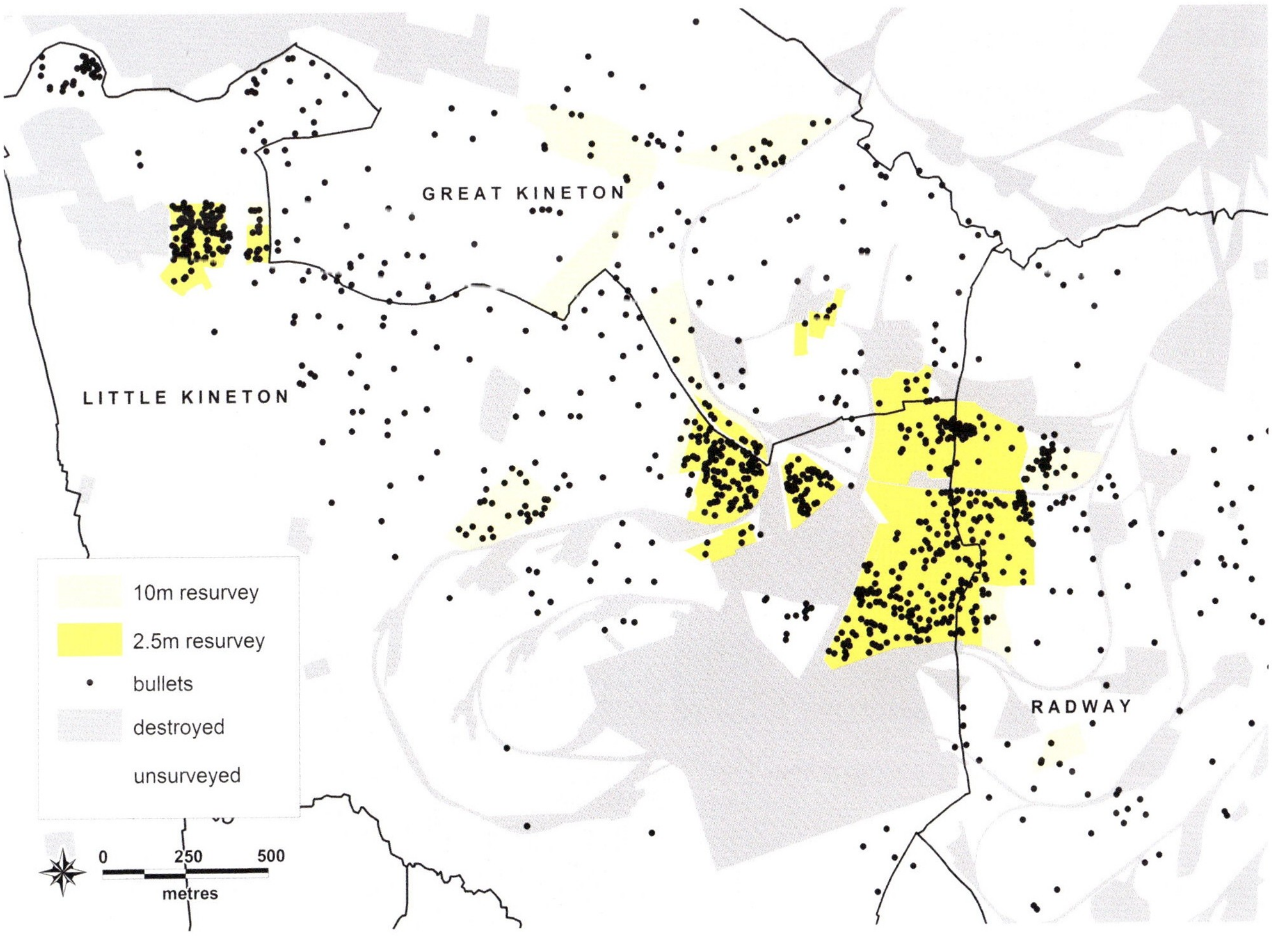
GREAT KINETON
LITTLE KINETON
RADWAY
10m resurvey
2.5m resurvey
bullets
destroyed
unsurveyed
0
250
500
metres

Fig 7.17 (above) Leather-covered wooden powder box, with a lead cap secured by a leather thong, from a musketeer's bandolier. This would have held a single charge of gunpowder (from a private collection)

Fig 7.18 A moulded lead powder box cap from Edgehill, diameter 23mm. Two distinctive loops can be seen, through which was passed the leather thong to secure cap and box to the bandolier

Fig 7.19 Moulded lead top from a priming flask, distinguished by its long spout for pouring fine powder into the priming pan. Also visible are the loops through which a leather thong attached it and the wooden flask to the musketeer's bandolier. The find is shown in the field immediately after retrieval at Edgehill, prior to cleaning (courtesy of D Beaumont)

Fig 7.20 Typical equipment carried by a Civil War musketeer, including a matchlock musket and a bandolier of twelve powder boxes, each with a single charge for the musket. Hanging from the bandolier, below the bullet bag, is a priming flask which carried the fine powder with which the musket's priming pan was charged prior to each firing

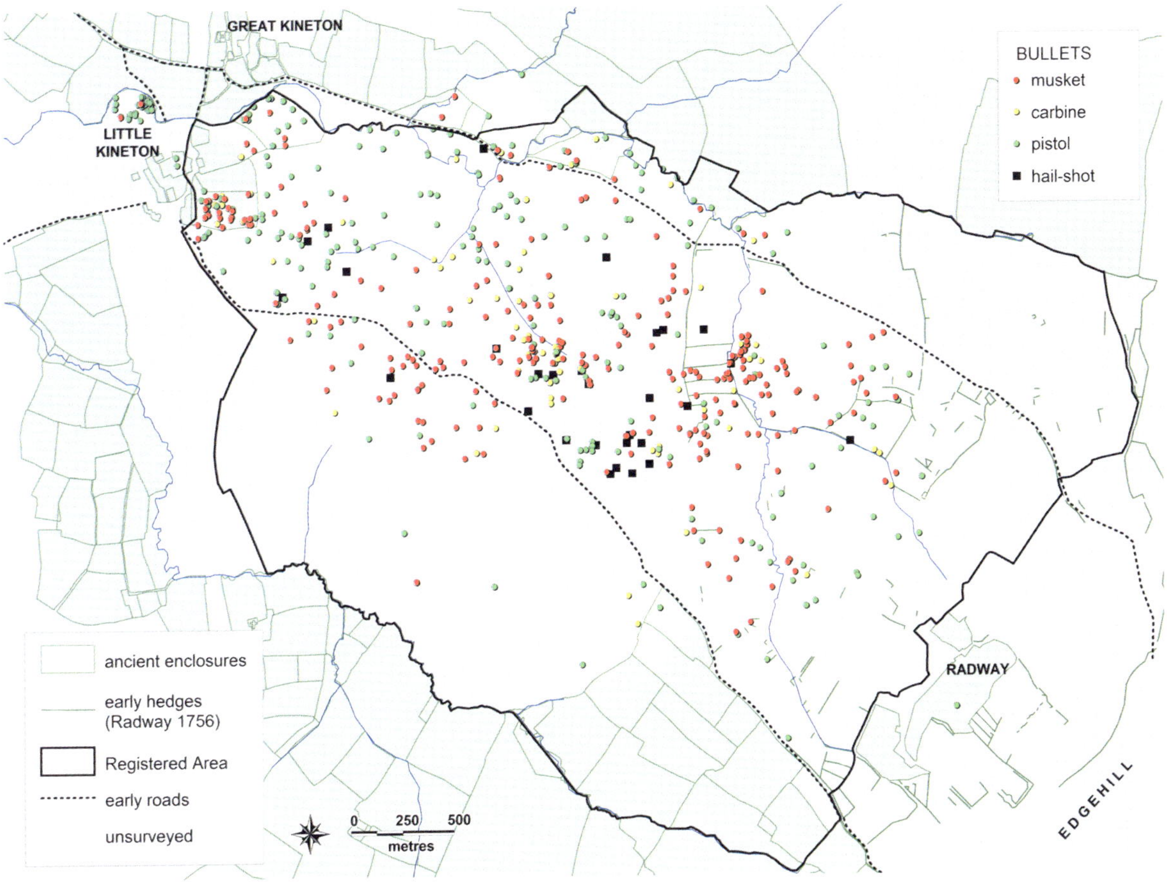

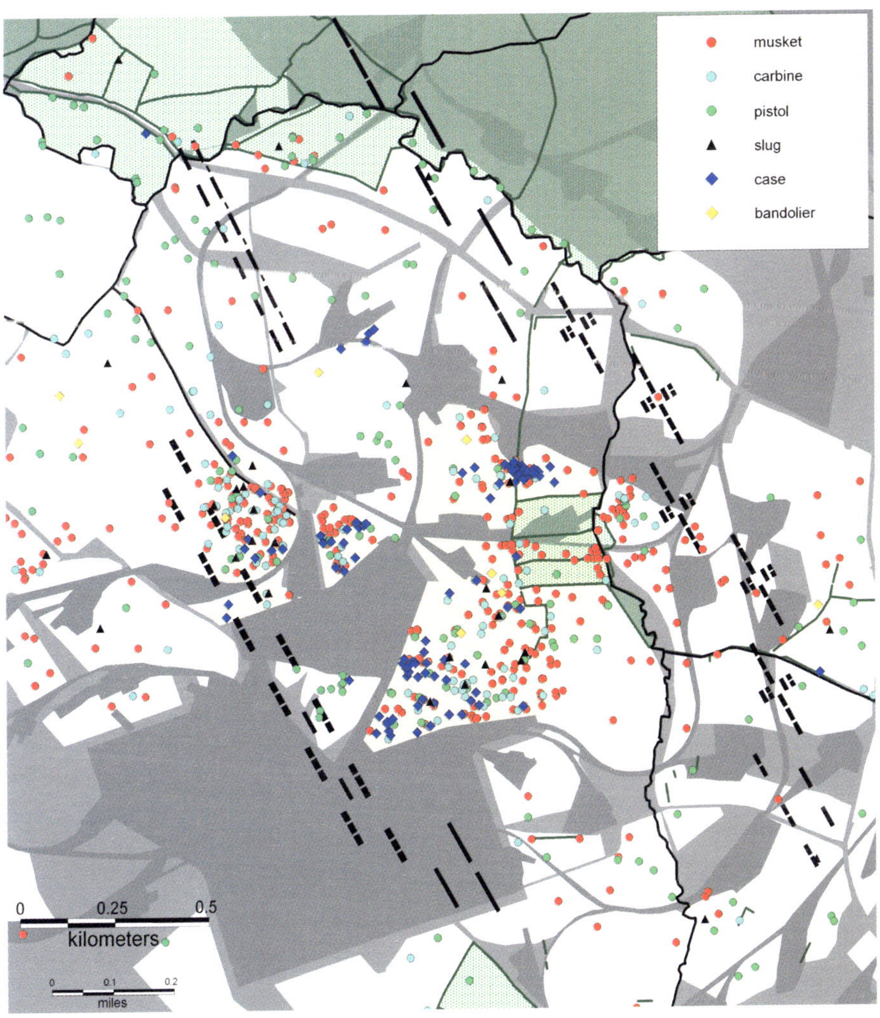

Fig 7.21 Map of Edgehill (1642) showing the distribution of the main bullet classes recovered in the 10m base survey, depicted against a background of the historic terrain derived from sources of various dates (Foard 2008c)

Fig 7.22 Map of the central area of Edgehill (1642), showing the distribution of the main types and calibres of bullet and the powder box caps from bandoliers. The background of terrain and other data is from Fig 7.21. The conjectural reconstruction of the battle deployment of both armies is based on the analysis of primary sources, terrain reconstruction, and battle archaeology. Significant uncertainties remain because much of the area of infantry action was destroyed by the creation of the munitions depot in the 1980s (Foard 2009)

was finally halted by artillery and musket fire from a ditch.

Pistol calibre bullets are found throughout the battlefield. Several distinct groupings are apparent. The concentrations in the northern part of the battlefield are interpreted as the initial attack by the right-wing royalist cavalry and their pursuit of fleeing parliamentarian cavalry. At the western end of this scatter the density increases as it approaches Little Kineton; as just discussed, this may represent the royalist cavalry attack on the baggage train. Two other scatters of pistol bullets, albeit far less clearly defined, lie in the south-eastern part of the battlefield, in an area largely restricted to parliamentarian cavalry operation.

Some cavalry carried carbines as well as pistols, although the picture is blurred because some pistols were of a carbine calibre. A carbine fired a larger bullet than a pistol and so was able to cause more damage, but was more difficult to fire than a pistol when on the move. For these reasons the carbine may often have been used in a different context to pistols. At Edgehill the carbine bullets are only sparsely associated with the wider cavalry action as defined by pistol bullets. Rather, they are found predominantly in association with musket bullets – both in the core infantry action and in the area around Little Kineton, suggesting that the carbine was the weapon favoured by cavalry when engaging infantry. The 34 slugs (see Fig 4.17) of carbine or pistol calibres also have a close association with infantry action where cavalry were engaged. This may, again, be an attempt on the part of the cavalry to increase the damage done by their firearms by increasing the mass of the projectile. A significant revelation of the Edgehill survey is the sheer quantity of carbine and especially of pistol bullets, in contrast to the evidence previously published for Naseby and Marston Moor (Foard 2007a; Foard 1995, 241–9). This suggests that assemblages produced by non-systematic collection grossly under-represents the smaller calibres, so giving a distorted picture of a battle.

In addition to small arms rounds, 127 bullets which had been fired as hailshot shot from artillery were found (see Fig 4.6). The sampling rate achieved with the 10m-transect survey means that several hailshot scatters were represented by just one or two bullets, and it is thus possible that some locations where hailshot was fired were not identified in the base survey. Hailshot distributions were clearly resolved only where resurvey was undertaken on 2.5m transects, revealing the orientation of most scatters and, with the benefit of experimental firing results to aid interpretation, in several cases suggesting the approximate gun position (see Fig 4.7). This hailshot evidence proved central in reconstructing the location and orientation of the original parliamentarian battle formation because, in this period, field artillery was typically placed in pairs between each battalion. At Edgehill, in addition, three artillery pieces were placed with the left wing of the cavalry. Only one of these three appears to have been located in the survey.

In the Edgehill survey all three elements of analysis have been employed: historic terrain reconstruction; re-analysis of the documentary accounts of the battle, enabling the deployments and events to be placed within the terrain reconstruction; and large-scale survey of the battle archaeology, leading to a revision of the overall interpretation (Fig 7.22). This work suggests that the battle lines need to be re-orientated by 90 degrees compared with those shown by studies based principally on the written accounts. It also appears to locate securely various elements of the action in relation to the terrain.

Despite the level of detail available from Edgehill, considerable uncertainty remains. While this is partly due to the degree of loss in the heart of the battlefield, it is also because of the current lack of comparative evidence. When other well-preserved Civil War battlefields have been explored in similar detail a more sophisticated interpretation of artefact distributions may be possible, which in turn may necessitate reinterpretation of Edgehill.

Sieges and related sites

While sieges originally lay largely outside the scope of the present study it was decided that those of the Civil War should be considered in some detail, as certain aspects of their archaeology are comparable to what is seen on battlefields of the same date – a characteristic which has thus far been insufficiently investigated. They contain five main types of evidence for military action: bullet scatters; impact scars on structures; siege works; destruction levels; and burials. The present discussion is offered as a scoping exercise, illustrating what might be achieved through more detailed investigation. It also confirms siege sites as an important class of monument, and one where the battle archaeology is vulnerable and currently not being effectively managed.

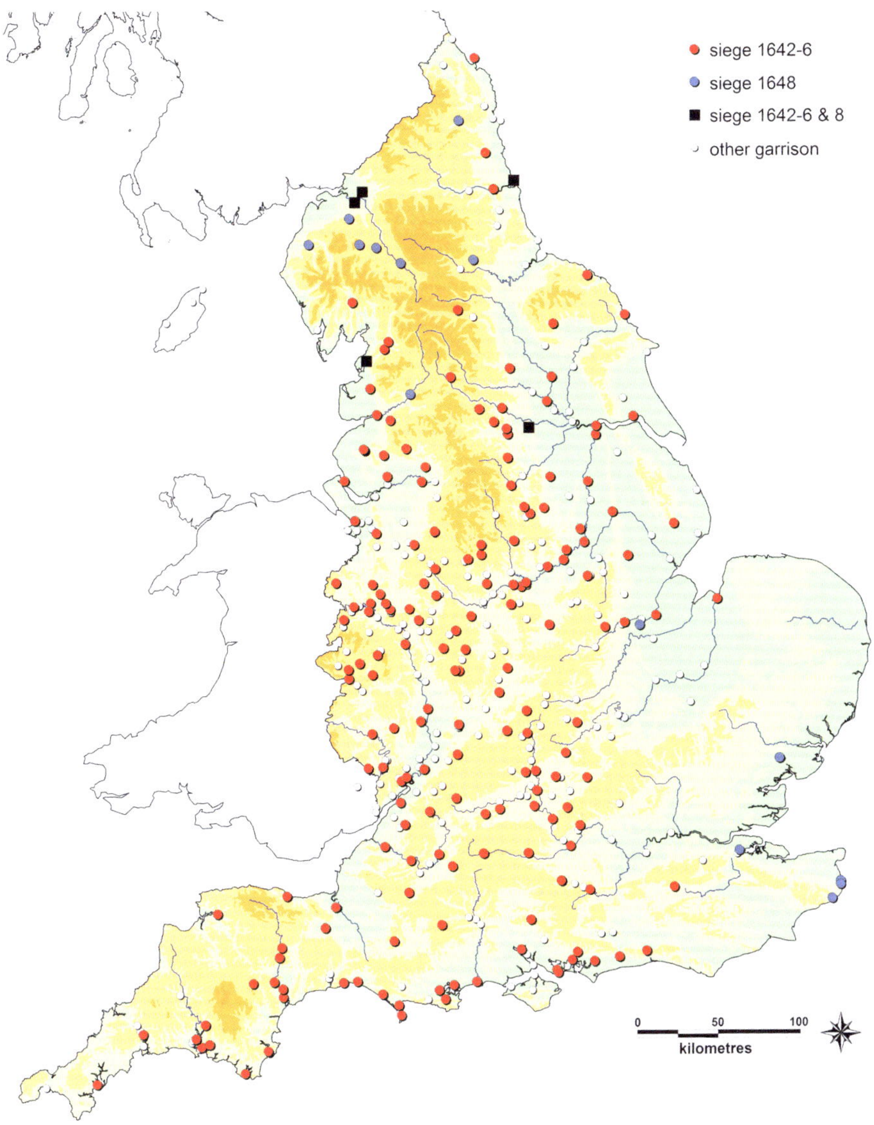

Fig 7.23 Map of siege sites and other garrisons in England from the Civil Wars

The Database includes 242 sieges in England, of which 223 are from the first Civil War (1642–46) and 19 from the second (1648) (Fig 7.23). There are, however, just 189 siege sites, as a number of garrisons were besieged more than once. Thus, for example, the major royalist garrison of Basing House was attacked in 1643, 1644, and 1645. Evidence from a siege will vary in nature according to the scale, duration, and character of the action; the size of the garrison and the attacking forces; and the scale of the defences. A siege that involved attempts at storming is more likely to have left complex and informative archaeological evidence; a total of 41 such events was identified, though this is likely to be a large underestimate.

Many sieges included the construction of offensive works, such as trenches to approach the defences or saps to undermine them. There were also camps for the attacking forces, some of which will have had their own defences. The scale and complexity of such works can be seen at Newark, where the remains appear to be the only major example of English Civil War offensive works to have seen extensive archaeological study (Royal Commission on Historical Monuments 1964). Some other sites have seen more limited investigation as part of wider studies, as at Plymouth (Pye and Woodward 1996). While no attempt has been made here to collect information on the detail of the siege works themselves, some information has been published (Harrington 2003, 35–9; Harrington 2004).

In addition, there are garrisons for which no record of a siege has been identified. These do not appear on the Fields of Conflict Database, but, as some of them may have seen action, a supplementary database of Civil War garrisons was developed (see Fig 7.23).[9] This is probably the most complete listing of garrisons and siege sites so far produced, but is still not exhaustive. There will also be a small number of sites which were not garrisons, as such, but which saw action. For example, the church at Canons Ashby, Northamptonshire, was used as a refuge by a 'tax-collecting' force from Northampton when attacked by troops from Banbury. The latter proceeded to launch an attack on the church, blowing the door with a petard and firing the tower – which, as a result, remains a floorless shell today (Page 1893). Additional garrisons and sites of lesser actions will be identified only by a systematic search of the secondary works on the War that have been produced at a county and regional level.

While there has been extensive study of defensive works in 17th-century England, there has been little archaeological investigation of the attacks upon these garrisons (Saunders 2004; Harrington 2003). This is surprising given that such attacks relate directly to the primary purpose of the sites, while their study may reveal a great deal about how, in practice, they were attacked and defended. Where recording has been undertaken it has been mainly though survey of earthworks, as at Newark, or through excavation of stratified evidence for saps and mines, as at Pontefract Castle. The two other types of evidence – impact scars and unstratified bullet scatters – have seen almost no investigation, and form the focus of the following discussion.

Impact scars

Impact scars on buildings resulting from fire-fights and artillery bombardments have long been known (Barrett 1896, 285) (Figs 7.24–7.26). Such marks have, however, usually been treated more as curiosities than as potential sources of information. Field inspection of 16th- and 17th-century battlefields in England for the present study revealed impact scar evidence only at Nantwich (on Acton church – see Fig 7.29) and Winwick Pass (on Winwick church). There are also reports of impact scars on Winwick church, which was used as a refuge by some routed troops during the battle of Winwick Pass (1648), although it was also part of a garrison in 1643 (M Rayner pers comm). Such cases are rare partly because few battles involved the use of buildings or walls for defensive purposes and partly because relatively few structures from the period have survived unaltered. For example, a detachment of royalist musketeers deployed behind isolated buildings and enclosures to slow down the parliamentarian advance at the beginning of the battle of Adwalton Moor in 1643 (see Figs 8.15 and 8.16) were driven off in a fire-fight by parliamentarian musketeers who

Fig 7.24 Bullet impact scars on sandstone walling at Ashby-de-la-Zouche castle, Leicestershire, which was besieged in the 1640s. The typical cup-shaped central hollow can be seen, surrounded by surface spalling, though here the edges have been smoothed by erosion. There is also evidence of radial fractures and of fragmentation where one impact was close to the edge of a stone. 100mm scale

Fig 7.25 Bullet impact scars on the church tower at Holmes Chapel, Cheshire. They may derive from a skirmish which followed the nearby battle of Middlewich in 1643. Here, as on many sites, the scars tend to concentrate from around knee height to a metre or so above head height – unless a higher window or other opening was being targeted (Reproduced by courtesy of G Garner)

Fig 7.26 A round shot impact scar from artillery fire against the exterior of Tong church, Shropshire, showing similar but more extreme evidence to that which results from bullet impacts. 100mm scale

fought from building to building. The action will almost certainly have left scars on the structures, but none of the buildings concerned appear to survive today (Foard 2003a; Foard 2010b; Johnson 2003).

In contrast, impact scars are far more common on siege sites, particularly castles and churches. Impact scars were identified in our assessment at 32 sites, though many more may be expected to produce comparable evidence.[10] Limited recording was carried out on several sites to assess where scars are likely to survive and what information may be drawn from them. While the vast majority should prove to be the result of Civil War action, a few may be the result of later activity. This must be the case with the scars on Lyveden New Build, a late 16th-century hunting lodge in Northamptonshire, as it was certainly never defended during the Civil War (Page 1893). It did, however, lie within a hunting landscape, while the site is also said to have been used, for a day or more, as a military camp in the 18th century. Both provide a possible context for the use of the building for target practice.

A scar is produced by bullet impact on all but the hardest stones, such as granite. Sandstone and limestone appear to provide the best evidence, although such masonry often weathers badly, resulting in the scars sometimes being obscured by erosion. In general, scars are most clearly defined on dressed stone and very difficult to recognise on rough-hewn stone or rubble; they can be several centimetres deep and typically have a cup-shaped central depression often surrounded by shallower irregular damage caused by surface spalling. Less often there are radial fractures, especially where the impact is close to the edge of a block of stone, and occasionally pieces of stone may have been broken off at the edge. Such attributes are quite distinct from the pitting of stone caused by natural erosion and other damage attributable to human activities. Normally, recognition is difficult only where stonework has been heavily weathered.

While most marks appear to be from musket fire, occasionally there are larger scars caused by artillery, as at Tong church, Shropshire (Fig 7.26). Round shot impact scars on the defences of Chester appear to be the only example of such evidence to have been recorded in detail (Ward 1987). Surviving evidence of structural damage from artillery fire is reported on

Fig 7.27 Detail of one of many impact scars on a brick outbuilding at the Carter House, Franklin, Tennessee, USA. The impacts are from firing, probably of Minié ball, in an assault during the American Civil War. 100mm scale

several other sites, including Lichfield Cathedral, which suffered two Civil War sieges (Gardiner 1893, 97–8, 108; B Meeson and W Rodwell pers comm).

Only one example of a round shot impact scar has been noted on brickwork. This is on the wall of the Grange, which lies within the outermost defences of Basing House (A Turton pers comm). The character of bullet impact scars on brick seems to be quite different from those on stone, having a far more jagged and fractured form, as demonstrated by Minié ball impacts from the American Civil War on Carter House in Franklin, Tennessee (Fig 7.27). However, a Minié ball will have had a higher velocity than a 17th-century musket bullet, while this American brick may have been harder than 17th-century English examples, perhaps leading to differences in the character of the scars.

Another variant is the bullet hole in timber. This is seen on various siege sites, including the timber-framed 'Siege House' at Colchester, the main door at Hillesden church, Buckinghamshire (Fig 7.28), and the tower doors of Berkeley church, Gloucestershire.

In the absence of any existing methodology for the recording of these scars, a simple method was employed here. Firstly they have been mapped in plan, to record the surviving distribution and thus give an indication of the intensity and direction of incoming fire. Two sample sites have been mapped in this way: Acton church, Cheshire, which was involved in the battle of Nantwich, 1644; and Morton Corbet castle and church, Shropshire, besieged in 1644. Secondly, a sample elevation of Morton Corbet Castle was recorded to present the vertical distribution of impact scars. Such elevations must accompany a plan, as distinctive vertical patterning has been noted on many sites (see Fig 7.25). There is a need to develop a more accurate and objective method of recording such evidence, to release its full potential. One option may be to record individual scars using a portable laser scanner, which would enable more detailed comparison of the form of original scars with those produced in firing experiments, where the angle of impact, bullet calibre, and amount of energy dissipated on impact are all known.

Acton churchyard appears to have formed the focus of the royalist baggage train during the battle of Nantwich in 1644 (National Army Museum 1995k). The documentary record shows that it came under parliamentarian attack – events witnessed by more than 50 bullet impact scars which survive on the building. A sketch plot of the distribution has been made from a series of photographs of the walls, although for full recording a measured survey would be required using photo rectification for each elevation. The plan presented here appears to indicate the scale and distribution of incoming fire (Fig 7.29). Additional information would be required to determine how much evidence may have been lost.

Salter's plan of the church shows that the addition of the 19th-century vestry will have obscured or destroyed scars on that part of the building. Other evidence may have been lost when the upper stages of the church were rebuilt in the later 18th century. It is possible that some impact scars have been lost through piecemeal refacing and stone replacement. Occasional

Fig 7.28 One of the bullet holes in the wooden door in the north porch of Hillesden church, Buckinghamshire. They are believed to be from the storming, in 1643, of the royalist garrison which encompassed both the church and the adjacent Hall

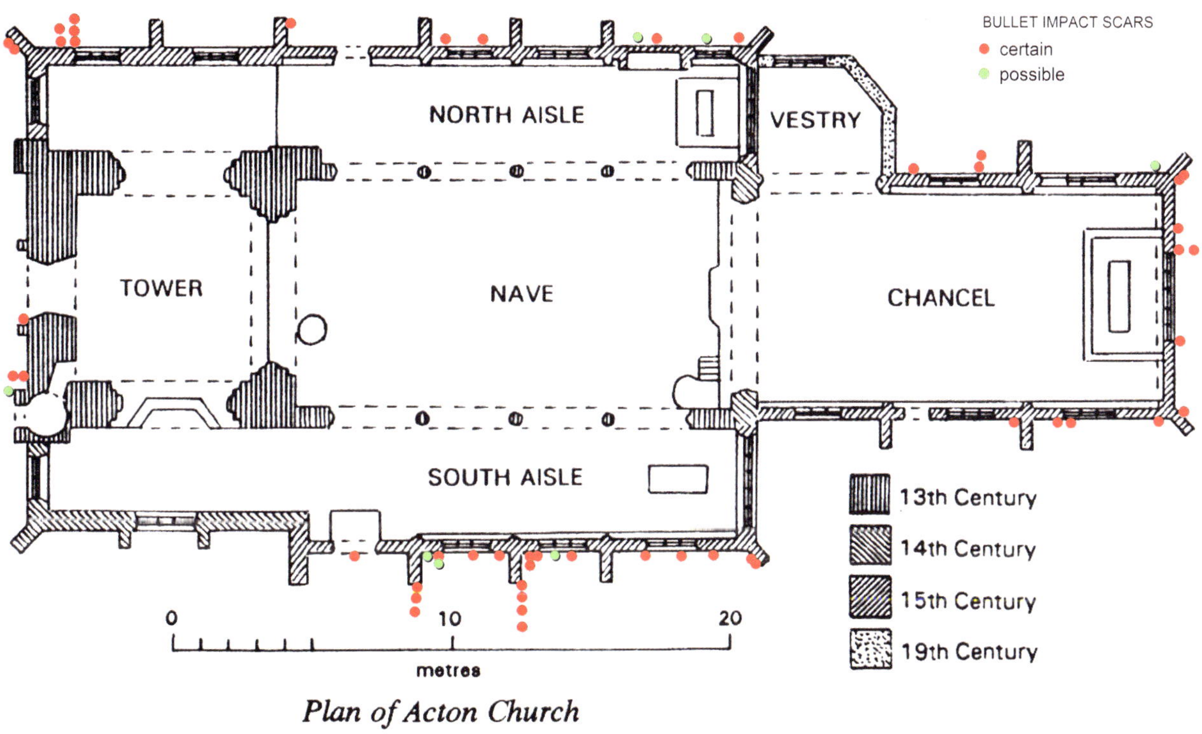

Fig 7.29 Plan showing the distribution of bullet impact scars on Acton church, which was attacked during the battle of Nantwich (1644). Each scar is indicated by a single red dot, with green dots indicating where evidence is equivocal due to erosion. Data collected by G Foard in 2007 and superimposed on a plan of the church taken from Salter 1995 (Reproduced by permission of M Salter)

patching to repair scars was noted, but a detailed stone-by-stone record with inspection at close quarters would be required to establish where stone has been replaced. Another uncertainty concerns the number of bullets which passed through windows. No impact scars were found within Acton church, but at Tong incoming rounds passed through one window and impacted on internal walls (Fig 7.30), probably during the 1644 royalist assault on the parliamentarian garrison in the adjacent castle (Auden and Frost 2007).

Further pilot recording of impact scars was undertaken at the English Heritage property of Morton Corbet Castle, Shropshire (Figs 7.31–7.33), a minor royalist garrison between 1643 and 1645. It was

Fig 7.30 Impact scars, one partly repaired, on the arch of the north aisle arcade at Tong church, Shropshire. They must be from rounds which passed through the windows

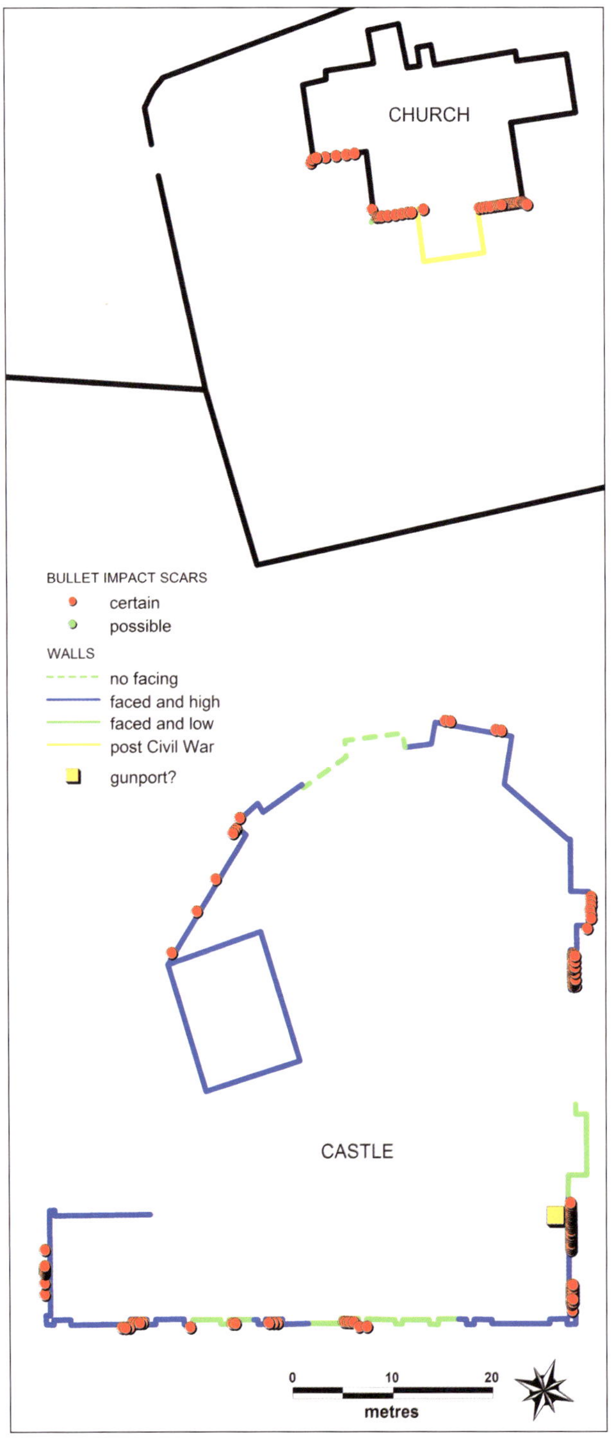

Fig 7.31 Plan showing the distribution of bullet impact scars on Morton Corbet castle and church

Fig 7.32 The largest concentration of impact scars on Morton Corbet castle is on the walling in the south-east corner. Here a circular opening, possibly a gun port for a small artillery piece, has been created. The small hole above and to the right may be a viewing point for the gunner

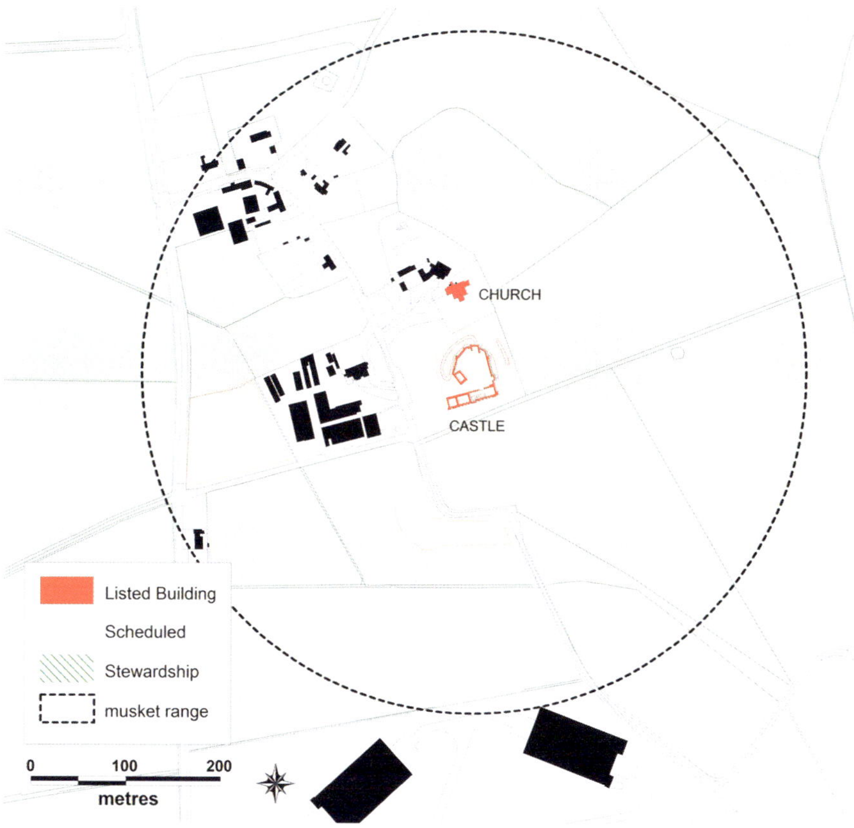

Fig 7.33 Map showing the Scheduled area, Listed Buildings and Entry Level Stewardship area, in 2010, around the Civil War siege site of Morton Corbet. Also depicted is the approximate final range of a musket bullet fired point blank from the castle – based on the Ashdown firing experiment in 2007 (Reproduced by permission of Ordnance Survey on behalf of HMSO. © Crown copyright and database right 2012. All rights reserved. Ordnance Survey Licence no. 100024900)

Fig 7.34 Impact scars on the gatehouse of Kenilworth Castle. The larger scars appear to be from bullet impacts and are accompanied by small scars which may be from hailshot fired from a handgun. They might derive from the firing of multiple loads, comprising a single bullet with a large collection of shot of small calibre placed above. A bullet from such a multiple load is shown in Fig 8.7. Alternatively they may prove to be two superimposed sets of scars as evidence of hailshot can be seen around the edges of the large scars. 130mm scale

stormed on the night of 8 September 1644, but was soon back in royalist hands and was not finally abandoned until late 1645 (Bracher and Emmett 2000). The assault presumably involved the attackers taking the adjacent church, for it too carries scars from bullets, though here fired solely from the direction of the castle. In contrast, the impact scars on the castle suggest that it was attacked primarily at the south-eastern corner, where there is also a possible makeshift gun port (see Fig 7.32). The distribution of scars is compromised, however, by the fact that large parts of the walls no longer survive, while some other sections remain only as unfaced or very low walling. Hence, the picture provided by the impact scars is unlikely to be wholly representative of the action.

Various distinctive attributes seen on different sites warrant further investigation. Thus, on one church in Devizes there is a grouping of very deep scars which have been suggested to be artillery hailshot impacts (Barrett 1896, 285). Another distinctive combination is seen at Kenilworth, where a small number of impact scars survive on the gatehouse and barn of Kenilworth castle (Fig 7.34). These are part of a wider spread of such evidence that extends to the remains of both the Abbey and the town church. On one part of the gatehouse there is an apparent association of bullet and small calibre hailshot impact scars. Although it is possible that the two types are coincidentally superimposed, they may come from a single weapon discharge, which would be further evidence for the use of an unusual combination of projectiles first suggested by a bullet recovered in the Sedgemoor survey (see Fig 8.7). Examples similar to that from Sedgemoor have subsequently been identified in the bullets from the siege of Wareham: these are of musket calibre and were fired as part of a multiple load, with small calibre hailshot resting immediately above. This may be a precursor of the 'buck and ball' multiple loads used in the 18th and 19th century in the USA (L Babits pers comm).

Fig 7.35 An impact scar from experimental firing against a sandstone block. Also seen is a fragment of the impacted bullet that caused the damage, which was recovered from a point several metres in front of the wall. The scar shows the typical irregular spalling and fracture lines, but the central 'cup' is less clearly defined than in most original examples

Impacted bullets

There are many situations in which impact scars do not survive. This may be because a structure has been demolished, rebuilt, or refaced, or because the stone was too hard to take an impact scar or too roughly dressed to enable their identification. Despite this, the intensity and distribution of incoming fire may still be recoverable from impacted bullets in front of the wall. Though some bullets will have been recovered later, many may remain in the ground where they fell after ricochet. Indeed, bullets in the ground around buildings are likely to be far more common than impact scars, yet they have scarcely been mentioned in archaeological literature and as far as we know there are no plans from excavated sites showing their distribution.

Various anecdotal reports refer to bullets recovered from standing structures. At Marston Moor (1644) there is even mention of bullets recovered from the trunks of trees on the York estate, on the south-east side of Long Marston village (Colonel York pers comm). Other places where embedded bullets might be sought include 'Cornish hedges' and similar forms of embanked boundary. Stratton battlefield, where intense fire-fights took place within an enclosed landscape of Cornish hedges, is one site which might produce such evidence (National Army Museum 1995p).

The effect on spherical bullets of impact with stone and other building materials has seen little or no research and, as a result, it is unclear how much useful evidence may be recovered (Foard 2008c). To gain an impression of the types of evidence involved

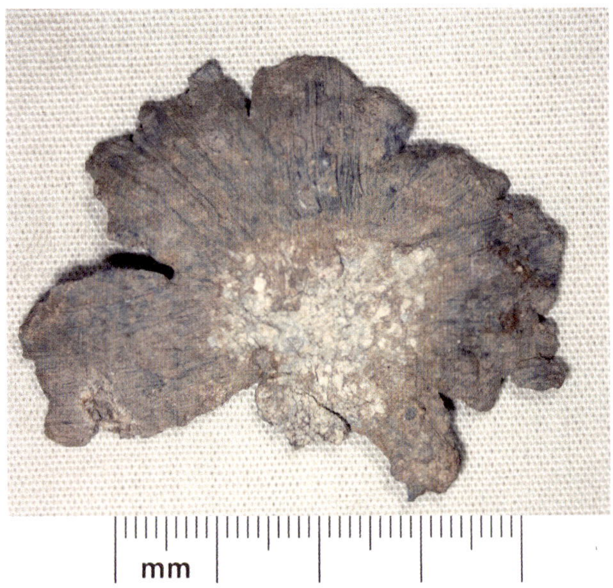

Fig 7.36 A massively impacted bullet from Beeston Castle excavations, showing the impact face. At the centre is an area with an irregular surface which here, unusually, is covered by a white deposit. This seems to comprise embedded grains from the impacted stone. Melted lead radiates from this core to the periphery, where some has been lost by spalling. The symmetrical form may indicate an impact at or near 90 degrees to the wall

we have examined assemblages from the excavations of Civil War siege sites at Beeston Castle and Sandal Castle (Ellis 1993; Mayes and Butler 1983). Both assemblages show a very high number of impacted bullets compared to battlefield assemblages, the evidence including attributes not previously encountered. For example, some bullets seem to provide evidence of their angles of impact, while other variations in the degree and character of impact damage

Fig 7.37 A massively impacted bullet from Sandal Castle excavations. The asymmetrical location of the core (below) and radial flow concentrating towards the top suggests an oblique impact

may reflect the range from which the bullet was fired and the type of surface impacted. Some bullets also appear have embedded particles from the impacted surface (Figs 7.35–7.37).

The true potential of such evidence will be determined only through a programme of detailed investigation on siege sites. This work should assess various aspects, among which should be the stone itself, to seek a correlation between hardness, which can be measured with a Schmit Hammer, and the depth of the scar (P Doyle pers comm). It would also need to be complemented by a programme of firing experiments.

Bullet scatters

On siege sites, just as on battlefields of the period, the archaeology of attack may often principally consist of a scatter of bullets. While most bullets lying close to the walls will be from incoming fire a more complex pattern may exist if there was a storming which breached the defences. Outgoing fire will extend at least 350m from the defences – a distance which firing experiments indicate is the approximate final range of a musket bullet, if fired point blank. While hailshot from artillery will have a similar range, round shot will have carried much further. There may also be wider scatters of bullets relating to ancillary action, where troops engaged in skirmishing beyond the defences.

Unlike battlefields, the background noise of non-projectile artefacts on most siege sites will be large. This is because a garrison may have been present for months or years, while the site may also have been occupied before and after the war. In such circumstances a higher proportion of non-projectile artefacts on siege sites is likely to derive from occupation rather than combat, making it more difficult than on a battlefield to distinguish battle-related artefacts.

At Grafton Regis, Northamptonshire, a dense bullet scatter extends well beyond 500m from the area of the garrison. Bullets have been recovered at a similar distance from the defences of Boarstall Tower, Buckinghamshire. In the environs of a garrison other buildings may have provided cover for attacking forces and these may yield impact scars and/or impacted bullets. One example is the pattern of impact scars on Morton Corbet church (see Fig 7.31), while another is the bullet scatter recovered within buildings at Hayes Barton during excavation in the 17th-century suburbs of Exeter, which was besieged several times in the Civil War (Henderson 1987).

A handful of other surveys, almost all of small scale, have been identified in the present review. At High Woods, Colchester, a bullet scatter relating to the 1648 siege was recorded (P Wise pers comm). Limited field survey undertaken on Prince Rupert's Mound at Lichfield, which was part of the defensive works around the cathedral, recovered a small number of munitions, including bullets and a cast-iron grenade fragment (Welch 1998). Small-scale systematic metal-detecting survey undertaken in 2001–02 in Farnham Park, Surrey, in an area north of the castle, recovered bullets of musket, carbine, and pistol calibres and several fired as hailshot from artillery. All presumably relate to the 1643 siege of the castle (D Graham pers comm). The case studies below illustrate various aspects of the evidence that may be available from siege sites.

Grafton Regis

Grafton Regis, Northamptonshire, was a small royalist garrison briefly besieged in 1643. It is the only siege site in England to have been subject to an extensive, systematic archaeological metal-detecting survey, during which the Midland Archaeological Research

Fig 7.38 Map of Grafton Regis, Northamptonshire, where a royalist garrison was besieged in the fortified manor house and church in December 1643. The distribution of bullets, recovered from systematic metal-detecting survey, is depicted against a reconstruction of the historic terrain. Some of the field boundaries undoubtedly post-date the siege, especially within the new deer park to the south-west of the village, which was disparked immediately after the Civil War[11]

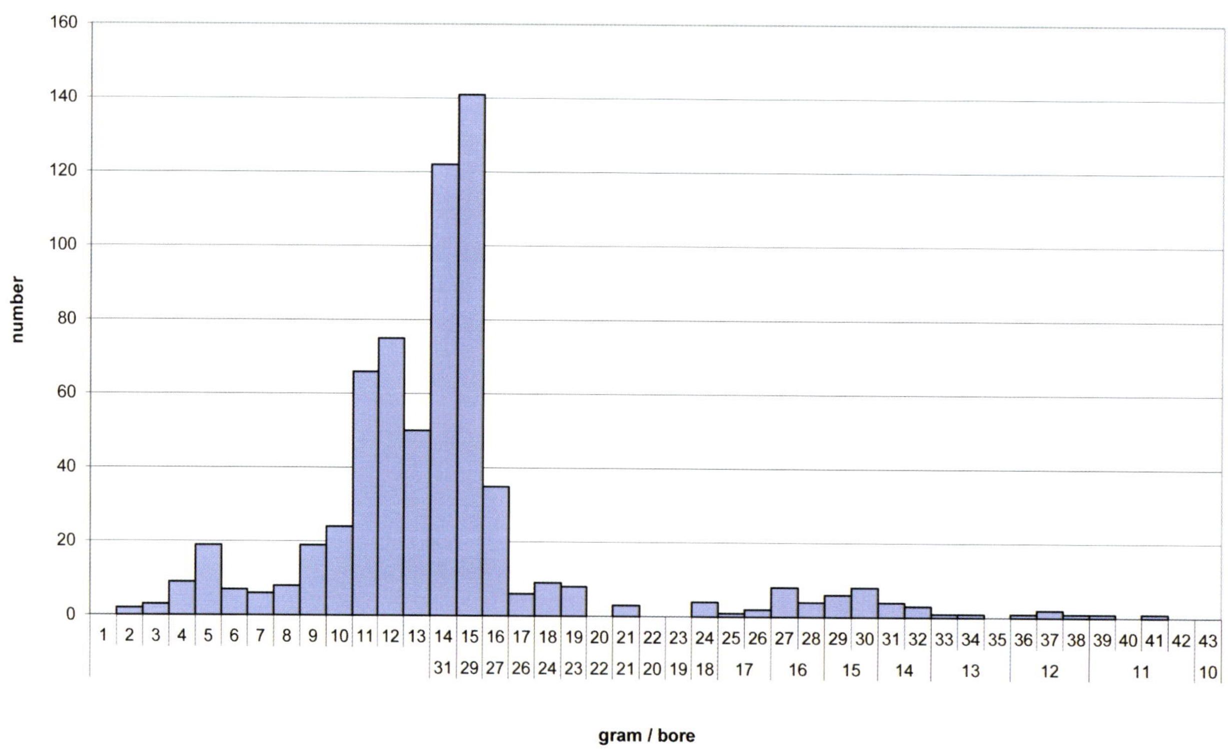

Fig 7.39 Graph of bullet calibre for the Grafton Regis (1643) siege site in Northamptonshire

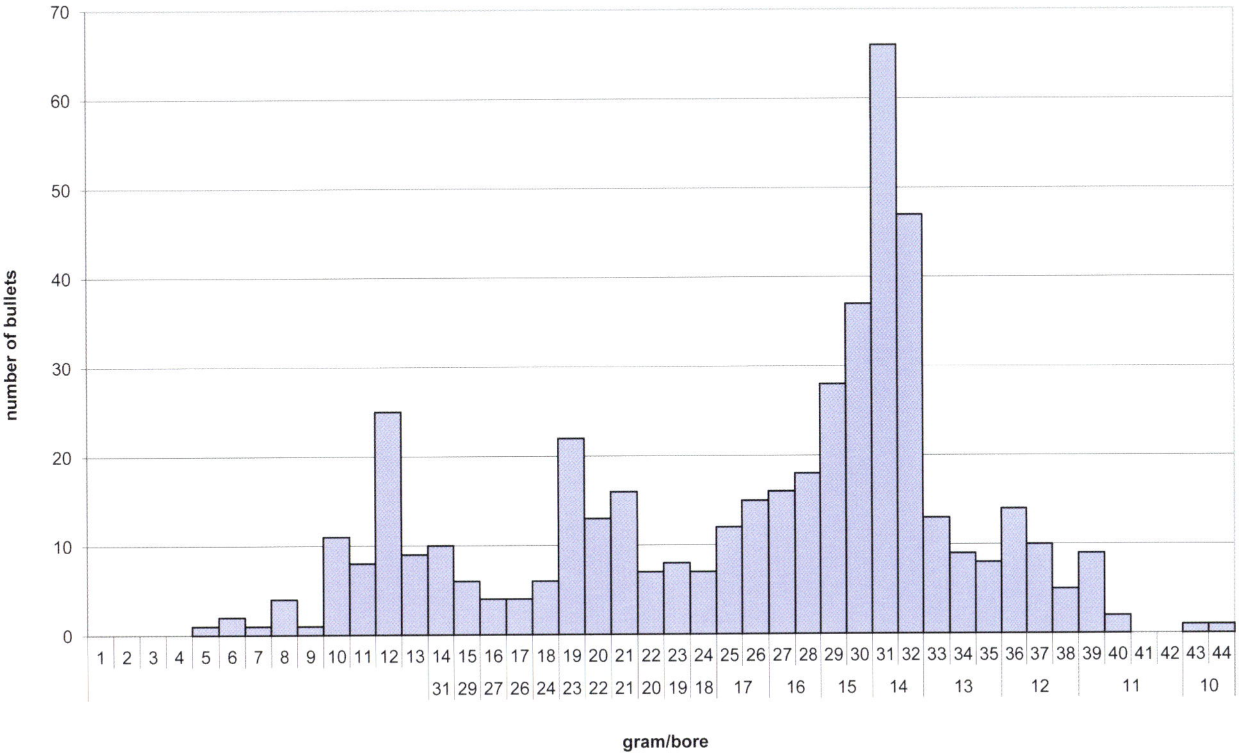

Fig 7.40 Graph of bullet calibre for finds collected by D Coppin immediately outside the defences of the royalist garrison of Basing House

Society recovered over 800 bullets. The survey, which took place in the late 1990s, was designed in collaboration with Bob Kings, who then supervised the investigation, while finds analysis was undertaken by Mark Curteis (Foard 2000; Foard 2001).

The area was divided into a grid of 20m × 20m squares, each of which was intensively searched by a detectorist on a series of overlapping parallel transects at about 1m intervals (not accurately measured or recorded) to give overlapping coverage of the whole square. Each artefact was separately bagged and sketch plotted at a large scale within each of the squares. Each find, together with the key attributes from finds analysis, was mapped in GIS to enable distribution maps to be compiled, and the data was then integrated with evidence for the historic terrain prepared from both historic map and written sources (Fig 7.38). A calibre graph was also prepared from the analysis by Curteis (Fig 7.39). The small calibre of most of the bullets at Grafton differs sharply from those shown on the graph for Basing House (Fig 7.40) and, while at present the full significance of such variations is not clear, it does indicate differences in the types of weapons being used by particular troops.

The investigation at Grafton was not completed because the survey was too intensive, demanding too great a commitment from the volunteers, especially in areas where few finds were being made. Among other things, this demonstrates the need for surveys to be undertaken at a sustainable level of intensity. Where more detailed investigation is required, this can best be achieved by follow-up resurvey of specific areas once the initial survey is complete.

Boarstall

Boarstall Tower was a fortified manor house within which a royalist garrison was established in 1643 as an outpost to the royalist capital at Oxford. It was abandoned soon afterwards, but then reoccupied by the parliamentarians in the spring of 1644. They surrendered in the face of a royalist assault a short time later and a royalist garrison was again installed. In late 1644 the site was briefly besieged by Sir William Waller. Another siege followed in late May 1645, when a large detachment of the New Model Army attempted a night assault. This failed and soon afterwards the siege was raised. The royalists then strengthened the fortifications, demolishing the church and all the surrounding buildings in the village to establish a clear field of fire; however, the garrison finally surrendered to another parliamentarian siege in 1646 (Page 1925, 10–11; Porter 1984, 86–90).

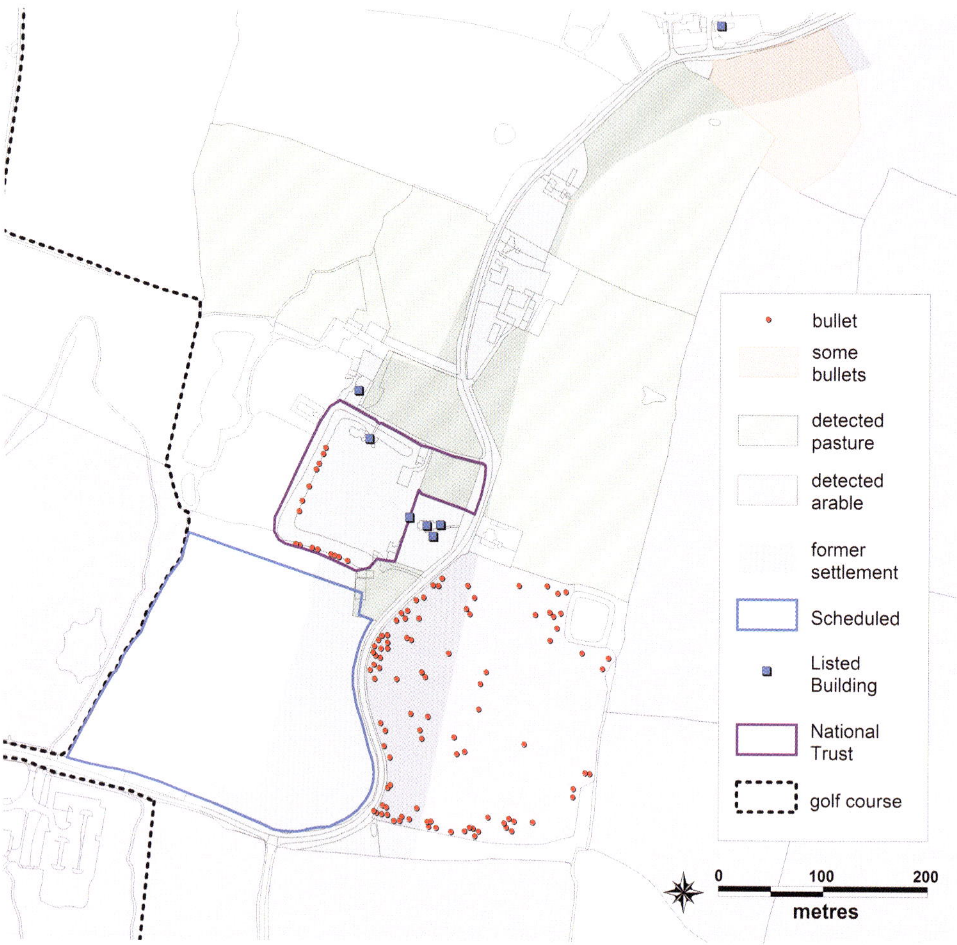

Fig 7.41 Map of Boarstall, Buckinghamshire, which held a royalist garrison that was besieged several times between 1643–6. The bullet distribution represents only a percentage of the finds that were made in the 1990s (Reproduced by permission of Ordnance Survey on behalf of HMSO. © Crown copyright and database right 2012. All rights reserved. Ordnance Survey Licence no. 100024900)

The site was subject to artefact collection in the 1990s by Les Rees, who recovered some 400 bullets plus various other artefacts. A sketch plan of the distribution, including just 115 of the bullets, was produced from memory in 1996–97. No subsequent finds were mapped, but were said to have come from the same general areas as before – particularly the field where Rees had earlier mapped bullet locations. The small number of bullets found on the north-eastern edge of the site was not mapped, but the general area involved was indicated by Rees. In addition, following dredging on the inner bank on the west side of the moat in August 1997, seven bullets were recovered, with a further nine being found in the same area in September of that year (L Rees pers comm; plan in Bucks HER). This evidence has been mapped here to a modern background (Fig 7.41).

The medieval and early modern settlement at Boarstall, as defined from aerial survey, fieldwalking, and a map of 1697, extended well beyond the moated manor (Beresford and St Joseph 1979, 111–12). The settlement was cleared, at least in part, during the refortification of the manor in 1645. The Tower was the gatehouse set on the northern arm of the moat; it is the only structure to survive from the time of the siege and shows no evidence of bullet or round shot impact scars. However, the concentration of bullets, particularly in the south-eastern part of the site, may indicate that the main assaults were via the then built-up area on the south. In this regard the absence of finds from the area of pasture (see Fig 7.41) is suspect, as the scatter extends from beneath it to both north and south. The lack of finds here may be a result of bullets being more deeply buried owing to the lack of recent cultivation.

While more than 400 bullets have already been removed from the site, most of them without record, there would still appear to be potential for the study of the archaeology of the sieges. Disentangling evidence from the three sieges will be difficult, although the fact that various buildings stood until late 1645 means that there may be a good stratigraphic association between artefacts and structures. This is a potential which may not exist on many siege sites, but it could only be realised as part of a large-scale excavation of the site for other purposes.

Subsequent to the detecting by Rees, an extensive area immediately to the west of the site was converted to a golf course. Earthmoving for tees, greens and bunkers may have distorted any bullet distribution pattern. Although Rees recovered no bullets in this area, the relative intensity of his survey in different parts of the site is unknown. The presence of a scheduled area, created purely to protect the remaining village earthworks, has incidentally protected part of the siege site from the golf course, cultivation, and collection of artefacts. Elsewhere the evidence of the siege has remained largely unprotected and unmanaged, despite the fact that part of the area is in the ownership of the National Trust.

Beeston Castle

A garrison was maintained in Beeston Castle, Cheshire, throughout the first Civil War and was subject to several sieges. Two substantial excavations have been carried out to examine the Civil War evidence (Ellis 1993, 159). The published report states that 70 bullets were recovered in this work, although rapid re-analysis of the collection has revealed that it actually contains 233 certain and 5 possible bullets. Of these, 223 are lead ball, including one certain and two possible burred bullets. At least 38 of the bullets show firing evidence, while a further 32 show impact damage, which is in most cases massive. If the collection were washed then further firing and impact evidence would probably become visible. The assemblage also contains ten hammered slugs and three possible slugs, plus two 'rods' of uncertain significance. Neither the burred balls nor the slugs were identified in the finds report, though one slug was identified there as a 'rod'. In addition, twelve headers from bullet casting were examined: two more than reported and one with a bullet attached. All had far smaller sprue spacing than the finds report states.

A calibre graph based on bullet weight has been produced from the re-analysis (Fig 7.42). This suggests that at least six discrete calibres were in use at the site during the Civil War, although confidence on this point is limited by the relatively small size of the assemblage. The pistol bullets centre on *c* 50 bore, but with a lesser grouping at *c* 37 bore. Carbine bullets centre on *c* 20 bore. Musket bullets focus on 13 bore, though a subsidiary peak at the lower end of 12 bore may be significant; there is also a minor grouping at 11 bore.

The whole Beeston assemblage should be re-analysed in detail, not least because it is one of the standard reference assemblages for Civil War bullets and related artefacts. Most of the impacted bullets that were identified in the original report appear to have come from the outer gateway and so, presumably,

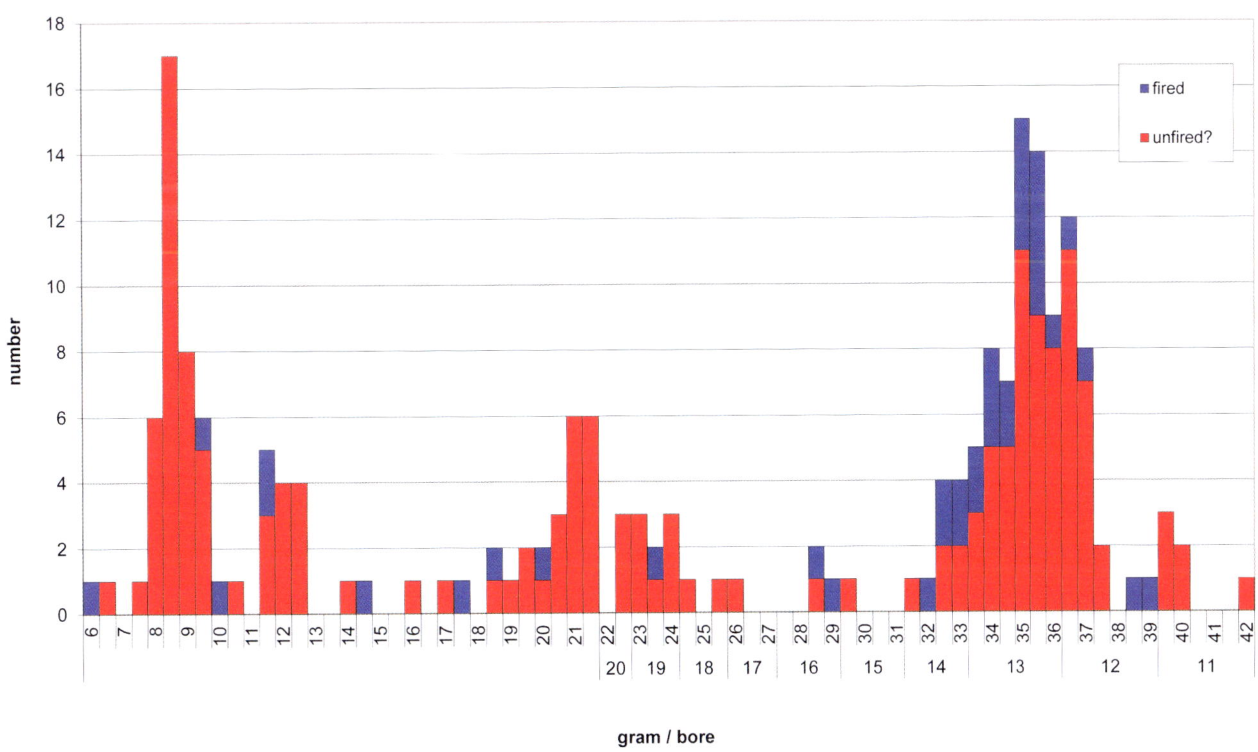

Fig 7.42 Graph of bullet calibre for finds from the excavations on Beeston Castle, Cheshire. The graph distinguishes, from impact and banding evidence, the bullets that have definitely been fired

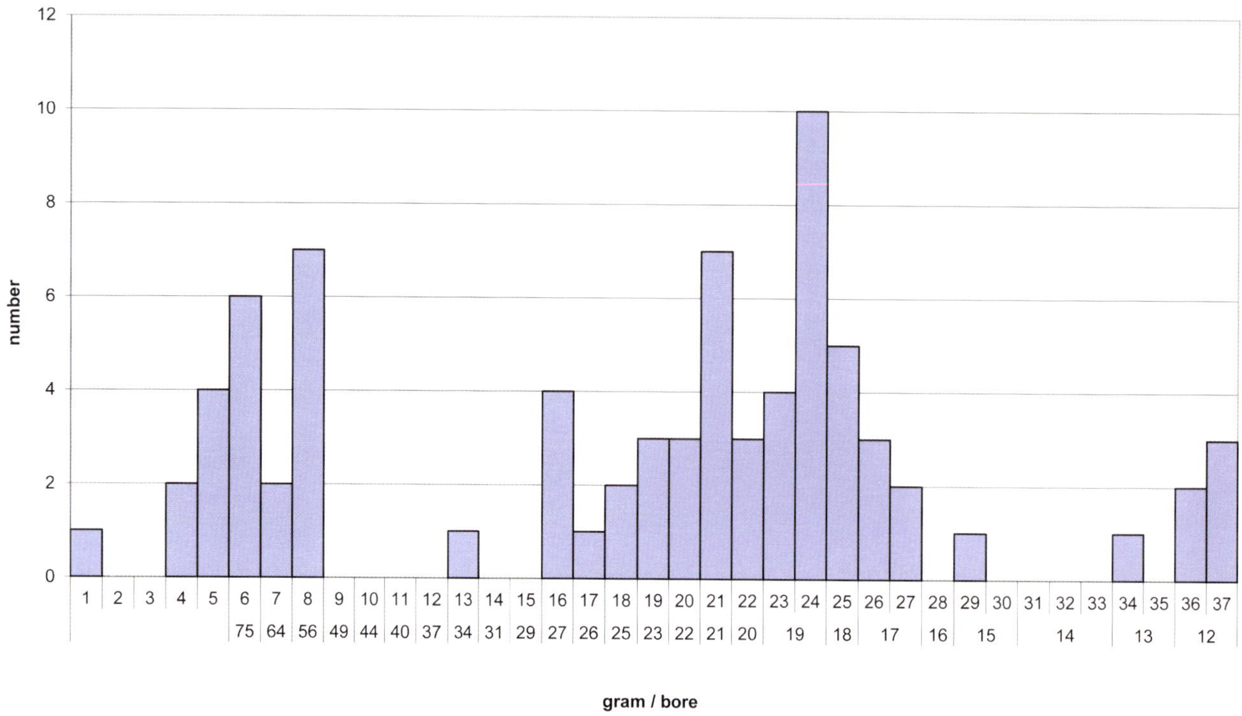

Fig 7.43 Calibre graph for un-impacted bullets from the Sandal Castle excavations

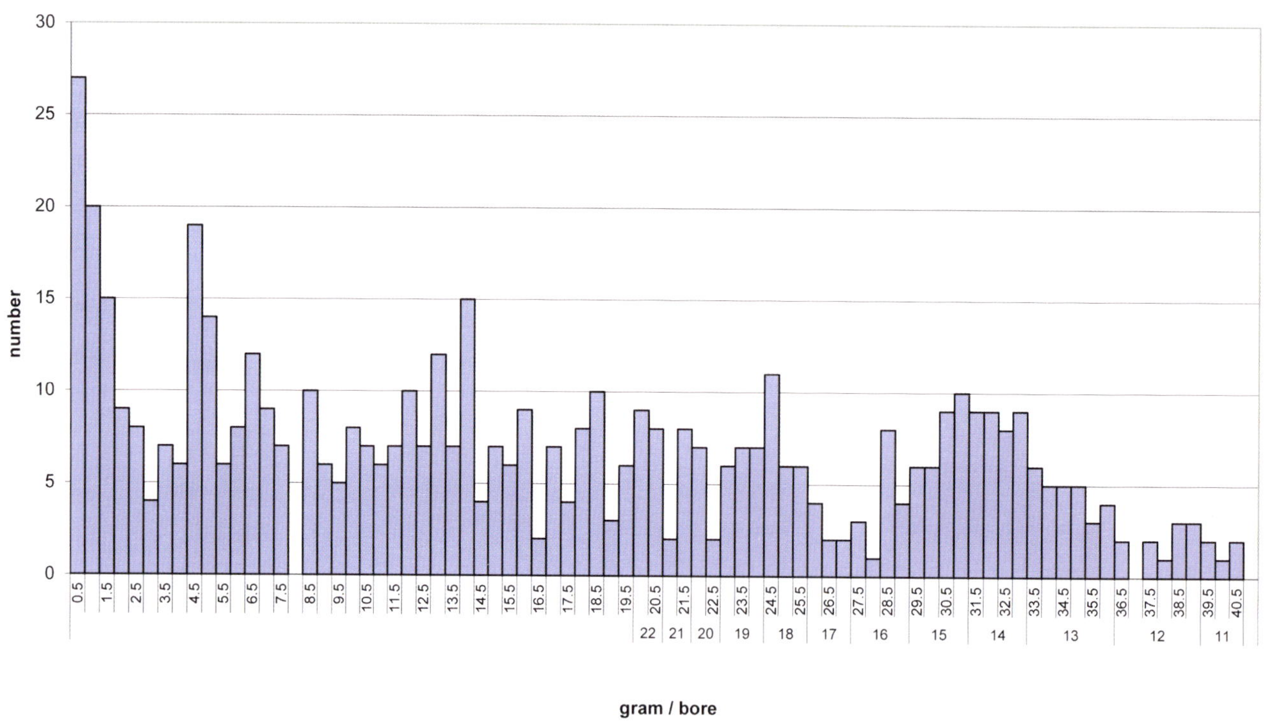

Fig 7.44 Graph of the calibre of bullets recovered on the Bestwall Quarry site, many of which probably derive from the Civil War sieges of Wareham, Dorset

relate to the various attacks on the castle. It is said that accurate three-dimensional recording was undertaken for all bullets during the excavation (Paul Courtney pers comm). If this record survives then a distribution plan should be produced to indicate each calibre and distinguish the fired and the impacted bullets. Such a plan would be the first of its kind for any siege site and may reveal useful new evidence.[12]

Sandal Castle

A royalist garrison was maintained in Sandal Castle, West Yorkshire, during the first Civil War, and the site saw a long and intensive siege in 1645. The castle was destroyed after the Civil War and today very little remains standing. Not surprisingly, despite careful examination, the fragments of wall that do survive failed to reveal more than one or two doubtful examples of bullet impact scars.

The site was subject to large-scale excavations between 1964 and 1973 in which 98 bullets were recovered together with a collection of iron round shot and grenados (Mayes and Butler 1983). The bullets were subject to rapid re-analysis in the present study, enabling preparation of a calibre graph of the un-impacted bullets (Fig 7.43). What this small assemblage most clearly demonstrates is the distinctive character of bullets that have impacted on stone structures (see Fig 7.37). Unfortunately, in the absence of accurate locations for each bullet, it is impossible to take the analysis any further. More importantly, a large part of the archaeology of the siege appears to have been destroyed, without record, in the 1970s, when much of the ground outside the walls was cleared by machine to 'restore' the earthworks. The work did not, apparently, include systematic collection and recording of artefacts, so many bullets, and possibly also round shot and grenados, will have been lost without record.

Wareham

A garrison in the town of Wareham, Dorset, was besieged several times during the Civil War. An assemblage of 558 bullets was recovered from several fields extending east from the defences of the town during a metal-detecting survey undertaken as part of the Bestwall Quarry investigation, both prior to and during the excavation, with the finds located to broad zones across the site (L Ladle pers comm). As part of the present study the collection was rapidly re-assessed and a calibre graph produced.

The assemblage demonstrates well the impact of soil chemistry on the condition of lead projectiles, as the bullets have lain in a highly acidic sandy soil (pH 4.6) and show high levels of corrosion which has destroyed most of the detail of manufacture and use that are normally expected (see Fig 8.10). Even the calibre graph appears to have been compromised by varying loss of mass, with a more random pattern than is seen in any other assemblage (Fig 7.44).

With this caveat registered, a number of observations can still be made from the graph. These include the near-absence of 12 bore bullets, with the main musket calibre apparently around 14 bore, and nor is there a clear peak from carbines, which would be expected at around 20 bore. The most distinctive feature is the presence of many very small bullets. They are small even for hailshot fired from small arms, which tends to be around 5–9g, so it is possible that the assemblage includes a significant amount of shot from later birding. However, as at Sedgemoor (see Fig 8.7), a single bullet shows clear evidence of having been fired as a multiple load with very small hailshot above. This might indicate that at least some of the very small bullets are indeed fine hailshot from the Civil War action – unless of course this practice itself relates to birding.

Notes

1. National Library of Scotland EMS.s.164.
2. In the 19th century Braddock (or Bradoc) included the manors of Braddock and Warleggan but was a parish united with Boconnoc. Boconnoc included the manors of Botelet, Langunnet, and Bodulgate. St Pinnock included the manors of Botelet, Penvvrane, Fursdon, and Trevillis. Lanreath, the northern extremity, extends into the East Down at Boconnoc, and includes the manors of Botolet, Langunnet, Lanreath, and Treire. St Winnow: at enclosure the St Winnow Down was contiguous with the West Down of Braddock, and also included the north-western part of Boconnoc Park. Documents in CRO: tithe maps and awards: Boconnoc: TM12 and TA12; Braddock: FS3/924 and TA17; Lanreath: TM113 and TA113; St Pinnock: TM189 and TA189; St Winnow: TM253 and TA253/1. Enclosure documents: Downs in Braddock, Boconnoc and St Winnow (2300 acres):

1809 enclosure act, AD593; 1822 enclosure award, QS/PDA1. Enclosure of Pollard's Down in St Pinnock (106 acres shown not to be on or near the battlefield): 1867 enclosure act; 1873 enclosure award, QS/PDA20; Commissioners' draft plan Boconnoc enclosure *c* 1821, F/326 – not seen, as unfit for production. Other historic maps: tracing of Bodargie in Bradoc with fields numbered (ref. P 17/3/2, no date); plan of Boconnoc, 'draught of the East Commons', *c* 1590, AD644 (bought by CRO from Grampound Antiques, Truro, but was from the sale of the contents of Ethy House, June 1977); plan of Boconnock Barton with woods, fields named, undated, F/3/map/21; enclosure of roads in Boconnoc, Bradoc, and St Winnow, 1811: F/325 – not seen, as unfit for production; plan of part of Boconnoc estate, *c* 1811–20, F/327/1; plan of Penventon platation and adjoining land, 1817, F/321/8; map of deer park in parishes of Boconnoc and St Winnow, F/327/27; Warleggan manor in Braddock – 18th-century, no land in Braddock identified, DDG1872. County maps: Gascoyne 1699, Martyn 1784 (appears to show church towns (church), other hamlets (circle), and isolated single farms or great houses (house)); Morden 1695; Greenwood 1826–27; Smith 1804. Extensive written sources exist for the Boconnoc estate which could not be consulted in the present study, including various deeds and leases from the 17th to the 19th centuries: DDR741–5; Fortescue Collection: summary catalogue only – an important large collection, mostly uncatalogued, extending at least from the 16th century onwards.

3. CEI was the Centre for Environmental Interpretation at Manchester Metropolitan University. Copies of all their reports on the landscape and interpretation issues for battlefields being considered for registration in 1994 are in English Heritage's 'Designation' file for each battlefield.
4. 'Draught of the East Commons', *c* 1590: Cornwall Record Office (CRO), map AD644.
5. Late 18th-century pre-enclosure map of King's Sedgemoor, Somerset Record Office: DD/AH Box 47, 11. Map of King's Sedgemoor re drainage and enclosure, 1795, TNA, CP43/851, after rot.276; tithe map of Westonzoyland, 1843, TNA, IR30/30/453.
6. RAF CPE/UK/1924/3035–8.
7. The 2007 work was undertaken in collaboration with Context One Archaeological Services, Wessex Water PLC and Somerset County Council. The work was requested by Somerset County Council in fulfilment of requirements in Local Plan Policy HE10 and County Structure Plan policy 10. The analysis of the finds from this work is in Foard 2008g.
8. Battle archaeology pre-2007 from plans provided by Glasgow University Archaeological Research Division (GUARD) and validated with reference to a plan from Somerset HER.
9. Sources included Gaunt 1987; Foard 1995; Atkin 1995; Bracher and Emmett 2000; Harrington 1992 and 2003; Kenyon and Ohlmeyer 1998; Baker 1986; Newman 1985; Marix Evans 1998.
10. Civil War sites with impact scars so far identified are: Acton church (Nantwich battlefield); Alton church; Apsley Castle; Ashby-de-la-Zouche castle and church; Berkeley castle and church; Bolsover Castle; Chester; Colchester; Devizes churches; Evesham church; Farndon bridge and church; High Ercall church; Hillesden church; Holt church; Kenilworth Abbey Barn and church; Knaresborough; Lichfield cathedral; Lilleshall Abbey; Moreton Corbet; Lowick church; Tonbridge castle; Tong church; Warick castle and church; Winwick church tower (battlefield). Other sites (not known garrisons) where scars may be from target practice include: Berkeswell church; Dodleston church; Hardwick Hall; Lyveden New Build; Marton Church; Misterton church; Norham church; Salisbury Cathedral; Holy Trinity church, Stratford on Avon; Gnosal church; Lady Chapel, Glastonbury Abbey.
11. Furlong pattern from Partida *et al* in prep. Enclosures and buildings from maps of 1721 and 1725 (Northamptonshire Record Office, Maps 4211, 463 and 457) edited with information from Survey of the manor of Grafton, 1650, TNA, E317/ Northamptonshire/20. Bullets from survey for Northamptonshire County Council by Midland Archaeological Research Society, supervised by Bob Kings in the late 1990s.
12. Information from Paul Courtney. The limitations of his report on the finds arise largely from the full assemblage not having been passed to him for study, and from the degree to which the study of bullets has advanced since the report was written.

8

Managing battlefields

The preceding survey has argued that battlefields, siege sites, and other fields of conflict form a significant part of England's historic environment. Such sites are not simply of commemorative and interpretative significance: they also have research value, with potential to contribute to the understanding of individual military actions and to the wider history of warfare.

The following discussion considers the current condition of English battlefields and examines the factors which affect the survival of their physical remains. It then reviews the way in which the resource has been designated and where improvements in the non-statutory Register might be made. Finally there is discussion of the mechanisms by which management can be achieved and current problems addressed, illustrated through a case study of Adwalton Moor (1643).

We have seen that physical evidence on battlefields is of three main types. Firstly, there is the terrain, comprising those elements of the historic landscape which are likely to have had tactical significance. Secondly, there is the battle archaeology, principally in the form of scatters of artefacts left by the action and its aftermath. Thirdly, there are the graves of the slain and, occasionally, the remains of temporary defensive features. Given the character and importance of this evidence it follows that battlefields need to be managed not just to preserve their visual integrity and setting but also to sustain their value as historic landscapes and archaeological sites.

Historic terrain

The first aspect of battlefield terrain is the form of the ground. Here management concerns will focus principally upon issues of inter-visibility between locations significant for the understanding of the battle.

Richard Holmes has frequently emphasised the importance of being able to walk the ground in order to understand a battle (Holmes 1997). Such appreciation is achieved through views of, from, and – most importantly – within the battlefield. This can give insights into, for example, commanders' decisions on how to deploy their troops by exploiting cover or taking advantage of rising ground. It may also reveal why particular tactical moves could take place without opposing troops being aware of them. Such views therefore have both an interpretative and a research value, and will become progressively more valuable as information technology improves, particularly 'augmented reality' via smart phones or similar equipment. When applied to the analysis and interpretation of battlefields, such technology should enable those man-made or man-altered elements of the battlefield terrain that are now lost to be superimposed upon the scene.

Man's impact on the landscape since an action will affect our ability to reconstruct its appearance at the time of battle. Earthmoving may alter the form of the land by, for example, removing high points that provided important prospects or created dead ground. The classic example is Waterloo in Belgium (1815): when Wellington himself revisited the battlefield in later years he is said to have decried the construction of the Lion Mound, the major monument to the battle, because a slight rise intentionally used to protect many of his troops from French artillery fire had been destroyed to construct the monument. As a result it was no longer possible to appreciate one of his main tactical decisions in choosing the ground on which to fight.

The insertion of new buildings or tree planting may also affect the inter-visibility of different parts of the battlefield. Such an impact is clearly seen on the Registered battlefield at Newburn (1640), where in 2010 new buildings for a rowing club were constructed and surrounded by associated tree planting (Foard 2010b). This broke the main visual link which remained within the battlefield – that between the approximate site of the English northern sconce and Newburn church, across the Tyne. It was from this church tower that Scottish artillery had rendered the forts controlling Newburn ford indefensible, so allowing their troops to cross the Tyne and defeat the heavily outnumbered English army. While such development comes within the planning process, those advising on the implications of development for a battlefield must be provided with appropriate information about what is significant if they are to recognise the threats and argue effectively for protection.

The second aspect of terrain concerns more superficial man-made or man-altered components which remain in the modern landscape, including features still functioning today, such as hedgerows; upstanding earthworks including hollow ways and boundary banks; and wholly levelled features, such as former drainage ditches, which survive now only as cut features beneath the topsoil.

The character of land use on most battlefields has altered greatly since the time the battle was fought. Changes have usually been greatest in formerly unenclosed landscapes, such as open field or moorland. A small number of battles were fought across wholly or largely enclosed landscapes. Here hedgerows, walls, or embanked Cornish hedges may survive, as at Stratton (1643) and Newbury I (1643). On other battlefields, which were largely unenclosed, more limited areas of enclosure had tactical significance. The greatest problems arise in distinguishing the early boundaries from later additions. While a methodology exists for the analysis of the Cornish boundary system (S Hartgroves pers comm), work at Edgehill demonstrates that, although it may be possible to distinguish broad phases of landscape development, in the absence of documentary sources of the right date it can be impossible to prove whether certain features existed at the time of the battle (see Fig 7.21). Yet, unless features from the time of the battle can be isolated from those of earlier or later date, they will often be of no more than local significance and it will not be possible to target conservation measures effectively.

Earthworks often relate to land use. One of the most common is ridge and furrow from open-field systems, and this can have had a significant impact on the battle, perhaps by stopping round shot from bouncing into the enemy ranks, as reported at Edgehill, or by slowing a cavalry attack, as reported at the 1547 battle of Pinkie (East Lothian, Scotland). Even where ridge and furrow had no direct tactical significance, its survival on a battlefield can demonstrate the open character of the landscape as it was at the time of the action; ridge and furrow is, however, very vulnerable to cultivation, disappearing rapidly after just a few years under modern arable. Other features surviving as earthworks or cut features may have affected the progress of battles, such as the pits that disrupted the parliamentarian left wing of cavalry at Naseby (Foard 1995, 253) or the drainage ditch which dissuaded the rebel infantry from advancing into hand to hand action at Sedgemoor (see Fig 7.9).

A review of all Registered battlefields as they appeared on early post-war RAF vertical air photographs has shown that in central England extensive ridge and furrow then still survived on several of them. Best preserved were the remains at Edgehill in Warwickshire and Cropredy in Oxfordshire, while Rowton and Nantwich in Cheshire also had extensive survival. Bosworth (Leicestershire), Naseby, and Northampton (both Northamptonshire) had far less, while others had just a few fields, as at Stoke (Nottinghamshire).

Today most of those earthworks have gone, with small areas remaining on just one or two battlefields. Of the Registered battlefields only one, Cropredy, retains extensive and continuous area of ridge and furrow (Fig 8.1).[1] Cropredy also embraces the adjacent alluvial areas on the valley floor, which lack ridge and furrow, having been used as meadowland, in at least one part of which palaeo-channels are visible. The Registered area at Cropredy is in two parts, reflecting the standard interpretation of the battle as having been fought in two discrete zones. Re-examination of the primary sources suggests that action may have extended across the intermediate zone. In either case, Cropredy is now the best example of an open-field landscape survival on any Registered battlefield. Its protection is of correspondingly high priority. Ridge and furrow surviving in permanent pasture is particularly vulnerable to arable conversion, and while temporary conservation can be achieved through agri-environment schemes the only currently available long-term conservation measure is scheduling (Hall 2001).

Even where ridge and furrow has been lost, David Hall's work has demonstrated that understanding can still be advanced. This is because when evidence from headlands is combined with air photographic and documentary sources this can be sufficient to enable reconstruction of the open-field system. Such reconstruction can also identify areas which never had furlongs, for instance because they were too wet, too steep, or the soils were too poor to be cultivated (Hall

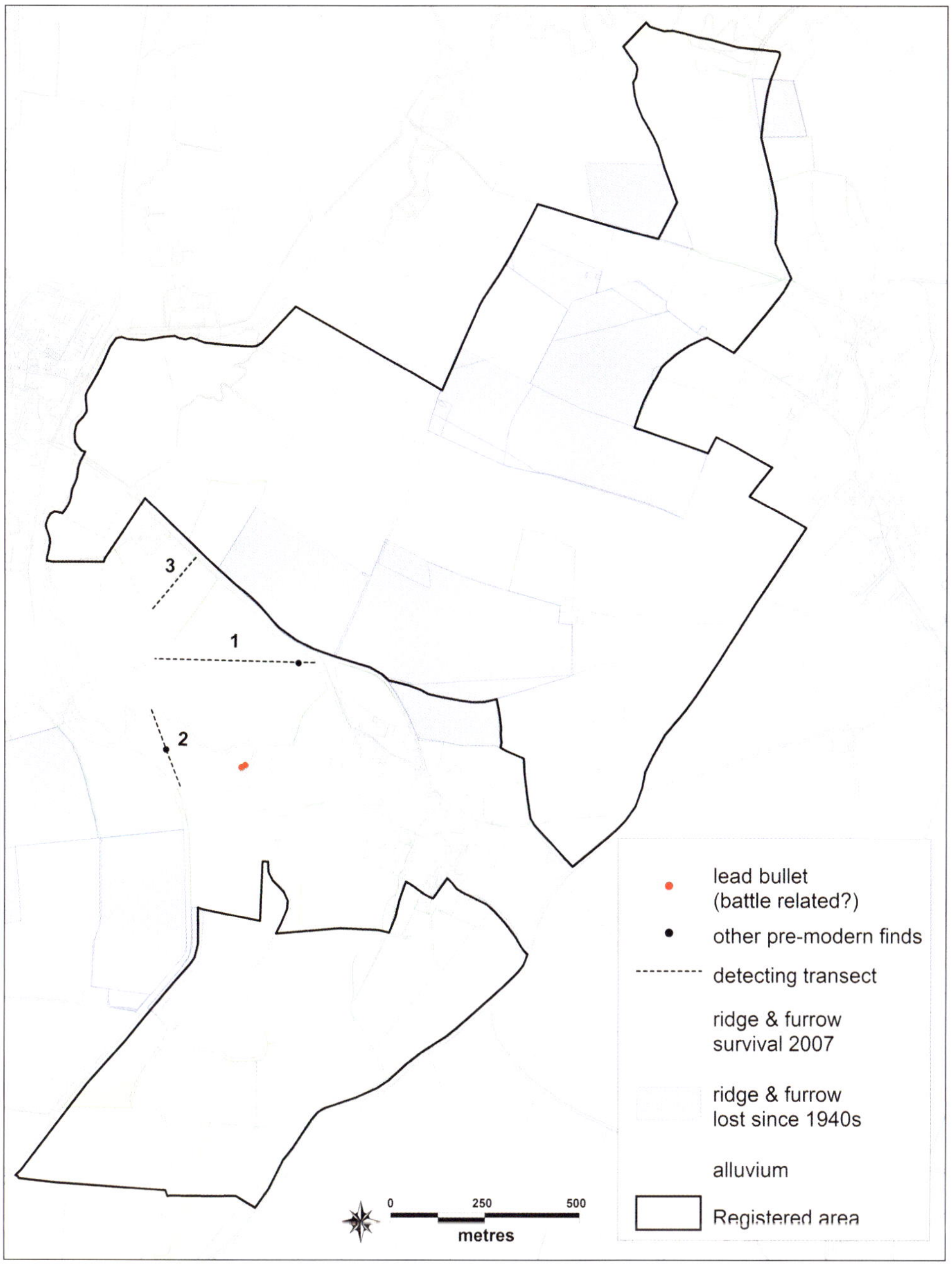

Fig 8.1 Map of Cropredy (1644) showing ridge and furrow survival in the 1940s and in 2007, togther with the location of metal-detecting transects

1995). Unfortunately the survival prospects for such evidence are precarious. In many cases headlands within modern arable are rapidly being eroded and need to be recorded before they are lost. To date, complete reconstructions have been carried out at Naseby, Northampton, Edgecote, and Bosworth, and partial reconstruction at Towton (Foard 1995; Hall 1980; Partida *et al* forthcoming) (see Figs 5.7 and 5.5). In addition to upstanding remains, the remnants of furrows between the strips can survive as shallow features beneath the topsoil in modern arable, as noted at Towton (Chapter 5).

Earthwork remains from extensive enclosed field systems exist on one or two battlefields. The best example is Lansdown, where an area of banks, ditches, hollow ways, and quarries on the slope falling northwards from the plateau may represent parts of the battlefield terrain. Smaller areas exist on other battlefields, as at East Stoke, where the village closes may be associated with the destruction of the rebel army in the rout (see Fig 2.16).

There may well be more battlefields where such features have been levelled but where buried evidence still survives. On battlefields that were partly or wholly outside any field system there may also be distinctive features such as drainage dykes, carrs, and causeways; examples discussed above include Sedgemoor and Northallerton (see Figs 7.9 and 3.16). These features may contain environmental evidence which can illuminate the wider terrain or specific wetland feature itself. Improvements in drainage pose a threat to such waterlogged deposits in ditches and former marshy areas.

Battle archaeology

The various types of battle archaeology – mass graves, unstratified metal artefact scatters, impact scars, and defensive structures – each face distinct problems of decay and destruction. Each accordingly calls for its own specialised management.

Mass graves pose particular problems. The evidence from Towton shows that the dead are not safe where they lie, because graves are often shallow and so vulnerable to cultivation. Yet on nearly all battlefields the graves remain unlocated (see pp 32–5). Hence, the most urgent need is to advance the methodology for locating them.

Once graves are found, scheduling will provide protection against most threats, including conversion from pasture to arable. However, it will not address existing agricultural impacts. These can be assessed in the light of the 2006 study on the effect of cultivation on scheduled monuments (Oxford Archaeology 2006). Appropriate responses are likely to involve either arable reversion or a minimum-till option, which can be facilitated through agri-environment schemes. However, the possible repercussions of such strategies for unstratified metal artefacts must also be taken into account: minimum-till may involve additional chemical application or the use of different cultivation equipment, which could accelerate their decay.

As we have seen, these scatters of unstratified metal artefacts are the principal type of archaeological evidence for battles. The rate at which different materials decay varies with ground conditions, meaning that the character of surviving assemblages will vary between one site and another. Organic materials will have been lost relatively quickly unless, exceptionally, they were deposited in waterlogged conditions. Over longer periods ferrous artefacts will also have suffered significant decay, especially if they remained in the topsoil, although the rates of decay will vary according to the soil chemistry. Other metals, such as copper alloy and lead, are likely to have survived far better.

The artefacts that remain are vulnerable to two largely invisible threats. Firstly, changes in agricultural practice during the later 20th century are believed to have accelerated the decay of metal objects in the soil. Secondly, and of even greater concern, is the collection of artefacts on a large scale as a result of the development of the hobby of treasure hunting during the last 40 years. Both impacts continue, even where battlefields are Registered. The following discussion aims to explain how and why losses occur and to demonstrate the conservation action required. In cases where effective mitigation is not possible, an intensive programme of recording action may be needed to recover representative samples from exemplar sites.

Losses to other processes tend to be more visible. Urban development, road construction, and mineral extraction will destroy or occasionally mask battle archaeology. For example, large-scale earthmoving during the 19th-century re-alignment of the Tyne at Newburn appears to have buried some areas of battle archaeology to a depth beyond the range of metal detectors (Foard 2010b). Piecemeal land-use change, such as incorporation into gardens, will cause fragmentation and render future survey impracticable. Even tree planting can obstruct survey and, in some contexts, may cause damaging changes in soil chemistry. Thus, Grave Ground Coppice at Edgehill, a surviving area in an otherwise destroyed zone at the heart of the battlefield, proved impossible to survey consistently on 10m transects because of the close spacing of trees and the density of undergrowth.

Such influences on a battlefield's condition can be assessed using modern and historic mapping and aerial photography. In most cases development threats can now be addressed through the planning process. Where change cannot be avoided then it is usually possible to ensure adequate recording to secure a representative sample of the artefact scatter. Problems can still arise in such situations, however, because the significance of a small part of a battlefield can only be understood from the overall distribution pattern of metal artefacts. This will cause difficulty with development-led evaluation of small areas, for, as we have seen (p 22), a low density of artefacts need not mean that the area in question saw no action or that the scatter is not worth detailed recording. We have also noted the need for consistency between investigations on different areas of a battlefield. If surveys are conducted by different contractors using different methodologies it may not be possible to reconstruct a consistent picture of the density and character of the scatter across the whole site. Yet the ability to do this is crucial to the understanding of the artefact scatters.

Stripping and redeposition of topsoil will, to a greater or lesser degree, redistribute artefacts and so destroy the detail of spatial patterning. The 1995 guidance for the Battlefields Register suggested that 'small-scale ground disturbance such as pipeline laying is unlikely to diminish the value of battlefields' (English Heritage 1995). We can now see that this was wrong. While it is true that the appearance of the site may not be compromised, the impact on battle archaeology may be significant; and while the probability that a pipeline might destroy a mass grave is low, topsoil disturbance will certainly distort the distribution pattern of the artefacts. Thus the removal of topsoil over a 20m-wide corridor along several pipelines across Sedgemoor battlefield may have caused significant distortion to the distribution patterns (see Fig 7.11).

Decay of artefacts

Since the vast majority of artefacts on our battlefields are of metal and lie within the plough zone we must understand the processes by which metals decay in the topsoil (Foard *et al* 2010). Metals can be divided into three groups according to their susceptibility to corrosion. Firstly, there are the corrosion-resistant metals, such as gold and silver. These are relatively rare among battlefield finds, where they are restricted mainly to silver coins, although other silver, gilded, and gold artefacts are occasionally recovered (see Fig 5.8). Gilding or silvering may also protect vulnerable ferrous artefacts from decay, as with the spurs reported from Towton. Secondly, there are the metals, particularly copper and lead, which are subject to initial rapid corrosion but which build up a layer of stable corrosion products, making the object resistant to further attack. In most environments artefacts of these metals will retain an extensive metallic core even after burial for hundreds of years. Indeed, in many cases the whole artefact survives in good condition, retaining its all-important surface detail. Most non-projectile finds from battlefields, including items such as buckles, buttons, and strap ends, are of copper alloy, although some are of lead. Lead is a more problematic metal than copper alloy and, because lead bullets are by far the most common and important type of find on early modern battlefields, it is considered in more detail below. Lastly, there are the metals, most notably iron, that corrode rapidly but do not form a layer of protective corrosion products. In aggressive environments over long periods artefacts made from these metals may either be totally lost or, where they remain, consist largely of corrosion with a much reduced metallic core. Other than bullets, ferrous objects probably represented the greatest proportion of artefacts that were originally deposited on our battlefields. However, because of their vulnerability to corrosion they are normally recovered in small numbers and, when retrieved, they are often in such poor condition that establishing their period and function can be difficult.

Smaller objects and those with complex forms tend to be more vulnerable to decay because of their greater surface area. Thus a large iron round shot is more likely to survive than the smaller, thinner, and elongated ferrous arrowhead. Recent metallurgical analysis has been conducted on arrowheads believed to be from the battle of Tewkesbury (1471) which were recovered from stratified contexts during large-scale excavation of a fortified manor house on the battlefield. The results illustrate the structural vulnerability of this artefact type to corrosion (Cubitt 2006). If we are to develop a more sophisticated predictive model of survival potential, then further baseline studies on key types of battlefield artefact from varied burial conditions are needed.

Rates of corrosion will depend not only upon the metal composition and time since deposition, but also on the soil chemistry and land-use history of the site. Cultivation causes mechanical damage to objects and also increases aeration, both of which can accelerate chemical action. Drainage may also have a significant impact, not just on the survival of organics preserved in waterlogged contexts but also on metal artefacts through increased aeration of the soil. During the last half century rates of decay have accelerated. In part this is due to large-scale conversion of pasture to arable during and following the Second World War (Stamp 1962, 962). It is also the result of subsequent changes in agricultural processes. Alterations in the scale and character of machinery and practices, such as subsoiling and the use of power harrows, have affected the depths of disturbance and the levels of mechanical damage. Most importantly, the application of agrochemicals is likely to have caused significant modifications to soil chemistry (Foard *et al* 2010).[2]

Soil chemistry

Metals buried in stratified contexts or in plough soil are subject to aqueous corrosion. This is an electrochemical process in the presence of water. Metal atoms lose electrons to become positively charged metal ions that go into solution. These then react with other chemical species in the soil groundwater to form solid corrosion products such as metal oxides, hydroxides, and sulfates. It is these solid corrosion products that often form a coloured matrix with soil particles around the corroding object (Cronyn 1990). The initial formation of the metal ions takes place at a site on the metal known as the anode, whereas the electrons produced are consumed by another reaction with an electron acceptor (the cathode). Owing to the electrical conductivity of metals the locations of the anode and cathode can be at different places on the metal surface. In the presence of water and oxygen the cathodic reaction is $O_2 + 2H_2O + 4e^- \rightarrow 4(OH^-)$. Where there are depleted oxygen levels, hydrogen ions act as the electron acceptors: $2H^+ + 2e^- \rightarrow H_2$. In the absence of oxygen, unless there is an abundance of hydrogen ions, for example in an acidic environment of pH 4 or below, corrosion rates are generally slow because the reaction at the cathode determines corrosion rate. However, aside from some situations of seasonal waterlogging, most shallow depositional environments (the bulk of battlefield contexts) will be sufficiently aerated for oxygen to act as the electron acceptor.

In addition to the metal itself, metallic corrosion is influenced by two key environmental parameters: redox potential and pH (Edwards 1996). Under high redox values (oxidising conditions) most metals will easily corrode, whereas under low redox values (reducing conditions) they will tend not to corrode. In addition, low pH (acidic conditions) will assist corrosion, whereas high pH (alkaline conditions) will tend to result in the formation of a stable corrosion matrix in most metals although, importantly for battlefield archaeology, not always in lead. These factors work by determining whether the metal ions form and, if they do form, whether they remain in solution and are dissipated from the metal surface or form stable corrosion films over the surface. The first of these situations, where ions do not form, is termed *immunity*. That where ions dissipate and the metal continues to corrode is termed *corrosion*. Finally, that where stable films are formed, preventing further corrosion, is termed *passivation*.

Marcel Pourbaix developed a series of equilibrium potential pH diagrams that predict the likelihood of corrosion based on thermodynamic stability (Pourbaix and Franklin 1966). The iron/water Pourbaix diagram (Figs 8.2 and 8.3) predicts that at low redox potentials ($E_H(V)$) metallic iron (Fe) will be the stable form, ie immunity. At higher redox potentials that are acidic, ferrous and ferric ions will be the stable forms (Fe^{2+} and Fe^{3+}), ie corrosion. Higher redox potentials under more alkaline conditions will result in the formation of haematite (Fe_2O_3) or magnetite (Fe_3O_4), ie passivation. A comparison of the iron and copper diagrams (Fig 8.4) demonstrates why on a wide range of sites the condition of copper alloy is often better than that

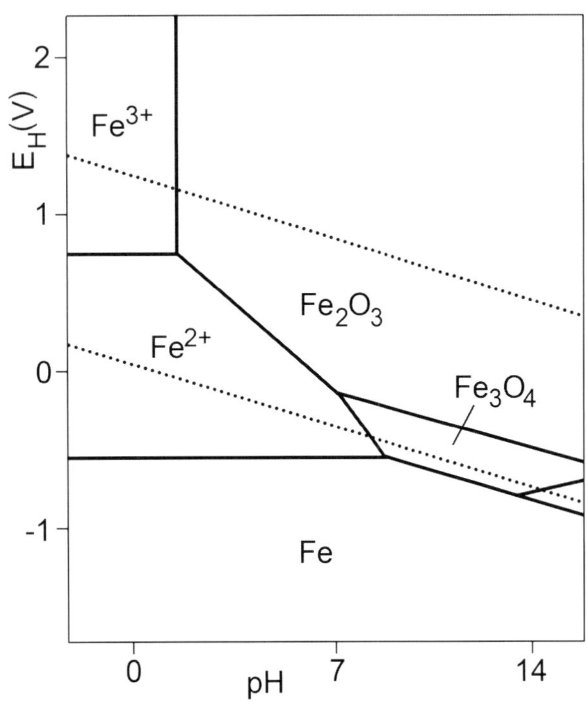

Fig 8.2 Simplified Pourbaix diagram (Potential –pH) for iron/water at 25°C. Fe, Fe_2O_3 and Fe_3O_4 are solids, while Fe^{2+} and Fe^{3+} are in solution

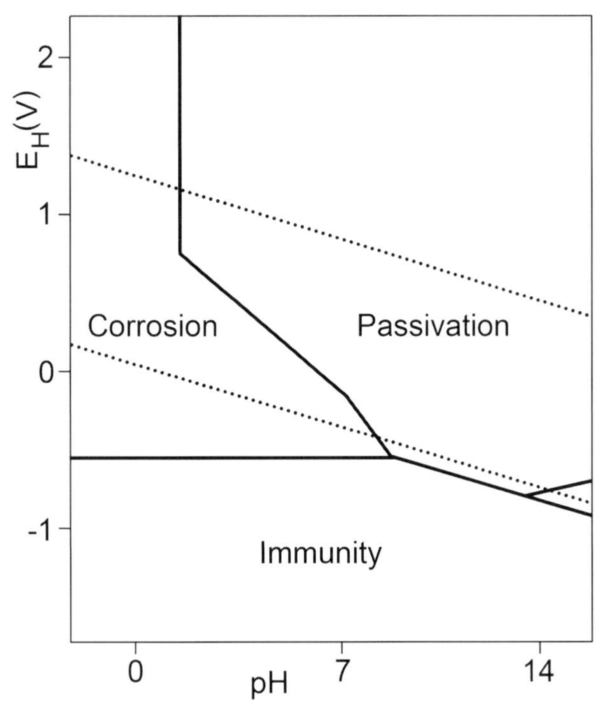

Fig 8.3 Theoretical conditions of corrosion, immunity, and passivation by the formation of oxides. This diagram is valid only in the absence of substances with which iron can form soluble complexes and insoluble compounds

of other metals. However, metal stability, especially the formation of passivation layers, is severely affected by the presence of chloride. This is one of a number of reasons why there is concern over the influence of field-scale application of agrochemicals during the last fifty years. In addition to the alteration of chloride levels by fertilisers, the application of organic manures or the top dressing of land will change the soil pH. As a result soil pH and probably also chloride levels may today be different to historic levels.

In Denmark and Sweden work with focus on the influence of soil type, groundwater, and pollution/acidification has been carried out on the survival of metal artefacts (mostly copper alloy) in agrarian landscapes (Brinch Madsen *et al* 2004; Nord *et al* 2000). The impact of fertiliser use on the corrosion of metal artefacts in stratified deposits within the vadose zone (ie above the water table and thus not permanently waterlogged) has also been explored through English Heritage-funded research (Pollard *et al* 2003; 2004; 2006). The need for this research arose because of evidence suggesting that the survival and condition of prehistoric metal artefacts varied according to when they were excavated, with more recent finds exhibiting a greater extent of metal corrosion than those found earlier (Brinch Madsen *et al* 2004). The composition and corrosion effects of commercial agricultural fertilisers (categorised according to their NPK value to enable farmers to calculate appropriate field application rate for different crops) is not fully understood, and the situation is further complicated because many are proprietary blends (Department for Environment, Food and Rural Affairs 2000). However, it is evident that soluble chemicals used as fertilisers alter the dissolved salt content in soil pore water, increasing conductivity and thus the corrosivity of soil. The solubility and rate of anion removal from fertilisers will vary. Those fertilisers incorporating a high mineral potash component, for instance, are dominated by highly mobile chloride ions which are frequently implicated in metal corrosion.

Given the role of oxygen in the decay process, the degree to which it diffuses to the location where the find lies will have a significant influence on the rate of decay. The deeper a find, the less oxygen will reach it, but this will also be influenced by how freely the soil drains. In clay and alluvium there are small spaces between particles and oxygen levels are correspondingly low. In contrast, sand has large particles and therefore high oxygen levels are found deep down the soil column as well as at the surface. Sandy soils also drain more easily, so soluble materials tend to flush through and strip ions out, hence creating acid conditions. It may be possible, therefore, to predict the gross impact of soil chemistry in the past from the underlying geology, although assessment would be more effective with soils data. For the same reasons one may expect that the installation of land drains, begun on a substantial scale in the 19th century, will have accelerated corrosion.

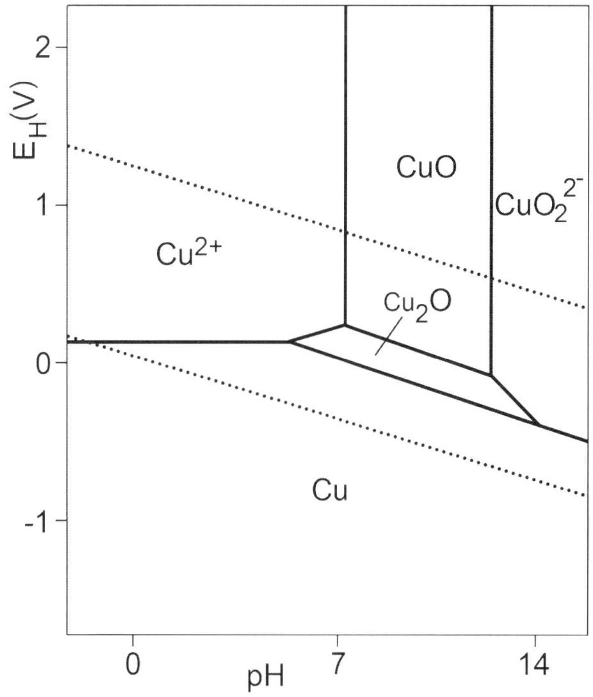

Fig 8.4 Simplified Pourbaix diagram (Potential –pH) for copper/water at 25°C. Cu, Cu_2O and CuO are in solid phase, while Cu^{2+} and CuO^{2-} are in solution

Cultivation can improve drainage and increase aeration of the soil, enabling oxygen to penetrate more deeply and so increasing the rate of corrosion. Cultivation also redistributes artefacts within the soil column, periodically exposing objects to increased oxygen levels at or close to the surface. In contrast, the longer a find has lain in permanent pasture the deeper down the topsoil column it is likely to have gravitated, halting at the top of the subsoil where it is furthest from the air. In addition, cultivation may result in increased abrasion as a result of the churning of the soil during ploughing and harrowing, the effects of which may be seen to varying degrees on the surface of lead bullets. In some cases the corrosion deposits, which have in the past protected the artefact from further corrosion, appear to have been actively stripped away, although the mechanisms causing this are not clear. Heavily corroded ferrous arrowheads will be more vulnerable to such mechanical damage – a process which appears to be at work at Towton (see Fig 2.10). Large lead objects may also suffer from direct impact by ploughshares, causing gouges and other effects, as has been noted on several of the larger round shot from Bosworth (Fig 8.5). Over time, as a result of corrosion, such impact marks may become difficult to distinguish from the evidence of impact damage which occurred at the time of firing. Anecdotal evidence also suggests that modern machinery such as power harrows may be responsible for far more severe impact damage and even the fragmentation of artefacts such as coins.

While mechanical damage will be absent where land is under pasture or other non-arable land use, this can be damaging for other reasons. Planting under coniferous woodland, for example, can reduce soil pH and thus increase the rate of decay.

Where artefacts lie in a stratified context beneath the topsoil they are protected from mechanical damage and the more aggressive effects of soil chemistry. Such a context may be one of secondary stratification, where artefacts in the topsoil have been buried beneath colluvium, alluvium, or in other deposits laid down by activity such as terracing. Secondary stratification may also have occurred in restricted areas, for instance through burial within remnant furrows of former ridge and furrow or in other cut features which were open at the time of the battle or subsequently, but are now infilled. If previously protected artefacts become incorporated into the topsoil by deep ploughing or subsoiling, then, for a limited period, an exceptional assemblage of artefacts may be recoverable from the topsoil. As noted, this may explain why ferrous arrowheads have been recovered from Towton (Fig 8.6). Investigation of such scatters which have been preserved by secondary stratification may indicate what has been lost in other circumstances.

Burial by colluviation may protect small pockets of battle archaeology. The identification of such locations will normally require field investigation. More extensive burial is likely where there has been alluviation. At first sight it might appear that such potential can be estimated with reference to the British Geological Survey 1:10,000 scale mapping. A rapid assessment of Registered battlefields reveals five with extensive alluvial areas in the core of the site: Sedgemoor (1685), Marston Moor (1644), Myton (1319), Mortimer's Cross (1461), and Newburn (1640). A further five have smaller but still significant alluvial areas: Cropredy (1644), Bosworth (1485), Worcester (1651), Boroughbridge (1315), and Maldon (AD 912). However, this is not a simple relationship, for much will depend on how much of the alluvium was deposited since the battle. At Sedgemoor, although most of the battlefield is alluviated, the battle archaeology is spread through the topsoil over large parts of the site, and the same appears true for the former moorland at Marston Moor. This suggests that in these cases alluviation largely or wholly pre-dates the battle. The earlier the battlefield the greater may be the potential for alluviation post-battle, for the major phase of

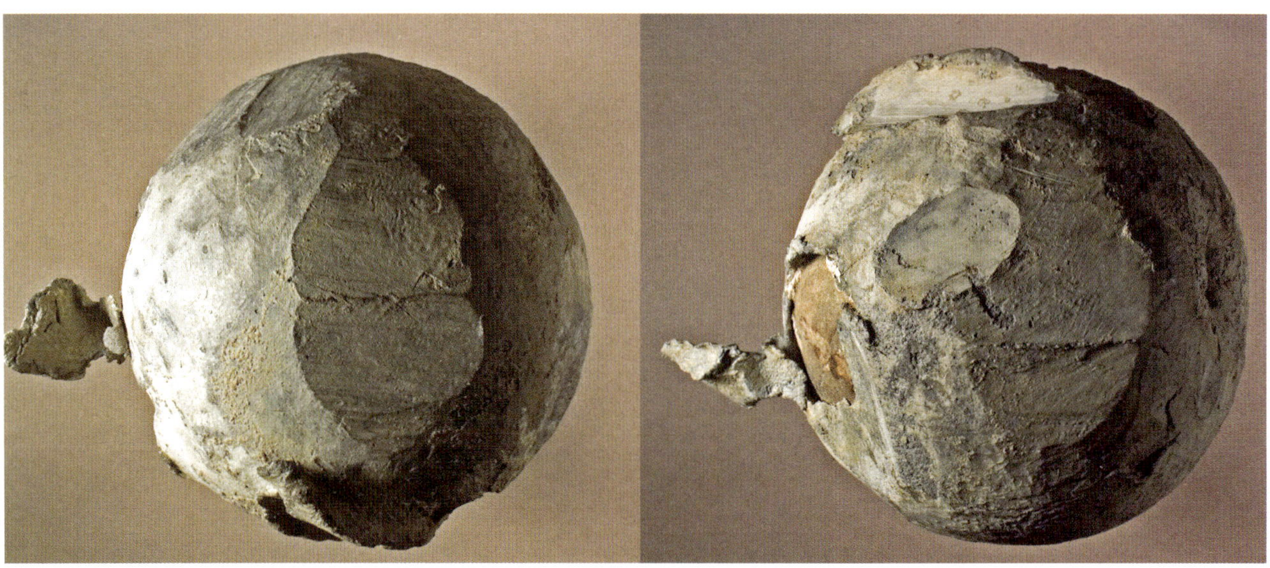

Fig 8.5 Lead composite round shot (diameter *c* 87mm) with a stone pebble core from Bosworth (1485). To the right is lead raised up by modern plough impact. To the top is a deep gouge likely to have occurred when the ball impacted after firing. To the fore is one of a set of banding facets, each with a central groove, thought to be the result of firing from a stave-built, wrought-iron gun

Fig 8.6 View of Towton battlefield looking east along Towton Dale. The effect of colluviation can be seen from the steep step from right to left at the field boundary along the bottom of the Dale, suggesting far more substantial colluviation on the right. It is from the field to the left that most of the ferrous arrowheads have been recovered, while the mass graves lie towards the further end of the same field

alluviation (at least in some Midland river valleys) occurred between the 10th and 14th centuries (Parry 2006).

On a small number of battlefields there may also be waterlogged deposits in palaeo-channels or wider areas of peat from former areas of fen. Here there is the potential for the preservation of artefacts made from organic materials. Such exceptional deposits need to be located so their potential can be conserved.

Decay of lead artefacts

To provide an initial indication of the impact of soil pH and land use on artefact condition a small-scale study was undertaken on five sites: Towton (1461), Bosworth (1485), Flodden (1513), Edgehill (1642), and the siege site at Wareham in Dorset (1643–44). The artefact class chosen for analysis was lead projectiles: they are present on most battlefields, even if in some cases they are not battle-related, and from the late 15th century onwards they are the principal artefact class for most sites. The condition of lead projectiles from each site was subjectively assessed.[3]

A small number of soil samples were analysed to establish soil pH on each site. The average pH was found to vary significantly between the five sites: it was neutral at Edgehill (7.2) and Towton (7.1) and decreased through Bosworth (6.6) and Flodden (6.0) to an acidic context at Wareham (4.6). To complement this information, land-use history was examined using a simple method developed in the Bosworth project. Arable, pasture, and other land uses were digitally mapped for three periods: the current landscape (assessed in the field and from Google Earth imagery); that of the early 1930s (based on a field-by-field survey in 1931–35); and, for some areas, that of the 1840s, which was based upon field-by-field information from the tithe surveys. Additional evidence for the long-term continuity of pastoral land use since the time of enclosure was provided by the 1940s' RAF vertical aerial photography, where this shows ridge and furrow.

Almost all bullets retrieved from the topsoil showed surface corrosion (Figs 8.7–8.10), usually conversion of the lead to lead carbonate. As already discussed (p 147), the build-up of such corrosion deposits will often protect the artefact from further corrosion, although the depth to which such corrosion has penetrated will vary significantly according to the conditions within which the object has lain. Where the corrosion deposit is thin then fine surface details left by manufacture, firing and impact will normally show clearly. More substantial features may also survive within the underlying uncorroded lead. Where there is a thicker corrosion deposit then finer detail may be masked or lost, but the major features will still be recognisable. In the latter circumstance most of the evidence may be preserved solely within the corrosion deposit, so erosion or the intentional removal of this will destroy the evidence. If corrosion has been more extreme, then all surface detail may be lost and the artefact may even begin to fracture and fragment. In such situations even the calibre, established from mass and/or diameter, may be significantly altered.

Fig 8.7 The light corrosion on this bullet from Sedgemoor (1685) means that remarkable surface detail survives. It is a lead ball of carbine calibre that was fired as the lower part of a multiple load. Above it were a large number of small lead shot, each a few millimetres in diameter, as revealed by the small polygonal compression marks which mirror the polygonal form of hailshot fired from artillery. Maximum diameter *c* 18.5mm

Fig 8.8 A thick lead carbonate corrosion deposit on this musket calibre bullet from Edgehill (1642) masks some detail. Despite this, the snip (a shallow scoop in the form of two hemispheres with a central bar) where the casting sprue has been removed is still visible. Maximum diameter *c* 19.5mm

Fig 8.9 The crazed surface on this bullet from Edgehill (1642) appears to represent the early stages of decay of a thick lead carbonate corrosion deposit. Maximum diameter *c* 16.5mm

Fig 8.10 This bullet, from the siege site at Wareham, Dorset (1640s) shows intense corrosion which has penetrated deep into the lead, causing it to fragment. Maximum diameter *c* 13mm

Fig 8.11 A bullet from Pinkie battlefield (East Lothian, 1547) which shows an exceptional degree of corrosion, analysed by R Janaway to establish its metal composition. It was half-sectioned to allow sampling from the uncorroded core, avoiding surface enrichment effects due to corrosion. At 6mm below the surface X-ray fluorescence (XRF) revealed a composition of 14% lead, 2% copper and 80% tin. The latter is a far higher percentage than would be expected if scrap pewter had been used to manufacture the bullet. This high tin content is almost certainly responsible for the excessive corrosion in this particular depositional environment (Foard 2008d). Maximum diameter *c* 15mm

Occasionally where a bullet shows a very high degree of corrosion this may be because it has been manufactured from an alloy rather than from 'pure' lead. This will not usually be apparent from visual inspection. The problem was revealed through analysis of the metal composition of several bullets from Pinkie (East Lothian, Scotland), which were examined because a few from the survey of a single field showed very different levels of corrosion for which no clear explanation could be found. The bullets were half sectioned so analysis could take place at several points on uncorroded metal as well as at the corroded surface (Fig 8.11). This revealed that the bullet showing the highest levels of corrosion, leading to fragmentation, was composed principally of tin, whereas the bullets showing lower levels of decay were composed largely of lead (Foard 2008d).

The majority of the Edgehill assemblage survives in excellent condition; hence most of the bullets have yielded evidence of manufacture and use. Their condition may be largely explained by soil pH, soil type, and land-use history. The underlying geology is clay (Charmouth Mudstone) and the soil generally remains wet, often being waterlogged in the winter. The land use in the 19th century is not known, as no tithe maps exist, but was almost all pasture in 1931–35, the presence of ridge and furrow over almost the whole battlefield in the late 1940s demonstrating that most of the land had remained uncultivated since the 18th century, when the open fields were enclosed. By 2004–07 land use was largely arable, although a small number of fields still contained intact ridge and furrow, indicating that they had still not been ploughed since enclosure. Several others had remnant ridge and furrow, showing that they had been cultivated only briefly in the late 20th century. Thus a high soil pH was combined with relatively low aeration of the clay soils and little mechanical damage and aeration over several centuries, until cultivation began at some point since the 1940s. What is not known is whether the condition of the Edgehill bullets is currently stable or if rapid decay has been initiated by recent conversion to arable.

At the other extreme is the siege site assemblage from Wareham. These bullets are in by far the poorest condition of any of the assemblages so far examined. They show deep corrosion which in some cases is leading to fragmentation (see Fig 8.10), and as a result the surface evidence of manufacture and use has usually been lost. Decay also appears to have altered significantly the bullets' mass and diameter. Their poor condition has rendered analysis almost meaningless; indeed, this is the only assemblage so far studied where distinctive calibre groupings are not distinguishable when graphed. The primary factor here is likely to be soil chemistry, for the site is on free-draining sandy soils and has a low pH. Decay may have been accelerated by mechanical damage and increased aeration as a result of cultivation, as the site was already under arable in 1931–35 and remained so immediately prior to mineral extraction in the 1990s. A complicating factor affecting the Wareham material is that storage conditions since recovery have not been ideal, with no steps taken to control humidity or minimise abrasion.

The other sites reveal a more complex picture. At Towton the average pH values are similar to those at Edgehill, but the bullets (believed to be from sporting activity subsequent to the battle) and the two lead round shot that are battle-related are in significantly poorer condition than projectiles from Edgehill. Geology and land-use history appear to provide a partial explanation: the soil at Towton, which overlies a limestone geology, appears to be very light and freely draining, and has also seen long-term arable use. Almost all fields described in the 1840s were under arable, as was most of the battlefield in the 1930s, and so it remains today (Foard 2010b).

At Bosworth the lead round shot from the battle are almost all in very good condition. The site has a marginally lower soil pH than Towton and Edgehill, so this does not seem to be a key factor; rather, the geology and land use seem to have been the influential factors here. The underlying geology is mixed, but mainly clay. Land use in the 1840s and 1930s was a mixture of pasture and arable, although most of the area producing the lead round shot is now arable. Even at Flodden, which has a slightly lower pH, the few lead bullets recovered (which may post-date the battle) and the three lead round shot which are battle-related are in better condition than those from Towton.

Thus a range of co-varying factors is implicated in the decay of metals in the soil, including metal type, the length of time an object has been in the ground, geology and soil type, historic land use, and agricultural regime. These will have been modified by human intervention in antiquity, but the greatest changes have been since the mid-20th century. Most worrying is the possibility that artefacts that are currently in good condition reflect past, rather than present, ground conditions, and that decay has accelerated in recent years.

While a great deal is known about how and why metals decay, we currently lack a clear understanding as to how the different factors interact in the topsoil.

Until science addresses this issue any assessment will remain speculative. Only when data are available to allow predictive modelling may it be possible to define appropriate sets of measures, applicable through agri-environment schemes, to mitigate the threats posed by modern agriculture. We should be open to the possibility that the conclusion of such work might be that the concept of preservation *in situ* may not always be applicable to battle archaeology. If so, the only viable strategy will be recording.

Collection

Metal detecting outside the framework of archaeological survey is almost certainly the greatest threat to historic battlefields in England. We have seen that the interpretation of battle archaeology depends upon analysis of relative densities in the scatter of unstratified metal artefacts across the landscape. Unrecorded or insufficiently recorded removal of artefacts distorts this all-important patterning, and does so especially where the intensity of that removal is not consistent across the landscape. This is an insidious threat, because there is no obvious sign in surviving distributions to show what has been lost. Over subsequent decades the collections themselves may be dispersed, discarded, or, as seen with material from Newburn, mixed up with finds from other sites (Foard 2010b). Where this happens it will be impossible to establish the character of the material that has been removed or the scale of loss. Indeed, as time passes, the very knowledge that removal has occurred is likely to fade, as collectors, landowners, and tenants move on or die.

The highest-profile threat is posed by metal-detecting rallies. Information from the PAS indicates that at least six rallies have been held on or immediately adjacent to nationally important battlefields; those held at Marston Moor led to parliamentary questions and national press coverage. The first was on 13 September 2003 (Keyes 2003); following discussion between English Heritage and the PAS, Finds Liaison Officers were present to make a record.[4] No information regarding the distribution of the finds was collected from this rally, and although there are anecdotal reports that more than a hundred bullets were found, only a small proportion of them are believed to have been shown to the Finds Liaison Officers. Detectorists claim that this was because they were not told that bullets were significant finds that should be recorded (T Sutherland pers comm). Subsequently, in response to a question in the Lords, Lord McIntosh of Haringey responded thus for the Government:

> My Lords ... [this] is why we have a review that includes historic battlefield sites as part of the general subject of listing and scheduling. At present, it is entirely unsatisfactory that we can do nothing about battlefields, metal detectorists or anybody else, if they operate with the permission of the landowner and avoid scheduled sites.[5]

Despite the furore over the first rally, a second rally was held on another part of the battlefield on 27–29 August 2005, promoted by the same landowner to raise money for charity. Despite approaches by English Heritage and others the rally went ahead, this time impinging on the Registered area. It involved about 300 detectorists and affected 540 acres, although it did see more substantial recording by Finds Liaison Officers. Among the potentially battle-related artefacts reported for recording were 60 bullets, including at least one piece of artillery hailshot, one round shot, and a sword guard. In addition, 136 other post-medieval finds, 37 coins from a hoard, and seven other coins were recorded. With the help of volunteers, GPS was used to record find locations, allowing a partial distribution plan to be compiled (Fig 8.12).

The evidence from the 2005 rally is thus more informative than that from 2003, and suggests that some action may have occurred well to the north of the published scatter. However, it is not known whether all the bullets found were reported, or the degree to which the concentrations reflect the intensity of detecting rather than a concentration of action. In addition, the information recorded for each find is limited because the bullets were not reported upon by an appropriate specialist, while re-analysis is not possible because the artefacts were taken away by the detectorists and so dispersed. Given that Marston Moor may have been the largest of all battles fought on English soil, with major military and political repercussions, it is remarkable that the attrition of its archaeological remains has been tolerated for recreational purposes. It is difficult to imagine the acceptance of such losses from other types of nationally important archaeological site.

Rallies on other battlefields have gone largely unnoticed. In the absence of any national consultation mechanism for battlefield issues and with no general guidance available, variable responses to them are not surprising. Thus, a rally took place on the north part of the battlefield at Nantwich in 2004 without the

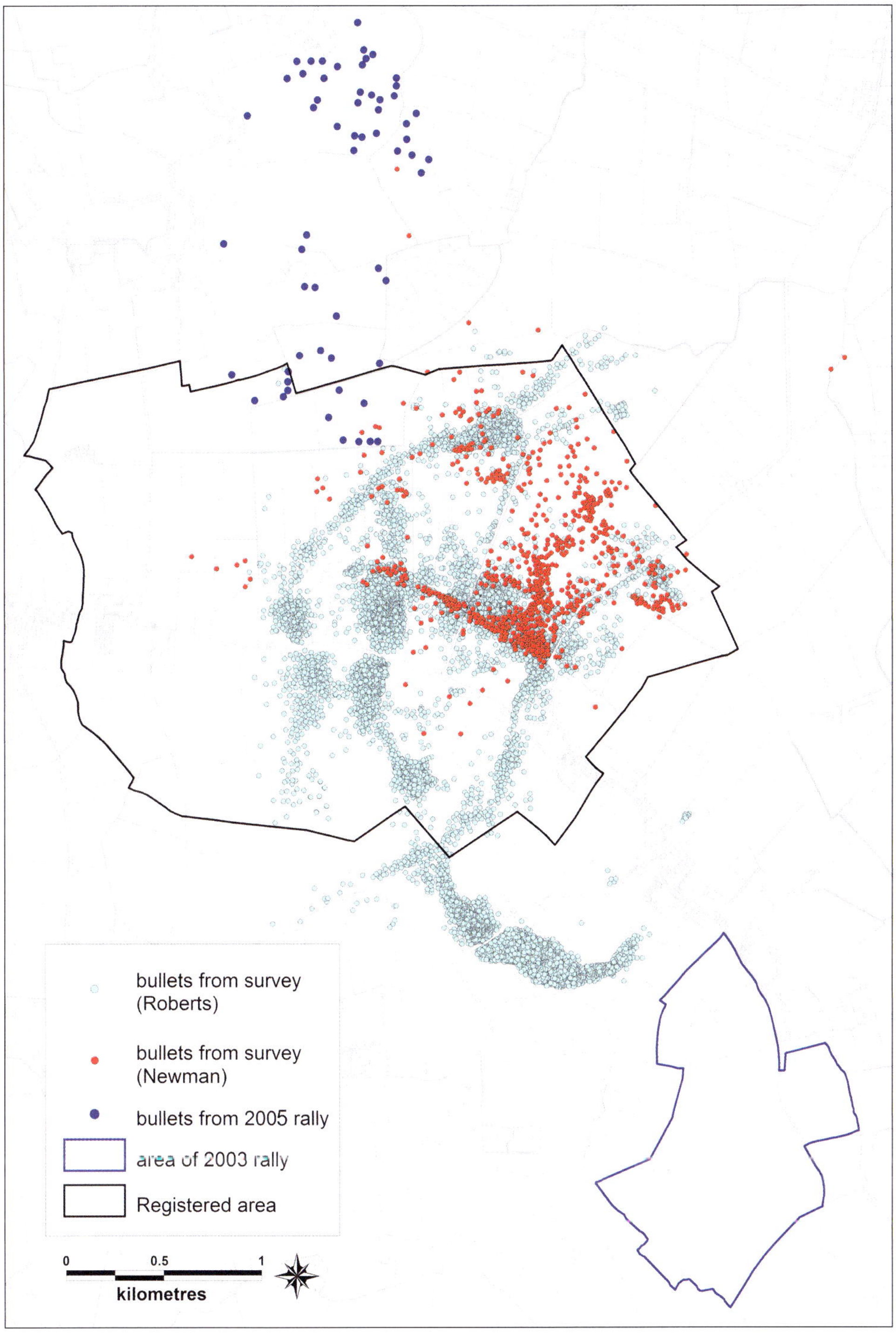

Fig 8.12 Map of Marston Moor (1644), comparing the Registered area with reported distributions of bullets from Newman's fieldwalking in the 1970s, Roberts' metal detecting 1984–2002, and the metal-detecting rally in 2005[6]

knowledge of battlefield archaeologists; there was no recording of finds because the involvement of the Finds Liaison Officer was rejected by the organisers.[7] On 5 August 2007 a second rally was held, this time in the heart of the Registered area. Again, this was without the knowledge of battlefield archaeologists, although the Finds Liaison Officer was allowed to record finds.[8] Another two rallies are reported which, although outside the Registered area, lay in close proximity to Acton church, where a parliamentarian attack took place against the royalist baggage train (see Fig 7.29).

Rallies are not necessarily the most destructive of metal-detecting impacts. Greater damage is probably caused by sustained detecting on battlefields over a long period by individuals or small groups. This can take two forms: treasure hunting to collect objects for their intrinsic value, and collection of material through a wish to understand a battlefield.

The former may be for the development of private collections or for sale. Reports from the PAS, museums, and HERs, together with published and anecdotal evidence, suggest that many battlefields have been so affected (Smith 2004; 2005; Bailey 2001). Some collectors detect on a battlefield without realising the significance of the land or their finds, and typically collect the material with little or no understanding of the archaeological evidence that they are destroying. Discussion with detectorists frequently reveals the 'bullet bucket' where they collect their 'musket balls'; although such objects are often treated as 'junk' they are normally still collected.

Detectorists have been developing collections from battlefields for several decades (Bailey 1992). More recently the sale of artefacts has increased, or at least (with the advent of eBay, where English battlefield finds are now regularly on sale) it has become more obvious. On 17 September 2003, for example, a search of eBay returned four lots: five bullets and six bullets from 'near' an unnamed Civil War battlefield, five from Newark, and three from Naseby. On 29 January 2008 another search returned fourteen lots comprising 'musket balls' in groups of up to 20 bullets, and one including a half pound iron cannonball. These included finds specified as coming from Cheriton battlefield and the siege sites at Newark and Pontefract Castle.

There is online promotion of such activities. One example first reproduces information from the Battlefield Trust's online UK Battlefields Resource Centre, then states:

> December 22, 2006 11:54 pm: I continue my blog on famous battlefields in England. Although as I have explained previously it is often illegal to Metal Detect on these fields, there is absolutely nothing wrong in contacting land owners in the vicinity and ask if you can detect on their land.[9]

Battlefields form part of the portfolio of sites used by commercial businesses that run metal-detecting holidays and related events which are advertised on the internet.[10] Battlefield detecting is also sometimes organised by metal-detecting clubs as 'club sites': for example, on the probable baggage train area at Marston Moor, a Manchester metal-detecting club is said to have paid the farmer for permission to detect, with about a dozen people at a time on site in the late 1990s (P Roberts pers comm).

The second type of collection, where the principal purpose is to understand the site, is marred by a failure to follow archaeological principles of systematic collection and detailed recording. The cumulative impact of such activity is far greater than a single rally. Published evidence for Marston Moor shows that the scale of removal can be substantial, with many thousands of bullets and other artefacts having been removed (Newman and Roberts 2003; Foard 2007a).

In the early 1990s such collecting could be argued to have been beneficial for raising awareness of the potential of battle archaeology. Today there is no longer any justification for unrecorded collecting. Some detectorists now use GPS to record the location of each find; where this is combined with individual bagging of finds and their submission for specialist analysis, the resulting increase in information is substantial. However, such collection still does not normally lead to deposition of the assemblage in an archive to enable re-analysis, and if the collection is not undertaken systematically with recording that includes information on intensity of survey, then information will be lost. Moreover, because the removal of artefacts will affect the total populations of artefacts that remain, inconsistent removal will distort the patterning obtained from any future re-survey.

The priority should be to retain assemblages *in situ*, so that more effective techniques can be developed to draw the greatest range of information from the scatters. As with scheduled monuments, artefacts should ideally be removed from Registered battlefields only as part of an archaeological research programme which addresses significant research questions and follows current best practice. This is particularly important because the number of battlefields in England is relatively small, in some cases with only one or two sites representing a particular phase of warfare.

The need for control of metal detecting on Registered battlefields could best be met through a licensing scheme, with permission given only for archaeological survey that follows current best practice (Department of Culture, Media and Sport 2008, clause 161). With this would go guidance which places a responsibility on all to seek English Heritage approval – a Written Scheme of Investigation – for any archaeological interventions on a Registered battlefield. Assessment of such schemes could then ensure that they follow current best practice in battlefield survey, that they are undertaken only by those with appropriate expertise, and that sufficient resources are available to enable analysis, publication, and archiving. While it could be argued that similar measures are needed on many other types of archaeological site, the difference with battlefields is that it is the artefact assemblage itself which forms the principal evidence.

Licensing will not stop nighthawks. As in the USA, illicit detecting will still occasionally occur on protected ground, and indeed there are already reports of this on the scheduled area of the Basing House siege site (Alan Turton pers comm). However, this problem may be more limited on battlefields than some other site types because the artefacts on most battlefields are of low monetary value. The nighthawking survey commissioned by English Heritage makes specific reference to battlefields and has important conclusions relevant to controlling the threat.[11]

With all this said, it is legal metal detecting which is far and away the greatest problem, as can be seen from the scale of removal at Marston Moor (see Fig 8.12). In such situations a licensing scheme should be largely effective because most detectorists, rally organisers, detecting club officials, and landowners are law-abiding people. Until legislative change to facilitate such control is forthcoming, interim measures are needed where there is a nighthawking problem or where collecting is taking place with landowner permission. The approach pioneered in 2010 at Towton provides a model. Here an agreement to control all metal detecting was achieved through intensive negotiation between community, landowners, police, detectorists, and archaeologists, all assisted by the English Heritage initiative on 'heritage crime'. This should not, however, be seen as an alternative to effective statutory control.

Battlefields where collecting is known to have taken place include Marston Moor, Sedgemoor, Naseby, Stratton, Shrewsbury, Barnet, Cropredy, Towton, Cheriton, Blore Heath, Newburn, Nantwich, and Edgehill. Work is needed to establish what has already been lost from each Registered battlefield. This may be achieved through consultation with collectors, landowners, and other members of the local community. Such work should ideally be complemented by research into the ways in which past non-systematic collection has distorted artefact distributions. It could consider whether any indicators can be isolated in scatters that remain for the scale or nature of the losses. Such research could be undertaken through experiment and by working with the collectors on exemplar sites, such as Naseby, where the individuals are known, are interested in the site, and have surviving collections.

It is sometimes said that metal-detected assemblages from battlefields are of no value if each object is not accurately and individually located. While most of the potential information will indeed have been lost, some useful data may still be retrieved. Assessments of such assemblages can reveal relative proportions of different bullet calibres, types of bullet, and the presence of other artefacts such as powder-box caps. Such information can give insights into the nature of the battlefield action and assist in understanding the nature of the distortion caused to the assemblage remaining *in situ*.

Contamination

It is not only the removal but also the addition of artefacts to battlefields that can compromise the potential of a site. In parts of continental Europe 20th-century warfare has caused massive contamination with munitions and other debris, as, for example, noted in survey work on the battlefields of the Crimean war (Wason 2003, 167). While nothing of this character is seen in England, modern activities of other sorts can cause significant problems. At Bosworth one pasture field had been in long-term use for stock car racing and is impossible to survey because of the vast number of small modern non-ferrous items that it contains. In fact, any activity which brings together large numbers of people on a battlefield is likely to lead to contamination of the site with modern artefacts. While these artefacts will rarely confuse the assemblage of battle archaeology, modern coins, ring-pulls, tent pegs and other small items can vastly outnumber battle artefacts and so will make systematic survey difficult, if not impossible.

Limited assessment of contamination has taken place at Cropredy, where part of the 1644 battlefield has been used for an annual folk festival since the 1970s. The festival, including camping and parking, has been held in the same location throughout. The site has been subject to some metal detecting; this appears to have been occasional. Visual inspection found no signs of ground disturbance. This was followed by small-scale sampling to assess any masking effects of artefacts deposited as a result of the folk festival, and the effect on the practicality of survey (see Fig 8.1).[12] Three fields were detected along single transects: fields 1 and 3, on the festival site, and field 2, immediately across the river. All artefacts were recorded but none was removed. The Edgehill survey provides comparative data. There, the number of metres detected per modern non-ferrous find was typically greater than 100m, and even in close proximity to a modern farm the total reduced to only 40m per find. At Cropredy, while the non-festival field (field 2) produced only double the maximum Edgehill density, the festival fields (fields 1 and 3) produced up to 20 times the average Edgehill density. The survey produced 77 modern finds but just two pre-modern finds, neither of which was battle-related.

Re-enactment is of even greater concern. The artefacts deposited during such events may, in future, be difficult to distinguish from historic artefacts. This problem will increase as knowledge about original manufacture advances and skills in replicating ancient technologies improve. Moreover, the longer the reproduction artefacts are in the ground and suffer decay, the harder it will be to differentiate them from original objects. This will be especially true of ferrous artefacts which, as we have seen at Towton, include one of the most important artefact classes on medieval battlefields – arrowheads.

In recognition of these and other problems of re-enactment, the US National Park Service (NPS) prohibits all forms of 'simulated warfare' on their sites because they

> create an atmosphere that is inconsistent with the memorial qualities of the battlefields and other military sites placed in the Service's trust. The safety risks to participants and visitors, and the inevitable damage to the physical resource that occurs during such events are also unacceptably high when seen in light of the NPS mandate to preserve and protect park resources and values (National Park Service 2006, section 7.5.9).

The NPS does, however, recognise the importance of re-enactment for the appreciation of historic events and so, in some circumstances, it does support re-enactment off the battlefield. This approach is followed by most US federal and state organisations with battlefield management responsibilities.[13]

In England the issue needs assessment, because organisations responsible for fields of conflict sometimes promote re-enactment in original locations. English Heritage, for example, holds an annual re-enactment on the Hastings battlefield. Other battlefields which have seen on-site re-enactment include Cheriton, Roundway Down, Naseby, and Worcester. On siege sites the National Trust has sponsored re-enactment at Corfe Castle, while Hampshire County Council does so at Basing House. New interpretative schemes are in place at Shrewsbury and planned at Naseby, where regular re-enactment is intended.

Management mechanisms

As with battlefield investigation, we can look to the United States for experience in conservation management. The first US National Military Parks were established in the 1890s for the Civil War battlefields of Chickamagua, Chattanooga, Shiloh, Gettysburg, and Vicksburg. By 1993 all or part of 31 Civil War battlefields were protected within a National Park of some kind, with most areas being of more than 1000 acres (405 ha) and the largest of more than 8000 acres (3237 ha) (Civil War Sites Advisory Commission 1993, 30–31). From the Revolutionary War there are other sites, with the greater part of the 1781 Yorktown battlefield in Virginia lying within the Colonial National Historical Park, managed by the National Parks Service. In addition, parts of other battlefields are managed by state and local battlefield preservation organisations, and there is collaboration between the various national organisations, through the American Battlefield Protection Program, to promote the conservation of fields of conflict across the USA (Greenburg 1997).

An example of a site managed at a local level is Piedras Marcadas Pueblo, on the outskirts of Albuquerque, New Mexico. This site contains exceptional battle archaeology from Coronado's campaign of 1540–41, and came under threat from urban expansion in 2007. The core of the site is managed as part of the Open Space Visitor Centre, but there is little potential for protection beyond this area of city land. As a result the main strategy under discussion is to restrict further encroachment by purchase of key areas of land.[14]

While acquisition is clearly the most effective of all management strategies, it is not one that has been pursued in England, nor is it likely to be viable in the future for more than a handful of sites. Just one battlefield, Hastings, is currently in national ownership, although, for incidental reasons, parts of a few other battlefields are in public ownership. Unfortunately, as the damage caused by earthmoving and tree planting on Northampton battlefield shows, in the absence of informed policy such public ownership does not necessarily lead to effective management. In contrast, a far greater number of siege sites are wholly or partly in the care of English Heritage (27) and the National Trust (6). It is not clear whether the conservation frameworks for any of these sites acknowledge the potential for battle archaeology.

In comparison with the successes of management via ownership, responses to development threats in the

USA have been less effective. Where government land is involved or where the government is the developer then evaluation and recording now normally take place prior to destruction, but on private land the mechanisms are generally far weaker than in England, though effectiveness varies between states and local authorities. In places, urban encroachment on major battlefields has been restricted by zoning, but there are far more cases where development has proceeded without restriction (Civil War Sites Advisory Commission 1993). Thus the American experience has only limited relevance to the management of battlefields in England.

The Register of Historic Battlefields

Management of battlefields in England is relatively recent. Yet with the launch in 1995 of the Register of Historic Battlefields, England has led Europe in this field, and for more than fifteen years it has been the only country to identify battlefields of national importance (English Heritage 1995). Building upon this pioneering initiative, a new generation of battlefield conservation measures is being developed in Scotland, Wales, Ireland, and Flanders.[15]

In 1994–95 English Heritage assessed 71 actions for inclusion on the Register. Of these, 43 fulfilled the criteria and were added to the Register. A further eight were considered to be in too poor a condition to justify inclusion, while five others could not be located with sufficient accuracy to be Registered. The remaining fifteen were discarded because they did not justify classification as battles.

For battlefields to be included on the Register they had to meet key criteria: political significance (the impact of the action should be traceable nationwide); military historical significance (such as use of tactics of particular note); and biographical significance (for example, it was the crowning glory of a military career, or where a famous leader was killed or captured). While these criteria have proved effective in most respects, they do not necessarily extend to archaeological potential, because there need be no correlation between a battle's political or military importance and the significance of its archaeological deposits. Some historically minor actions, for instance, may have high archaeological potential because of the special quality of physical and/or documentary evidence.

Based on the criteria discussed in the preceding chapters, our analysis has provided a graded list of battles (see Appendix 1). Few battlefields in the higher levels of our scoring are excluded from the Register. Of those omitted, most were left out either because information on their location was inadequate or because the sites were largely destroyed. Our analysis suggests that, for a few of these, there may now be sufficient information to justify re-assessment. It also suggests that several battles which were not considered in 1995 should now be assessed to ensure that the Register is properly representative.

Maldon (AD 991) was the only battlefield from before 1066 to be included on the Register in 1995. Our assessment has confirmed that, over the last fifteen years, no other early battlefield has been located with sufficient certainty to enable it to be added.

Of the 31 medieval battles, just nineteen were included on the Register in 1995. St Albans I (1455), St Albans II (1561), and Wakefield (1460) were assessed but excluded because the sites were considered too heavily developed. Lincoln I (1141) and Lincoln II (1217) were presumably excluded because the sites were developed, although no justification for their exclusion was identified in the records of the 1995 assessment held in the relevant English Heritage files. Our assessment supports these decisions in most cases, although very limited areas of the Wakefield battlefield might survive undeveloped. The one exception is Lincoln I, which may warrant re-examination. While one site for the battle, lying close to the medieval city walls, has been wholly developed, an alternative site lies further to the west and appears largely intact. Mortimer's Cross (1461), Hexham (1464), Edgcote (1469), and Empingham (1470) were omitted in 1995 because their sites were too poorly located to enable a boundary to be defined. A similar problem may explain the exclusion of Fulford (1066) and Hedgeley Moor (1464). Our review suggests that for three of these (Edgcote, Mortimer's Cross, and possibly Fulford), sufficient information may now be available to allow their inclusion on the Register. Unfortunately, in the case of Fulford it is probably too late, because extensive development has now been permitted.

It is unclear why Piper Dene (1435) was not assessed in 1995. There is a strong case for this battle to be considered because it represents a class of site not adequately covered by the Register. It was one of the larger engagements in England to have developed out of a border raid, with perhaps as many as 8000 troops involved. While it is little discussed in secondary works, the site appears intact and may have high potential. Moreover, it lies in close proximity to a series of later medieval battlefield, siege, skirmish, and probably also raid sites. Taken together, these may cast new light on late medieval warfare on the Anglo-Scottish border.

Of the possible battles only Bramham Moor (1408) was assessed for the Register, but was excluded at an early stage for unknown reasons. Most of the remainder are poorly located and some are likely to be heavily developed. Two in particular are worthy of re-examination: Fornham St Genevieve (1173) and Alnwick I (1093).

Of the 29 actions from the Civil War that are classified here as battles, 20 were Registered in 1995. Our re-assessment has confirmed that little if any of Preston I (1648) or Newark (1644) remains undeveloped, but in contrast, there is potential for surviving areas of both Newbury II (1644) and possibly also Torrington II (1646), while Ripple (1643) appears to be wholly undeveloped. Given the scale and importance of Newbury II, and its vulnerability to the expansion of the town of Newbury, a re-examination of that battlefield seems particularly urgent. Of those never assessed for the Register, both Selby (1644) and Maidstone (1648) are wholly developed, but Winwick (1648) should be reconsidered; though subsidiary to the major battle in and around Preston the day before, it was of a scale greater than many Registered battlefields. The site is almost completely undeveloped and apart from small-scale mineral extraction it seems to be largely intact. In addition, Winwick church, to which some royalist forces were driven back, shows bullet impact scars (M Rayner pers comm). It is also the only battlefield from the Second Civil War which appears to survive in a good state of preservation and may, for example, provide information about the character of the archaeological record created by the small arms and artillery then in use by the New Model Army.

The most remarkable omission is the battle of Lostwithiel (1644), which was one of the most significant battles of the entire Civil War period (Brooks 2005, 448–5). It was a large, complex action that involved some 25,000 troops and extended across more than 6km. It saw the destruction of the parliamentarians' most important field army, and together with the abortive action at Newbury II it led to major political upheaval in parliament which ultimately resulted in the establishment of the New Model Army – with far-reaching military and political results. Lostwithiel was also one of the few major battles of the war that was fought in an almost wholly enclosed landscape. Hence, the character of this action is very different from most others, comprising a number of subsidiary actions over several days and across a wide landscape. As such, it would be a valuable comparator for the many other battles of the war which were fought in wholly or largely open landscapes and over just a few hours.

Lostwithiel included the capture of Restormel Castle (now an English Heritage property) and the destruction of the church in the town of Lostwithiel when the powder magazine exploded. The most substantial event was the engagement around Castle Dore, a prehistoric earthwork which is now publicly accessible. A number of these locations are well preserved and are likely to have good surviving battle archaeology and terrain evidence;[16] and yet the battle is said to have been excluded from the Register precisely because it was not a simple, single action and so would be difficult to encompass within one boundary (John Childs pers comm). Scale and complexity cannot, however, be adequate grounds for the exclusion of one of the major military events in English history. Indeed, the unusual character of the event reinforces the case for its inclusion on the Register as the most intact example of its type. Battles with some similarity in terms of complexity are the Registered battlefield at Worcester (1651), which survives only in part, and Preston I (1648), which was excluded because of its condition.

There are several other actions involving large numbers which may not warrant registration. Blackheath (1497) was an ill-organised urban action fought during the Cornish rebellion of 1497 and involving as many as 20,000 combatants. Though not adequately understood, the main clash appears to have taken place at the river crossing at Deptford Bridge. Thus, despite there being extensive open ground remaining on Blackheath itself, the greater part of the battlefield lay to the north and is wholly built over (Rayner 2004). Turnham Green in Middlesex (1642) and Ludford Bridge in Shropshire (1459) are also excluded because neither seems to have included significant fighting. Penrith in Cumbria (1715) saw only small-scale fighting between Scottish forces and the local militia despite the large numbers said to have been present. Hilton in County Durham (1644) is a disputed site, where uncertainty might be resolved by a review of the primary sources in the context of terrain reconstruction. However, such work does not seem justified as on present evidence most of the alternative sites appear to be built up. Preston I (1648) was another complex action with several widely spread component actions. However, as noted above, it appears largely built over. So too is the site of Maidstone (1648), which was essentially an urban fight. Selby (1644) was also partly fought in an urban area, while the rest of the site is now built over.

Alton (1644) was a street fight; hence, despite the large numbers involved, little seems likely to remain. However, there are bullet impact scars on Alton church and scatters of impacted bullets will presumably accompany them in the soil of the churchyard. Investigation of this small component of the action might be of value for the light it could cast on the nature and significance of impact scars in the study of early modern warfare. In addition, there may be potential for interpretation to the public. Alton thus provides a good example of a site which, when assessed as a whole seems to possess little of conservation value and does not deserve registration, even though specific elements of the action might warrant stewardship through the planning process. Such partial objectives may best be achieved through inclusion on the relevant HER, as discussed below.

Discussion in preceding chapters reveals several other themes which warrant further consideration to ensure that the Register represents the full range of warfare in England. The clearest examples of these themes come from the 16th century, for which the Register includes only two sites, both international battles on the Anglo-Scottish border. As we have seen, however, this is a critical period of transition in the technology of war, when handguns were beginning to appear in large number in English armies. The two major rebellions fought in 1549 included substantial battles (see Chapter 6), and one battle from each of these has been identified as having high potential: Sampford Courtney in Devon and Dussindale in Norfolk. Both justify assessment for inclusion on the Register, though the latter has suffered extensive development.

The adequacy of Register boundaries

The effectiveness of management of Registered battlefields will be determined, first of all, by the adequacy of boundaries. As we have seen, defining the extent of a battlefield is difficult. As a basic definition a battlefield can be regarded as that area where the troops deployed and fought while in battle array. Once the formations were lost, as in a rout and pursuit, then it can be argued that the action becomes a subsidiary skirmish, because such fighting was typically piecemeal and could be widely scattered. However, these subsidiary events frequently had a dramatic influence on the outcome and significance of a battle, while key archaeological evidence may be found in this wider zone – as shown by the mass grave in Towton village. A related problem is seen at Bosworth (1485), where part of the round shot scatter is currently interpreted as overshot (see Fig 5.9). These may lie hundreds of metres beyond the initial deployments in areas that never saw hand to hand action. They can nonetheless still provide crucial evidence for the tactical deployment of both the guns and of the armies as a whole. Together with the other projectiles from the battlefield, they may also define the character of the artillery in use and the intensity of fire they laid down. It is our view that when defining a zone for purposes of management, much of this wider area of manoeuvre, rout and overshot, should be encompassed by a single battlefield boundary.

The Register boundaries drawn in 1995 were defined on the basis of evidence then available. This comprised 'documentary, archaeological and topographical and landscape history'. In each case the boundary was taken to be 'the outer reasonable limit to the area within which the bulk of the fighting took place' (English Heritage 1995). Only where extensive development or mineral extraction had taken place were parts of the battlefield excluded.

We have visited all 43 Registered battlefields and examined the battle reports by the National Army Museum and the landscape reports by CEI, upon which the Register was based. In some cases we have supplemented the terrain evidence with additional historic map and other evidence and, where practicable, have brought together the available archaeological data. The most significant examples have been discussed in the preceding chapters. The combined evidence indicates the need for revision of some Register boundaries, while for others it points to significant uncertainties that need to be addressed.

For English battlefields before the 1450s we have seen that only terrain analysis is currently effective in advancing understanding. In several cases, however, such work has provided sufficient information to suggest the need for the revision of Registered areas. The clearest example is Northallerton, where the boundary may need to be extended to take in a more southerly English deployment and important terrain features to both east and west (see Fig 3.16). In contrast, for actions from the 1450s onwards battle archaeology can be brought to bear in defining boundaries. However, at present, only a handful of battlefields have seen sufficient survey of their archaeology for this to assist in the definition of boundaries, and for most of these later battlefields we are still principally dependent upon terrain-related analysis.

In some cases the revisions required appear to be relatively small. For example, terrain analysis for Sedgemoor (1685) appears to confirm the general accuracy of the Register boundary, which is also supported by the limited archaeological information that is currently available (see Figs 7.8–7.13). However, both the probable site of Penzoy Pound and the crossing of the Langmore Rhyne – the latter a key feature in the events of the battle – are excluded from the Registered area. It is not yet clear if results of as-yet unpublished collection of artefacts will suggest significant action beyond the Register boundary to the north-west.[17]

Minor but potentially significant amendments may be appropriate at Edgehill (see Figs 7.15–7.16 and 7.21–7.22). The current boundary appears to include all the core cavalry and infantry action and much of both royalist and parliamentarian rout. The main omission is part of the attack on the parliamentarian baggage train in Little Kineton. Survey is incomplete

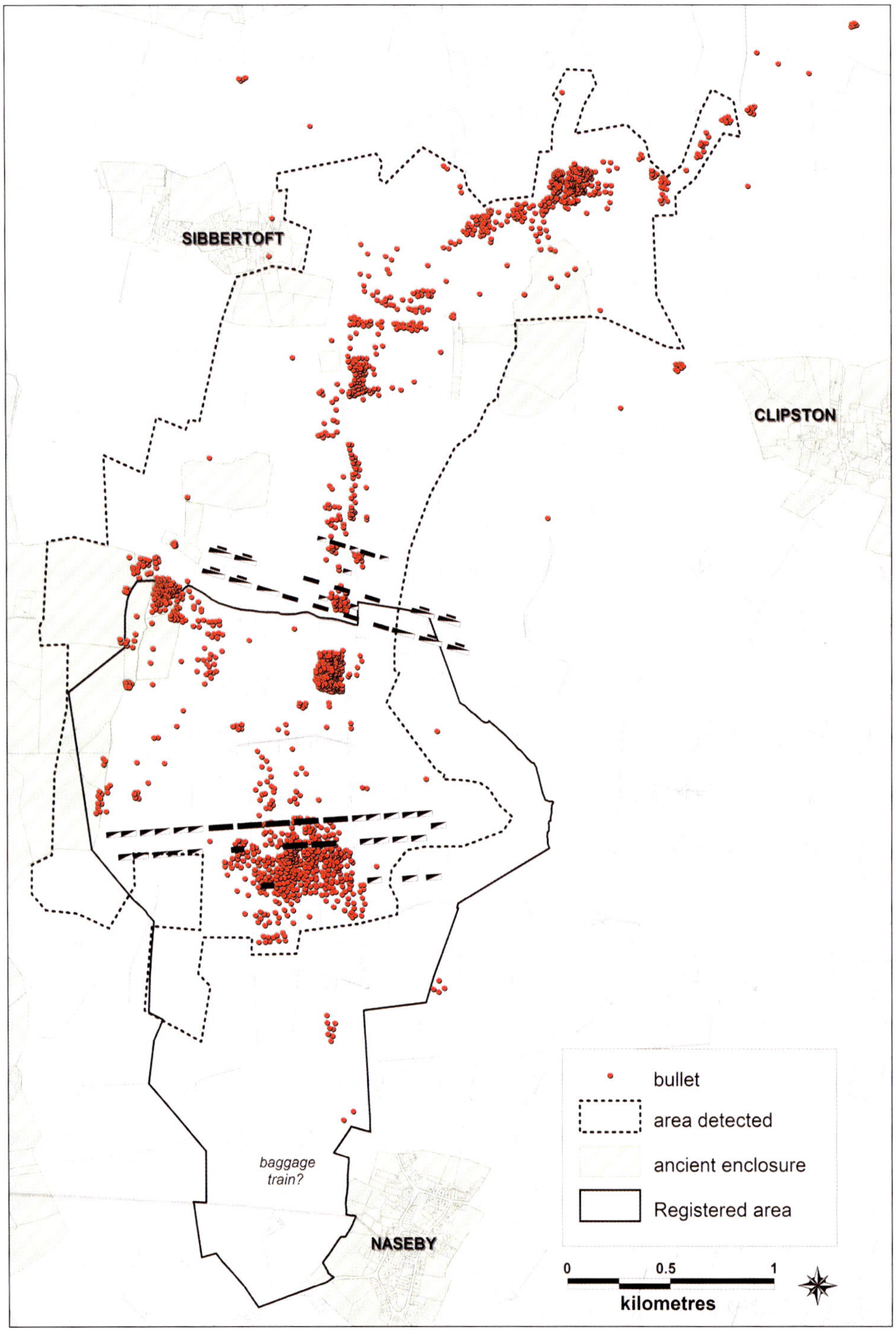

Fig 8.13 Map comparing the Registered area at Naseby with the bullet scatter from non-systematic collection and the probable extent of enclosed land in 1645. The Parliamentarian deployment is to the south and the royalist to the north, both with infantry in the centre and cavalry on either flank[18] (Reproduced by permission of Ordnance Survey on behalf of HMSO. © Crown copyright and database right 2012. All rights reserved. Ordnance Survey Licence no. 100024900)

on other parts of the periphery of the battlefield, so it is possible that other minor modifications of the boundary will be necessary in future.

Several other battlefields have extensive battle archaeology and/or terrain analysis suggesting that the action extended beyond the Registered area. However, the evidence is often less reliable or incomplete. Thus, while the evidence shows that the boundaries require adjustment, it is insufficient to define where the new boundaries should run. For example, at Naseby the Register currently includes the main action and, to the south, the probable area of the attack on the parliamentarian baggage train. In contrast, to the north, the probable area of the royalist deployment is partly excluded, while the bullet scatter runs for over a kilometre beyond the Registered boundary. This scatter appears to represent a major phase of the battle which saw the destruction of the royalist infantry and the plundering of the royalist baggage train (Foard 1995). This was the critical outcome at Naseby, for it was the destruction of the king's 'old infantry' that made it impossible for him to continue to fight the war effectively.

Only the battle archaeology can give full definition to this wider area at Naseby (Fig 8.13). Unfortunately, because the map of the bullet scatter derives from non-systematic collection (see p 126) it almost certainly under-represents the true spread of battle archaeology. For instance, the narrow width of the bullet scatter extending north through Sibbertoft township, together with the lack of pistol and carbine calibre bullets, suggests this may be only a partial picture of the full extent of the assemblage. With such uncertainty it is difficult to suggest exactly where a revised boundary for the Register should be drawn. A similar situation exists at Marston Moor, where substantial battle archaeology lies well beyond the Registered area but the plan derives from non-systematic collection and its accuracy and completeness are accordingly in question (see Fig 8.12).

The information from Towton is far more reliable. As we have seen, this is particularly true of the extent of the artefact scatter on the east side of the battlefield. With this caveat, only limited revision of the Register boundary appears to be needed. This would involve inclusion of the mass grave excavated in 1996 and the associated chapel, which lie just to the north of the Registered area, and the addition of an area to the south-east of the current boundary in which a detached artefact scatter is interpreted as a subsidiary action in Dintingdale (see Fig 5.6).

At the other extreme, there are at least two cases where new studies indicate that the wrong site has been Registered. The clearest example is Bosworth (1485) (see Chapter 5). The other is Barnet (1471), where the evidence has come mainly from terrain analysis (see Fig 5.3). It is likely that these are not unique cases, for it was only when intensive research was conducted that the true situation was revealed.

Very different issues arise over the definition of boundaries when part of a battlefield has been affected by development or other destructive processes. In such cases it may not be appropriate to include poorly preserved areas within the Register boundary. The logical response would be to define an outer zone, delineated by a broken line, where the presence of battle and terrain archaeology is still possible. This would act as a guide to planners and others as to where significant remains might be expected outside the Registered area.

The 1995 Register tentatively pioneered this approach on seven Registered battlefields, where the original Register map defined an outer zone that typically took in land which had been affected by development.[19] At Adwalton the failure to define the relevance of this outer zone, or to maintain this mapping principle when the new digital maps of Registered battlefields were delivered online, has meant that its significance has been overlooked. The implications of this decision for the effective management of the site are discussed in the Adwalton case study below.

Historic Environment Records and SHINE

The vast majority of battlefields and all other fields of conflict are omitted from the Register. Nonetheless, many of them will have significant archaeological potential. In order that their significance is recognised, the sites should be recorded on the appropriate Historic Environment Record (HER).

Consultation with all English HERs formed a part of the Database enhancement in 2007, and a comparison of the returns with our complete data set enabled a crude assessment of the completeness, although not the quality, of each HER's information. Figure 8.14 reveals the degree to which enhancement was then required to ensure that all known fields of conflict exist on the HERs. Many HERs have now assimilated the data provided to them on completion of our project.

The more important sites should also be identified as polygons on the Selected Heritage Inventory for Natural England (SHINE).[20] These will comprise unregistered sites, including well-preserved siege and skirmish sites, as well as any currently unregistered but intact areas of Registered sites. SHINE aims to create a single, nationally consistent data set of undesignated historic environment features that could benefit from management within the Environmental Stewardship scheme, discussed below. The project has created a methodology that allows local authority HERs to contribute information directly into the national SHINE database. Using SHINE, the local authority can define the features and how they should best be managed. This may lead to a farmer agreeing to adopt a specific management option for a particular resource; even if it does not, the added benefit is that, by being shown on the map, the feature is automatically protected from deliberate damage or removal as part of 'cross compliance' conditions.

Siege sites

Siege sites form another distinct area that requires management. At present none is included on the Register, while their coverage in HERs is variable. Indeed, certain terms such as 'siege' are not present in the national thesaurus to enable fields of conflict to be classified adequately in HERs.

In 1995 sieges were recognised as being of potential national importance. Despite this, they were excluded from the Register because it was then believed that 'they are usually associated with physical remains which can be conserved through existing statutory mechanisms such as scheduling or listing' (English Heritage 1995). The evidence presented above (Chapter 7) suggests that, for early modern siege sites at least, this view was wrong. Defensive works, siege-works,

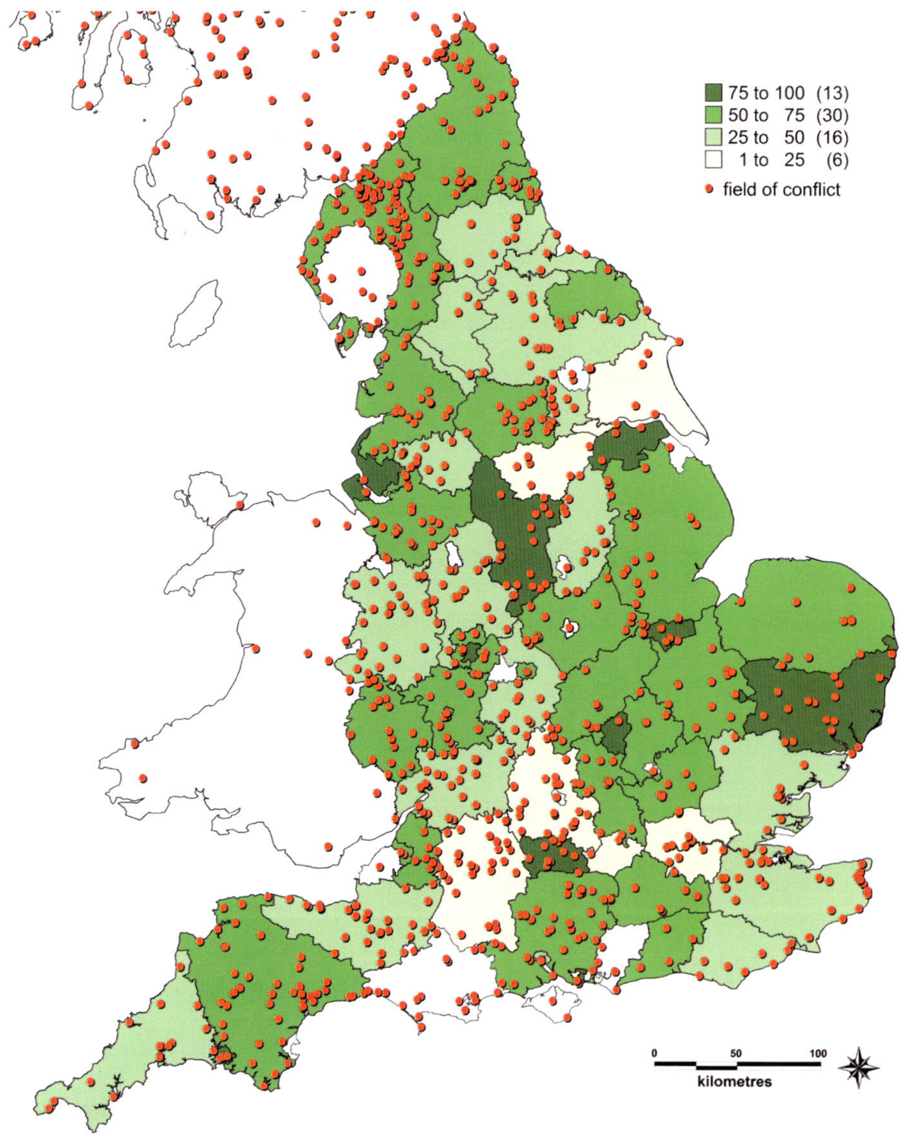

Fig 8.14 Map showing the percentage of fields of conflict on the Database that was also on the relevant Historic Environment Records in 2007

and related evidence may be effectively covered by scheduling and listing, but other aspects of the archaeology of the sieges are not.

Bullet impact scars on structures might be expected to be embraced by listing, but they can be managed effectively only if there is awareness of their presence and significance. Even then, straightforward like-for-like repair, which presents a major threat to this evidence, does not call for Listed Building Consent. Likewise, it is true that scatters of bullets and other artefacts within or close to defensive works may be embraced by a scheduled area. Yet this will have practical effect only if their presence is catered for by schemes of management. This is demonstrated by the case of Kenilworth Castle, where the former garden immediately north of the slighted wall of the keep, within the scheduled area, was excavated in 2005–06 on behalf of English Heritage. Despite the fact that the castle was known to have held a Civil War garrison and there are bullet impact scars on the surviving structures, the research design for this investigation did not provide for the metal-detecting survey that would have been appropriate to record a bullet scatter. It is rumoured that bullets were identified by informal metal detecting of the spoil heaps, but this remains unconfirmed. Evidence in the ground beyond the defences at Kenilworth and other such sites is unprotected, except where siege works have been scheduled. As on battlefields, the aspects most in need of protection are these bullet scatters which in this case are expected to extend well over 300m from the defences. On some sites the scatter may extend much further, as demonstrated at Grafton Regis (see Fig 7.38).

Morton Corbet provides a further illustration of the management issues (see Figs 7.31–7.33). Scheduling covers only the defended area of the castle, plus two small detached areas, while Listing applies to the standing structures of church and castle. However, neither the impact scars nor the bullet scatter that is to be expected in the adjacent ground is defined in the Schedule and List descriptions. As a result, it is unlikely that either the management of the guardianship monument and scheduled area or faculty jurisdiction covering the church will adequately take the siege archaeology into account. We have indicated a buffer zone of 300m from the walls as being the minimum area within which combat evidence should be expected (see Fig 7.33). This is based on the final range, after bounce and roll, of bullets fired experimentally from a 12 bore barrel (see Fig 4.19). Artillery hailshot may be expected to have travelled a similar distance (see Fig 4.7). Round shot are likely to have travelled considerably further, as also could bullets fired from small arms set high on the building. Most of this zone lies well beyond the scheduled area, and although there are Stewardship arrangements in place for most of the land, because this is at Entry Level it offers no significant protection for unstratified artefact scatters.

A rapid assessment was undertaken to establish which siege sites of the Civil War are in public ownership or control and thus amenable to direct management. English Heritage own or manage all or part of 27 sites and the National Trust at least six.[21] It has not been possible to examine issues of survival on these sites, but work by Harrington has already shown that much of the bullet and round shot evidence on several was removed when the sites were prepared for display in the first half of the 20th century. At Helmsley Castle, for example, there was massive loss of stratified and unstratified scatters (Harrington 2006). As we have seen, continuing official indifference in the 1970s led to comparable loss on the local-authority-controlled site of Sandal Castle.

A significant number of the remainder of the sieges sites are buildings in private, local government, or ecclesiastical ownership. Many of them are either scheduled or listed, and the provision of appropriate guidance to those who operate these controls is a clear priority. The Chester Diocesan Advisory Committee (DAC) was consulted regarding bullet impact scars because, in addition to Acton (see Fig 7.29), they have a number of other churches that bear such evidence. The DAC acknowledged awareness of the issue. Indeed, in one case, at Dodleston, the church's inspecting architect had made a rudimentary record of the impact scar locations on the north elevation of the tower when identifying works required.[22] However, the DAC does not have a list of churches in the diocese which display such evidence, and neither English Heritage nor the Council for the Care of Churches have issued guidance on what effective management might involve. Identical problems and opportunities will exist for once-besieged country houses and castles in private ownership.

Implementation

The Register gives non-statutory guidance and information. Management of these sites, along with all other fields of conflict recorded on the HERs and

SHINE, is achieved through a plethora of other mechanisms, including the planning process (now guided by Planning Policy Statement 5), agri-environment grant schemes managed by Natural England, and Woodland Grants (Department for Communities and Local Government 2010). The method by which management is achieved through the planning process is well understood so need not be reviewed here, although some problems are considered in the Adwalton case study. The other schemes are beginning to be used to positive effect in the conservation of battlefields, with recent initiatives on sites such as Towton and Bosworth. However, there is much more that we need to know about the detailed nature of the threats posed, particularly by modern agriculture, if these mechanisms are to be implemented to full effect (Foard 2010b; Foard *et al* 2010).

Management can often be fully effective only when it is undertaken in partnership between the different bodies involved in the administration of grant schemes. It is essential, too, that community organisations are fully involved – at the national level the Battlefields Trust, and at a local level individual battlefield and local history societies. Experience from sites such as Towton and Boroughbridge demonstrates that it is only when the local community is fully engaged and committed to the conservation and interpretation of their battlefield that the most effective management is achieved. Conversely, it is at battlefields where formal groups do not exist, as at Adwalton Moor, that problems have gone unrecognised or pressure has not been brought to bear to ensure that issues are adequately addressed.

An important recent initiative which helps to ensure that the threats to battlefields are recognised is the inclusion of battlefields on the At Risk Register. This has highlighted a small number of battlefields where there is evidence of significant damage. In 2010, six of the 43 Registered battlefields were considered to be at risk from the pressures of modern development and other threats.[23] The accurate ranking of risk is important because it enables effective targeting of action under Stewardship schemes and shows where further information is needed to counter threats.

The main mechanism by which agri-environment schemes can assist in the conservation of fields of conflict is Stewardship. Entry Level Stewardship has only limited usefulness: it cannot either influence agricultural practices or, in most contexts, metal detecting, nor can it facilitate improvements of access and interpretation. The one exception may be its potential to control metal detecting where land is under permanent pasture, if this requirement is actively enforced. In contrast, Higher Level Stewardship has the potential to advance all these strands, and can provide the opportunity for enhancement on some battlefields. This may include the removal of features which obscure views or change the landscape character, and the reinstatement or repair of other features, such as the gapping-up of hedgerows which existed at the time of the battle to enhance the appearance of the battlefield. Unfortunately, to date, there is little sign of achievements through Stewardship in terms of the conservation of either battle archaeology or terrain features, although various mechanisms do exist which could be applied; an example is arable reversion, which may be suitable for the protection of both mass graves and suspected reservoirs of ferrous arrowheads, as at Towton. The various alternatives are given in the handbooks for the land-based schemes in the online information for farmers and land managers on the Natural England website.

We have seen that a major stumbling block is inadequate understanding of the threats posed to battle archaeology by modern agriculture. As a result, appropriate sets of measures suitable for conservation in particular circumstances cannot be defined; implementation of some measures without such knowledge might even be counter-productive. For example, minimum-till might be appropriate for protection of secondary or primary stratified deposits, as suggested above for part of Towton battlefield. However, the use of machinery such as power harrows, which may accompany such a regime, has the potential to increase mechanical damage to metal artefacts in the topsoil.

Adwalton Moor: a case study

Adwalton lies in an urban fringe on the edge of Bradford; over the last fifteen years it has been one of the most threatened of England's Registered battlefields. In 2010 it was one of those that was considered to be at high risk, and with seven other At Risk battlefields it was the subject of an assessment commissioned by English Heritage (Foard 2010b). What follows here is a summary that draws upon that assessment, presented to exemplify some of the general problems faced by English battlefields.

The battle was fought in 1643 for control of the north of England. It began as a royalist army moving to attack Bradford encountered a parliamentarian army marching south-eastward out of the town to attack the royalist camp. The king's forces responded by deploying on Adwalton Moor. However, according to the parliamentarian leader Sir Thomas Fairfax, they also

> manned divers houses standing in the enclosed grounds betwixt Bradford and Atherton moor with musketeers, and sent out great parties of horse and foot by the lanes and enclosed grounds to give us fight.

Parliament's forlorn hope, an advance guard of musketeers, advanced up Wiskeard Hill – today known as Westgate Hill – to drive the royalists from the enclosures. According to Slingsby, a Yorkshire royalist landowner and MP, the royalists at first stopped the parliamentarian advance, but then

> they c[a]me on fiercer, and beat the enemy (the royalists), from one hedge, from one house to another; at last they were driven to retreat and we (the royalists) recover[ed] the moor …'
>
> (Johnson 2003; National Army Museum 1995a)

The parliamentarian army was now able to deploy on moorland on the north-western edge of the plateau, and from here advanced towards the enemy. A second area of enclosures lay between the two forces. The parliamentarians advanced and took these enclosures. While fighting from the security of the hedgerows they had the advantage in firepower, because their army was dominated by musketeers. In contrast, when they ventured forward into the open ground they were at a severe disadvantage, as the royalists were far stronger in cavalry. Successive royalist attempts to break into the enclosures were repulsed. Finally, in one last desperate attack, the royalist infantry, supported with artillery fire and seconded by cavalry, drove back the defenders on the parliamentarian left. Here sheer weight of numbers finally told. Thanks in part to the failure of the parliamentarians to commit their reserves, the royalists broke into the enclosures. Their cavalry were also now able to make an outflanking move on that side of the field. On the left and in the centre parliamentarian resistance collapsed and the troops fell back in disarray, north-westward towards Bradford. On the right Sir Thomas Fairfax's forces were cut off and had to retreat, still in good order, south-westward towards Halifax.

The historic terrain has been partially reconstructed from documentary sources (Fig 8.15). The best-understood area is that to the north-west; here the

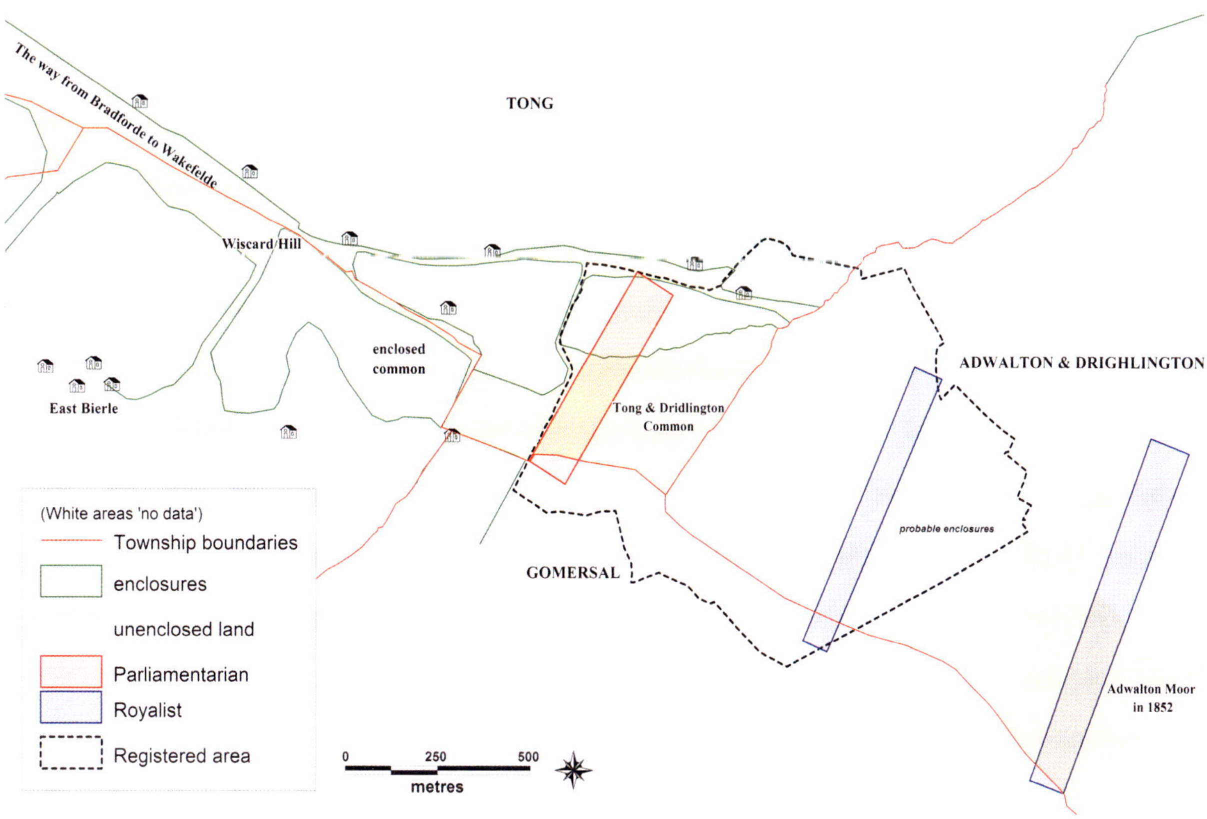

Fig 8.15 Map of Adwalton Moor (1643), showing the western area of the battlefield as it was in 1599, together with the extent of Adwalton Moor, as defined on the 1852 Ordnance Survey map. Inadequate evidence is so far available to map the areas left white on the plan (Foard 2003)

complex landscape of moorland, enclosures, and buildings must be the ground where the troops fought from house to house and enclosure to enclosure. The main action seems to have taken place further to the south-east, on the north-western edge of Adwalton Moor. It is in this general area that the antiquary Scatcherd reported an extensive distribution of battle-related finds in the 19th century.

Only small areas of the enclosures and moorland on the north-western part of the battlefield remain undeveloped. Most lie outside the Registered area, yet these fragments may contain sufficient archaeological evidence to locate the initial fire-fight. Similarly, on the south-eastern part of the battlefield a large tract of Adwalton Moor remains undeveloped, yet it too is excluded by the Register. While part of the Moor is disturbed by small pits, some of these might pre-date the battle, since mention of coal pits is made in the battle accounts. Surviving battle archaeology in this area could place elements of the main action, in which parliamentarian forces pushed forward out of the enclosures almost as far as the royalist guns. The greatest problems arise because of the uncertainty over where the north-western boundary ran between the moor and the enclosures in 1643. As a result, it is unclear how much of the main action has been lost beneath 19th- and 20th-century development, and how much is within the large tract of pasture immediately to the north-west (Fig 8.16).

Adwalton demonstrates how the Register boundary determines what is and what is not achievable in managing a battlefield in the face of development pressure. At the north-western end of the Registered area large-scale development in the late 1990s was resisted with some success. However, the local planning archaeologist reports that

> [t]he main problem with Adwalton Moor is that the area of the Registered Battlefield does not fully reflect the area of the battle. The eastern part of the battlefield, where the Royalists probably drew

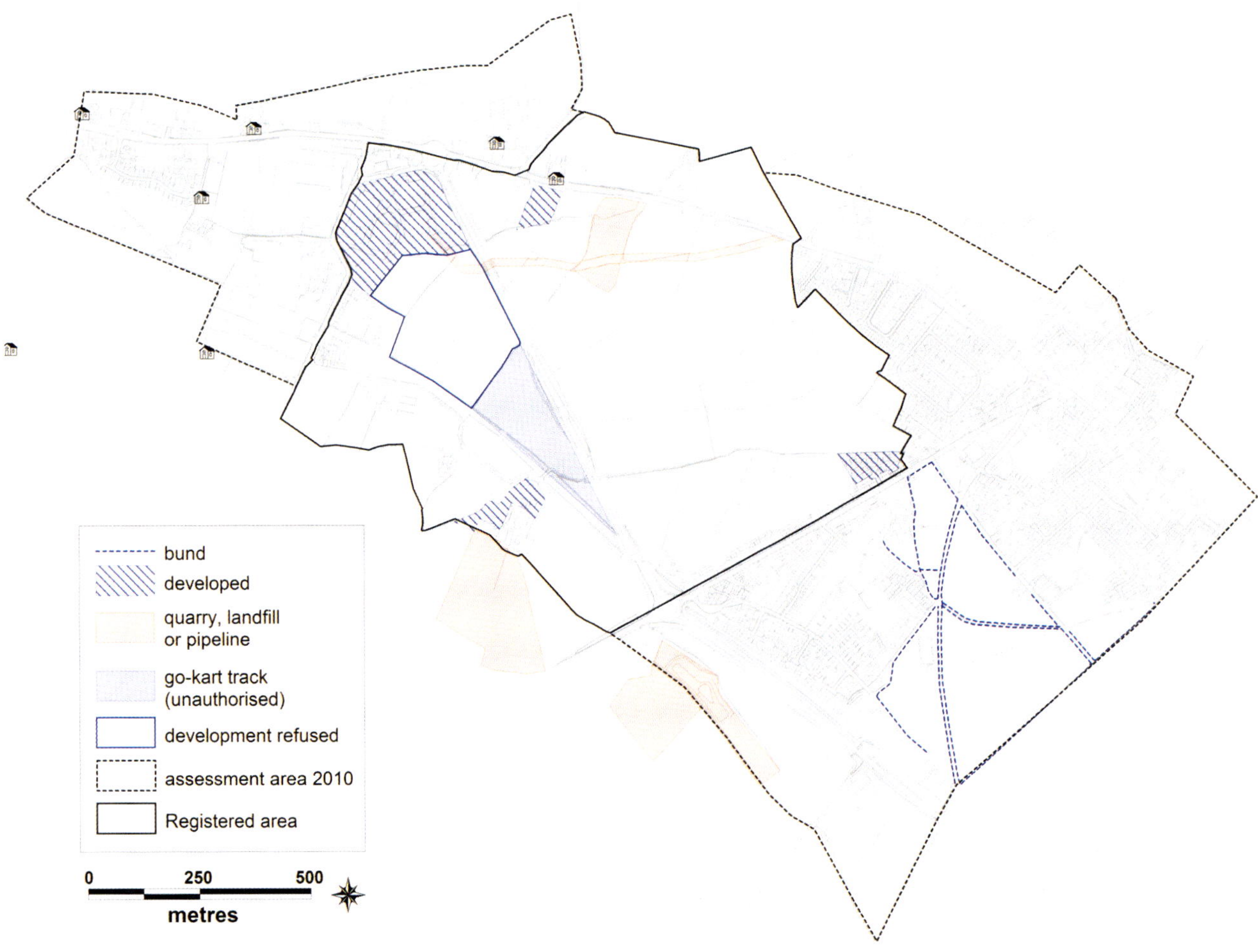

Fig 8.16 Map of Adwalton Moor (1643), showing the state of development in 2010 and indicating key changes since 1995 (Foard 2010b). (Reproduced by permission of Ordnance Survey on behalf of HMSO. © Crown copyright and database right 2012. Ordnance Survey Licence no. 100024900)

> up on the ridge and repelled a Parliamentarian advance, is not within the Registered area. [Part of this land] has relatively recently been landscaped into playing fields without any archaeological work carried out (as far as we are aware) although this was what we had recommended. We find it difficult to recommend refusal in these circumstances because the boundaries drawn by English Heritage are further west and English Heritage has conceded industrial development within the Registered area
>
> (I Sanderson pers comm).

There is also pressure for incremental development, including house building in larger gardens. In some cases it has proved possible to achieve a watching brief and metal-detecting survey, with some development-led work yielding small quantities of artefacts, such as the six lead bullets, a powder box cap, a decorative lock cover, and three buttons that came from a pre-development metal-detector survey in 2003 in Moorside Road, Drighlington. This is just beyond the south-eastern edge of the surviving moor (indicating that action extended right up on to the hilltop, beyond the edge of the area mapped on Figure 8.16) and shows how important it can be to undertake fieldwork on even small-scale developments outside a Registered area.

In contrast, much of the work undertaken at Adwalton in advance of development has proved negative. This cannot yet be taken as indicating that battle archaeology did not exist in these areas because the standard of the work was variable. In some cases detecting was conducted without the retrieval of artefacts, and by present standards the work was piecemeal and poorly documented, once again demonstrating why guidance on best practice in battlefield survey is required. Adwalton also shows the need for large-scale survey to provide a context within which the results of smaller-scale evaluations can be interpreted.

Other pressures arise as a result of Adwalton's location in an urban fringe. For example, one field was used, without permission, for a go-kart track; the earthmoving involved will have disturbed artefact patterning. Other problems have been exacerbated by the fragmentation of the battlefield: the construction of a bypass, permitted before the Register was created, has reinforced the effects of the earlier railway embankment, dividing up the area and making access to certain parts of the battle difficult, while other small areas feel almost unsafe, encouraging further degradation from activities such as fly tipping.

Guidance

Battlefields are clearly an exceptional class of monument which pose unusual, contentious, and often unfamiliar issues. In the preceding chapters we have identified a range of research that is needed both on individual sites and on general issues to enable effective investigation and conservation of English battlefields. There is also the need for steps to enable the threat of uncontrolled metal detecting to be tackled.

However, many of the problems which currently arise do so simply as a result of the fact that expertise in the study and conservation of battlefields is not widely available in the archaeological profession. This is inevitable with a new area of enquiry. There is thus a need for provision to the discipline of guidance and training in the developing techniques of battlefield archaeology and conservation. The most urgent requirement is for a guide to best practice in the location, investigation, and conservation management of battlefields and siege sites. Training is also needed for the instruction of those conducting, designing, and commissioning surveys of battlefields. This could usefully be complemented by guidance for a wider audience, including the owners of sites. This might take the form of a publication by Natural England of an additional Farming Leaflet for Stewardship which addresses historic battlefields.

Such action needs to be part of a national strategy for the management and investigation of battlefields that ensures appropriate evaluation and recording on important sites when they come under threat. Battlefields should be included within all the Regional Research Frameworks (eg Cooper 2006). If this is to be effective, a mechanism is required to enable all those involved in the management of sites to obtain specialist advice; at present, such matters lie outside the remit of the English Heritage Battlefields Panel, and there is no recognised equivalent of a Period Society which has the resources to provide such advice.

Valuable guidance is given to metal detectorists by the Finds Liaison Officers of the Portable Antiquities Scheme, who are well placed to encourage detectorists to report finds from non-Registered sites and to promote best practice in battlefield detecting. To facilitate this, Finds Liaison Officers and others involved in management need access to appropriate guidance on survey methodology for and analysis of battlefield finds. This would complement the *Code of Practice for Responsible Metal Detecting* – the voluntary agreement drawn up between the National Council for Metal Detecting, the Federation of Independent Detectorists, National Farmers' Union, and various heritage organisations.[24]

Finally, there is a requirement for specific guidance on individual sites, so that those responsible for their management understand the resource, its research and interpretative potential, its vulnerabilities, and its conservation needs. At present there are no model Conservation Statements for Registered battlefields or siege sites in England. Exemplars should be produced which take account of the distinct requirements of different periods, types of battle, and terrain, and reflect the main types of potential and threat. Given limited resources, it would be inappropriate to produce elaborate Conservation Plans modelled on those used for designed landscapes, which focus on man-made or man-modified elements of the landscape. For most battlefields in England the resource is very different, as are the management requirements. Rather, shorter and more concise documents are called for which should draw upon specialist expertise in military history, battlefield archaeology, and landscape history to ensure a clear focus on the distinctive, important aspects of each battlefield. Only when these documents exist, and the wider guidance and advice mechanisms are available, will the battlefields of England be as effectively managed as most other aspects of England's historic environment.

Notes

1. RAF vertical air photos 1947: CPE UK 1994/1107, 1109 and 1019; CPE UK 1926/1072. Modern survival from vertical photography is available at http://www.flashearth.com/ (accessed 10 April 2011) and complemented by field inspection in 2007.
2. Much of the following technical text on soil chemistry and its impact on artefacts has been edited from a contribution provided by Rob Janaway and Andy Wilson.
3. Lillian Ladle provided bullets and three soil samples from areas adjacent to her Bestwall Quarry excavations at Wareham; Tim Sutherland provided 69 soil samples for analysis from Towton. At Flodden three soil samples were taken from the centre of the battlefield during the 2007 metal-detecting survey. At Edgehill three samples and at Bosworth 22 samples were taken as part of battlefield surveys there. Analysis was undertaken by Bradford University under the direction of Rob Janaway.
4. Recording by S Holmes and D Evans, then, respectively, the North and East Yorkshire Finds Liaison Officers.
5. Hansard, 17 September 2003, 230917–02.
6. Roberts' detecting data from the CD published with Newman and Roberts 2003. Data for the 2005 rally from the PAS database. Extent of the 2003 rally from the PAS advisor for Yorkshire. Newman's survey data from Foard 2007a.
7. Information from Sally Worrell, paper to Battlefield Archaeology seminar held by the Battlefields Trust at the Royal Armouries, Leeds, 2005.
8. Information from Frances McIntosh, Finds Liaison Officer for Cheshire.
9. http://detecting.merseyblogs.co.uk/english_battlef/ Accessed 10 April 2011.
10. www.metaldetectingholidays.co.uk Accessed 2007. 'Hands on History' tours where groups paid to detect on 500 acres of Lansdown battlefield: http://website.lineone.net/-handsonhistory Accessed 14 December 1999.
11. http://www.helm.org.uk/server/show/nav.20434 Accessed 10 April 2011.
12. Field inspection 19 May 2007. Metal detecting by L Macfarlane 29 August and 3 September 2007. Field 1: transect 425m long, modern finds >32, metres per modern find 13m. Field 2: 228m long, 11 modern finds, 21m per find. Field 3: 183m long, 34 modern finds, 5m per find.
13. National Park Service Living History and Re-enactments Policy; information from Douglas Scott.
14. Information from Dr Matt Schmader, Open Space Assistant Superintendent, City of Albuquerque.
15. In Scotland preparation of reports to underpin the Inventory began in 2006 and in December 2010 Historic Scotland consulted on the planned Inventory. http://www.historic-scotland.gov.uk/index/heritage/battlefields.htm Accessed 10 April 2011. Preparation of battlefield reports to underpin the Irish Battlefields Register began in 2008. In Wales the first list of battlefields was produced by the RCAHMW in 2006. Cadw subsequently commissioned an assessment of Welsh battlefields (CADW 2011). In 2011 the Flemish Heritage Institute commissioned a database of Flemish battlefields with a view to advancing their conservation.

16. Substantial numbers of bullets and other artefacts have been collected around Tywardreath, Cornwall HER PRN178062.
17. Information from John Pettet, a collector on Sedgemoor battlefield, and from Natasha Ferguson, University of Glasgow.
18. The data are from Foard 1995 but with limited additions to the bullet scatter from Marix Evans *et al* 2002, 152.
19. Adwalton, Boroughbridge, Neville's Cross, Newbury I, Stamford Bridge, and Tewkesbury.
20. http://www.myshinedata.org.uk/ Accessed 10 April 2011.
21. National Trust: Boarstall House, Buckland Abbey, Corfe Castle, Dunster Castle, Lacock House, Saltram House. English Heritage guardianship: Abbotsbury; Ashby-de-la-Zouche Castle; Beeston Castle; Bolingbroke Castle; Bolsover Castle; Carlisle Castle; Chester walls; Christchurch; Colchester Castle; Dartmouth; Donnington Castle; Farnham Castle; Goodrich Castle; Helmsley Castle; Lilleshall Abbey; Moreton Corbet; Nunney Castle; Pendennis Castle; Plymouth; Portsmouth; Restormel Castle; Scarborough Castle; Sherborne Castle; South Wingfield; Stokesay Castle; Tynemouth; Wardour Castle.
22. Information from Richard Mortimer, Chester DAC Secretary.
23. http://www.english-heritage.org.uk/caring/heritage-at-risk/registered-battlefields-at-risk/ Accessed 10 April 2011.
24. http://www.britarch.ac.uk/conservation/portant/detecting Accessed 28 April 2011.

9

Conclusions

The study of battlefields and other fields of conflict is a recent branch of archaeological investigation. Today we are only just struggling to pull clear of the amateur phase of unsystematic collection – a phase that many other areas of archaeological research left behind long ago. This is why a good deal of the evidence presented in the preceding pages is incomplete, problematic, or awaits fresh survey and experiment to release its potential.

The purpose of this book has been to bring together the often disparate strands of evidence that form the corpus of the archaeological investigation of battlefields in England. Parallel studies will undoubtedly soon follow in other European countries. When they do, a broader view will be practicable.

We have attempted here to outline the nature of the resource and methods that have been developed to investigate it. The picture presented is necessarily biased to certain periods and themes. This is, in part, a reflection of where the study of battlefields actually sits at the present time. More could have been said of some themes, such as the investigation of human remains, but this is a specialised area which already has a well-developed methodology. Instead, our focus has been upon the areas where new initiatives are needed – most particularly in the study of metal artefact scatters.

A challenge to the very survival of the physical evidence on our battlefields is the background against which this work has been prepared. At times the priorities for action come thick and fast; this is inevitable when there is so much that needs to be done so quickly. We must be able to identify and conserve the resource before it is destroyed by the very piece of prospecting equipment that has made possible the systematic study of the sites in the first place.

The usefulness of this book will perhaps best be judged by how quickly it becomes out of date – as the issues it highlights are rapidly tackled and, we hope, resolved. At present the research potential seems great, but only time will tell whether this promise can be realised. Among the many uncertainties one thing is crystal clear. If effective action to limit the decay and destruction of the evidence is not taken soon, in as few as ten or twenty years little of value will be left to study.

Appendix 1 English battles listed by name

Names in italics are 'antique' and have sometimes fallen from use; dates in italics are suspect, usually stemming from the late Saxon *Anglo-Saxon Chronicle*

Action name	Name alternatives, early names	Historic county	Year (AD)	Type	Register
Aclea	Ockley	Hampshire	851	battle?	
Adwalton Moor	Atherton Moor	Yorkshire W. Riding	1643	battle	Registered
Aethelingadene	Alton; East or West Dean	Hampshire	1001	battle?	
Alnwick I		Northumberland	1093	battle?	
Alnwick II		Northumberland	1174	Siege / battle?	
Alton		Hampshire	1643	Battle / skirmish	
Alutthelia	Bishop Auckland	Durham	844	battle?	
Archenfield	*Ircingafeld*	Herefordshire	914	battle?	
Arthuret	Arderyth, *Arfderydd*	Cumberland	573	battle?	
Ashdown	*Aescesdun*	Berkshire	871	battle	
Ashingdon	*Assundun*; Assingdon; *Assandun; Assendun*	Suffolk	1016	battle	
Aylesford	*Aegelesthrep*	Kent	455	battle?	
Badon	Mount Badon; *Mons Badonicus*	Wiltshire	500	battle	
Barbury	*Deranbyrg*; *Baranburh*; Bera's Stronghold; Barbury Castle, *Beranburh*	Wiltshire	556	battle?	
Barnet		Middlesex	1471	battle	Registered
Basing		Hampshire	871	battle?	
Bea's Mount	*Beandun*	Devon	614	battle	
Beda's Head	*Biedanheafde*; Bedwyn	Wiltshire	675	battle?	
Bedcanford	*Biedcanford*	Bedfordshire	571	battle	
Bedford		Bedfordshire	917	battle?	
Benfleet	*Bleamfleote*	Essex	893	battle?	
Benson	Bensington	Oxfordshire	779	battle?	
Beorgford	Burford?; *Beorhford*	Oxfordshire	752	battle?	
Billingham		Durham	800	battle?	
Blackheath	Deptford Bridge	Kent	1497	battle?	
Blore Heath		Staffordshire	1459	battle	Registered
Boliegh		Cornwall	936	battle?	
Boroughbridge		Yorkshire W. Riding	1322	battle	Registered
Bosworth	Redemore	Leicestershire	1485	battle	Registered
Boudicca		Middlesex	61	battle	
Braddock Down	Lostwithiel	Cornwall	1643	battle	Registered
Bradford on Avon	*Bradenforda*	Wiltshire	652	battle?	
Bramham Moor		Yorkshire W. Riding	1408	battle?	assessed
Brentford		Middlesex	1016	battle?	
Burgh by Sands		Cumberland	1031	battle?	

Action name	Name alternatives, early names	Historic county	Year (AD)	Type	Register
Buttington			893	battle	
Camlann		Cumberland	511	battle?	
Canterbury		Kent	851	battle?	
Carham		Northumberland	833	battle?	
Carham		Northumberland	1016	battle	
Carham		Northumberland	1028	battle?	
Carham		Northumberland	1018	battle	unlocated
Carrum	Carhampton	Somerset	843	battle?	
Castleford		Yorkshire W. Riding	948	battle?	
Catterick	*Catraeth; Kaltraeth; Gododin; Cor-eiddin; Kaltrae*	Yorkshire N. Riding	600	battle	
Cerdic's Ford	Charford	Hampshire	519	battle?	
Cerdic's Shore	*Cerdicesora*		514	battle	
Cerdic's Shore	*Cerdicesora*		495	battle	
Cerdic's Wood	*Cerdicesleag*	Wiltshire	527	battle?	
Cheriton	Alresford	Hampshire	1644	battle	Registered
Cherrenhul		Berkshire	820	battle	
Chester	Caerlegion, Caer Legionis	Cheshire	604	battle?	
Chesterfield		Derbyshire	1266	battle?	
Cirencester		Gloucestershire	628	battle?	
Clitheroe		Lancashire	1138	battle?	
Clyst St Mary	Clyst Heath	Devon	1549	battle	
Corbridge	Bloody Acres	Northumberland	918	battle	
Corbridge		Northumberland	913	battle?	
Creacanford	Crayford, *Crecganford*	Kent	456	battle?	
Cropredy Bridge		Oxfordshire	1644	battle	Registered
Cymen's Shore	*Cymenesora*		477	battle	
Cynwit	Bloody Corner; Countisbury Hill; Northam	Devon	878	battle	
Deal Beach		Kent	1495	battle?	
Denisesburn or Heavenfield	Denisesburn; Heaven Fields; Heavenly Plain; Hefnfelth	Northumberland	633	battle	
Dexastan	Florida; *Degastan*; Dexa Stone; *Degsastan*; Dalston; *Daegsastan*	Cumberland	603	battle	
Dunmail Raise		Westmorland	945	battle?	
Durham		Durham	1069	battle?	
Durham		Durham	1006	battle?	
Dussindale	Ossian's Vale	Norfolk	1549	battle	
Dyrham	*Deorham*	Gloucestershire	577	battle?	
East Kennet	Cynetan	Wiltshire	1007	battle?	
Edgcote	Banbury; Danesmoor; Danes Moor; Edgecot	Northamptonshire	1469	battle	unlocated
Edgehill	Kineton fight	Warwickshire	1642	battle	Registered
Ellandun	*Ellendun*; Wroughton	Wiltshire	825	battle	
Empingham	Losecote Field; Stamford?	Rutland	1470	battle	unlocated
Englefield	*Englafeld*	Berkshire	870	battle?	

Action name	Name alternatives, early names	Historic county	Year (AD)	Type	Register
Ethandun	Edington, *Aethandune*	Berkshire	878	battle	
Evesham		Worcestershire	1265	battle	Registered
Farnham		Surrey	893	battle?	
Fenny Bridges	Fenny Meadow	Devon	1549	battle	
Fethanleag	Battle Wood, Stoke Lyne	Oxfordshire	584	battle?	
Flodden	Branxton Moor; Branston Moor	Northumberland	1513	battle	Registered
Fornham St Genevieve		Suffolk	1173	battle?	
Fulford	Gate Fulford; Fulford Gate	Yorkshire E. Riding	1066	battle	
Fulhope Law			1400	battle?	
Galford	*Creodantreow; Creadantreow; Gafulford, Gafolford*	Devon	825	battle?	
Gillingham		Kent	1016	battle?	
Guoloph		Hampshire	437	battle?	
Halidon Hill		Northumberland	1333	battle	Registered
Hastings	Senlac; Senlac Hill	Sussex	1066	battle	Registered
Hatfield Chase	Hatfield; Heathfield; *Haethfelth*; Campodonum?	Nottinghamshire	632	battle?	
Hedgeley Moor		Northumberland	1464	battle	assessed
Hereford		Herefordshire	1067	battle?	
Hereford		Herefordshire	1055	battle?	
Hexham		Northumberland	1464	battle	unlocated
Hilton	Hylton	Durham	1644	battle	
Hingston Down	*Hengestesdun; Hengestdun*	Devon	838	battle?	
Holme	Holm		904	battle	
Homildon Hill	Humbleton Hill	Northumberland	1402	battle	Registered
Hopton Heath		Staffordshire	1643	battle	Registered
Hoxne	Hellesdun	Suffolk	869	battle?	
Kempsford	*Cynemuersford*	Gloucestershire	802	battle?	
Langport		Somerset	1645	battle	Registered
Lansdown		Gloucestershire	1643	battle	Registered
Lewes		Sussex	1264	battle	Registered
Lincoln I		Lincolnshire	1141	battle	assessed
Lincoln II	*Nundinae*; Lincoln Fair	Lincolnshire	1217	battle	
London		Middlesex	994	battle?	
London		Middlesex	1013	battle?	
London		Middlesex	851	battle?	
London		Middlesex	886	battle	
Lostwithiel	Castle Dore	Cornwall	1644	battle	assessed
Luton		Bedfordshire	913	battle?	
Maidstone	Gabriel's Hill	Kent	1648	battle	
Maldon		Essex	991	battle	Registered
Marston Moor		Yorkshire W. Riding	1644	battle	Registered
Maserfield	*Maserfelth; Maserfeld*; Havenfield	Gloucestershire	641	battle?	
Mearcred's Burn	*Mearcredesburna*; Mercred's Stream	Sussex	485	battle	
Medway		Kent	43	battle	

Action name	Name alternatives, early names	Historic county	Year (AD)	Type	Register
Meretun		Wiltshire	871	battle?	
Mortimer's Cross		Herefordshire	1461	battle	unlocated
Myton	White Battle; Myton on Swale	Yorkshire N. Riding	1319	battle	Registered
Nantwich		Cheshire	1644	battle	Registered
Naseby		Northamptonshire	1645	battle	Registered
Neville's Cross		Durham	1346	battle	Registered
Newark		Nottinghamshire	1644	battle	destroyed
Newburn Ford		Durham	1640	battle	Registered
Newbury I		Berkshire	1643	battle	Registered
Newbury II		Berkshire	1644	battle	destroyed
Northallerton	Battle of the Standard	Yorkshire N. Riding	1138	battle	Registered
Northampton		Northamptonshire	1460	battle	Registered
Old Sarum	Salisbury; Searoburh	Wiltshire	552	battle?	
Otford	Dane Bottom; Ottanford	Kent	1016	battle?	
Otford	Ottanford	Kent	776	battle?	
Otterburn	Chevy Chase	Northumberland	1388	battle	Registered
Penselwood		Somerset	1016	battle?	
Penselwood	*Pen; Peonnan, Peonnum*	Somerset	658	battle?	
Pinhoe	Poltimore; Peonho	Devon	1001	battle?	
Piper Dene	Piperdean	Northumberland	1435	battle	
Poole Harbour			896	battle?	
Porlock	Polock	Somerset	1052	battle?	
Portland	Port	Dorset	840	battle?	
Portsmouth	Porchester Castle, Portesmutha	Hampshire	501	battle	
Posbury	Posbury; *Posentesburh*	Devon	661	battle?	
Preston I	Ribbleton Moor	Lancashire	1648	battle	destroyed
Reading		Berkshire	871	battle?	
Ringmere	Ringmere Pit; Wretham Heath; Rymer	Norfolk	1010	battle?	
Ripple Field		Worcestershire	1643	battle	assessed
River Idle	Idle	Yorkshire W. Riding	617	battle	
River Lea		Hertfordshire	895	battle?	
River Parrett		Somerset	848	battle?	
River Trent		Lincolnshire	679	battle	
Rochester		Kent	999	battle?	
Romney marsh			841	battle	
Roundway Down		Wiltshire	1643	battle	Registered
Rowton Heath	Rowton Moor	Cheshire	1645	battle	Registered
Salisbury		Wiltshire	1143	battle?	
Sampford Courtenay		Devon	1549	battle	
Sedgemoor		Somerset	1685	battle	Registered
Selby		Yorkshire W. Riding	1644	battle	
Sherston		Wiltshire	1016	battle?	
Shidlaw		Northumberland	833	battle?	
Shrewsbury		Shropshire	1403	battle	Registered
Solway Moss	Sollom	Cumberland	1542	battle	Registered

Action name	Name alternatives, early names	Historic county	Year (AD)	Type	Register
Southampton		Hampshire	840	battle?	
Southwark		Surrey	1066	battle?	
St Albans I		Hertfordshire	1455	battle	destroyed
St Albans II		Hertfordshire	1461	battle	destroyed
Stainmoor	Stainmore	Westmorland	950	battle?	
Stamford Bridge		Yorkshire E. Riding	1066	battle	Registered
Stockbridge		Yorkshire W. Riding	1141	battle?	
Stoke Field	East Stoke; Stoke	Nottinghamshire	1487	battle	Registered
Stow on the Wold		Gloucestershire	1646	battle	Registered
Stratton	Stamford Hill	Cornwall	1643	battle	Registered
Tettenhall	*Uodnesfelda Campo*; Wednesfield Heath	Staffordshire	910	battle?	
Tewkesbury		Gloucestershire	1471	battle	Registered
Thames			43	battle	
Thanet	Tenet	Kent	853	battle?	
Thetford		Norfolk	1004	battle?	
Torrington II		Devon	1646	battle	destroyed
Towton		Yorkshire W. Riding	1461	battle	Registered
Tynemoore	Tynemoor		921	battle	
Vortigern's Burg			652	battle	
Wakefield		Yorkshire W. Riding	1460	battle	destroyed
Whalley	Billingahoth; Bullasey Ford; Hwaelleage	Lancashire	798	battle?	
Wibbandun	Wibba's Mount	Surrey	568	battle	
Wicganbeorg	Weekaborough, Wigborough?	Devon	851	battle	
Wichum	Wych	Flintshire (part)	1146	battle?	
Wilton		Wiltshire	1143	battle?	
Wilton		Wiltshire	871	battle?	
Winceby		Lincolnshire	1643	battle	Registered
Winchester		Hampshire	860	battle?	
Winwaed	*Winwedfeld; River Winwaed; Winwoed; Maes Gai, Winwidfeld*	Yorkshire W. Riding	655	battle?	
Winwick Pass	Red Bank	Lancashire	1648	battle	
Wipped's Creek	Wippedesfleot, Ebbsfleet	Kent	465	battle	
Wirtgernesburh	Bradford on Avon?	Wiltshire	665	battle	
Woden's Barrow	Adam's Grave, Alton Priors; Wodnesburh (second battle)	Wiltshire	715	battle?	
Woden's Barrow	Adam's Grave, Alton Priors; *Wodnesbeorh*	Wiltshire	592	battle?	
Woodbury Hill		Worcestershire	1405	battle?	
Worcester		Worcestershire	1055	battle?	
Worcester		Worcestershire	1651	battle	Registered
York		Yorkshire W. Riding	1069	siege/battle?	
York		Yorkshire W. Riding	1069	battle?	
York		Yorkshire W. Riding	866	battle?	

Appendix 2 Battles 1066–1685 listed by bibliographic score

Bibliographic score	Action name	Year	Type of action	Designation
141	Bosworth	1485	battle	Registered
88	Flodden	1513	battle	Registered
80	Tewkesbury	1471	battle	Registered
66	Marston Moor	1644	battle	Registered
64	Shrewsbury	1403	battle	Registered
63	Naseby	1645	battle	Registered
59	Towton	1461	battle	Registered
54	Hastings	1066	battle	Registered
52	Otterburn	1388	battle	Registered
50	Worcester	1651	battle	Registered
49	Wakefield	1460	battle	Destroyed (site b)
47	Barnet	1471	battle	Registered
46	Newbury I	1643	battle	Registered
46	Edgehill	1642	battle	Registered
44	Sedgemoor	1685	battle	Registered
43	Lewes	1264	battle	Registered
42	Neville's Cross	1346	battle	Registered
40	Blore Heath	1459	battle	Registered
37	Northallerton	1138	battle	Registered
36	Evesham	1265	battle	Registered
35	Stamford Bridge	1066	battle	Registered
34	Stoke Field	1487	battle	Registered
33	Newbury II	1644	battle	Destroyed? (site b) reassess
33	Cheriton	1644	battle	Registered
32	Halidon Hill	1333	battle	Registered
32	Lansdown	1643	battle	Registered
31	Roundway Down	1643	battle	Registered
30	St Albans I	1455	battle	Destroyed (site b)
29	Newburn Ford	1640	battle	Registered
29	Mortimer's Cross	1461	battle	Unlocated (site a) reassess
29	Hexham	1464	battle	Unlocated (site a) reassess
29	Adwalton Moor	1643	battle	Registered
28	Boroughbridge	1322	battle?	Registered
27	Winceby	1643	battle	Registered
26	Homildon Hill	1402	battle	Registered
26	Solway Moss	1542	battle	Registered
26	Langport	1645	battle	Registered
25	Cropredy Bridge	1644	battle	Registered
24	St Albans II	1461	battle	Destroyed (site b)
24	Lostwithiel	1644	battle	Assess
24	Northampton	1460	battle	Registered
23	Rowton Heath	1645	battle	Registered

Bibliographic score	Action name	Year	Type of action	Designation
23	Stratton	1643	battle	Registered
23	Nantwich	1644	battle	Registered
22	Braddock Down	1643	battle	Registered
20	Edgcote	1469	battle	Unlocated (site a) reassess
20	Hopton Heath	1643	battle	Registered
18	Hedgeley Moor	1464	battle	Unlocated?
17	Newark	1644	battle	Unlocated (site b)
16	Myton	1319	battle	Registered
15	Lincoln II	1217	battle	Destroyed (site b)
15	Preston I	1648	battle	Destroyed (site b)
15	Torrington II	1646	battle	Destroyed (site b)
13	Fulford	1066	battle	Unlocated (site a)
11	Bramham Moor	1408	battle?	Unlocated?
11	Stow on the Wold	1646	battle	Registered
9	Lincoln I	1141	battle	Assess
8	Ripple Field	1643	battle	Assess
8	Empingham	1470	battle	Unlocated (site a)
7	Chesterfield	1266	battle?	
7	Selby	1644	battle	
7	Winwick Pass	1648	battle	Assess
7	Alnwick I	1093	battle?	
6	Maidstone	1648	battle	
6	Alnwick II	1174	siege/battle?	
5	Durham	1069	battle?	
4	Sampford Courtenay	1549	battle	Assess
4	Piper Dene	1435	battle	Assess
3	Dussindale	1549	battle	Assess
3	Hilton	1644	battle	
3	Blackheath	1497	battle?	
1	York	1069	battle?	
1	York	1069	battle?	
1	Alton	1643	battle/skirmish	
0	Stockbridge	1141	battle?	
0	Wilton	1143	battle?	
0	Fornham St Genevieve	1173	battle?	
0	Fulhope Law	1400	battle	
0	Woodbury Hill	1405	battle?	
0	Deal Beach	1495	battle?	
0	Clyst St Mary	1549	battle	
0	Fenny Bridges	1549	battle	
0	Salisbury	1143	battle?	
0	Hereford	1067	battle?	
0	Winchester	1141	Siege/battle?	
0	Wichum	1146	battle?	
0	Southwark	1066	battle?	

Appendix 3 Civil War battlefields including terrain and condition

A list of Civil War battlefields indicating the main and subsidiary type of terrain and state of development (4 indicates near-complete while 1 is wholly developed).

Action name	Historic terrain	State of development
Adwalton Moor	Open moor, enclosures	3
Braddock Down	Open pasture, (enclosures)	4
Cheriton	Open pasture, enclosures (wood)	4
Cropredy Bridge	Open field	3
Edgehill	Open field	3
Hopton Heath	Open heath, (enclosures)	3
Langport	Open field, enclosures	3
Lansdown	Open pasture, enclosures, open field	4
Lostwithiel	Enclosures?	3
Maidstone	Unclassified	1
Marston Moor	Open field, open moor, (enclosures)	4
Nantwich	Enclosures, (settlement)	4
Naseby	Open field, (enclosures)	4
Newark	Unclassified	1
Newburn Ford	Open meadow, (enclosures), fortifications	2
Newbury I	Enclosures, open heath, open field	3
Newbury II	Unclassified	2
Preston I	Enclosures, open moor?	1
Ripple Field	Open field?	4
Roundway Down	Open pasture	4
Rowton Heath	Open heath, enclosures	3
Sedgemoor	Open moor	4
Selby	Unclassified	1
Stow on the Wold	Open field?	4
Stratton	Enclosures	3
Torrington II	Unclassified	2
Winceby	Open field	4
Winwick Pass	Unclassified	3
Worcester	Open meadow?, enclosures, settlement	2

Bibliography

Aalen, F, 2006 *England's landscape: the North East.* London: English Heritage

Allen, D & Anderson, S, 1999 *Basing House, Hampshire: excavations, 1978–1991.* Hampshire County Council

Allen Brown, R, 1984 *The Norman Conquest of England: sources and documents.* Woodbridge: The Boydell Press

Allsop, D & Foard, G, 2008 Case shot: an interim report on experimental firing and analysis to interpret early modern battlefield assemblages, in T Pollard & I Banks (eds) *Scorched earth: studies in the archaeology of conflict* (*Journal of Conflict Archaeology*, **3**). Leiden: Brill, 111–46

Arnold, T F, 2001 *The Renaissance at War.* London: Cassell

Atkin, M, 1995 *The Civil War in Worcestershire.* Stroud: Alan Sutton

Auden, J E & Frost, J, 2007 *Notes on the history of Tong from the parish books.* Bury St Edmonds: Arima

Bailey, G, 1992 Collecting Civil War relics. *Orders of the Daye (Sealed Knot Society magazine)*, **24**, 16–18

Bailey, G, 2001 Troubled times, *Treasure Hunting*, May, 28–32

Baker, A, 1986 *A battlefield atlas of the English Civil War.* Shepperton: Ian Allan

Baker, G, 1822 *The history and antiquities of the county of Northampton.* London: Nichols

Baker, J, Brookes, S and Reynolds, A (eds), in press *Landscapes of defence in the Viking age*, Studies in the Early Middle Ages series 28. Turnhout: Breols

Barrett, C R B, 1896 *Battles & battlefields in England.* London: Innes & Co

Bayley, A R, 1910 *The Great Civil War in Dorset 1642–1660.* Taunton: Barnicott and Pearce

BBC, 2010 *Parts of guns found at Towton War of Roses site.* BBC News North Yorkshire. Available: http://www.bbc.co.uk/news/uk-england-york-north-yorkshire-11810487 Accessed 7 April 2011

Beresford, M W & St Joseph, J K S, 1979 *Medieval England: an aerial survey.* Cambridge: Cambridge University Press

Bessinger, J B, 1963 Maldon and the Oláfsdrápa: an historical caveat, in S B Greenfield (ed) *Studies in Old English literature.* Eugene, 23–35

Bewley, B S C, Grady, Damian and Horne, Pete 2003 Flying over Roman Britain: recent results from the National Mapping Programme, *The Archaeologist*, **48**, 12–13

Blackmore, D, 1990 *Arms and armour of the English Civil Wars.* London: Royal Armouries

Blackmore, H L, 1976 *The armouries of the Tower of London: The Ordnance.* London: HMSO

Boardman, A W, 2000 *The Battle of Towton.* Stroud: Sutton Publishing

Bonsall, J, 2000 Archaeological applications to Dark Coppice Field: a scene of retreat from the 1644 Battle of Cheriton. Dissertation, King Alfred's College

Bonsall, J, 2008 The study of small finds at the 1644 Battle of Cheriton, in T Pollard & I Banks (eds) *Scorched earth: studies in the archaeology of conflict* (*Journal of Conflict Archaeology*, **3**). Leiden: Brill, 29–52

Border Archaeology, 2010 Lincoln Green and the battle of Tewkesbury: Detailed Archaeological Assessment, unpublished report for Lioncourt Homes Ltd

Bracher, T & Emmett, R, 2000 *Shropshire in the Civil War.* Shrewsbury: Shropshire Books

Bradbury, J, 1998 *Stephen and Matilda: the Civil War of 1139–53.* Stroud: Sutton Publishing

Brinch Madsen, H, Andersen, J H & Andersen, L B, 2004 Deterioration of prehistoric bronzes as an indicator of the state of preservation of metal antiquities in the Danish agrarian landscape: preliminary results, in T Nixon (ed) *Preserving archaeological remains in situ?* London: MOLAS/ English Heritage, 50–57

Brooks, F W, 1956 *The Battle of Stamford Bridge.* York: East Yorkshire Local History Society

Brooks, R, 2005 *Cassell's battlefields of Britain and Ireland.* London: Weidenfeld & Nicolson

Broxap, E, 1910 *The Great Civil War in Lancashire, 1642–1651.* Manchester: Manchester University Press

Buck, C, 1996 An archaeological assessment of Braddock Down. Truro: Cornwall County Council, a report to County Environmental Services by Cornwall Archaeological Unit. Unpublished report in HER

Burley, P, Elliott, M & Watson, H, 2007 *The battles of St Albans.* Barnsley: Pen and Sword

Burne, A & Young, P, 1959 *The Great Civil War*. London: Eyre & Spottiswoode

Burne, A H, 1950 *The battlefields of England*. London: Methuen

Burne, A H, 1952 *More battlefields of England*. London: Methuen

CADW, 2011 *Historic battlefields: consultation on the establishment of a register of historic battlefields in Wales*. Cardiff: CADW

Carman, J (ed), 1997 *Material harm: archaeological studies of war and violence*. Glasgow: Cruithne Press

Carpenter, D, 1987 *The battles of Lewes and Evesham 1264/65*. Keele: Mercia Publications Ltd

Carter, A, 1984 The site of Dussindale. *Norfolk Archaeology*, **39**, 54–62

CEI (Centre for Environmental Interpretation), 1994a Battle of Stamford Bridge, 1066: Battlefield Landscape Report. London: English Heritage (unpublished)

CEI (Centre for Environmental Interpretation), 1994b Braddock Down 1643, Battlefield Landscape Report. London: English Heritage (unpublished)

Champion, M, 2001 Kett's Rebellion 1549: a Dussindale eyewitness? *Norfolk Archaeology*, **43**, 642–5

Chandler, D, 1990 *The art of warfare in the age of Marlborough*. Staplehurst: Spelmount

Chandler, D, 1994 *The Oxford history of the British army*, 2003 edn. Oxford: Oxford University Press

Chandler, D, 1999 *Sedgemoor 1685: from Monmouth's Invasion to the Bloody Assizes*. Staplehurst: Spellmount

Childs, J, 2001 *Warfare in the seventeenth century*. London: Cassell

Civil War Sites Advisory Commission, 1993 *Report on the nation's Civil War battlefields*. Washington: National Parks Service

Clunn, T, Cheeseman-Clunn, A & Cheeseman, U, 1999 *In quest of the lost legions: the Varusschlacht*. London: Minerva

Cockle, M J D, 1957 *A bibliography of British military books up to 1642*. London: Holland Press

Cole, R, 1999 Liskeard To Maudlin pipeline: an archaeological evaluation and watching brief. Truro: A report to Transco by Cornwall Archaeological Unit. Unpublished report in HER

Connor, M & Scott, D D, 1998 Metal detector use in archaeology: an introduction. *Historical Archaeology*, **32**, 73–82

Cooper, J, 1993 *Battle of Maldon: fiction and fact*. London: Hambledon Press

Cooper, N E, 2006 *The archaeology of the East Midlands: an archaeological resource assessment and research agenda*. Leicester: University of Leicester Archaeological Services

Cornwall County Council, 1996 *Cornwall Landscape Assessment 1994*. Truro: Landscape Design Associates

Coulston, J, 2001 The archaeology of Roman conflict, in P W M Freeman & T Pollard (eds) *Fields of conflict: progress and prospect in battlefield archaeology*, BAR Int Ser. **958**. Oxford: Archaeopress, 23–49

Cox, D C, 1988 *The Battle of Evesham: a new account*. Evesham: Vale of Evesham Historical Society

Cronyn, J M, 1990 *The elements of archaeological conservation*. London: Routledge

Cross, J, 2011 *The Wars of the Roses:* Time Team *Special*. First broadcast 16 March 2011, directed by J Cross. Channel 4

Cruickshank, C, 1990 *Henry VIII and the invasion of France*. Stroud: Alan Sutton

Cubitt, R S, 2006 Determining the function of late medieval ferrous arrowheads. Unpublished MSc, University of Bradford

Cunliffe, B, 1984 *Danebury: Iron Age hillfort in Hampshire: the excavations, 1969–1978: the site*. York: Council for British Archaeology

Cunliffe, B, 2006 *England's landscape: the West*. London: English Heritage

Cunliffe, B, Bartlett, R, Morrill, J, Briggs, A & Bourke, J, 2001 *The Penguin atlas of British & Irish history*. London: Penguin

Currie, C & Lewis, C P (eds), (1994) *English county histories: a guide*. Stroud: Alan Sutton

Curry, A, 2005 *Agincourt: a new history*. Stroud: Tempus

Delano-Smith, C & Kain, R J P, 1999 *English maps: a history*. London: The British Library

Delbruck, H, 1923 *Medieval warfare*, 1982 edn. Lincoln: University of Nebraska

Department for Communities and Local Government, 2010 *Planning Policy Statement 5: Planning for the Historic Environment*. London: TSO

Department for Environment, Food and Rural Affairs, 2000 *Fertiliser recommendations for agricultural and horticultural crops (RB209)*. London: The Stationery Office

Department of Culture, Media and Sport, 2008 *Draft Heritage Protection Bill*. London: TSO

DeVries, K, 1999 *The Norwegian invasion of England in 1066*. Woodbridge: The Boydell Press

Dodgson, John McNeal, 1991 The site of the battle of Maldon, in D Scragg (ed) *The battle of Maldon, AD 991*. Oxford: Blackwell, 170–79

Douglas Smith, R & DeVries, K, 2005 *The Artillery of the Dukes of Burgundy, 1346–1477*. Woodbridge: The Boydell Press

Dugdale, W, 1675 *The baronage of England, or, an historical account of the lives and most memorable actions of our English nobility*. London: Printed by Tho. Newcomb

Edwards, P, 2000 *Dealing in death: the arms trade and the British civil wars, 1638–52*. Stroud: Sutton

Edwards, R, 1996 The effects of changes in ground-water geochemistry on the survival of buried metal artefacts, in M Corfield, P Hinton, T Nixon & M L Pollard (eds) *Preserving remains in situ*. London: MOLAS, 86–92

Eickhoff, S, Grothe, A & Jungklaus, B, 2011 Their last battle – a mass grave and the battlefield of Wittstock 1636. Paper given at the Fields of Conflict Conference, Osnabruck, 2011

Ellis, P, 1993 *Beeston Castle, Cheshire: a report on the excavations 1968–85 by Laurence Keen and Peter Hough*. London: English Heritage

Emery, P, 2000 Report on an archaeological evaluation at Busseys Garage, Palace Street, Norwich, Norfolk Archaeological Unit Report 498

English Heritage, 1995 *Register of historic battlefields*. London

English Heritage, 2008 *Conservation principles: policy and guidance for the sustainable management of the historic environment*. London: English Heritage

Eyers, V, 2006 Ballistics of Matchlock Muskets. Unpublished MSc, Cranfield University

Fergusson, J S, 1947 1547: The rough wooing. *Blackwood's Magazine*, 183–94

Fergusson, S J, 1963 *The White Hind and other discoveries*. London: Faber and Faber

Fiennes, C & Morris, C, 1949 *The journeys of Celia Fiennes*. London: Cresset Press

Fiorato, V, Boylston, A & Knusel, C, 2000 *Blood red roses: the archaeology of a mass grave from the Battle of Towton AD 1461*. Oxford: Oxbow Books

Fleming, A, 2007 Don't Bin Your Boots! *Landscapes*, **8**, 85–99

Foard, G, 1995 *Naseby: the decisive campaign*. Whitstable: Pryor Publications

Foard, G, 2000 The Civil War siege, in C Fitzroy & K Harry (eds) *Grafton Regis: the history of a Northamptonshire village*. Cardiff: Merton Press, 49–63

Foard, G, 2001 The archaeology of attack: battles and sieges of the English Civil War, in P W M Freeman & T Pollard (eds) *Fields of conflict: progress and prospect in battlefield archaeology*, BAR Int Ser. **958**. Oxford: Archaeopress, 87–103

Foard, G, 2003a The forgotten battle: the campaign and battle of Adwalton Moor – 1643, *Battlefields Review*, **23**, 39–46

Foard, G, 2003b Sedgemoor, 1685: historic terrain, the 'archaeology of battles' and the revision of military history, *Landscapes*, **4**, 5–15

Foard, G, 2006 A group of lead bullets from Hadley Wood, Barnet. Unpublished report for The Battlefields Trust

Foard, G, 2007a English battlefields 991–1685: a review of problems and potentials, in D D Scott, M Haecker Charles & L Babbits (eds) *Fields of conflict: battlefield archaeology from the Roman Empire to the Korean War*. Westport, CT: Praeger Security International, 133–59

Foard, G, 2007b *Battle of Ancrum Moor, 27th February 1545*. Historic Scotland. Available: http://data.historic-scotland.gov.uk/ Accessed 9 April 2011

Foard, G, 2007c *Battle of Pinkie, 10th September 1547*. Historic Scotland. Available: http://data.historic-scotland.gov.uk/ Accessed 9 April 2011

Foard, G, 2008a *Conflict in the pre-Industrial Landscape of England: A Resource Assessment*. University of Leeds/English Heritage. Available from 2012 at http://ads.ahds.ac.uk/

Foard, G, 2008b Early modern small arms munitions from archaeological investigation at Weedon Hill, Aylesbury, Buckinghamshire. Unpublished report for Wessex Archaeology

Foard, G, 2008c Integrating the physical and documentary evidence for battles and their context: a case study from 17th century England. Unpublished PhD, University of East Anglia

Foard, G, 2008d Lead munitions and other metal finds from the AOC Investigation at Inveresk of part of Pinkie battlefield. Unpublished report for AOC

Foard, G, 2008e Lead munitions and other metal finds from the CFA Investigation at Wallyford in 2005 & 2007 of part of Pinkie battlefield. Unpublished report for CFA Archaeology

Foard, G, 2008f Lead munitions and other metal finds from the East Lothian Council Investigation at Wallyford of part of Pinkie battlefield. Unpublished Report for East Lothian Council

Foard, G, 2008g Sedgemoor Battlefield Survey 2007: Report on lead bullets. Unpublished report for Context One Archaeological Services

Foard, G, 2009 The investigation of early modern battlefields in England, in H Meller (ed) *Schlachtfeldarchaeologie: Battlefield Archaeology*. Halle, Germany: Lamdesmuseums fur Vorgeschichte, 117–25

Foard, G, 2010a Discovering Bosworth. *British Archaeology*, **112**, 26–31

Foard, G, 2010b High Risk Battlefields Management Strategy: Yorkshire & the Humber & North East Regions. Unpublished report for English Heritage

Foard, G & Curry, A, in preparation *Bosworth Battlefield rediscovered*

Foard, G & Partida, T, 2005 *Scotland's historic fields of conflict: an assessment*. Historic Scotland. Available: http://www.battlefieldstrust.com/resource-centre/battlefieldsuk/periodpageview.asp?pageid=827 Accessed 9 April 2011

Foard, G & Walton, S, in preparation A study of the barrels of late 15th and early 16th century small artillery and hand guns

Foard, G, Hall, D & Partida, T, 2009 *Rockingham Forest: an atlas of the medieval and early modern landscape.* Northampton: Northamptonshire Record Society

Foard, G, Janaway, R & Wilson, A, 2010 *The scientific study and conservation of battlefield artefact assemblages.* http://www.battlefieldstrust.com/resource-centre/battlefieldsuk/periodpageview.asp?pageid=853&parentid=199 Accessed 9 April 2011

Foss, P, 1990 *The Field of Redemore: the Battle of Bosworth, 1485.* Headingley: Rosalba Press

Foss, P, 1998 *The Field of Redmore: the Battle of Bosworth, 1485.* Newtown Linford: Kairos Press

Fraser, G M, 1974 *The Steel Bonnets: the story of the Anglo-Scottish border reivers.* London: Pan

Fraser, J, 2005 *The Roman conquest of Scotland: The Battle of Mons Graupius AD 84.* Stroud: Tempus

Freeman, E A, 1869 *The history of the Norman Conquest of England: its causes and its results.* Oxford: Clarendon Press

Gale, R, 1781 An historical account of the borough of Northallerton in the North Riding of the County of York, in J. Nichols (ed) *Bibliotheca Topographica Britannica*, vol. 3. London, 200–212

Gardiner, S R, 1893 *History of the Great Civil War, 1642–44.* London: Longman

Gaunt, P, 1987 *The Cromwellian gazetteer: an illustrated guide to Britain in the Civil War and Commonwealth.* Gloucester: Alan Sutton

Geschwinde, M, Haßmann, H, Lönne, P, Meyer, M & Moosbauer, G, 2009 Roms vergessener Feldzug. Das neu entdeckte Schlachtfeld am Harzhorn in Niedersachsen, in *2000 Jahre Varusschlacht: Konflikt.* Stuttgart: Konrad Theiss Verlag, 228–32

Geschwinde, M, Haßmann, H, Lönne, P, Meyer, M & Moosbauer, G, 2011 The Harzhorn Incident. Archaeological research on a late Roman battlefield near Northeim, Lower Saxony. Paper given at the Fields of Conflict Conference, Osnabruck, 2011

Gover, J E B, Mawer, A & Stenton, F M, 1933 *The Place Names of Northamptonshire.* Cambridge: Cambridge University Press

Greenburg, R M, 1997 *Altogether fitting and proper: saving America's battlefields, Cultural Resources Management*, **20**(5) (special issue)

Griffiths, M, 1997 Moor Lane, Stamford Bridge: an appraisal for Barratt York. Unpublished report, Mike Griffith and Associates

Grummitt, D, 2008 *The Calais garrison: war and military service in England, 1436–1558.* Woodbridge: The Boydell Press

Grummitt, D, 2010 The Procurement and Organisation of Royal Ordnance in England, c.1422–1485. Unpublished paper delivered at International Medieval Congress, Leeds

Haigh, P A, 1995 *The military campaigns of the Wars of the Roses.* Godalming: Bramley Books

Haigh, P A, 1997 *Where both hosts fought: the rebellions of 1469–1470 and battles of Edgecote and Lose-cote-field.* Stockton on Tees: Battlefield Press

Hall, B, 1997 *Weapons and warfare in Renaissance Europe.* Baltimore: The Johns Hopkins University Press

Hall, D, 1980 Hardingstone parish survey 1972, *Northamptonshire Archaeology*, **15**, 119–32

Hall, D, 1982 *Medieval fields.* Princes Risborough: Shire Publications

Hall, D, 1995 *The open fields of Northamptonshire.* Northampton: Northamptonshire Record Society

Hall, D, 2001 *Turning the plough: midland open fields: landscape character and proposals for management.* Northampton: Northamptonshire County Council and English Heritage

Hall, D, forthcoming *The open fields of England*

Halsall, G, 2003 *Warfare and society in the barbarian west, 450–900.* London: Routledge

Harkins, S, 2010 The application of modern forensic techniques to battlefield archaeology. Unpublished MSc, Cranfield University

Harnecker, J, 2004 *Arminius, Varus and the battlefield at Kalkriese.* Bramsche: Rasch

Harrington, P, 1992 *Archaeology of the English Civil War.* Princes Risborough: Shire

Harrington, P, 2003 *English Civil War fortifications 1642–51.* London: Osprey Publishing

Harrington, P, 2004 *English Civil War archaeology.* London: Batsford

Harrington, P, 2006 Civil War siege evidence from early castle clearances. Unpublished paper delivered at Fields of Conflict IV, Leeds

Henderson, C G, 1987 Excavations at Hayes Barton, St Thomas, *Exeter Archaeology 1985/6*, 53–4

Higham, N J, 1997 The context of Brunanburh, in A R Rumble & A D Mills (eds) *Names, places and people: an onomastic miscellany in memory of John McNeal Dodgson.* Stamford: Paul Watkins, 144–56

Hildred, A, forthcoming *Weapons of warre: the ordnance of the* Mary Rose. Oxford: Oxbow Books

Hind, J G F, 2005 The watchtowers and fortlets on the North Yorkshire Coast, *Yorkshire Archaeological Journal*, **77**, 17–24

Hodges, G, 2001 *Ludford Bridge and Mortimers Cross.* Little Logaston: Logaston Press

Hodgkins, A, 2008 Reappraising the battles of the Prayer Book Rebellion. Dissertation, University of Leeds

Hollowell, S, 2000 *Enclosure records for historians.* Chichester: Phillimore

Holmer, P L, 1977 Studies in the military organisation of the Yorkist kings. Unpublished PhD, University of Minnesota

Holmes, R, 1997 *War walks 2: from the Battle of Hastings to the Blitz*

Hooke, D, 2006 *England's landscape: the West Midlands*. London: English Heritage

Hunn, J R, 1991 A reconstruction and measurement of landscape change: a study of six parishes in the St Albans area. Unpublished PhD, University of Southampton

Hutton, R & Reeves, W, 1998 Sieges and supply, in J Kenyon & J Ohlmeyer (eds) *The Civil Wars*. Oxford: Oxford University Press, 234–71

Jagger, J, 2010 Harvest and heritage – a working partnership, in Surviving the peace: public access, conservation and military heritage. Culloden Visitor Centre (unpublished)

Johnson, D, 2003 *Adwalton Moor 1643: the battle that changed a war*. Pickering: Blackthorn Press

Johnson, W, 1917 Caesar's Ford: the claims of Battersea. *Transactions of the London and Middlesex Archaeological Society*, **3**, ns, 438

Jones, C, 2011 *Finding Fulford: The search for the first battle of 1066*. York

Jones, R & Page, M, 2006 *Medieval villages in an English landscape: beginnings and ends*. Bollington: Windgather

Jones, R W, 2010 *Bloodied banners: martial display on the medieval battlefield*. Woodbridge: The Boydell Press

Kain, R, 2006 *England's landscape: the South West*. London: English Heritage

Kelly, J, 2004 *Gunpowder: alchemy, bombards and pyrotechnics: the history of the explosive that changed the world*. New York: Basic Books

Kempers, R T W, 1983 Haquebuts from Dutch collections, *The Journal of the Arms and Armour Society*, **11**, 56–89

Kenyon, J & Ohlmeyer, J, 1998 *The Civil Wars: a military history of England, Scotland and Wales*. Oxford: Oxford University Press

Keyes, D 2003 The fight to save battlegrounds from invasion of metal detectors, *The Independent*, Monday 22 September 2003

Keynes, S, 1991 The historical context of the battle of Maldon, in D Scragg (ed) *The battle of Maldon, AD 991*. Oxford: Blackwell, 81–113

Kinross, J, 1988 *Walking and exploring the battlefields of Britain*. Newton Abbot: David and Charles

Knarrstrom, B, 2009 On the trail of early use of gunpowder weapons: evidence from Swedish battlefields. Unpublished paper delivered at the International Congress on Medieval Studies, Kalamazoo

Laborde, E D, 1925 The site of the battle of Maldon, *English Historical Review*, **40**, 161–73

Lawson, M K, 2002 *The Battle of Hastings 1066*. Stroud: Tempus

Lawton, I G, 1997 The Roman roads around Stamford Bridge: recent work, *Forum* (*CBA Yorkshire Annual Newsletter*), 23–9

Lawton, I G, 1999 Dervention – Roman Stamford Bridge update. *Forum* (*CBA Yorkshire Annual Newsletter*), 7–11

Leadman, A D H, 1891 *Battles fought in Yorkshire*. London: Bradbury, Agnew & Co

Lee, J W I, 2001 Urban combat at Olynthos, 348 BC, in P Freeman & A Pollard (eds) *Fields of conflict: progress and prospects in battlefield archaeology*. Oxford: Archaeopress, 11–22

Liddiard, R & McGuicken, R, 2007 *Beeston Castle*. London: English Heritage

MacBain, A & Kennedy, J, 1892 *Reliquiae Celticae: texts, papers and studies in Gaelic literature and philology*. Inverness

McConnell, 2007 Land to the North of Westonzoyland Sewage Treatment Works, Westonzoyland, Somerset: an archaeological programme of works: phase 1 – metal detecting survey. Wincanton: Context One Archaeological Services (unpublished report)

Machiavelli, N, 1521 *The art of war*, 2001 edn. Cambridge, MA: Da Cappo Press

McLachlan, S, 2010 *Medieval handgonnes: The first black powder infantry weapons*. Oxford: Osprey

McNeill, P G B & MacQueen, H L, 1996 *Atlas of Scottish History to 1707*. Edinburgh: The Scottish Medievalists & Department of Geography, University of Edinburgh

Marix Evans, M, 1998 *The military heritage of Britain and Ireland*. London: Andre Deutsch

Marix Evans, M, 2007 *Boudicca's last battle*. Oxford: Osprey

Marix Evans, M, Burton, P & Westaway, M, 2002 *Naseby: June 1645*. Barnsley: Leo Cooper

Mason, D, 2001 Battle victims found at Heronbridge, *The Past Uncovered: Chester Archaeology, Design and Conservation News*

Mason, D, 2006 AD 616: The Battle of Chester, *Current Archaeology*, **202**, 517–24

Mayes, P & Butler, L, 1983 *Sandal Castle Excavations 1964–1973*. Wakefield: Wakefield Historical Publications

Meller, H (ed), 2009 *Schlachtfeldarchaeologie: battlefield archaeology*. Halle: Lamdesmuseums fur Vorgeschichte

Mercer, R J, 1981 Excavations at Carn Brea, *Cornish Archaeology*, **20**, 67

Mercer, R J, 1999 The origins of warfare in the British Isles, in J Carman & A F Harding (eds) *Ancient warfare*. Oxford: Oxbow Books, 143–56

Mercer, R J, 2006 By other means? The development of warfare in the British Isles 3000–500 BC, *Journal of Conflict Archaeology*, **2**, 118–51

Merriman, M, 2000 *The rough wooings: Mary Queen of Scots 1542–1551*. East Linton: Tuckwell Press

Miller, D P, 2010 Ballistics of 17th century muskets. Unpublished MSc, Cranfield University

Mills, A D, 2003 *Dictionary of British place names*. Oxford: Oxford University Press

Mills, P, 1996 The Battle of London 1066, *London Archaeology*, **8**, 59–62

Morillo, S (ed), 1996 *The Battle of Hastings*. Woodbridge: The Boydell Press

National Army Museum, 1995a *Battle of Adwalton Moor 1643*. English Heritage. Available: http://www.english-heritage.org.uk/caring/listing/what-can-we-protect/battlefields-offline/battle-of-adwalton-moor Accessed 9 April 2011

National Army Museum, 1995b *Battle of Barnet, 1471*. English Heritage. Available: http://www.english-heritage.org.uk/caring/listing/what-can-we-protect/battlefields-offline/battle-of-barnet Accessed 9 April 2011

National Army Museum, 1995c *Battle of Blore Heath 1459*. English Heritage. Available: http://www.english-heritage.org.uk/caring/listing/what-can-we-protect/battlefields-offline/battle-of-blore-heath Accessed 9 April 2011

National Army Museum, 1995d *Battlefield Register Report: Braddock 1643*. London

National Army Museum, 1995e *Battlefield Register Report: Edgcote 1469*. London

National Army Museum, 1995f *Battlefield Register Report: Evesham, 1265*. English Heritage. Available: http://www.english-heritage.org.uk/caring/listing/what-can-we-protect/battlefields-offline/battle-of-evesham Accessed 9 April 2011

National Army Museum, 1995g *Battle of Flodden 1513*. English Heritage. Available: http://www.english-heritage.org.uk/caring/listing/what-can-we-protect/battlefields-offline/battle-of-flodden Accessed 9 April 2011

National Army Museum, 1995h *Battle of Halidon Hill 1333*. English Heritage. Available: http://www.english-heritage.org.uk/caring/listing/what-can-we-protect/battlefields-offline/battle-of-halidon-hill Accessed 9 April 2011

National Army Museum, 1995i *Battle of Lewes 1264*. English Heritage. Available: http://www.english-heritage.org.uk/caring/listing/what-can-we-protect/battlefields-offline/battle-of-lewes Accessed 9 April 2011

National Army Museum, 1995j *Battle of Maldon 991*. English Heritage. Available: http://www.english-heritage.org.uk/caring/listing/what-can-we-protect/battlefields-offline/battle-of-maldon Accessed 9 April 2011

National Army Museum, 1995k *Battle of Nantwich 1644*. English Heritage. Available: http://www.english-heritage.org.uk/caring/listing/what-can-we-protect/battlefields-offline/battle-of-nantwich Accessed 9 April 2011

National Army Museum, 1995l *Battle of Northampton 1460*. English Heritage. Available: http://www.english-heritage.org.uk/caring/listing/what-can-we-protect/battlefields/battle-of-northampton Accessed 9 April 2011

National Army Museum, 1995m *Battle of Otterburn 1388*. English Heritage. Available: http://www.english-heritage.org.uk/caring/listing/what-can-we-protect/battlefields/battle-of-otterburn Accessed 9 April 2011

National Army Museum, 1995n *Battle of Shrewsbury 1403*. English Heritage. Available: http://www.english-heritage.org.uk/caring/listing/what-can-we-protect/battlefields/battle-of-shrewsbury Accessed 9 April 2011

National Army Museum, 1995o *Battle of Solway Moss 1542*. English Heritage. Available: http://www.english-heritage.org.uk/caring/listing/what-can-we-protect/battlefields/battle-of-solway-moss Accessed 9 April 2011

National Army Museum, 1995p *Battle of Stratton 1643*. English Heritage. Available: http://www.english-heritage.org.uk/caring/listing/what-can-we-protect/battlefields/battle-of-stratton Accessed 9 April 2011

National Army Museum, 1995q *Battle of Towton 1461*. English Heritage. Available: http://www.english-heritage.org.uk/caring/listing/what-can-we-protect/battlefields/battle-of-towton Accessed 9 April 2011

National Park Service, 2006 *Management policies 2006: the guide to managing the National Park System*. Washington DC: Department of the Interior

Neff, L C, 2002 *Archaeological survey and soil testing at Washita Battlefield Historic Site, Roger Mills County, Oklahoma*. Tucson, AZ: US Dept of the Interior, National Parks Service

Newman, J, 1996 New light on old finds – Bloodmoor Hill, Gisleham, Suffolk, *Anglo-Saxon Studies in Archaeology and History*, **9**, 75–9

Newman, P, 1978 *Marston Moor, 2 July 1644: the sources and the site*. York: Borthwick Institute of Historical Research

Newman, P, 1979 Marston Moor 1644–1979: the study of a Civil War battlefield, *Journal for Army Historical Research*, **57**, 137–43

Newman, P, 1981 *Battle of Marston Moor, 1644*. Chichester: Bird

Newman, P, 1985 *Atlas of the English Civil War*. New York: Macmillan

Newman, P & Roberts, P R, 2003 *Marston Moor 1644: the battle of the five armies*. Pickering: Blackthorn Press

Nicholson, H, 2004 *Medieval warfare*. London: Palgrave Macmillan

Nord, A G, Ullén, I, Tronner, K, Sjöstedt, J & Runesson, H, 2000 *The deterioration of archaeological metal artefacts in soil*. Stockholm: National Heritage Board

Nye, N, 1647 *The art of gunnery*. London: William Leak

Ogilby, J, 1675 *Britannia*. London: Ogilby

Oman, C W C, 1898 *A history of the art of war in the Middle Ages*. London: Methuen

Oman, C W C, 1937 *A history of the art of war in the sixteenth century*. London: Methuen & Co

Osgood, R, 2005 The dead of Tormarton: Middle Bronze Age combat victims? in M Parker Pearson and I J N Thorpe (eds) *Warfare, violence and slavery in prehistory: proceedings of a Prehistoric Society conference at Sheffield University*, BAR Int Ser. **1374**. Oxford: Archaeopress, 139–44

Oxford Archaeology, 2006 *Conservation of scheduled monuments in cultivation (COSMIC)*. English Heritage and DEFRA. Available: http://randd.defra.gov.uk/Document.aspx?Document=BD1704_3769_FRA.pdf Accessed 9 April 2011

Page, J T, 1893 The Great Civil War in Northamptonshire, *East London Magazine*, **1**, 285–320

Page, W, 1925 *The Victoria History of the county of Buckingham*. London: St Catherine Press

Paris, M & Luard, H R E, 1884 *Matthaei Parisiensis, monachi Sancti Albani, Chronica majora*. London: Longman & Co

Parry, S J, 2006 *Raunds Area Survey: an archaeological study of the landscape of Raunds, Northamptonshire 1985–94*. Oxford: Oxbow Books

Partida, T, Foard, G & Hall, D, forthcoming *An atlas of the medieval and early modern landscape of Northamptonshire*. Oxford: Oxbow Books

Patten, W, 1548 *The Expedicioun*. London: Richard Grafton

Petty, G & Petty, S, 1993 A geological reconstruction of the site of the battle of Maldon, in J Cooper (ed) *The battle of Maldon: fiction and fact*. London: Hambledon, 159–69

Petty, G R & Petty, S, 1976 Geology and the Battle of Maldon, *Speculum*, **51**(3) 435–46

Phillips, G, 1999 *The Anglo-Scots Wars, 1513–1550: a military history*. Woodbridge: Boydell Press

Pisan, C D, 1489 *The book of fayttes of armes and of chyaulrye*. London: William Caxton

Plummer, C, 1896 *Venerabilis Baedae Opera Historica*, 2 vols. Oxford

Pollard, A M, Wilson, L, Wilson, A S & Hall, A J, 2003 *Influence of agrochemicals on the rate of metal corrosion in the vadose zone in arable burial environments*. London, Report PNUM 3138

Pollard, A M, Wilson, L, Wilson, A S, Hall, A J & Shiel, R, 2004 Assessing the influence of agrochemicals on the rate of copper corrosion in the vadose zone of arable land. Part 1: field experiments, *Conservation and Management of Archaeological Sites*, **6**(3 & 4), 363–75

Pollard, A M, Wilson, L, Wilson, A S & Hall, A J, 2006 Assessing the influence of agrochemicals on the rate of copper corrosion in the vadose zone of arable land – Part 2: laboratory simulations. *Conservation and Management of Archaeological Sites*, **7**, 225–39

Pollard, T, 2003 The value of enmity: remaking and revisiting historic battlefields in the United States and Britain, *Landscapes*, **4**, 25–34

Pollard, T (ed), 2009 *Culloden: the history and archaeology of the last clan battle*. Barnsley: Pen and Sword

Pollard, T & Oliver, N, 2002 *Two men in a trench: battlefield archaeology – the key to unlocking the past*. London: Michael Joseph

Pollard, T & Oliver, N, 2003 *Two men in a trench II: uncovering the secrets of British battlefields*. London: Michael Joseph

Porter, P, 2000 *Medieval warfare in manuscripts*. London: British Library

Porter, S, 1984 The Civil War destruction of Boarstall, *Records of Buckinghamshire*, **26**, 86–91

Pourbaix, M & Franklin, J A, 1966 *Atlas of electrochemical equilibria in aqueous solutions*. Oxford/New York: Pergamon Press

Powlesland, D, 2008 Why bother? Large-scale geomagnetic survey and the quest for 'real archaeology', in S Campana and S Piro (eds), *Seeing the unseen: geophysics and landscape archaeology*. London: Taylor & Francis, 167–82

Prestwich, M, 1996 *Armies and warfare in the Middle Ages: the English experience*. New Haven/London: Yale University Press

Pye, A & Woodward, F, 1996 *The historic defences of Plymouth*. Truro: Cornwall County Council

Raine, J (ed), 1864 *Priory of Hexham*. Durham: Surtees Society

Ramsay, S J H, 1892 *Lancaster and York: a century of English history, A.D. 1399-1485*. Oxford: Clarendon

Ramsay, S J H, 1908 *The dawn of the constitution: or the reigns of Henry III and Edward I 1216–1307*. London: Macmillan

Raymond, J, 2007 *Henry VIII's military revolution: the armies of sixteenth century Britain and Europe*. London: Tauris Academic Studies

Rayner, M, 2004 *English battlefields: an illustrated encyclopaedia*. Stroud: Tempus

Reynolds, A, 2009 *Anglo-Saxon deviant burial customs*. Oxford: Oxford University Press

Reynolds, C, 2000 *A short history of Bernard's Heath*. Tring: Codil Language Systems

Richmond, C, 1985 The battle of Bosworth, *History Today*, **35**, 17–22

Roberts, B K & Wrathmell, S, 2000 *An atlas of rural settlement in England*. London: English Heritage

Roberts, K, 2010 *Pike and shot tactics 1590–1660*. Oxford: Osprey

Rodwell, W, 1993 The battle of Assandun and its memorial church: a reappraisal, in J Cooper (ed) *The Battle of Maldon: fact and fiction*. London: The Hambledon Press, 127–58

Roe, A, 2009 A Romano-British landscape at Moor Lane, Stamford Bridge, *East Riding Archaeologist*, **12**, 70–86

Rowland, T H, 1994 *Medieval castles, towers, peles and bastles of Northumberland*. Warkworth: Sandhill

Roy, I, 1964 *The Royalist ordnance papers 1642–1646*. Oxford: Oxfordshire Record Society

Roy, I, 1975 *The Royalist ordnance papers: May 1643–1646*. Oxford: Oxfordshire Record Society

Royal Commission on Historical Monuments, 1964 *Newark on Trent: the Civil War siegeworks*. London: HMSO

Salter, M, 1995 *The Old Parish Churches of Cheshire*. Malvern: Folly Publications

Saunders, A, 2004 *Fortress builder: Bernard de Gomme, Charles II's military engineer*. Exeter: University of Exeter Press

Scott, D & Mcfeaters, A, 2011 The archaeology of historic battlefields: a history and theoretical development in conflict archaeology. *Journal of Archaeological Research*, **19**, 103–32

Scott, D D, Fox, R A, Connor, M A & Harmon, D, 1989 *Archaeological perspectives on the battle of the Little Bighorn*. Oklahoma: University of Oklahoma Press

Searle, E (ed), 1980 *The chronicle of Battle Abbey*, Oxford: Oxford University Press

Short, B, 2006 *England's landscape: the South East*. London: English Heritage

Sivilich, D M, 2007 What the musket ball can tell: Monmouth Battlefield State Park, in D Scott, L Babits & C Haecker (eds) *Fields of conflict: battlefield archaeology from the Roman Empire to the Korean War*. Westport, CT: Praeger Security International, 84–101

Sivilich, D M & Sivilich, E, 2011 Surveying, statistics and spatial mapping: predictive modelling of 18th century artillery at Monmouth Battlefield State Park, New Jersey. Paper given at the Fields of Conflict Conference, Osnabruck, 2011

Smail, D, 2009 Beyond the great divide, *History Today*, **59**, 21–3

Smalley, R, 2008 Geophysical survey report: Battle Well Field, Evesham. Stratascan (unpublished report)

Smith, R D & DeVries, K, 2005 *The artillery of the dukes of Burgundy, 1363–1477*. Woodbridge: Boydell Press

Smith, T, 2004 Detector surveys of battlefield sites, *Treasure Hunting*, October, 64–8

Smith, T, 2005 Detector surveys on battlefield sites, *Treasure Hunting*, January, 56–9

Stamp, D, 1931–5 *Land utilisation survey of Britain*. http://digimap.edina.ac.uk/landuse/index.jsp Accessed 31 March 2011

Stamp, L D, 1962 *The land use of Britain*. London: Longmans

Starkey, D, Ward, P & Hawkyard, A, 1998 *The inventory of King Henry VIII: Society of Antiquaries MS 129 and British Library MS Harley 1419*. London: Society of Antiquaries of London

Starley, D & Cubitt, R S, 2006 Tudor arrowheads: battlefield finds under the microscope. Unpublished paper delivered at Fields of Conflict IV, Leeds

Stenton, F M, 1947 *Anglo-Saxon England*. Oxford: Clarendon Press

Stocker, D, 2006 *England's landscape: the East Midlands*. London: English Heritage

Strickland, M & Hardy, R, 2005 *The great warbow: from Hastings to the* Mary Rose. Stroud: Sutton Publishing

Sutherland, T L, 2000a The archaeological investigation of the Towton battlefield, in V Fiorato, A Boylston & C Knusel (eds) *Blood red roses: the archaeology of a mass grave from the Battle of Towton AD 1461*. Oxford: Oxbow Books, 155–68

Sutherland, T L, 2000b Recording the grave, in V Fiorato, A Boylston & C Knusel (eds) *Blood red roses: the archaeology of a mass grave from the Battle of Towton AD 1461*. Oxford: Oxbow Books, 36–44

Sutherland, T L, 2000c The rings of the lords: non military artefacts as battlefield indicators, in P W M Freeman & A Pollard (eds) *Fields of conflict: progress and prospect in battlefield archaeology*, BAR Int Ser **958**. Oxford: Archaeopress, 297

Sutherland, T L, 2002 Locating and quantifying the dead from the Battle of Towton: analysing the available data. Unpublished paper delivered at Fields of Conflict II, Åland, Finland

Sutherland, T L, 2005 The Battle of Agincourt: an alternative location? *Journal of Conflict Archaeology*, **1**, 245–63

Sutherland, T L, 2009 Archaeological evidence of medieval conflict – case studies from Towton, Yorkshire, England (1461) and Agincourt, Pas de Calais, France (1415), in H Meller (ed) *Schlachtfeldarchaeologie: battlefield archaeology*. Halle: Landesmuseums fur Vorgeschichte, 109–15

Sutherland, T L, 2011 Guns at Towton, *Battlefield* (the magazine of The Battlefields Trust), **16**(1), 13

Sutherland, T L & Richardson, S, 2007 Arrow point to mass grave: finding the dead from the Battle of Towton, 1461 AD, in D Scott, L Babits & M Haecker Charles (eds) *Fields of conflict: battlefield archaeology from the Roman Empire to the Korean War*. Westport, CT: Praegar Security International, 160–73

Sutherland, T L & Schmidt, A, 2003 Towton, 1461: an integrated approach to battlefield archaeology. *Landscapes*, **4**, 15–25

Syse, B, 2002 A mass grave from the Battle of Good Friday in 1520, Uppsala, Sweden. Unpublished paper delivered at Fields of Conflict II, Åland, Finland

Tate, W E & Turner, M E, 1978 *A domesday of English enclosure acts and awards*. Reading: University of Reading

Thomas-Stanford, C, 1910 *Sussex in the Great Civil War and the Interregnum 1642–1660*. London: Chiswick Press

Thordeman, B, 1939 *Armour from the Battle of Wisby*, 2001 edn. Union City, CA: Chivalry Bookshelf

Twemlowe, F R, 1912 *The Battle of Blore Heath*. Wolverhampton: Whitehead Brothers

Walker, R & Hildred, A, 2000 Manufacture and corrosion of lead shot from the flagship 'Mary Rose', *Studies in Conservation*, **45**, 217–25

Ward, S, 1987 *Excavations at Chester: the Civil War siege works*. Chester: Chester City Council Grosvenor Museum

Warren, B, 2002 The chapel for the dead of the Battle of Barnet, *Journal of the Potters Bar and District Historical Society*, **2**, 1–8

Warren, B, 2009 *Reappraisal of the Battle of Barnet, 1471*. Potters Bar: Potters Bar & District Historical Society

Wason, D, 2003 *Battlefield detectives*. London: Granada

Webster, G, 1981 *Rome against Caratacus: the Roman campaigns in Britain, AD 48–58*. London: Batsford

Webster, G, 1993 *Boudicca: the British revolt against Rome AD 60*. London: Batsford

Webster, G & Dudley, D R, 1973 *The Roman conquest of Britain*. London: Pan

Welch, C, 1998 Prince Rupert's Mound: a Civil War earthwork in Lichfield. Environmental Planning Unit Research Report 3, Staffordshire County Council

Wiedemer, J E, 1967 Arms and armour in England, 1450–1471: their cost and distribution. Unpublished PhD, University of Pennsylvania

Wilbers-Rost, S, 2007 Total Roman defeat at the Battle of Varus (9 AD), in D Scott, L Babits & C Haecker (eds) *Fields of conflict: battlefield archaeology from the Roman Empire to the Korean War*. Westport, CT: Praeger Security International, 121–32

Wilbers-Rost, S, 2009 The site of the Varus Battle at Kalkriese. Recent results from archaeological research, in N H A Morillo and E Martin (eds) *Limes XX, Roman frontier studies. Anejo de Gladius*. Madrid, 1347–52

Williamson, T, 2006 *England's landscape: East Anglia*. London: English Heritage

Wilton, R, 1985 Some notes on the Battle of Braddock Down, *Devon and Cornwall Notes and Queries*, **35**, 246–53

Wilton, R, 1992 The site of the Battle of Braddock Down, *Devon and Cornwall Notes and Queries*, **41**

Winchester, A, 2006 *England's landscape: the North West*. London: English Heritage

Wood, I, 2008 Monasteries and the geography of power in the age of Bede, *Northern History*, **45**, 11–25

Young, P, 1967 *Edgehill 1642: the campaign and the battle*. Kineton: The Roundwood Press

Young, P & Adair, J, 1979 *From Hastings to Culloden*. Kineton: The Roundwood Press

INDEX

Entries in bold refer to the Figures